Detecting Texts

Detecting Texts

The Metaphysical Detective Story
from Poe to Postmodernism

Edited by Patricia Merivale
and Susan Elizabeth Sweeney

PENN

University of Pennsylvania Press
Philadelphia

10 9 8 7 6 5 4 3 2 1

Published by
University of Pennsylvania Press
Philadelphia, Pennsylvania 19104-4011

Library of Congress Cataloging-in-Publication Data
Detecting texts : the metaphysical detective story from Poe
to postmodernism / edited by Patricia Merivale and
Susan Elizabeth Sweeney.
p.   cm.
Includes bibliographical references and index.
ISBN 0-8122-3469-3 (cloth : alk. paper). — ISBN 0-8122-1676-8
(pbk. : alk. paper)
1. Detective and mystery stories—History and criticism.
2. Experimental fiction—History and criticism.   3. Fiction—20th
century—History and criticism.   4. Metaphysics in literature.
5. Fiction—Technique.   I. Merivale, Patricia.   II. Sweeney, Susan
Elizabeth, 1958–
PN3448.D4D39   1998
809.3'872'0904—dc21   98-27815
                                                            CIP

. . . that metaphysical art in which the souls of all mysteries lie. —EDGAR ALLAN POE,
reviewing Charles Dickens's *Barnaby Rudge*

Contents

Postmortem: Modern and Postmodern

Forging Identities

In Place of an Ending

Preface

Detecting Texts first began as a panel at the 1990 Modern Language Association convention, chaired by Susan Elizabeth Sweeney and entitled "Metaphysical Detective Stories." Several years later, we are delighted to present this volume of essays as that panel's long-awaited dénouement.

Beth would like to dedicate her work on *Detecting Texts* to four people who have died since this project began: her friend, critic and detective novelist Richard H. Rodino (coauthor of the Easy Barnes mysteries), who had an important role in the book's early stages; her father and mother, Daniel J. Sweeney and Dorothy Daub Sweeney; and especially her beloved sister, D. J. Sweeney Kimball, who taught her where the meaning is. Beth also wishes to thank, for their kindness, generosity, and encouragement, her husband, Michael Chapman; her friends and colleagues, especially Shirley Adams, Laurie Brown, Tina Chen, Laurence Enjolras, Katharina Gerstenberger, Richard Matlak, Jack O'Connell, Kay O'Connor, Carol Singley, and Sarah Stanbury; and her students in "Detective Fiction," "Borges and Nabokov," "The American Detective Story," and "The Metaphysical Detective Story" at Holy Cross College.

Pat would like to thank her several support teams: in Carmel, Chris, Ann, Anne, and Dennis; in Vancouver, Cheryl, James, Ryszard, and Michele; in Toronto, Helga, David, Patrick, and Norma. And particularly, also, those colleges and persons who lent much needed and treasured study space: Rick Asals at New College, Jay Macpherson at Victoria, Colin Visser and Lise-Lone Marker at University College, and Brian Corman at 7 KCC. Special thanks to Ingrid Harder for computerizing the genealogy, thereby making many a crooked line straight. She dedicates her share of this book to the memory of her parents, who made it all possible: her father, who introduced her to Chesterton, Doyle, H. G. Wells, and the life of the mind, and her mother, a Friend, in the Josephine Tey mode, of Richard the Third. We are both grateful to our contributors for their fine essays, as well as for their patience during the process of bringing this volume into print. Thanks, too, to Jerry Singerman, Ellen Fiskett, and Alison Anderson at the University of Pennsylvania Press for the care they took with *Detecting Texts*.

Because we want this book to be useful to readers of several languages and literatures, we have quoted foreign-language texts in English or included parenthetical translations. Texts that are well known in English, like Borges's "Death and the Compass," are cited according to their English-language titles; in the list of works cited, however, we include the original title and publication date. Conversely, we refer to less familiar foreign-language works by their original titles; if they have been translated into English we include the English title in the list of works cited. Occasionally, an essayist refers to both the original and the translation; in those instances, we provide full bibliographical information for both.

We hope that *Detecting Texts* will lead to further and more sophisticated criticism of this narrative genre. Therefore, in keeping with the spirit of the metaphysical detective story—which, by definition, adds to a mystery rather than resolving it—we have chosen to outline some generally unexplored areas of investigation in our introductory essay, and to conclude the volume with recommendations for additional reading on detective fiction and on metaphysical detective stories.

The Game's Afoot
On the Trail of the Metaphysical Detective Story

Patricia Merivale and
Susan Elizabeth Sweeney

> Then we sallied into the streets, arm in arm, continuing the top-
> ics of the day, or roaming far and wide until a late hour, seeking,
> amid the wild lights and shadows of the populous city, that infinity
> of mental excitement . . .
> —Edgar Allan Poe, "The Murders in the Rue Morgue" (415)

This collection of critical essays is the first to track down the metaphysical detective story, a genre of largely twentieth-century experimental
fiction with a flamboyant yet decidedly complex relationship to the detective story, and a kinship to modernist and postmodernist fiction in
general. The metaphysical detective story is distinguished, moreover,
by the profound questions that it raises about narrative, interpretation,
subjectivity, the nature of reality, and the limits of knowledge. For these
reasons, the aims of our volume are different from—and indeed, go far
beyond—those of other books that have been published on detective fiction, pop culture, postmodernist discourse, twentieth-century literature,
or literary theory. *Detecting Texts* traces the evolution of the metaphysical
detective story from its beginnings in Edgar Allan Poe's tales of mystery
and imagination to recent works by Umberto Eco, Georges Perec, Paul
Auster, and many others. Our volume also identifies the characteristic
themes and formal properties of the metaphysical detective story; develops new theoretical frameworks with which to analyze its unsettling
effects; and points the way for future investigations of the genre.

Definitions

A metaphysical detective story is a text that parodies or subverts traditional detective-story conventions—such as narrative closure and the
detective's role as surrogate reader—with the intention, or at least the
effect, of asking questions about mysteries of being and knowing which
transcend the mere machinations of the mystery plot. Metaphysical detective stories often emphasize this transcendence, moreover, by becoming self-reflexive (that is, by representing allegorically the text's own
processes of composition). Margaret Atwood's "Murder in the Dark"
(1983) provides a good illustration of the playful self-reflexiveness that
characterizes such stories:

> If you like, you can play games with this game. You can say: the murderer is the
> writer, the detective is the reader, the victim is the book. Or perhaps, the mur-
> derer is the writer, the detective is the critic and the victim is the reader. In that
> case the book would be the total *mise en scène*. . . .
>   In any case, that's me in the dark. I have designs on you, I'm plotting my sin-
> ister crime, my hands are reaching for your neck. . . . I wear boots with very soft
> soles, you can see the cinematic glow of my cigarette, waxing and waning in the
> fog of the room, the street, the room, even though I don't smoke. Just remem-
> ber this, when the scream at last has ended and you've turned on the lights: by
> the rules of the game, I must always lie.
>   Now: do you believe me? (30)

Atwood's tale concludes with a question rather than an answer—and
this sort of ending is typical of the genre. As Michael Holquist explains,
"the metaphysical detective story . . . is not concerned to have a neat
ending in which all the questions are answered, and can [therefore]
be forgotten" (170). Rather than definitively solving a crime, then, the
sleuth finds himself confronting the insoluble mysteries of his own interpretation and his own identity. (Metaphysical detectives are almost
invariably male, an issue that we will address later.) Patricia Merivale defines "a real metaphysical detective story," for example, as one "where
the detective hero himself becomes . . . the murderer he has been seeking" ("Flaunting" 210). In other such stories, the sleuth may fail to solve
the crime altogether—or do so only by accident. The detective's apparent inability to decipher the mystery (except solipsistically, in terms of
himself, his perceptions, and his mistaken assumptions) inevitably casts
doubt on the reader's similar attempt to make sense of the text. As Kevin
J. H. Dettmar puts it, a metaphysical detective story induces the reader
to read "like a detective a tale which cautions against reading like a detective" (156).

Literary critics have devised other names for this genre besides "metaphysical detective fiction." In 1972, William V. Spanos coined the term

"anti-detective story" to describe narratives that "evoke the impulse to 'detect'. . . in order to violently frustrate it by refusing to solve the crime" (154). Dennis Porter refined Spanos's term in 1981 (245–59); and Stefano Tani, who published, in 1984, the first book on what we call metaphysical detective fiction, analyzed, itemized, and further categorized such narratives under the general rubric of "anti-detective fiction." Yet the adjective "anti-detective" remains slightly misleading. These stories do subvert traditional detective-story conventions, but not necessarily as, in Tani's words, "a deliberate negation" of the entire detective genre (24). Rather, these stories apply the detective process to that genre's own assumptions about detection.

More recently, in 1987, Patrick Brantlinger identified as "deconstructive mysteries" certain novels, like Kafka's *The Trial* (1925), in which embedded texts " 'deconstruct' the crime-and-detection genre in parodic ways" (25); but this phrase unduly emphasizes the narrower category of "deconstruction" over the more capacious "metaphysics." In 1990, William J. Scheick coined the term "ethical romance" to describe how G. K. Chesterton's detective stories invite readers to examine their own epistemological assumptions (90); but this term fails to acknowledge that such tales are an extension of the detective-story tradition. That same year, Kevin Dettmar justified still another name, "postmodern mystery," by explaining that "according to all commentators this perverted detective tale is a postmodern genre" (cf. Richter, De Los Santos). Yet "postmodernism" itself is a hotly debated, polyvalent term that is as Protean as it is Procrustean (Merivale, "Austerized"), and that can be defined historically as well as formally. It inevitably leads Dettmar to such contradictions as, for example, attempting to apply the label "postmodern mystery" to a story written before World War I (154). Michel Sirvent, confronting a similar imbroglio of historical and formal distinctions in an essay written for this volume, has resolved it with the useful term "post-*nouveau roman* detective novel." Unfortunately, however, Sirvent's term necessarily applies to novels written within the last twenty years or so, and only French ones at that. Joel Black, in his essay for this volume, suggests a more precise and more accurate variant of the "anti-detective" label: "a hermeneutic mode that nevertheless reveals anti- or even post-hermeneutic features" (see p. 79). John T. Irwin, meanwhile—in a 1994 book on the subject, and an essay drawn from it that is reprinted in this volume—has proposed the category "analytic detective fiction" to differentiate Poe's and Jorge Luis Borges's tales from those that more or less straightforwardly narrate a detective's adventures. Irwin's rubric is appealing, because it accurately reflects such stories' self-reflexive concern with their own search for meaning; but it does not distinguish between Poe's early detective stories and the later, often subversive or even parodic refinements of the genre that he invented. Finally, Elana Gomel's 1995 coinage, "ontological detective story," neatly addresses both the genre's metafictional concerns and its affinity with science fiction. The "ontological" designation may be too narrow, however, to include those tales that focus explicitly on epistemology.

We have chosen the name "metaphysical detection," instead of these other designations, because it indicates explicitly how late modernist (sometimes proto-postmodernist) and postmodernist writers have altered the detective story. Such writers have used Poe's ratiocinative process to address unfathomable epistemological and ontological questions: What, if anything, can we know? What, if anything, is real? How, if at all, can we rely on anything besides our own constructions of reality? In this sense, metaphysical detective stories are indeed concerned with metaphysics. They evoke, moreover, the oddly abstract conceits of seventeenth-century "metaphysical" English poets and the eerie images of twentieth-century "metaphysical" Italian surrealist painters: works which use fabulous symbols, elaborate ironies, incongruous juxtapositions, and self-reflexive pastiche to indicate that "reality" is ultimately unknowable or at least ineffable (Cawelti 196; Tisdall 7–9). Metaphysical detective stories—composed in equal parts of parody, paradox, epistemological allegory (Nothing can be known with any certainty), and insoluble mystery—self-consciously question the very nature of reality, just as those metaphysical poems and paintings do.

In any case, "metaphysical detective story," the phrase first coined by Howard Haycraft in 1941 to describe the paradoxical plots and philosophico-theological intentions of Chesterton's Father Brown tales, and later refined by Merivale (in "The Flaunting of Artifice," 1967) and Holquist (1971–72), is the oldest and by now the most frequently used term for such literature. Age has its privileges.

Histories

The metaphysical detective story began with Poe's self-reflexive, philosophical, consciously literary detective stories in the 1840s; Arthur Conan Doyle's adventures in positivistic detection, in the 1890s, which provided material for later writers to question and parody; and Chesterton's early twentieth-century tales, wherein earthly crimes were solved while divine mysteries were acknowledged as beyond human understanding. Chesterton's brand of "metaphysical" detective fiction began to flourish again in the 1930s and 1940s, secularized by Borges and other proto-postmodernist writers of experimental fiction like Felipe Alfau, Vladimir Nabokov, and Flann O'Brien (Sweeney, "Aliens" 207–9). The metaphysical detective story was again renewed and redefined in the 1950s by

Alain Robbe-Grillet and his fellow writers of the French *nouveau roman*. And when Borges's exemplary fictions were finally translated from Spanish into English in the early 1960s, they inspired similar revisionist detective stories by Donald Barthelme, Robert Coover, Thomas Pynchon, and other American postmodernists—even as another generation of Latin-American writers, most notably Julio Cortázar and Gabriel García Márquez, continued to work primarily from the Borgesian model.

In the decades since Robbe-Grillet's and Borges's fictions became widely known, the metaphysical detective story has flourished in American, British, Canadian, French, Swiss, Italian, several Latin-American, German, Polish, Russian, and Japanese literatures, in novels and stories by Kobo Abe, Peter Ackroyd, Martin Amis, Hubert Aquin, Paul Auster, Julian Barnes, Barthelme, Thomas Berger, Richard Brautigan, Italo Calvino, Coover, Cortázar, Don DeLillo, José Donoso, Ariel Dorfman, Jean Echenoz, Umberto Eco, Timothy Findley, Max Frisch, Carlos Fuentes, Carlo Emilio Gadda, García Márquez, Witold Gombrowicz, William Hjortsberg, Sebastien Japrisot, Allen Kurzweil, Jean Lahougue, Stanislaw Lem, Patrick Modiano, Lawrence Norfolk, Joyce Carol Oates, Benoît Peeters, Georges Perec, Roberto Piglia, Manuel Puig, Pynchon, Ishmael Reed, Jean Ricardou, Ernesto Sábato, Leonardo Sciascia, Carol Shields, Gilbert Sorrentino, Graham Swift, Antonio Tabucchi, and many others. We discuss most of these writers in *Detecting Texts*, or at least locate them in our taxonomic genealogy of the metaphysical detective story (see p. 18).

By now, in fact, this quirky, bookish, decidedly highbrow genre may be ready for a mainstream audience—or, indeed, the mainstream audience may be ready for it. Brian McHale, discussing Cyberpunk (that is, postmodernist science fiction) in *Constructing Postmodernism*, points out that sophisticated and erudite fictional genres reciprocally invade and are invaded by more popular ones. Accordingly, elements of the metaphysical detective story may be seeping back into the popular mystery genre. Consider, for example, *The Singing Detective* (1986), Dennis Potter's successful television miniseries, or *Umney's Last Case* (1993), a fine metaphysical detective story by Stephen King, who is perhaps the most popular (in both senses) author of our day. One could also point to films such as *Angel Heart* (1987), based on William Hjortsberg's *Falling Angel* (a stunning blend of Gothic horror, hard-boiled detection, and metaphysical identity quest); or *Face/Off* (1997), which was advertised with the highly "metaphysical" slogan, "In order to catch him, he had to become him," and turned out to be a flabby techno-thriller with a shapely little metaphysical detective story inside it, trying to get out. Such "interface" or "reciprocity," in McHale's terms, between literary and popular detective genres is a thought-provoking development that deserves further study.

In order to trace the metaphysical detective story's evolution, this book is organized more or less chronologically. We examine metaphysical extensions or inversions of detective fiction's major types: Doyle's nineteenth-century tale of positivistic detection; Agatha Christie's Golden Age "puzzle" story; and Dashiell Hammett's and Raymond Chandler's hard-boiled detective novel. We also investigate some remarkable cases of literary influence, such as Christie's effect on French writers' compositional strategies or Chandler's impact on other authors as a stylistic model and even as a fictional character. The most remarkable case, however, may be that of Poe—the inventor of detective fiction—who determined the course of the genre not only with his famous Dupin tales, as everyone knows, but also, our essayists suggest, with his earlier stories "William Wilson" (1839) and "The Man of the Crowd" (1840). Poe, furthermore, originated such key generic tropes as the armchair detective, the purloined letter, the spurious text, the gumshoe, and the missing person—tropes which essays in our volume trace from his tales to the present. Indeed, Poe may well have invented not only classical detective fiction and its offshoot, the metaphysical detective story, but also the kind of playfully self-reflexive storytelling that we now call "postmodernist."

Theories

The metaphysical detective story (like the detective story proper) also plays a major part in the history of literary theory. As shown by the suggestions for further reading that conclude our volume, the poetics of traditional detective fiction has long been a popular and provocative topic among literary critics. Theorists have always been fascinated by the genre, of course, from Poe's own classic essays on literary closure to Roger Caillois's formalist study of the detective story as game, Geraldine Pederson-Krag's Freudian reading of it as repetition of the primal scene, and Ernst Kaemmel's Marxist analysis of it as product of capitalism. But recent critical interest in the detective genre dates, in particular, from Jacques Lacan's famous reading of Poe's story in "The Seminar on 'The Purloined Letter'" (1956; trans. 1972), which generated not only a notorious chain of ripostes—by Jacques Derrida, Barbara Johnson, and John Irwin, among others—but also new critical approaches to deconstruction, intertextuality, and psychoanalytic criticism. Other theorists have used detective fiction to illustrate the "hermeneutic code" (Barthes 75–77, 84–88), the importance of closure in Western culture (Kermode 19–21), the ways in which narratives tell stories (Brooks 23–27), and the ways in which readers read them (Prince 238). Heta Pyrhönen's recent book, *Murder from an Academic Angle*, systematically analyzes such theoretical approaches to the genre. And two previous essay collections have documented the extent to which traditional detective stories and literary theories mutually illuminate each other: Most and Stowe's *The Poetics of Murder: Detective Fiction and Literary Theory* and Walker and Frazer's *The Cunning Craft: Original Essays on Detective Fiction and Contemporary Literary Theory*.

Detecting Texts builds upon and expands these critical foundations in its work with the "newer" metaphysical genre, one that is inherently linked to literary theory. Metaphysical detective stories themselves explicitly speculate about the workings of language, the structure of narrative, the limitations of genre, the meanings of prior texts, and the nature of reading. Indeed, some literary theorists have even chosen the metaphysical genre as a rhetorical mode in which to advance their theories: consider Eco's *The Name of the Rose* (1980) or Norman Holland's *Death at a Delphi Seminar: A Postmodern Mystery* (1995). For these reasons, metaphysical detective stories present special challenges to literary critics. As Richard H. Rodino has remarked, critics must "try to match the fluid relations, risk-taking, uncouth energies, and nonpositivistic hermeneutics of metaphysical detective fiction with exegetical activity that is equally energetic and rigorous . . . and [that] engages in dialogical relations with the fresh orthodoxies promulgated by these works." Accordingly, the contributors to *Detecting Texts* use an eclectic range of approaches in order to analyze the already self-analytical genre of metaphysical detective fiction: literary history and influence; genre theory; reader-response and reception theory; deconstruction, hermeneutics, intertextuality, and narratology; phenomenology; psychoanalysis; cultural studies; and the philosophical insights of Blanchot, Foucault, Freud, Heidegger, Lacan, and Peirce, among others.

These various approaches also help to situate the metaphysical detective story within the ongoing critical debate about postmodernity. The genre offers a useful way to understand postmodernism as a theory, a practice, and a cultural condition. Holquist speculates, intriguingly, that postmodernist literature—which he places after World War II—uses detective fiction as a recurrent narrative subtext in much the same way that modernism uses mythology (165). Certainly, the writers who are most identified with postmodernism's formal characteristics (even if, like Borges and Nabokov, they began writing at the height of modernism) also helped to create the metaphysical detective story. The genre exemplifies postmodernism's concern with intertextuality, pop-culture pastiche, metafiction, and what John Barth famously called "the literature of exhaustion" (29). The metaphysical detective story's affinity for self-reflexive hermeneutics is also typically postmodernist (Hutcheon 81–82). Indeed, Spanos labels this genre "the paradigmatic archetype of the postmodern literary imagination" (154). And Tani even suggests that because metaphysical detective fiction "frustrates the expectations of the reader, transforms a mass-media genre into a sophisticated expression of avant-garde sensibility," and replaces positivistic interpretation with an acknowledgment of mystery, it is "the ideal medium of postmodernism" (40)—and, furthermore, that "Good contemporary fiction and anti-detective fiction are for the most part the same thing" (148).

The essays in this volume extend, question, and qualify such pronouncements. Several contributors in particular—Stephen Bernstein, Michael Sirvent, Jeanne C. Ewert, Raylene Ramsay, and Anna Botta—apply specific definitions of postmodernism to the genre or elucidate specific aspects of its postmodernist practice. Bernstein compares postmodernist intertextuality to nineteenth-century American allegorical romances and twentieth-century French existentialism. Sirvent studies the witty intertextual generative practices of the French novel after Robbe-Grillet, and Ramsay, examining Robbe-Grillet's own recent works, reveals some personal and cultural skeletons in the postmodernist closet. Ewert qualifies McHale's contrast between (modernist) epistemological and (postmodernist) ontological dominants in *Postmodernist Fiction* (1987), arguing that metaphysical detective fiction displays ontological concerns within an epistemological genre. (In *Constructing Postmodernism*, McHale himself qualifies that earlier distinction.) Botta, meanwhile, distinguishes the hermeneutics of space in recent novels from the hermeneutics of time in modernist texts. All these investigations help calibrate the genre's relationship to postmodernist modes and movements.

Themes and Structures

This volume also surveys the characteristic themes of the metaphysical detective story: (1) the defeated sleuth, whether he be an armchair detective or a private eye; (2) the world, city, or text as labyrinth; (3) the purloined letter, embedded text, *mise en abyme*, textual constraint, or text as object; (4) the ambiguity, ubiquity, eerie meaningfulness, or sheer meaninglessness of clues and evidence; (5) the missing person, the "man of the crowd," the double, and the lost, stolen, or exchanged identity; and (6) the absence, falseness, circularity, or self-defeating nature of any kind of closure to the investigation.

The first section is devoted to the armchair detective, whose investigation—like that of the protagonist in Cortázar's marvelous miniature metaphysical detective story, "Continuity of Parks" (1963)—consists solely of the act of reading. The second section is devoted to the gumshoe, who shadows his quarry throughout the mean streets of hard-boiled metaphysical detective stories, as Patricia Merivale shows in her essay on "Poe's 'The Man of the Crowd' and his Followers." But in these stories the armchair detective cannot escape from the text he is reading (or reading with), and the private eye cannot establish anyone's identity—not even his own.

In metaphysical detective fiction, in fact, the mystery is a maze without an exit. The armchair detective confronts a labyrinthine literary text; the private eye, a convoluted entanglement of streets—like the aerial view of a city that Pynchon's Oedipa Maas sees in *The Crying of Lot 49* (1966). Our contributors analyze such riddling configurations in detail. John Irwin proposes a seventeenth-century cabalistic design as a model for one of Borges's stories, and Robert L. Chibka recounts his experiences in the mazelike confusion of textual variations and variants generated by another; Joel Black examines the elusive library in *The Name of the Rose*; and Merivale follows the gumshoe, in his urban labyrinth, from Poe to the present. In later sections of the book, Ewert, echoing Eco, cites the rhizome structure—that is, an endlessly interlaced network rather than a bifurcated tree—as a paradigm of postmodernist detection; Hanjo Berressem, disentangling the temporal loops in Poe, Hitchcock, and Gombrowicz, critiques Lacan's use of the Borromean knot as a figure for human reality; and Botta surveys the perplexing topographies of Modiano's Paris and Tabucchi's Genoa. All of these mazes, moreover, are temporal as well as spatial.

Robert Rawdon Wilson has suggested that the metaphysical detective story itself is designed in the form of a textual labyrinth. Certainly the genre is preoccupied with perplexing, purloined, missing, and abyssal texts. Several essays in our volume trace the influence of Poe's classic tale "The Purloined Letter" (1844) on literary theory (Irwin, Berressem) and on later metaphysical detective stories (Irwin, Black, Sirvent, Ewert). Other essays trace the formal tradition, from Poe to the post-*nouveau roman*, of textual constraints that generate the very text of a metaphysical detective story (Irwin, Sirvent, Ewert, Ramsay). Contributors to *Detecting Texts* also manage to identify oddly shaped documents that mislead their would-be readers (Black); to enumerate multiply embedded texts that are incomplete or virtually indistinguishable (Sirvent); to uncover attempted forgeries by sleuths as well as criminals (Sweeney); and to delineate the process by which detectives disappear, at the story's end, into the words of its title (Botta).

In many metaphysical detective stories, letters, words, and documents no longer reliably denote the objects that they are meant to represent; instead, these texts become impenetrable objects in their own right. Such a world, made up of such nameless, interchangeable "things," cries out for the ordered interpretation that it simultaneously declares to be impossible. Robbe-Grillet articulates this problem in explaining why his intensely psychological novels are so concerned with surfaces, items, and artifacts. The world itself resembles a detective story, he says, in which "you have to keep coming back to the recorded evidence: the exact position of a piece of furniture, the shape and frequency of a fingerprint, a word written in a message. The impression grows on you that nothing else is *true*. Whether they conceal or reveal a mystery, these elements that defy all systems have only one serious, obvious quality—that of being *there*" (56; original emphasis). Our volume includes several meditations on the unalterable thing-ness of things: Jeffrey T. Nealon's explication of the nameless artifacts littering the streets of Auster's *City of Glass* (1985); Botta's account of passports, name tags, photographs, and other objects that are supposed to identify their owners in Modiano's and Tabucchi's novels, but instead remain obstinately ambiguous; Berressem's analysis of the "real" physical evidence in Gombrowicz's fictions, which must be changed to reflect the imaginary; and Susan Elizabeth Sweeney's description of physical traces that stubbornly remain despite the stories that are substituted for them.

Subjectivity presents a special problem for metaphysical sleuths. Detecting a singular identity is difficult in a postmodern world of forged papers and empty names, as Sirvent confirms with the parodic onomastics of the post-*nouveau roman*, Ramsay with the extensive variations upon the name "Morgan" in Robbe-Grillet's fiction, and Botta with the ambiguous referents in Modiano's *Rue des Boutiques Obscures* (1978). The central generic trope of "missing persons" is usefully defined in Merivale's essay. Merivale, like Botta, shows that the gumshoe detective's search for another is a definitively unsuccessful search for himself: he is the principal missing person for whom the reader, too, is forced to search. In other essays, Nealon traces relationships among author, narrator, detective, and fictitious detective novelist; Ramsay shows how author, investigator, and criminal are interrelated in Robbe-Grillet's fiction; and Sweeney studies staged deaths in which one character tries to appropriate another's identity.

The detective's failure to identify individuals, interpret texts, or, even more to the point, solve mysteries, is characteristic of the metaphysical genre. All of our essays deal, in one way or another, with what Black calls "(de)feats of detection." The detective's failure means, moreover, that the mystery remains unsolved and the text incomplete. This absence of closure is necessarily discussed in every essay, but is central to the arguments of Nealon, Sirvent, Ewert, and Botta.

The metaphysical detective story's most striking aspect, however, may be the inherently unresolvable nature of its own self-reflexiveness. Essays by Irwin, Chibka, Black, Sirvent, and Ewert address the problems of interpreting such a self-reflexive text. Other essays trace complicated patterns of intertextuality among different authors, such as Borges's revision of Poe's Dupin trilogy (Irwin); Eco's revision, in turn, of Poe, Chesterton, Christie, and Borges (Black); Auster's revision of American romanticism and Beckettian existentialism (Bernstein); and several post-*nouveaux romanciers*' revisions of classic tales by Christie and others (Sirvent). All the essays in *Detecting Texts* reveal, in these various ways, the extent to which the metaphysical detective story endlessly investigates the mysteries of narrative and interpretation, as well as the mysteries of its own narrative and its own interpretation.

To illustrate the historical development, critical significance, and generic concerns of the metaphysical detective story, we have divided this collection's twelve essays into the following sections: "Armchair Detecting, or the Corpus in the Library"; "Hard-Boiling Metaphysics"; "Postmortem: Modern and Postmodern"; and "Forging Identities."

Armchair Detecting, or the Corpus in the Library

The opening essay, John T. Irwin's "Mysteries We Reread, Mysteries of Rereading: Poe, Borges, and the Analytic Detective Story," brilliantly elucidates the taxonomy, the family relationships, as it were, of the most important branch of the metaphysical detective story. Irwin traces the derivation, from Poe's Dupin stories, of not only the "classical" detective story as a whole, and its "locked-room" and "armchair-detective" paradigms in particular, but also the metaphysical variants thereon—as seen in three of Borges's tales, "The Garden of Forking Paths" (1941), "Death and the Compass" (1942), and "Ibn Hakkan al-Bokhari, Dead in His Labyrinth" (1951). Irwin's widely acknowledged critical masterpiece, *The Mystery to a Solution: Poe, Borges, and the Analytic Detective Story* (1994), connects these tales to Poe's Dupin stories as tautly and neatly as is humanly possible. His book is a marvel of the comparative method, and a long overdue tribute to Poe as the "onlie begetter" of so much in postmodernist narrative structure. "Mysteries We Reread, Mysteries of Rereading," an excerpt from Irwin's book, provides a splendid beginning to our volume as well as an appropriate introduction to the next two essays.

In "Borges's Library of Forking Paths," Robert L. Chibka writes his own autobibliographical detective story in the form of a witty critical essay on Borges's tale "The Garden of Forking Paths." Chibka uses seemingly trivial variations in English texts cited by Borges, and in English translations of Borges's own text, as a model for analyzing the "proliferant variations" that are central to the thematics—but not, as he wisely reminds us, to the structure—of the tale itself (see p. 63). In his reading of "The Garden of Forking Paths," Chibka shows how the wistful theory of bifurcation collides with the heartbreaking fact of convergence—to result, via linear narrative, in what *one* English translation of Borges's text calls his protagonist's "infinite penitence and sickness of the heart" (101).

Joel Black's essay, "(De)feats of Detection: The Spurious Key Text from Poe to Eco," begins with the "spurious key texts" of Poe, subtly distinguishing "key" from "prize" texts and unreadableness (of various kinds) from incomprehensibility. Black shows how Chesterton adapts elements of "The Purloined Letter" in his story "The Wrong Shape" (1911), in which Father Brown determines from the medium (an oddly cut piece of paper) the falsity of the supposed message. And Borges, as we know from Irwin, also went back to Poe—but, as Black points out, via both Chesterton's story and Christie's *The ABC Murders* (1936)—in elaborating his own version, in "Death and the Compass," of spurious key texts. Eco, in turn, borrows this device in *The Name of the Rose* (1980) and *Foucault's Pendulum* (1988): in both novels, detectives fail to obtain a prize text because they misread the key text. Black concludes by briefly extending this theme into the postmodernist territory of Pynchon's *V.* (1963) and *The Crying of Lot 49* (1966), and DeLillo's *Ratner's Star* (1976).

These first three essays stress the historical and thematic development of the metaphysical detective story's self-reflexive intertextuality. Together, they show how the investigation of textual relationship links Poe to Borges (Irwin); characterizes our rereadings of Borges's rereadings (Chibka); and connects Borges, in turn, back to Chesterton, his favorite author, and ahead to Eco, the highly self-conscious contemporary heir of the Poe-Borges tradition (Black).

Hard-Boiling Metaphysics

The next three essays survey the dark, lonely world of the modernist and postmodernist private investigator. Indeed, in the last thirty years private eyes have become even more important to metaphysical detective fiction than armchair detectives—especially in the United States and in France (where, as we will see later, Chandler and the *roman noir* have saturated the culture of the twentieth century almost as much, perhaps, as Poe pervaded that of the nineteenth).

Patricia Merivale's essay, "Gumshoe Gothics: Poe's 'The Man of the Crowd' and His Followers," argues that Poe not only initiated the classical, "soft-boiled," amateur-sleuth story with his three Dupin tales, but also invented the "hard-boiled" detective story with his lesser-known earlier tale, "The Man of the Crowd" (1840). Merivale shows that this tale is actually a *metaphysical* hard-boiled detective story—a genre she calls "Gumshoe Gothic." Many gumshoe gothics explore the trope of the missing person, "a person sought for, glimpsed, and shadowed, gum-

shoe style, through endless, labyrinthine city streets, but never really
Found—because he was never really There" (see p. 105). Poe's gumshoe, shadowing his enigmatic eponymous hero, is shadowed, in turn,
by the readers of "The Man of the Crowd," as well as by the writers who
followed the model of this story: Chesterton, in "The Painful Fall of
a Great Reputation" (1905); Graham Greene, in "A Day Saved" (1935);
Kobo Abe, in *The Face of Another* (1964) and *Inter Ice Age 4* (1970); and
Paul Auster, in his *New York Trilogy* (1985, 1986, 1986). Merivale's pursuit
of "The Man of the Crowd" (and its followers) leads, in our genealogi-
cal taxonomy (see p. 18), from Poe to Auster—the most "European" of
contemporary American authors.

Auster's *New York Trilogy* is necessarily the high point of any inquiry
into the postmodernist private eye story. Stephen Bernstein and Jeffrey
T. Nealon, in their satisfyingly complementary essays, give complementary answers to what Auster calls "the question [which] is the story
itself" (3). In a subtly "worked" analysis of Auster's philosophical context, Nealon shows that "work" in *City of Glass* (1985), as well as "Work,"
the fictional detective invented by Auster's protagonist, can best be
understood in terms of the writer's "work," or labor, as defined by Blanchot. The dilemma of Auster's protagonist—a writer and would-be detective—is a philosophical one: how to proceed from the raw material
of words to transcendent metaphysical work. This problem is reiterated,
moreover, by the criminal's search for the prelapsarian language in our
world of fallen languages, where words no longer correspond to objects.
Language's stubborn indeterminacy can be read in two ways: Heidegger suggests that words, like objects, always point to other latent possibilities, whereas Blanchot points out that words therefore preclude the
possibility of any true meaning or end. Auster agrees with Blanchot, according to Nealon: in *City of Glass*, the detection process, the writing
process, the case, and the text itself yield nothing but "the revelation of
a dissembling endlessness" (see p. 123).

Bernstein focuses on both writing and reading by tracing the triple
intertextuality of Auster's *New York Trilogy*, in which European and
nineteenth-century American subtexts meld with echoes from Auster's
own works. Bernstein rightly emphasizes the analogues whereby Hawthorne's, Poe's, and Thoreau's texts can be seen to "invade" Auster's. The
play of "light" and "darkness" in the mode of the American Renaissance,
along with a specifically postmodernist anxiety related to Beckettian
self-negation, produce a trilogy that is, Bernstein believes, a revision of
Beckett's (in much the same sense, perhaps, that Irwin reads Borges's
detective-story triptych as a revision of Poe's). As Bernstein points out,
the internal echoes in Auster's works include Beckettian "scenes of writing," doubling characters not only with each other but with the au-

thor (as in Perec), in order to yield the "metafictional aesthetic" of Auster's self-reflexiveness. Bernstein asserts, in lapidary summary, that it is Auster's "unique mixture of a brooding nineteenth-century American pessimism and a brooding postmodernist French solipsism" that characterizes *The New York Trilogy* (see p. 150).

These various routes from Poe to Auster, braided together, comprise the primary strand of our collective inquiry in this collection. The "metaphysical art" that Poe found lacking in Dickens' *Barnaby Rudge* (244), he notably originated and skillfully developed in his own work, bequeathing it in full measure to his literary heirs: all the writers of the detective story, whether classical, hard-boiled, metaphysical, or some other category yet to be devised.

Postmortem: Modern and Postmodern

As the metaphysical detective story developed from its origins in Poe's armchair detective (Dupin) and his gumshoe (the narrator of "The Man of the Crowd"), it shaped and was shaped by modernism and postmodernism. The next three essays in our collection investigate the historical, formal, and thematic connections that link metaphysical detection to these two movements.

In "Reader-Investigators in the Post-*Nouveau Roman*," Michel Sirvent sees modernists Agatha Christie and Georges Simenon as sources of generative constraints. When combined with *nouveau-roman* strategies for deconstructing the detective story—such as multiple intertexts and textualized Oedipal plots (as in Robbe-Grillet), or a detective-as-criminal and a narrator playing each detective-story function in turn (as in Claude Ollier's recursively circular *La Mise en scène* [1958])—these generative constraints produce what Sirvent calls "the post-*nouveau roman*." He shows how hard- and soft-boiled detective stories alike are rewritten in witty texts by Benoît Peeters, Jean Lahougue, and (the best-known) Georges Perec. Peeters writes fictions based on Christie's classic detective stories. The very title of his *La Bibliothèque de Villers* (1980) generates the anagram of the culprit: one is meant to find *l i v r e [s]*, or the book itself, to be guilty. Lahougue's work rewrites Simenon's in a similar way. Simenon, as a highly influential heir of Chandler, and in some ways a bridge between Christie and Chandler, is parent to all the brooding, meditative policemen in recent detective fiction (like P. D. James's poet-policeman, Inspector Dalgliesh). Lahougue's levels of intertextual reworking link Simenon's themes with Robbe-Grillet's poetics to form a narratological critique challenging both memory and identity. Perec's *"53 jours"* (1989) sets up intertextual reading as investigation, again with Christie's help. The novel's narrative structure could be described, says

Sirvent, as a box with four false bottoms made up of *mises en abyme* and overlapping narratives. Elements of autobiography, detective story, and puzzle combine so that "Perec" himself appears as the final investigator. Like other post-*nouveaux romans*, "*53 jours*" does not include a solution to the mystery; therefore, the reader is forced into a textual investigation by way of a re-reading, "detecting" scattered textual signs by seeking clues in the narration rather than in what is narrated.

While Sirvent sees such textual constraints as characteristic of the change from modernist to postmodernist detective stories, Jeanne C. Ewert applies McHale's definition of the change from modernism to postmodernism as a shift from primarily hermeneutical to primarily ontological concerns. In her essay, " 'A Thousand Other Mysteries': Metaphysical Detection, Ontological Quests," Ewert finds that "bodies of dead detectives (and their victims) warn the reader away from the quest for knowledge" in the metaphysical detective stories of Borges, Friedrich Dürrenmatt, Heimito von Doderer, Robbe-Grillet, Eco, and especially Perec (see p. 181). She focuses on Perec's lipogrammatic detective novel, *A Void* (*La Disparition*, 1969), which is a tour de force in French, as well as in its English translation, because both versions surmount the trickiest challenge imaginable in any lipogram: composing without recourse to the commonest letter in either language, the *e*. *A Void* parodies Dupin's strategy for seeking a "purloined letter," and playfully indicates the forbidden (and thus fatal) knowledge of that letter's identity; in this way, it provides a complex example of the artifice of an ontologically oriented text. As proto- and postmodernist writers have refined the metaphysical detective-story tradition, Ewert argues, the nature of the game has changed: in books like Flann O'Brien's *The Third Policeman* (1967) and Gilbert Sorrentino's *Odd Number* (1985), the familiar labyrinth becomes a rhizome of infinite possibility and uncertainty, in accordance with the ontologies of unfamiliar universes with unnervingly porous boundaries. And hidden within that fantastic structure, Ewert adds, may be fictional representations of historical crimes, like the Holocaust, which provoke profound moral and metaphysical questions.

In "Postmodernism and the Monstrous Criminal," Raylene Ramsay, too, finds that such crimes produce, in metaphysical detective stories, a lingering sense of complicity that is characteristic of the postmodern era. She also shows how pathologies of projection in Robbe-Grillet's fiction, in particular, lead to the post-Sadean literature of misogynistic yet aestheticized violence against women, about which we will say more below when we look (albeit briefly) at metaphysical detective fiction in a feminist context. Ramsay traces the image of a "cell"—variously figured as a prison chamber, writer's study, secret room, heart, hollow, or void—throughout Robbe-Grillet's later fiction. This cell, Ramsay argues, is the domain of several different but oddly interrelated figures in Robbe-Grillet's version of the metaphysical detective story: the detective, the scientist, the sexual voyeur, the criminal, and the author himself. She examines, in particular, the multiple appearances of one inhabitant of the cell—the sinister Dr. Morgan—in several novels. Morgan, the sadistic voyeur, represents both an "I" (Robbe-Grillet's sense of himself) and a "we" (his sense of postmodernist identity, in an age influenced by scientific principles of "complementarity" and by shared responsibility for genocide, racism, and other collective crimes).

Forging Identities

Ramsay's essay provides a useful introduction to postmodernist concepts of subjectivity. The essays in our last section build upon her insights, demonstrating how efforts to establish identity in metaphysical detective stories are confounded by solipsism, self-projection, and the inability to position oneself in time or space or even one's own narrative.

Anna Botta's comparative study of Antonio Tabucchi and Patrick Modiano, "Detecting Identity in Time and Space," examines how these writers deploy the trope of "missing persons," that is, missing identities. Modiano's detective in *Rue des Boutiques Obscures* (1978) is an amnesiac searching for his own identity, which is lost in time; Tabucchi's detective in *Il Filo dell'orizzonte* (1986) must identify an anonymous corpse. Manipulating detective-story codes in this Foucauldian version of the contemporary world—one in which spatial precision tries in vain to compensate for temporal uncertainty—both protagonists seek, and fail to find, the linear narratives (or "solutions") proper to a detective story. Their way is blocked, Botta argues, by "the essential impasse of a hermeneutical project founded on a traditional concept of time" (see p. 222) and by the fundamentally unreliable nature of names as clues to identity. "[D]ead ends and trap doors," in Tabucchi's phrase (54), mark the labyrinthine topographies of Modiano's Paris and Tabucchi's Genoa: their hermeneutics of spatial, no longer temporal, detection ultimately yields an itinerary rather than an identity.

Hanjo Berressem's essay further studies postmodernist subjectivity by linking pathology, obsession, sexuality, violence, and death, and by following what inevitably emerges as the twisted and inconclusive patterns of the "return of the repressed." " 'Premeditated Crimes': The Dis-Solution of Detective Fiction in Gombrowicz's Works" uses Alfred Hitchcock's film *The Trouble with Harry* (1955) and a tale by the expatriate Polish writer Witold Gombrowicz, "A Premeditated Crime" (1936), as "primal scenes" for a Lacanian reading of Gombrowicz's novel *Cosmos* (1965). Berressem identifies Lacan's three-part structure of human reality (the symbolic, the imaginary, and the real) with three aspects of detective fiction: the detective, the criminal, and the evidence, respectively. It is the evidence, in particular—"in ninety-nine cases out of a hundred, a corpse —which has to be accounted for as the alien parameter in the symbolic universe" (see p. 232). Berressem examines the criminal's attempt to account for such evidence—belatedly, after the fact—by tracing the logical and temporal loops that dominate the structure of Hitchcock's film and Gombrowicz's fictions. In these works, as in Robbe-Grillet's *The Erasers*, paranoid systems already in place provide crimes committed after the fact—crimes that can, that is, be made to have "already happened."

In " 'Subject-Cases' and 'Book-Cases': Impostures and Forgeries from Poe to Auster," Susan Elizabeth Sweeney concludes our volume by examining the detective's efforts to imagine, conjecture, or borrow another's identity in order to solve a crime. In some tales, this practice leads to the detective's or criminal's attempt to substitute another's identity for his own. Sweeney links such substitution to the staged self-murder, a motif that she traces from Poe's "William Wilson" (1839) and Doyle's "The Man with the Twisted Lip" (1891) to its full development in metaphysical detective stories by Felipe Alfau ("Identity" [1936]); Vladimir Nabokov (*The Eye* [1930] and *Despair* [1934]); Borges ("The Form of the Sword" [1942] and "Theme of the Traitor and Hero" [1944]); and Auster (*The Locked Room* [1986]). The would-be criminal or detective masterminds of these metaphysical tales attempt, in each "case," to steal someone else's identity within the plot (what Sweeney calls a "subject-case"), and also to attain metafictional immortality within the narration (what Sweeney calls a "book-case"). These attempts are failures, however—as are most of the other detective enterprises described in our volume.

Leads for Further Investigation

Like all texts, the essays in this book suggest, in their gaps and aporias, further explorations that will map the territory of the metaphysical detective story more fully—in its relation, for instance, to such neighboring genres as the metaphysical spy story, mystery story, conspiracy novel, and cyberpunk techno-thriller, or indeed to the whole webbed texture of postmodernist, or perhaps Po(e)st-modernist fiction in which it is embedded.

A book on the metaphysical detective story without an entire essay on Thomas Pynchon will be seen in some quarters as *Hamlet* without the Prince. *V.* (1963), *The Crying of Lot 49* (1966), and sections of *Gravity's Rainbow* (1973) are all massively influential encyclopedic texts, in which failed searches for truth, certainty, and identity, where the world can only be interpreted by means of paranoid patterns, establish, at the very

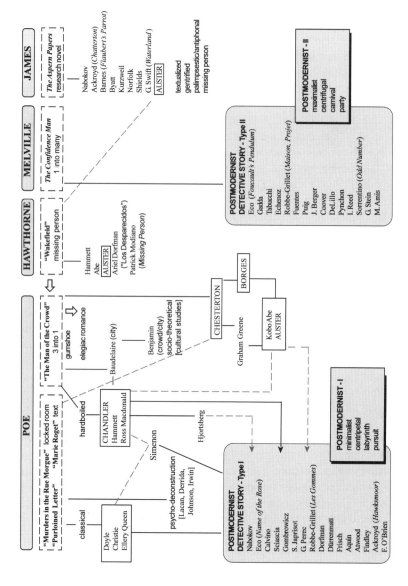

Figure 1. The metaphysical detective story: a tentative genealogy.

least, "metaphysical" conspiracy fiction. The problem with Pynchon is not the "metaphysical" but the "detective story" part of our rubric: not the mode, but the genre. Only Black, linking *V.* and *The Crying of Lot 49* with the trope of the "spurious key text," and Nealon, briefly discussing the latter novel's lack of closure, have found a way out of this difficulty. Other, more venial, omissions are simply due to the limits of space, opportunity, and availability. African-American novels like Ishmael Reed's *Mumbo Jumbo* (1972) remain largely unexplored, despite their metafictional detection of cultural history. Botta's account of Tabucchi and the readings of Eco by Black and Ewert are, regrettably, our only contributions to the study of the rich harvest of Italian metaphysical detective stories, where Sciascia the minimalist, Gadda the maximalist, and Eco the self-conscious postmodernist tower in significance. And the Hispanic, especially the Latin-American, metaphysical detective story— characterized by Donoso, Dorfman, Fuentes, Piglia, Puig, and many others (the homegrown progeny of García Márquez as well as of Borges), and represented here only in work on Borges himself (by Irwin, Chibka, Black, Ewert, and Sweeney)—raises further questions about the genre's links to other literary modes: magic realism, surrealism, fantasy, and the neoexpressionism of many recent, intensely psychologized crime fictions.

The Poe-to-Auster line—minimalist, labyrinthine, where plural identities are reduced into one, usually by pursuit—is, in studies by Irwin and others, the maze most fully mapped out. But it has come to dominate discussion of the metaphysical detective story in a way that blurs possibly useful distinctions with at least two other types, as shown in Figure 1. In addition to the minimalist tradition, then, the taxonomy sketched out in this chart suggests two other major postmodernist groupings of metaphysical detective stories that deserve further study: the maximalist (Sorrentino, Echenoz) and the pseudobiographical (Ackroyd, Byatt), which are only obliquely discussed in this volume. The merging of two popular genres, the detective story and the historical novel, is emphatically metaphysical in Eco and Ackroyd (and also, for instance, Peter Greenaway), and though somewhat less so in Norfolk, Kurzweil, Caleb Carr, Iain Pears, and many others, the grouping would repay investigation. Gilbert Sorrentino, for instance, exemplifies a very different type of metaphysical detective story from those in the Poe-to-Auster line. *Odd Number* (1985) is carnivalesque in mode, maximalist in style, and centrifugal in structure. It has far too much plot, leaves loose ends all over the place, and supplies everyone with identities as uncertain as they are multiple (see Ewert's essay for an account of this novel). Future work on the metaphysical detective story might include, then, a comparative study of authors like Gadda (*That Awful Mess on the Via Merulana* [1957]), the middle Robbe-Grillet (*La Maison de Rendez-vous* [1965] and *Project for a Revolution in New York* [1970]), Reed (*Mumbo Jumbo* [1972]), Coover (*Gerald's Party* [1986]), and Eco (not in *The Name of the Rose* [1980] but in *Foucault's Pendulum* [1988]), who have all written such stories.

Peter Ackroyd's *Chatterton* (1987), for instance, although largely about "forgers and plagiarists," is also, as Sweeney's essay points out, an example of the "research novel"—a subgenre which constitutes antiphonal pseudobiography as a form of metaphysical detection, in which finding the "missing person" characteristically leads, as in other instances of fictional stalking, to discovering that *we* are him or her. Literary biography thus becomes the metatext of palimpsested identity. The research novel is by far the most flourishing branch of the metaphysical detective story, at least in economic (bestseller) terms, perhaps because it is the least flamboyantly postmodernist; and it is quite markedly the type of metaphysical detective story that has appealed most to female writers, possibly for the same reason. The most notably "metaphysical" of female detectives are the academic women in A. S. Byatt's *Possession* (1991) and Carol Shields' *Swann* (1987). The latter, for example, is an excellently metaphysical detective story of a poet's identity built up of nothing but the steadily more doubtful "text," with both mysteries spoiled, for the purist, by two solutions: "Who stole it?" (the ex-boyfriend); "Who wrote it?" (everybody). *Swann* also provides a rare example of the *feminist* metaphysical detective story, as Sweeney has shown elsewhere ("Formal").

Future work on the metaphysical detective story should indeed include feminist approaches to the genre. Joyce Carol Oates's series of Gothic mysteries, set in nineteenth-century America, which defy ratiocinative solutions—especially *Mysteries of Winterthurn* (1984)—deserves further investigation, for example. But the female authors who really get into the spirit of the metaphysical detective story, albeit in miniature, are Margaret Atwood (cited above) and Gertrude Stein (cited below). A feminist response to the genre, while clearly necessary, is fraught with difficulties. With the exception of the pseudobiographical mode just mentioned, the authors of metaphysical detective stories are almost exclusively men—a fact made more curious by the notoriously dominant role of women in writing classical detective stories (Agatha Christie, Dorothy Sayers, P. D. James, and many others), as well as women's recent and much-annotated forays into the hard-boiled and police procedural genres (see, for example, Irons and others on Sue Grafton, Sara Paretsky, Barbara Wilson, and many more). At the same time, male authors like Robbe-Grillet (in his later novels) and Hubert Aquin have turned the metaphysical detective story into a branch of highbrow pornography, thus making it, perhaps unintentionally, a feminist concern. They and many others provide material for Patricia Smart's central question as she investigates patriarchy in Québécois literature, where (as elsewhere) it has both embodied and erased the woman:

Where Have They Put the Bodies?
    If patriarchal culture has imprisoned women in a prescribed bodily mold, feminist artists may choose to escape that representational trap by emphasizing the (female) body's absence from history and culture, its effective non-existence when objectified by the male gaze. For Louky Bersianik (who has frequently acknowledged her debt to Luce Irigaray), this "disappeared" female body has been the primary structuring element in human history: "L'histoire de l'humanité qu'on nous a donnée pour vraie est . . . un grand roman policier . . . plein de meurtres anonymes où l'on a fait disparaître le corps, où l'on a parfaitement fait disparaître les taches de sang, de sorte que les gens ne croient pas à la réalité de ces meurtres."
    ("The history of humanity that they gave us as the truth is . . . an enormous detective story . . . full of anonymous murders in which the bodies have been made to disappear, in which the traces of blood have been utterly made to disappear, in such a way that people do not believe in the reality of those murders" [Bersianik, *Pique-nique* 75–76; our trans.]). (Smart 18–19)

As long as *bodies* are still unaccounted for in such investigations, much work remains to be done.
    Although *Detecting Texts* is the first volume of essays devoted solely to metaphysical detective fiction, then, it cannot claim to issue any definitive solutions. Gertrude Stein, describing (in 1937) one of her own modernist experimental novellas, may have had the first word on the problem of closure in metaphysical detective fiction: "It had a good name it was *Blood on the Dining-Room Floor* and it all had to do with that but there was no corpse and the detecting was general . . . it was such a good detective story but nobody did any detecting except just conversation . . . so finally I concluded that . . . on the whole a detective story . . . has to have an ending and my detective story did not have any" ("Why" 148–49). Indeed, Stein's *Blood on the Dining-Room Floor* (1935) may be counted among the earliest metaphysical detective stories. But the last word on closure—according to the very nature of this genre—is not yet, or perhaps never, to be spoken . . .

Works Cited

Ackroyd, Peter. *Chatterton.* New York: Grove, 1987.
Angel Heart. Dir. Alan Parker. Perf. Mickey O'Rourke, Robert De Niro, and Lisa Bonet. 1987.
Atwood, Margaret. "Murder in the Dark." *Murder in the Dark: Short Fictions and Prose Poems.* Toronto: Coach House Press, 1983. 29–30.
Auster, Paul. *The New York Trilogy.* [1985, 1986, 1986]. New York: Penguin, 1990.
Barth, John. "The Literature of Exhaustion." *Atlantic,* August 1967: 29–34.

Barthes, Roland. *S/Z*. [1970]. Trans. Richard Miller. New York: Hill and Wang, 1974.

Bersianik, Louky. *Le Pique-nique sur l'Acropole*. Montreal: VLB Editeur, 1979.

Borges, Jorge Luis. "The Garden of Forking Paths." ["El Jardín de senderos que se bifurcan," 1941]. Trans. Helen Temple and Ruthven Todd. *Ficciones*, ed. Anthony Kerrigan. New York: Grove, 1962. 89–101.

Brantlinger, Patrick. "Missing Corpses: The Deconstructive Mysteries of James Purdy and Franz Kafka." *Novel* 20, 1 (1987): 24–40.

Brooks, Peter. *Reading for the Plot*. New York: Random, 1984.

Byatt, A. S. *Possession*. New York: Random, 1991.

Caillois, Roger. "The Detective Novel as Game." [1941]. Trans. William W. Stowe. Most and Stowe 1–12.

Cawelti, John G. "Artistic Failures and Successes: Christie and Sayers." In *Detective Fiction: A Collection of Critical Essays*, ed. Robin W. Winks. Englewood Cliffs, N.J.: Prentice-Hall, 1980. 186–99.

Coover, Robert. *Gerald's Party*. New York: Simon and Schuster, 1985.

Cortázar, Julio. "Continuity of Parks." ["Continuidad de los parques," 1963]. *Blow-Up and Other Stories*. [1965]. Trans. Paul Blackburn. New York: Pantheon, 1990. 63–65.

De Los Santos, Oscar. "Auster vs. Chandler or: Cracking the Case of the Postmodern Mystery." *Connecticut Review* 18, 1 (1994): 75–80.

Dettmar, Kevin J. H. "From Interpretation to 'Intrepidation': Joyce's 'The Sisters' as a Precursor of the Postmodern Mystery." Walker and Frazer 149–65.

Face/Off. Dir. Paul Verhoeven. Perf. John Travolta and Nicolas Cage. 1997.

Gadda, Carlo Emilio. *That Awful Mess on the Via Merulana*. [*Quer pasticciaccio brutto de Via Merulana*, 1957]. Intro. Italo Calvino, trans. William Weaver. New York: George Braziller, 1984.

Gomel, Elana. "Mystery, Apocalypse, and Utopia: The Case of the Ontological Detective Story." *Science Fiction Studies* 22, 3 (1995): 343–56.

Haycraft, Howard. *Murder for Pleasure: The Life and Times of the Detective Story*. New York: Appleton-Century, 1941.

Holland, Norman. *Death at a Delphi Seminar: A Postmodern Mystery*. Albany, N.Y.: SUNY Press, 1995.

Holquist, Michael. "Whodunit and Other Questions: Metaphysical Detective Stories in Post-War Fiction." [1971–72]. Reprinted in Most and Stowe 149–74.

Hutcheon, Linda. *A Theory of Parody: The Teachings of Twentieth-Century Art Forms*. New York: Methuen, 1985.

Irons, Glenwood, ed. *Feminism in Women's Detective Fiction*. Toronto: University of Toronto Press, 1995.

Kaemmel, Ernst. "Literature Under the Table: The Detective Novel and Its Social Mission." [1962]. Trans. Glenn W. Most. Most and Stowe 55–61.

Kermode, Frank. *The Sense of an Ending*. New York: Oxford University Press, 1967.

King, Stephen. *Umney's Last Case*. [1993]. New York: Penguin, 1995.

Lacan, Jacques. "Seminar on 'The Purloined Letter.'" [1956]. Trans. Jeffrey Mehlman. *Yale French Studies* 48 (1972): 39–72.

McHale, Brian. *Constructing Postmodernism*. New York: Routledge, 1992.

———. *Postmodernist Fiction*. New York: Methuen, 1987.

Merivale, Patricia. "The Austerized Version." Review of *Beyond the Red Notebook*, ed. Dennis Barone; Paul Auster issue, *Review of Contemporary Fiction*, ed. Dennis Barone; and *L'Oeuvre de Paul Auster*, ed. Annick Duperray. *Contemporary Literature* 38, 1 (1997): 185–97.

————. "The Flaunting of Artifice in Vladimir Nabokov and Jorge Luis Borges." In *Nabokov: The Man and His Work*, ed. L. S. Dembo. Madison: University of Wisconsin Press, 1967. 290–324. Reprinted in *Critical Essays on Jorge Luis Borges*, ed. Jaime Alazraki. Boston: G. K. Hall, 1987. 141–53.

Modiano, Patrick. *Rue des Boutiques Obscures*. [*Missing Person*]. Paris: Gallimard, 1978.

Most, Glenn W. and William W. Stowe, eds. *The Poetics of Murder: Detective Fiction and Literary Theory*. New York: Harcourt, 1983.

Oates, Joyce Carol. *Mysteries of Winterthurn*. New York: Dutton, 1984.

Pederson-Krag, Geraldine. "Detective Stories and the Primal Scene." [1949]. Most and Stowe 13–20.

Poe, Edgar Allan. "*Barnaby Rudge* by Charles Dickens." [1842]. *Edgar Allan Poe: Essays and Reviews*. New York: Library of America, 1984. 224–44.

————. "The Murders in the Rue Morgue." [1841]. *Tales of Mystery and Imagination*, ed. Graham Clarke. London: Dent, 1984. 411–44.

Porter, Dennis. *The Pursuit of Crime: Art and Ideology in Detective Fiction*. New Haven, Conn.: Yale University Press, 1981.

Potter, Dennis. *The Singing Detective*. [BBC, London, 1986]. Boston: Faber and Faber, 1986.

Prince, Gerald. "Notes on the Text as Reader." In *The Reader in the Text: Essays on Audience and Interpretation*, ed. Susan R. Suleiman and Inge Crosman. Princeton, N.J.: Princeton University Press, 1980. 233–46.

Pynchon, Thomas. *The Crying of Lot 49*. Philadelphia: Lippincott, 1966.

————. *Gravity's Rainbow*. New York: Viking, 1973.

————. *V.* [1963]. New York: Bantam, 1964.

Pyrhönen, Heta. *Murder from an Academic Angle: An Introduction to the Study of the Detective Narrative*. Columbia, S.C.: Camden House, 1994.

Reed, Ishmael. *Mumbo Jumbo*. [1972]. New York: Bard, 1978.

Richter, David H. "Murder in Jest: Serial Killing in the Post-Modern Detective Story." *Journal of Narrative Technique* 19, 1 (1989): 106–15.

Robbe-Grillet, Alain. *La Maison de Rendez-vous*. [*The House of Assignation*]. Paris: Minuit, 1965.

————. "A Path for the Future Novel." ["Une Voie pour le roman futur," 1956]. *Snapshots* and *Towards a New Novel*, trans. Barbara Wright. London: Calder and Boyars, 1965. 50–57.

————. *Projet pour une révolution à New York*. [*Project for a Revolution in New York*]. Paris: Minuit, 1970.

Rodino, Richard H. Concluding Remarks. Session on Metaphysical Detective Stories. Modern Language Association Convention, Chicago, Ill., 1990.

Scheick, William J. "Ethical Romance and the Detecting Reader: The Example of Chesterton's *The Club of Queer Trades*." Walker and Frazer 86–97.

Shields, Carol. *Swann: A Mystery*. [1987]. New York: Viking, 1989.

Smart, Patricia. "The Body Seen Through a Distorting Lens: Feminist Grotesque in the Art of Jana Sterbak and Louky Bersianik." In *Literature and the Body*, ed. Anthony Purdy. Amsterdam: Rodopi, 1992. 13–28.

Spanos, William V. "The Detective and the Boundary: Some Notes on the Postmodern Literary Imagination." *Boundary 2* 1, 1 (1972): 147–60. Reprinted in *Repetitions: The Postmodern Occasion in Literature and Culture*. Baton Rouge: Lousiana State University Press, 1987. 13–50.

Stein, Gertrude. *Blood on the Dining-Room Floor*. [1935]. Ed. John Herbert Gill. Berkeley, Calif.: Creative Arts, 1982.

———. "Why I Like Detective Stories." [1937]. *How Writing Is Written*, ed. Robert Bartlett Haas. Los Angeles: Black Sparrow Press, 1974. 146–50.

Sweeney, Susan Elizabeth. "Aliens, Aliases, and Alibis: Felipe Alfau's *Locos* as a Metaphysical Detective Story." *Review of Contemporary Fiction* 13, 1 (1993): 207–14.

———. "Formal Strategies in a Female Narrative Tradition: The Case of *Swann: A Mystery*." In *Anxious Power: Reading, Writing, and Ambivalence in Narrative by Women*, ed. Carol J. Singley and Susan Elizabeth Sweeney. Albany, N.Y.: SUNY Press, 1993. 19–32.

Tabucchi, Antonio. *Il Filo dell'orizzonte*. [*The Edge of the Horizon*, trans. Tim Parks, New York: New Directions, 1990]. Milano: Feltrinelli, 1986.

Tani, Stefano. *The Doomed Detective: The Contribution of the Detective Novel to Postmodern Italian and American Fiction*. Carbondale: Southern Illinois University Press, 1984.

Tisdall, Caroline. "Historical Foreword." In *Metaphysical Art*, comp. Massimo Carrà, Patrick Waldberg, and Ewald Rathke, trans. Caroline Tisdall. London: Thames and Hudson, 1971. 7–16.

Walker, Ronald G. and June M. Frazer, eds. *The Cunning Craft: Original Essays on Detective Fiction and Contemporary Literary Theory*. Macomb: Western Illinois University Press, 1990.

Wilson, Robert Rawdon. "Godgames and Labyrinths: The Logic of Entrapment." *Mosaic* 15, 4 (1982): 1–22.

Armchair Detecting, or the Corpus in the Library

Chapter 1
Mysteries We Reread, Mysteries of Rereading
Poe, Borges, and the Analytic Detective Story
John T. Irwin

Let me start with a simple-minded question: How does one write analytic detective fiction as high art when the genre's basic structure, its central narrative mechanism, seems to discourage the unlimited rereading associated with serious writing? That is, if the point of an analytic detective story is the deductive solution of a mystery, how does the writer keep the achievement of that solution from exhausting the reader's interest in the story? How does one write a work that can be reread by people other than those with poor memories?

I use the term "analytic detective fiction" here to distinguish the genre invented by Poe, in the Dupin tales of the 1840s, from stories whose main character is a detective but whose main concern is not analysis but adventure, stories whose true genre is less detective fiction than quest romance, as one of the masters of the adventure mode, Raymond Chandler, implicitly acknowledged when he gave the name "Mallory" to an early prototype of his detective Philip Marlowe. For Chandler, the private investigator simply represents a plausible form of modern knight-errant. In his essay "The Simple Art of Murder," he says that a detective story is the detective's "adventure in search of a hidden truth, and it would be no adventure if it did not happen to a man fit for adventure" (398). The emphasis in Chandler's remarks, as in his fiction, is on the detective's character and his adventures, with the revelation of a hidden truth simply serving as a device to illuminate the former and motivate the latter. But in the pure analytic detective story the matter is otherwise. As a character, Dupin is as thin as the paper he's printed on. As for his adventures, they amount to little more than reading newspaper accounts of the crime and talking with the Prefect of police and the narrator in the privacy of his apartment. What gives the analytic detective genre its special appeal is that quality which the Goncourt brothers noted on first reading Poe. In an 1836 journal entry they described Poe's stories as "a new literary world" bearing "signs of the literature of the twentieth century—love giving place to deductions . . . the interest of the story moved from the heart to the head . . . from the drama to the solution" (Poe, *Collected* 2: 521n). Precisely because it is a genre that grows out of an interest in deductions and solutions rather than in love and drama, the analytic detective story shows little interest in character, managing at best to produce caricatures—those monsters of idiosyncrasy from Holmes to Poirot. In its purest form it puts all its eggs in the basket of plot, and a specialized kind of plot at that. The problem is that this basket seems to be one that can be emptied in a single reading. Related to this difficulty is another. If the writer does his work properly, if he succeeds in building up a sense of the mysterious, of some dark secret or intricately knotted problem, then he has to face the fact that there simply exists no hidden truth or guilty knowledge whose revelation will not seem anticlimactic compared to an antecedent sense of mystery and the infinite speculative possibilities it permits. Borges, one of the contemporary masters of the analytic detective story, acknowledges this difficulty in his tale "Ibn Hakkan al-Bokhari, Dead in His Labyrinth" (1951). He says that one of his characters, "steeped in detective stories, thought that the solution of a mystery is always less impressive than the mystery itself" (123). But if in the analytic detective story the solution is always in some sense an anticlimax that in dissipating the mystery exhausts the story's interest for us, an interest in speculative reasoning which the mystery empowers, then how does one write this kind of story as a serious, that is, rereadable, literary form? How does one both present the analytic solution of a mystery and at the same time conserve the sense of the mysterious on which analysis thrives?

Given the predictable economy of a critical essay, I think the reader is safe in assuming that if I didn't consider Poe's Dupin stories to be, on the one hand, archetypes of analytic detective fiction, and on the other, serious literary works that demand and repay rereading, there would be no reason for my evoking at this length the apparent incompatibility of these modes and thus the writer's problem in reconciling them. All of which brings me to the task of uncrumpling that much crumpled thing, "The Purloined Letter" (1844), to consider the way that this problem of a mystery with a repeatable solution, a solution that conserves (because it endlessly refigures) the sense of the mysterious, lies at the very origin of the analytic detective story.

I

My approach to "The Purloined Letter" will be along what has recently become a well-worn path. I want to look briefly at three readings of the story that form a cumulative series of interpretations, each successive reading commenting both on the story and on the previous reading(s) in the series. They are Jacques Lacan's "Seminar on 'The Purloined Letter'" (1957), Jacques Derrida's "The Purveyor of Truth" (1975), and Barbara Johnson's "The Frame of Reference: Poe, Lacan, Derrida" (1978). Each of these essays presents a lengthy, complex argument in which "The Purloined Letter" is treated as a pretext, which is to say, read as a parable of the act of analysis. However, I am not so much interested here in following the convolutions of their individual arguments as in isolating a thread that runs through all three, a clue to conduct us through labyrinthine passages. And that thread is the position that each essay takes on what we might call the numerical/geometrical structure of the story.

Let us begin with Lacan. He says that the story consists of "two scenes, the first of which we shall straightway designate the primal scene, and by no means inadvertently, since the second may be considered its repetition" (41). The first or primal scene takes place in "the royal *boudoir*" (41), the second scene in "the Minister's office" (42). And according to Lacan, each of these scenes has a triangular structure: each is composed of "three logical moments" (43), "structuring three glances, borne by three subjects, incarnated each time by different characters":

The first is a glance that sees nothing: the King and the police.
  The second, a glance which sees that the first sees nothing and deludes itself as to the secrecy of what it hides: the Queen, then the Minister.
  The third sees that the first two glances leave what should be hidden exposed to whoever would seize it: the Minister, and finally Dupin. (44)

Thus, in the royal boudoir, the King does not see the incriminating letter which the Queen in her haste has hidden in the open, leaving it with its address uppermost in plain sight on a table. And the Queen, seeing that the King doesn't see the letter, mistakes his blindness for the letter's concealment, thus leaving herself vulnerable to the Minister, who sees both the King's glance and the Queen's and realizes that the letter can be seized before the Queen's very eyes precisely because she dare not do anything to attract the King's attention to it. Similarly, in the second scene, at the Minister's residence, the letter, having been turned inside out and readdressed in a female hand, is once again hidden in plain sight in a card rack on the mantelpiece. And this time the police, who have searched the Minister's quarters repeatedly without noticing the letter, represent the first glance which sees nothing; the Minister, who mistakes the blindness of the police for the concealment of the letter, represents the second glance, and Dupin represents the third glance that sees what the first two miss, that is, that the letter hidden in the open is his for the taking. The figure who participates in both these triangular scenes is the Minister, and his shifting from the position of the third glance in the initial scene to that of the second glance in its repetition exhibits the special vulnerability to self-delusion, to a blind spot, which the possession of the letter conveys.

Consider, now, Derrida's critique of this reading, keeping in mind that in his essay "The Purveyor of Truth" Derrida is motivated less by an interest in Poe or "The Purloined Letter" than by a desire to score points off Lacan. As Johnson points out, Derrida, in a lengthy footnote to his book *Positions*, sketches the argument that will become "The Purveyor of Truth" and cites in this context Lacan's multiple *"acts of aggression"* against him since the publication of *De la grammatologie* in *Critique* in 1965 (Johnson 118). Obviously, Derrida takes the case of "The Purloined Letter" for one of the same reasons that Dupin did—the Minister once did Dupin "an evil turn" ("Purloined" 993) at Vienna, and Dupin sees the affair of the letter as an opportunity to get even. The wit of Derrida's essay lies in the way that it uses Lacan's reading of "The Purloined Letter" against itself, for if Lacan believes that with his interpretation of the story he has, as it were, gained possession of Poe's "Purloined Letter," has made its meaning his own, then Derrida will show him that the possession of that letter, as Lacan himself pointed out, brings with it a blind spot. In his essay Derrida sets out to repeat the encounter between Dupin and the Minister, with himself in the role of Dupin and Lacan in the role of the Minister.

Derrida attacks Lacan's reading of the story on a variety of points, but the one that concerns us has to do with Lacan's notion of the triangular structure of each of the two scenes in the tale. Derrida agrees that the story consists of two scenes, but not the two on which Lacan focuses. He points out that the scene in the royal boudoir and the subsequent scene at the Minister's residence are two narrated scenes within the framing artifice of the story, but that the story itself consists of two scenes of narration—the first scene being the Prefect's initial visit to Dupin during which the Prefect recounts the events in the royal boudoir, and the second scene being the Prefect's subsequent visit during which Dupin recounts the events at the Minister's residence. While the narrators of the two *narrated scenes* in the royal boudoir and at the Minister's residence are respectively the Prefect and Dupin, the narrator of the two *scenes of narration* at Dupin's lodgings is Dupin's unnamed companion. Thus, according to Derrida, Lacan reduces the four-sided structure of the scene of narration—what Derrida calls "the scene of writing"—to the three-sided structure of the narrated scene "by overlooking the narrator's position, the narrator's involvement in the content of what he seems to be recounting" (100). In ignoring the presence of the narrator of "The Purloined Letter," Lacan cuts "a fourth side" out of the narrated figure "to leave merely triangles" (54). And he does this, says Derrida, precisely because, as a psychoanalyst, Lacan projects upon Poe's story the structure of the Oedipal triangle in his desire to read "The Purloined Letter" as an allegory of psychoanalysis or "*an allegory of the signifier*" (Johnson 115).

Now, since in his critique of Lacan's interpretation of "The Purloined Letter" Derrida aims to get even with Lacan by being one up on him, and since Lacan in his reading of the numerical structure of the tale has already played the numbers one, two, and three (the tale is composed of two scenes, the second of which, by repeating the triangular structure of the first, creates a sameness or oneness between the two), then being one up on Lacan means playing the next open number (four); and that is what Derrida does in arguing that the structure of the scenes is not triangular but quadrangular. However, whether Derrida arrives at this quadrangular structure by adding one to three or by doubling two is a problematic point, a point on which Johnson focuses in her critique of Lacan's and Derrida's readings of the tale's numerical structure.[1]

As with Derrida's reading of Lacan, the wit of Johnson's reading of Derrida lies in the way that she doubles Derrida's own insights back upon themselves to make them problematic. Thus in dealing with Derrida's attempt to be one up on Lacan by playing the number four to Lacan's three, Johnson assimilates their opposed readings of the numerical structure of the tale to the game of even and odd, the game which Dupin proposed as an illustration of the way that one doubles the thought processes of an opponent in order to be one jump ahead. Derrida opts for a quadrangular structure, that is, he plays the even number four, in order to evoke the uncanniness, the oddness of doubling; while Lacan opts for a triangular structure by playing the odd number three, in order to enforce the regularizing or normalizing effect of the dialectical triad. In this game of even and odd, Derrida and Lacan end up as reciprocal opposites, as specular doubles of one another: Derrida asserts the oddness of evenness, while Lacan affirms the evenness of oddness. Given the destabilizing reversal-into-the-opposite inherent in doubling, Johnson sees the opposition between Derrida's and Lacan's interpretations as an "oscillation" between the former's "unequivocal statements of undecidability" and the latter's "ambiguous assertions of decidability" (146).

As to Johnson's own position on "The Purloined Letter," her reading of Lacan and Derrida is meant to free her from having to take a position on the numerical structure of the tale, or more exactly, to free her from having to take a *numerical* position on that structure. She does not intend, for example, to play the next open number (five); for since she has reduced Lacan's and Derrida's readings of the numerical structure of the story to the specular game of even and odd, there exist only two numerical positions that one can take on that structure—even or odd—and these, Johnson contends, have already been played by Derrida and Lacan without any clear conclusion. Johnson's strategy is to call into question the whole concern with numbers. At one point she asks, "But can what is at stake here really be reduced to a mere numbers game?" and a bit later she answers, "Clearly, in these questions, the very notion of a number becomes problematic, and the argument on the basis of numbers can no longer be read literally" (121). As Johnson sees it, taking a position on the numerical structure of the tale means, for Lacan and Derrida, taking a numerical position, choosing a number, but that means playing the game of even and odd, the game of trying to be one up on a specular, antithetical double. And playing that game means endlessly repeating the structure of "The Purloined Letter" in which being one up inevitably leads to being one down. For if the structure created by the repeated scenes in the tale involves doubling the thought processes of one's opponent in order to use his own methods against him—as Dupin does with the Minister, as Derrida does with Lacan, and as Johnson does with Derrida—then the very method by which one outwits one's opponent, by which one comes out one up, is the same method that will be employed against oneself by the next player in the game, the next interpreter in the series, in order to leave the preceding interpreter one down.

Is it possible, then, to interpret "The Purloined Letter" without duplicating in the interpretive act that reversal-into-the-opposite inherent in the mechanism of seizing the letter as that mechanism is described in the tale? Is it possible to generate an insight without a blind spot in it, a flaw that allows the insight subsequently to be turned against itself? Clearly, the desire for such an invulnerable insight is at work in Johnson's essay, and accounts for the at times disconcerting level of self-consciousness which she tries to maintain regarding her own methodological stance, her own critical assumptions.[2]

At the very start of her essay Johnson sets the tone for all the self-including statements that are to follow when she remarks that in Poe's tale, Lacan's reading, and Derrida's critique, "it is the *act of analysis* which seems to occupy the center of the discursive stage, and the *act of analysis of the act of analysis* which in some way disrupts that centrality. In the resulting asymmetrical, abyssal structure, no analysis—including this one

—can intervene without transforming and repeating other elements in the sequence, which is thus not a stable sequence, but which nevertheless produces certain regular effects" (110). The key phrase, of course, is "no analysis—including this one." It has about it the brisk American quality of Mark Twain's "No general statement is worth a damn—including this one"—a general statement worth a damn only if general statements aren't worth a damn. The very fact that Johnson makes an analytic statement that includes itself—which is to say, an analysis of her own analysis—in the sentence immediately following her statement that it is the act of analysis of the act of analysis that skews analysis in Poe, Lacan, and Derrida, is her way of announcing her strategy at the start. It is not that Johnson will do anything different in her essay from what Lacan and Derrida have done in theirs. Indeed, it is not clear that she thinks that anything different can be done at this point, inasmuch as Lacan and Derrida have already replayed the structure of the tale in a critical register by acting out the game of even and odd in their opposing positions. What will be different in her version is that these positions will be repeated with a complete awareness of their implications, a total critical self-consciousness that aims to create an insight without a blind spot; for what is at issue here is not so much whether one's critical argument is logically true or false, or one's reading of the tale perceptive or dull, but whether one's interpretive stance is methodologically self-aware or methodologically naive. In its translation from fiction to criticism, the project of analyzing the act of analysis becomes in effect the program of being infinitely self-conscious about self-consciousness. Or put another way, if the structure that we find in "The Purloined Letter" involves doubling an opponent's thought processes in order to turn his own methods against him, then the only defense against having the same strategy repeated against oneself by the next player is to produce an insight or take a position that is already self-consciously doubled back upon itself, as is the case with the type of self-including statement that says one thing grammatically but conveys its opposite rhetorically. For a position that knowingly includes itself and its opposite seems to leave no ground on which it can be undermined.

II

The commitment to an increasingly self-conscious analytic posture that animates this cumulative series of interpretations produces at last a kind of intellectual vertigo, a not uncharacteristic side effect of thought about thought—the rational animal turning in circles to catch itself by a tale it doesn't have. And certainly no one enjoyed creating this vertiginous effect more than did Poe, an effect that he imaged as dizziness at the edge of a vortex or on the brink of a precipice. That the giddy, self-dissolving effect of thought about thought—what Johnson calls the "asymmetrical, abyssal structure" of analyzing the act of analysis—forms the continuing theme of the Dupin stories is announced in the opening sentence of the first tale, "The Murders in the Rue Morgue" (1841). The story begins with the narrator's lengthy prefatory remarks on the nature of the analytical power, remarks that conclude by presenting the detective story as a "commentary upon the propositions just advanced" (531). But those prefatory remarks start with this curious proposition: "The mental features discoursed of as the analytical are, in themselves, but little susceptible of analysis" (527). Now inasmuch as this statement initiates the narrator's own brief analysis of the analytical power, it is self-reflexive: as an analytic statement about the nonsusceptibility of analysis to being analyzed, the statement is included in the class of things to which it refers, but what the statement says in effect is that analytic statements cannot wholly include themselves. In analyzing the act of analysis, self-conscious thought doubles back upon itself to discover that it cannot absolutely coincide with itself. This insight about the nature of thought is, of course, at least as old in our tradition as the philosophies of Zeno and Parmenides and as new as Gödel's proof and Borges's (and Carroll's and Royce's) map of natural size. It is the paradoxical insight that if one considers the act of thinking and the content of thought as two distinguishable things—as it seems one must in dealing with self-consciousness, with thought that is able to represent itself to itself, able to take itself as its own object—then the attempt to analyze the act of analysis, to include wholly the act of thinking within the context of thought, will be a progression of the order $n + 1$ to infinity. Which is to say that there will always be one more step needed in order to make the act of thinking coincide with the content of thought.

Since the self-including gesture of analyzing the act of analysis involves a doubling back in which self-consciousness, attempting to be absolutely even with itself, finds that it is originally and essentially at odds with itself, it is not surprising that Dupin, in illustrating the way that one doubles the thought processes of an opponent, gives as an example "the game of 'even and odd'." In this game "one player holds in his hand a number of marbles and demands of another whether that number is even or odd. If the guess is right, the guesser wins one; if wrong, he loses one." Dupin then tells the story of an eight-year-old boy who was so good at this guessing game that he won all the marbles at his school. The boy's "mode of reasoning" involved "an identification of the reasoner's intellect with that of his opponent" (984), and this doubling of the opponent's thought processes was achieved by a physical doubling of his appearance. The boy explained to Dupin: "I fashion the expression of my face, as accurately as possible, in accordance with the expression" of the opponent "and then wait to see what thoughts or sentiments arise in my mind or heart, as if to match or correspond with the expression" (984–85). The narrator comments that "the identification of the reasoner's intellect with that of his opponent, depends, . . . upon the accuracy with which the opponent's intellect is admeasured" (985); and Dupin, agreeing with this observation, adds that "the Prefect and his cohort fail so frequently, first, by default of this identification, and, secondly, by ill-admeasurement, or rather through non-admeasurement, of the intellect with which they are engaged. They consider only their *own* ideas of ingenuity; and, in searching for anything hidden, advert only to the modes in which *they* would have hidden it . . . but when the cunning of this individual felon is diverse in character from their own, the felon foils them, of course. This always happens when it is above their own, and very usually when it is below. They have no variation of principle in their investigations" (985).

Now what is going on here? Dupin cannot be the close reasoner that he is reputed to be and not realize that what he has just said undermines his use of the game of even and odd as an illustration of the way one doubles the thought processes of an opponent in order to be one up on him. First of all, if "the identification of the reasoner's intellect with that of his opponent, depends, . . . upon the accuracy with which the opponent's intellect is admeasured," then it cannot be that the Prefect and his men fail, "first, by default of this identification, and, secondly, by ill-admeasurement, or . . . non-admeasurement," for if the identification follows from admeasurement, the Prefect's first failure would have to be in admeasuring the opponent's intellect. And if the reason that the Prefect and his men fail so frequently in this admeasurement is that "they consider only their *own* ideas of ingenuity," that they are unable to imagine or conceive of the workings of a mind "diverse in character from their own" (always the case when the level of the mind is above their own and usually the case when it is below), then is there anything that occurs in the rest of Poe's tale that would lead us to believe this observation of Dupin's about the reason for the Prefect's failure? Which is to say, if the Prefect and his men can only catch felons whose minds are similar to their own and if what they need in this case is the ability to imagine the workings of a mind radically different from their own, then does Dupin's method of outwitting the Minister provide us with any evidence that this ability to imagine a mind radically different from one's own really exists? In fact, isn't all of the tale's emphasis on the resemblance between Dupin and the Minister, on their possessing the same dual creative/resolvent power, part of a plot line in which Dupin outwits the Minister only because their minds are so much alike? Isn't it precisely because the Minister has hidden the letter at his residence in the same way that the Queen hid it in the royal boudoir—by turning it over and leaving it out in the open—that Dupin already knows where to look for the letter when he visits the Minister? And doesn't Dupin recover the letter by replaying the same scenario by which the Minister originally stole it?

Isn't all this simply a device to make us realize that it is impossible to imagine or conceive of a mind whose workings are radically different from one's own? We don't have any direct access to another's thoughts. Our ideas of the workings of another person's mind may be derived from what that person says or does or tells us he or she is thinking, but our ideas of another's mind are still our ideas, a projection that we make of another mind's otherness to one's own based on the only immediate experience that one's mind has of psychic otherness, the self's original otherness to itself, that difference that constitutes personal identity. In his story "Morella" (1835) Poe quotes Locke's definition of personal identity as "the sameness of a rational being" (226). But one immediately thinks, "Sameness as opposed to what?" For in differential terms, it makes no sense to speak of the rational being's continuing sameness with itself unless there is also a sense in which the rational being is continually different from itself. In "Morella" Poe says, "Since by person we understand an intelligent essence having reason, and since there is a consciousness which always accompanies thinking, it is this consciousness which makes every one to be that which he calls 'himself'—thereby distinguishing him from other beings that think, and giving him his personal identity" (226). It is this difference of thought from itself—which Poe evokes here as the difference between thinking and "a consciousness which always accompanies thinking"—that enables the rational being to recognize its sameness with itself and thus recognize its difference from others, distinguish itself "from other beings that think." It is precisely because the self's thought of another mind's otherness to it reflects the otherness of thought to itself that the effort to imagine the thought processes of an opponent produces a specular, antithetical double of the self, the self's own projection of psychic difference. And consequently, for all that "The Purloined Letter" purports to be about the way in which one effects "an identification of the reasoner's intellect with that of his opponent," it is in fact about that psychic difference which permits thought to be identified with itself, that difference which constitutes self-identity but which prevents thought from ever absolutely coinciding with itself, indeed, which constitutes self-identity precisely *because* it prevents thought from being absolutely even with itself. And it is this difference, this condition of self-conscious thought's being originally and essentially at odds with itself, that Poe evokes at the very start of the Dupin stories when he says that the "mental features discoursed of as the analytical are, in themselves, but little susceptible of analysis" ("Murder" 527).

As is often the case in his fiction, Poe, using the picture language of radicals, emblematizes this latent meaning on the level of etymology, a level to which he explicitly directs our attention in "The Purloined Letter" when he has Dupin, in arguing against those who equate analysis with algebra, remark, "If a term is of any importance—if words derive any value from applicability—then 'analysis' conveys 'algebra' about as much as, in Latin, *'ambitus'* implies 'ambition,' *'religio,'* 'religion,' or *'homines honesti,'* a set of honorable men" (987). Since in each of these examples an English word has a meaning different from that of its Latin root, the inference seems clear: in "The Purloined Letter," "if a term is of any importance," we should submit that term to philological analysis to see if the root from which it derives has different or additional meanings compared to its English form, meanings that might alter, reverse, or deepen the significance of the passages in which these words appear.

Let me apply this principle suggested by Dupin's remark to two interlocking pairs of words in the tale. On his first visit, the Prefect introduces the affair of the letter like this: "The fact is, the business is *very* simple indeed, and I make no doubt that we can manage it sufficiently well ourselves: but then I thought Dupin would like to hear the details of it, because it is so excessively *odd.*" To which Dupin replies, "Simple and odd" (975). Dupin's emphatic repetition of the words is meant to fix them in our minds so that later when he describes the game of even and odd, we hear the echo and link the pairs. And to make sure that we don't miss the connection, Dupin, immediately after mentioning the game of even and odd, says, "This game is simple" (984).

"Simple," "even," "odd"—what are their roots? The word "simple" comes from the Latin *simplex,* meaning "single," "unmixed," "uncompounded." The word "even" derives from the Anglo-Saxon *efne,* meaning "flat," "level," and ultimately from the Indo-European base **im-nos-,* meaning "what is the same," and containing the adverbial base **im-,* meaning "just like" (503). The word "odd" derives from the Old Norse *oddi,* meaning a "point of land, triangle, hence (from the third angle) odd number" (1017). Three words and at the root of each a number—simple, single, *one;* even, things just alike, *two;* odd, a triangular point of land, *three.* And these three words are grouped into two pairs—simple/odd, even/odd—that contain, as it were, four syntactic places between them which the three words fill by having one of the words repeated. The doubling of the word "odd" links the two pairs; it gives them their element of sameness, evoking that condition of being at odds with itself, that difference with itself, which constitutes the sameness of a rational being (a condition of being at odds with itself that is most clearly perceived when thought tries to be absolutely even with itself). The three words—both through their meanings and through the way that they are paired and linked—are an emblem of the numerical structure that governs the tale, which is to say, of the numerical steps or geometrical patterns that self-consciousness goes through in trying to analyze itself.

Dupin says that the game of even and odd is simple, and throughout the Dupin stories Poe associates simplicity with the highest, purest form of ratiocination. It is in this vein that Dupin suggests to the Prefect on his first visit that "the very simplicity" of the affair of the letter constitutes its oddness: "Perhaps the mystery is a little *too* plain . . . A little *too* self-evident" (975). And later Dupin says that the Minister, in hiding the letter, "would be driven, as a matter of course, to *simplicity*, if not deliberately induced to it as a matter of choice." As in that "game of puzzles . . . played upon a map" (989), the Minister would choose a hiding place that would "escape observation by dint of being excessively obvious," relying on the fact that "the intellect suffers to pass unnoticed those considerations which are too obtrusively and too palpably self-evident." But what is that simple thing whose very simplicity makes it so odd, that thing which is so mysterious because so obvious, hiding out in the open "immediately beneath the nose of the whole world" (990)? What but self-consciousness, that condition of being at odds with itself that constitutes the sameness, the singleness, the simplicity of a rational being?

By definition a number is odd if, when the number is divided by two, there is a remainder of one. And by that definition the first odd number is three. In that simple game of even and odd in which self-consciousness analyzes itself, the question inevitably arises as to whether, when the mind's desire to be absolutely even with itself is divided into the mind's essential condition of being at odds with itself, the one that is always left over is the same as the number one that precedes two, that is, the same as that mythic, original, undivided unity prior to all pairing/pairing. Or put another way, when the mind tries to make the act of thinking coincide absolutely with the content of thought, only to find that there is always one more step needed to achieve this coincidence, is the infinite progression that results simply the mirror image, the antithetical double, of a Zenonian infinite regression which, by dividing a quantity in half, then dividing the half in half, then dividing the quarter in half, and so on to infinity, seeks a lower limit, a part that cannot be halved again, a thing so small that, being indivisible, it represents an undivided unity, an original one? Poe is too good both as philosopher and philologist not to know that the simple thing that is self-consciousness could never be as simple as that. Indeed, if the mind were ever able to make the act of thinking and the content of thought coincide absolutely so that there was no difference between them, then self-consciousness, that self-identity constituted by thought's difference from itself, would simply go out like a light. Such an undifferentiated one would be indistinguishable from zero. Though the root of the word "simple," the Latin *simplex*, means "single," "unmixed," "uncompounded,"[3] the roots of the word *simplex*—the Latin words *semel*, meaning "once," "a single time," and *plico*, meaning "to fold, fold together" (Simpson 556)—make it clear that to be unmixed or uncompounded does not mean to be undifferentiated. For in the picture language of these radicals we can see that a thing which is singlefold is something—like a sheet of paper, a letter—that in being folded a single time is doubled back upon itself. That the image of self-consciousness as a *simple* fold doubling an inscribed surface back on itself was in Poe's mind, when he plotted the folding/refolding of the purloined letter, can be inferred from an 1845 poem on folding money called "Epigram for Wall Street," attributed to him:

I'll tell you a plan for gaining wealth,
    Better than banking, trade or leases—
Take a bank note and fold it up,
    And then you will find your money in *creases*!
This wonderful plan, without danger or loss,
    Keeps your cash in your hands, where nothing can trouble it;
And every time that you fold it across,
    'Tis as plain as the light of the day that you *double* it! (378)

The infinite progression implicit in the analysis of the act of analysis is evoked at the end of "The Purloined Letter" with the revelation of Dupin's revenge on the Minister, for this attempt by a mastermind to get even with his specular double clearly serves as a figure of the analytic mind's attempt at mastery, its attempt to be absolutely even with itself. Knowing that the Minister "would feel some curiosity in regard to the identity of the person who had outwitted him," Dupin leaves him a clue by substituting for the purloined letter one containing a quotation from Crébillon's *Atrée* copied out in Dupin's own handwriting, a hand with which the Minister "is well acquainted" (993). In signing his deed, Dupin marks it as revenge, which is to say, he insures that the Minister will interpret his actions not simply as the paid intervention of a gifted amateur sleuth or a duel of wits between two of the cleverest men in Paris, but as a repayment for the evil turn which the Minister did Dupin at Vienna. For I take it that the satisfaction of revenge requires—except in those cases where it is carried out on a substitute—a moment of revelation in which the object of revenge learns by whom, and for what, he is being paid back, a point that Poe underlines by

having Dupin choose his quotation-signature from just such a revelatory moment in an eighteenth-century revenger's tragedy. And yet from
what we know of the Minister it is inconceivable that once he learned of
Dupin's revenge he would let the matter rest there—and equally inconceivable that his double would not know this. For though it might seem
that with Dupin's revenge the score between them is even at one apiece
(one bad turn at Vienna repaid by one bad turn at Paris), if the Minister allows Dupin's trick to go unanswered, then Dupin will have had the
last turn; and as proverbial wisdom assures us, the last word or the last
laugh is not just one word or one laugh like any other. The power to say
the last word or have the last laugh, the power to bring a series of reciprocal actions to an end, like the power to originate, involves the notion
of a one that is simultaneously more than one. Consequently, we are left
with the paradoxical situation in which Dupin's outwitting of the Minister will constitute an evening of the score between them at one apiece
only if the Minister *does not* allow Dupin's trick to end the series, does
not allow it to be that one last turn which in its finality is always more
than one. It is not so much that one bad turn deserves another, as that
one bad turn demands another if it is to be experienced as simply one
turn. All of which emphasizes the mutually constitutive contradictori-
ness of seeking *to get even* with a specular double *by being one up on him.*

In using the affair of the letter to even an old score, Dupin gives up
his "objective" fourth position as an apparently disinterested observer
of the triangular structure of King, Queen, and Minister described by
the Prefect, in order to insert himself for personal reasons into the third
position of an analogous triangle in which the police and the Minister
occupy, respectively, the first and second positions. Similarly, in describing this triangular structure in which Dupin shifts the Minister from the
third to the second position, Lacan would himself appear to occupy an
"objective" fourth position as a disinterested observer outside the triangle. Yet to a supposedly more objective observer of Lacan's position
such as Derrida, Lacan's description is not disinterested at all, but simply
a psychoanalyst's imposition of the structure of the Oedipal triangle on
a double story, an imposition that, though it seems to be made from an
objective fourth position outside the triangle, has the effect of inserting
Lacan into the third position of a triangle in which the psychoanalyst's
"objective" unmasking of the personal motive that lies behind Dupin's
"disinterested" involvement in the affair of the letter shifts Dupin into
the second position and his double, the Minister, into the first. Or so
says Derrida from a fourth position outside Lacan's triangle, a fourth
position that will itself be shifted in turn. This mechanism by which the
shifting from the third to the second position within the triangle is extended (as a supposedly more objective point of view is assumed from

which to observe the subjective triangle), and thus becomes the shifting from a fourth position outside the triangle to the third position within it, evokes the infinite regression that, in this quest for absolute self-consciousness, accompanies infinite progression as its shadow image. For while the progressive series moves in one direction in its flight from subjective involvement, in its termless search for an absolutely objective point of view from which to examine the self, it only exists *as a series* because of the regressive movement of consciousness, because of the retrospective gaze that keeps all the earlier terms of the series in view so that they are perceived as related, as serial in character. Thus the mental step that one takes in order to separate the self from itself, to distinguish absolutely the observer from the observed, is always a backward step, a step in the opposite direction from the one in which we are looking.

III

In the sardonic name of simplicity let me add one more, final (or else one, more final) element to this discussion. So far we have looked at three analytic readings of "The Purloined Letter" by Lacan, Derrida, and Johnson, and then gone back to consider Poe's own self-conscious thematizing within the story of the numerical/geometrical structure enacted in its interpretation. I would now like to look at a literary reading of Poe's tale that antedates the earliest of the three analyses we have considered by some fifteen years: the reading that Borges gives of "The Purloined Letter" when he rewrites its numerical/geometrical structure in his own detective story "Death and the Compass" (1942). In the story's opening paragraph Borges explicitly links the tale to Poe's Dupin stories, remarking that his detective Erik Lönnrot "thought of himself as a pure logician, a kind of Auguste Dupin" (65). "Death and the Compass" concerns a series of murders. All the obvious clues suggest that the number in the series will be three, but all the less than obvious clues—the kind that police inspector Treviranus would miss, but Erik Lönnrot wouldn't—suggest that the number of murders will be four. We learn at the end of the story that the series of crimes has been planned by Lönnrot's archenemy, the criminal Red Scharlach, who, seeking to lure Lönnrot unawares to his own destruction, has counted on the fact that the detective would solve the arcane clues which Inspector Treviranus missed, and that Lönnrot's intellectual pride would blind him, would make him think that because he was one jump ahead of the police, he was one jump ahead of the criminal as well. In effect, Borges reworks the triangular structure from "The Purloined Letter." He has Scharlach create a situation in which Lönnrot's apparent solution to the crimes constitutes that second glance whose observation of blindness in the first glance (Treviranus's apparent misreading of the clues) becomes itself a blind spot in the observer by convincing him that he sees everything. In the meantime Scharlach occupies the position of the third glance (hidden at the fourth point of the compass), seeing the blindness of the first glance, the blind spot in the second, and the fact that the object he seeks—Lönnrot's life—is his for the taking.

Lönnrot and Scharlach are, of course, doubles of one another, as their names indicate. In a note to the English translation of the tale Borges says, "The end syllable of Lönnrot means red in German, and Red Scharlach is also translatable, in German, as Red Scarlet" ("Commentaries" 269). Elsewhere Borges tells us that Lönnrot is Swedish, but neglects to add that in Swedish the word *lönn* is a prefix meaning "secret," "hidden," or "illicit." Thus Lönnrot, *the secret red*, pursues and is pursued by his double, Red Scharlach (Red Scarlet), *the doubly red*. Scharlach's motive is revenge. In their final confrontation, Scharlach reminds Lönnrot that three years earlier the detective had arrested Scharlach's brother in a gambling dive and that in the ensuing shootout Scharlach had escaped, as he says, with "a cop's bullet in my guts" (75). In hiding, delirious with fever for nine days and nights, "I swore," says Scharlach, "by the god who looks with two faces and by all the gods of fever and of mirrors that I would weave a maze around the man who sent my brother to prison" (76). I take it that this elaborate revenge on "a kind of Auguste Dupin" for the arrest of a brother is an allusion to the fact that in "The Purloined Letter" the Minister D—— has a brother with whom he is sometimes confused because they "both have attained reputation in letters" (986). Since Dupin gets even with the Minister, are we to see Scharlach's revenge on Lönnrot as an attempt to even the score for that earlier revenge on a brother criminal?

The maze that Scharlach weaves around the detective begins with the murder of Rabbi Marcel Yarmolinsky on the third of December at a hotel in the north of the city. Yarmolinsky is a Talmudic scholar, and among his effects the police find "a treatise. . . on the Tetragrammaton" (67) and a sheet of paper in his typewriter bearing the words, "*The first letter of the Name has been uttered*" (67). The second murder occurs on the night of January 3 in the west of the city. The victim, Daniel Simon Azevedo, is found lying on the doorstep of a paint store beneath "the shop's conventional red and yellow diamond shapes" (68–69). Chalked across the diamond shapes are the words, "*The second letter of the Name has been uttered*" (69). The third murder occurs on the night of February 3 in the east of the city. The victim, whose name is either Gryphius or Ginzberg, telephones Treviranus offering to give him information about the murders of Yarmolinsky and Azevedo, but the call is interrupted by the arrival of two men who forcibly remove Gryphius-Ginzberg from the sailor's tavern where he has been staying. It is Carnival time and the two men are wearing harlequin "costumes of red, green, and yellow lozenges" (70). Tracing the interrupted phone call, Treviranus arrives at the tavern to find scrawled on a market slate in front, "*The last letter of the Name has been uttered*," and in Gryphius-Ginzberg's room a star-shaped spatter of blood and "a 1739 edition of Leusden's *Philologus Hebraeo-Graecus*" with the following passage underlined: 'the Jewish day begins at sundown and ends the following sundown' " (71). On the night of March 1 Treviranus receives a sealed envelope, containing "a letter signed by one 'Baruch Spinoza' " (72) and a map of the city. The letter writer predicts that on the third of March there will not be a fourth murder because the locations of the three previous crimes in the north, west, and east form "the perfect sides of an equilateral and mystical triangle" (72), as demonstrated by a triangle drawn in red ink on the map.

Appropriately, the letter predicting that only three men will be killed is sent to Treviranus, the first two syllables of whose name recall the Latin words for "three" and "man"—*tres, vir*. The Inspector's name probably alludes as well to the *tresviri capitales*, a group of three magistrates who "exercised general control over the city police" in republican Rome. According to the eleventh edition of the *Encyclopaedia Britannica*, "Caesar increased their number to four, but Augustus reverted to three. In imperial times most of their functions passed into the hands of the *praefectus vigilum*" (27: 254)—an etymological-historical link between Borges's Treviranus and Poe's Prefect. Not to mention the fact (which Borges must have noticed) that the emperor who restored the number of the *tresviri capitales* from four to the original three also gave his name to the detective C. (César) Auguste Dupin. In "An Autobiographical Essay" (1970), Borges reports that he used part of the proceeds from a literary prize he received in 1929 to acquire "a secondhand set of the Eleventh Edition of the *Encyclopaedia Britannica*" (233), by no means an insignificant detail in the life of a writer obsessed with the image of the encyclopaedia, a writer who says that some of his earliest memories are of "the steel engravings in *Chambers's Encyclopaedia* and in the *Britannica*" in his father's library (209). It is worth noting that in the eleventh edition of the *Britannica* the entry for *tresviri* occurs on the page facing the entry for Gottfried Reinhold Treviranus (1776–1837), a German naturalist. Not unpredictably, Inspector Treviranus's first words in the story point to the numerical image that lies at the Latin root of his name: " 'We needn't lose any time here looking for three-legged cats,' Treviranus said, brandishing an imperious cigar. 'Everyone knows the Tetrarch of Galilee owns the world's finest sapphires. Somebody out to steal them probably found his way in here by mistake. Yarmolinsky woke up and the thief was forced to kill him" (66). The only historical Tetrarch of

Galilee, as the entry for *tetrarch* in the Britannica informs us, was Herod Antipas—the Herod of the gospels—whose reign (4 B.C.-39 A.C.) began under the emperorship of Augustus Caesar (hence Treviranus's "imperious cigar") and bracketed the life of Christ. At the death of Herod the Great in 4 B.C., his realm was divided among his three sons: half went to Archelaus, with the title "ethnarch"; a quarter to Philip, with the title "tetrarch"; and a quarter to Herod Antipas, with the same title. As with Treviranus's initial image of a four-legged animal with only three legs, his reference to the Tetrarch of Galilee—with its historical resonance of a quadripartite realm divided among three people by doubling the portion of one of them—evokes the numerical structure that governs the tale. That Borges intends the historical allusion (and intends for us not to miss it) seems clear from an exchange between Lönnrot and the editor of a Yiddish newspaper at the scene of Yarmolinsky's murder: "'Maybe this crime belongs to the history of Jewish superstitions,' Lönnrot grumbled. 'Like Christianity,' the editor from the *Judische Zeitung* made bold to add" (67). Need I add that the entry for *tetrarch* in the eleventh edition of the *Britannica* occurs on the page facing the entry for *Tetragrammaton?*

Treviranus sends the map with the red triangle and the letter suggesting that the number of murders will be three to Lönnrot, who now has, he believes, the final clue needed to capture the murderer. Since the letters in the Tetragrammaton are four rather than three, and since the Jewish day begins at sundown so that the three murders were committed not on the third but the fourth day of each month, and since in both the second and third murders a diamond shape is prominently displayed, Lönnrot concludes that the series of murders is not threefold but fourfold and that the shape which the locations of the crimes describe on the map is not a triangle but a diamond. Using a pair of dividers and a compass, Lönnrot pinpoints the location of the planned fourth murder in the south of the city, "the deserted villa Triste-le-Roy" (73); and he arrives there well in advance, so he thinks, of the murderer to catch him in the act. But, of course, at the villa of Triste-le-Roy—a building of intricate doublings, a kind of House of Usher designed by Zeno the Eleatic—Scharlach is already lying in wait and easily captures Lönnrot. Completing his triumph, Scharlach explains the maze to his prisoner. "The first term of the series came to me by pure chance," says Scharlach. He and some of his associates—among them Daniel Azevedo, the second victim—had planned to commit a jewel robbery at the hotel where Rabbi Yarmolinsky was staying. Double-crossing his friends, Azevedo tried to commit the robbery a day early, got into Yarmolinsky's room by mistake, and killed the rabbi when he tried to ring for help. From the newspaper accounts of the crime, Scharlach learned that Lönnrot was seeking the key to Yarmolinsky's death in the rabbi's writings, and so he planned the series of murders to encourage Lönnrot's belief that Yarmolinsky had been sacrificed by a group of Hasidic Jews in search of the secret and unutterable Name of God, a ruse to keep Lönnrot looking in the wrong direction while being led to his own destruction. Appropriately, the second victim was the double-crosser Azevedo, while the third murder was simply a ruse with Scharlach himself doubling as the victim, Gryphius-Ginzberg. Borges gives us a clue to the type of cabalistic design on which Scharlach's labyrinth is based when he tells us that among the books written by Yarmolinsky, and found in his room at the time of his death, there was "a *Study of the Philosophy of Robert Fludd*" (67), the seventeenth-century English physician and Christian cabalist whose work on geomancy ("a method of divination by means of marking the earth with a pointed stick" [Poe, *Collected* 2: 420n20]) Poe had included a century earlier in his catalogue of Roderick Usher's favorite reading ("Fall" 409). In Fludd's major work, *Utriusque cosmi majoris scilicet et minoris metaphysica, physica atque technica historia* (1617–19), we find the diagram shown in Figure 1, illustrating the mirror-image relationship between God and the universe.[4]

At the center of the upper triangle (whose angles represent the three persons of the Trinity) is the Tetragrammaton, and along one side a Latin legend reading "That most divine and beautiful counterpart visible below in the flowing image of the universe" (Heninger 83). In the lower triangle are "the three regions of the universe—empyreal, ethereal, and elemental" which correspond to "the triangular form of the trinitarian deity," and along one side of this is the Latin legend: "A shadow, likeness, or reflection of the insubstantial triangle visible in the image of the universe," the lower triangle being "a projection of an idea" in the divine mind and thus a mirror image of the deity (83–84). Surrounding both triangles is a flamelike effulgence suggesting at once the radiant nature of this Platonic projection or emanation, the symbolic character of the deity as fire or pure light (that is, as mind), and the traditional imagistic association (going back at least to the Egyptians) of the triangle with the tip of a flame (pyramid and obelisk being stone flames above a grave) and thus with eternal life. Since Scharlach knows from the newspaper accounts that Lönnrot began his investigation of the murders by reading Yarmolinsky's works on cabalism, and since one of these is a study of Robert Fludd's mystical philosophy, it seems likely that the type of schema shown below was the model for Scharlach's labyrinth and that it is this cabalistic design which Lönnrot believes he is tracing on the landscape, when in his initial surprise at finding Scharlach waiting at the fourth point of the compass he asks, "Scharlach, are you after the Secret Name?" (Borges, "Death" 75).

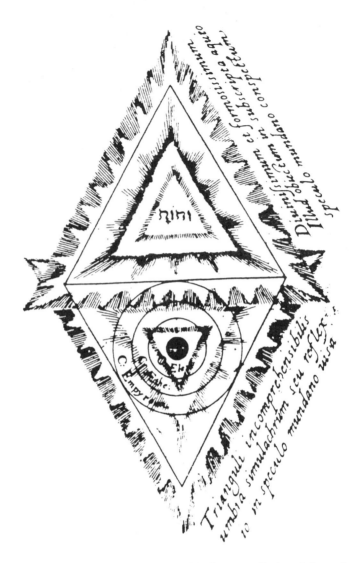

Figure 1. Mirror-image relationship between God and the universe. From Robert Fludd, *Utriusque cosmi majoris scilicet et minoris metaphysica, physica atque technica historia* (1617–19), reprinted in S. K. Heninger, Jr., *The Cosmographical Glass: Renaissance Diagrams of the Universe*, p. 83, fig. 52b.

Realizing that he has been outwitted and that he is about to be killed, Lönnrot tries to have the last word by finding a flaw in Scharlach's maze. Using a favorite ploy of mathematicians and logicians—that Scharlach's plan, though successful, violates the principle of economy of means—Lönnrot says, "In your maze there are three lines too many. . . . I know of a Greek maze that is a single straight line. Along this line so many thinkers have lost their way that a mere detective may very well lose his way. Scharlach, when in another incarnation you hunt me down, stage (or commit) a murder at A, then a second murder at B, eight miles from A, then a third murder at C, four miles from A and B halfway between the two. Lay in wait for me then at D, two miles from A and C, again halfway between them. Kill me at D, the way you are going to kill me here at Triste-le-Roy" (78). In his note to the tale, Borges identifies "the straight-line labyrinth at the story's end" as a figure taken from "Zeno the Eleatic" ("Commentaries" 269). This closing image of infinite regression as the endless subdivision of a line inverts, of course, the figure of infinite progression evoked in the tale by the movement from a triangular to a quadrangular maze, which is to say, the figure of infinite progression as the endless addition of sides to a polygon—the figure that symbolizes the attempt to integrate the process of thinking into the content of thought as the attempt to incorporate an "objective" point of view outside a structure (for example, the fourth point from which one views a triangle) into a more inclusive, more self-conscious formulation by making that viewpoint another angle of the structure (for example, the progression from triangle to quadrangle).

As we noted earlier, in the mind's quest to comprehend itself totally, to be absolutely even or at one with itself, infinite progression and infinite regression represent reciprocal paths to the idealized ground of the self, to its original, essential unity—infinite progression pursuing an absolute unity figured as totality, infinite regression pursuing an absolute simplicity figured as indivisibility. Part of the numerical mystery of individual self-consciousness is that though it is only one thing in a world of many things, for its individual possessor it is one thing that is everything. And this absoluteness of individual self-consciousness for its possessor not only underlies the absolute means employed in quest of the self's origin (that is, infinite progression/regression) but also projects itself naturally into the quest for a universal origin figured as a personified Absolute Consciousness, that Infinite Being whose consciousness is the one thing that is everything for every thing. Translated into a religious context, infinite regression and infinite progression, as reciprocal modes of seeking an ultimate origin conceived as either a lower or an upper limit of consciousness, suggest the *via negativa* and the *via positiva* of mystical theology. In the *via negativa* one seeks an unmediated encounter with the divine origin by subtracting attributes from, by denying affirmative predicates to, the idea of God, until one finally achieves a personal experience of the transcategorial nature of Being. Of this method, Borges remarks, "To be one thing is inexorably not to be all the other things. The confused intuition of that truth has induced men to imagine that not being is more than being something and that, somehow, not to be is to be everything" ("From" 148). In the *via positiva* one takes the opposite path, constantly adding affirmative predicates to the concept of God until that concept becomes an absolute totality; though what one experiences in this path is once again the transcategorial nature of Being. In his 1950 essay "From Someone to Nobody," in which he sketches the historical oscillations of the concept of the Judaeo-Christian God, Borges describes the reciprocal character of these two methods as "magnification to nothingness" (147).

Given Borges's interest in the way that the classical pursuit of a microcosmic and a macrocosmic limit becomes the religious quest for the origin and end of all things, it is not surprising that as Lönnrot gets caught up in the quest for the sacred and unutterable name of God, the meeting at the fourth point of the compass (a proleptic figure of infinite progression) comes to seem like a face-to-face encounter with the one, infinite, divine origin of all things. And inasmuch as Lönnrot will die at that fourth point, it does turn out to be the place where he will meet his maker (his mental double). Agreeing to Lönnrot's request that he trap him in a straight-line labyrinth in their next incarnation, Scharlach takes a step back and shoots the detective with his own gun—shoots him in the head, one would guess, the right spot to drop a pure logician. In his note to the tale, Borges says, "The killer and the slain, whose minds work in the same way, may be the same man. Lönnrot is not an unbelievable fool walking into his own death trap but, in a symbolic way, a man committing suicide" ("Commentaries" 269). What with the presence of the color red in the names of slayer and slain, and their talk of repeating their duel in another incarnation, one is reminded of Emerson's poem "Brahma," which Borges cites in his 1947 essay on Whitman ("Note" 69):

If the red slayer think he slays,
  Or if the slain think he is slain,
They know not well the subtle ways
  I keep, and pass, and turn again.

Far or forgot to me is near;
  Shadow and sunlight are the same;
The vanished gods to me appear;
  And one to me are shame and fame.

One question, however, still remains to be settled. Does Borges, in rewriting the numerical/geometrical structure of "The Purloined Letter" in "Death and the Compass," see that structure as threefold and triangular (as does Lacan) or fourfold and quadrangular (as does Derrida)? Certainly Scharlach's labyrinth seems to be fourfold and diamond shaped. But inasmuch as the murder of Gryphius-Ginzberg was a ruse in which the criminal doubled as the victim, there were really only three crimes, and these three—the murders of Yarmolinsky in the north, Azevedo in the west, and Lönnrot in the south—form a triangle on the map. And if the labyrinth is really threefold and triangular, then all the obvious, all the simple clues indicating that there would only be three crimes are the correct ones. But if the correct number is three, then what becomes of the name that is being uttered letter by letter? If it is not the four-letter name of God that Borges means to evoke, then is it the three-letter name of Poe, the creator, the origin, of the detective genre?

Before deciding, however, that the structure is threefold and triangular, we should recall that there finally turn out to be three crimes only because one of the doubles correctly interprets all the arcane clues and presents himself at the fourth point at the expected moment. Is the numerical structure that Borges rewrites from "The Purloined Letter," then, that of the two interlocking pairs of words (simple/odd, even/odd), a structure in which three things are made to fill four spaces by doubling one of them—and all as part of the mind's quest for an original undivided one, for a mythic absolute simplicity? Inasmuch as Lönnrot's search for God's "Secret Name" (75) at the fourth point of the quadrangle symbolizes this quest for an original undivided one, it is significant that the Tetragrammaton, "God's unspeakable name" (68), has the same structure in all its various spellings (JHVH, IHVH, IHWH, YHVH, YHWH) as that of the two interlocking pairs of words in "The Purloined Letter," which is to say that three different letters are made to fill the four spaces of the name by doubling one of them (H). It is also worth noting that in the case of both the sacred name and the interlocking pairs of words, the repeated letter or word occupies the second and fourth spaces—the numbers characteristically associated with doubling. (One might also note, given the quadrangular aspect of Scharlach's maze, that two is the only number for which doubling and squaring are the same operation.)

Borges's rewriting of the numerical/geometrical structure of "The Purloined Letter" in "Death and the Compass" assumes an even greater significance when we realize that it was part of a larger project, in which he set out to double Poe's three Dupin stories a century later with three detective stories of his own. But with this difference: where Poe's detective solves the mystery and outwits the culprit, Borges's detectives or pursuers are outwitted by the people they pursue, are trapped in a labyrinth fashioned from the pursuer's ability to follow a trail until he arrives in the chosen spot at the expected moment. (We should note, however, that in these stories Borges consistently undercuts the notion that the culprit's triumph, his being one up on his opponent, ultimately makes any real difference. "And one to me are shame and fame" might almost be the motto of these encounters.) The first Dupin story, "The Murders in the Rue Morgue," was published in 1841; Borges's first detective story, "The Garden of the Forking Paths," was published exactly one hundred years later in 1941. As the historian of the detective genre Howard Haycraft notes, there were "several events which marked the Centennial of the Detective Story in 1941" (xxi): one was the first issue of *Ellery Queen's Mystery Magazine,* another was the publication of Haycraft's own magisterial *Murder for Pleasure: The Life and Times of the Detective Story.* And yet another, it seems certain, was the publication of Borges's first detective story, which, he recalls, "won a second prize in *Ellery Queen's Mystery Magazine*" ("Commentaries" 273). The second Dupin story, "The Mystery of Marie Rogêt," first appeared in 1842–43 in serial form; while Borges's second detective story, "Death and the Compass," was first published in 1942. This story was also submitted to *Ellery Queen's Mystery Magazine* but, as Borges ruefully notes, "was flatly rejected" (273). The third Dupin story, "The Purloined Letter," was published in 1844, but Borges's third story, "Ibn Hakkan al-Bokhari, Dead in His Labyrinth," was not published until 1951. In his note to the story Borges accounts for this break in the pattern, commenting that after his "first two exercises of 1941 and 1942" his third effort "became a cross between a permissible detective story and a caricature of one. The more I worked on it, the more hopeless the plot seemed and the stronger my need to parody" ("Commentaries" 274). It is as if in reaching the third term of this series Borges realized that his effort to double Poe's three analytic detective stories—perhaps with the idea of going one up on the inventor of the genre—had gone awry and that he was himself trapped in the triangular/quadrangular labyrinth that Poe had constructed in "The Purloined Letter."

Certain it is that in Borges's final detective story the allusions to "The Purloined Letter" are numerous, culminating in an explicit reference. In the tale, two friends, Dunraven and Unwin, try to decipher the mystery of Ibn Hakkan al-Bokhari's death in his own labyrinth. At one point Unwin says, "Don't go on multiplying the mysteries. . . . They should be kept simple. Bear in mind Poe's purloined letter, bear in mind Zangwill's locked room." To which Dunraven replies, "Or made complex. . . . Bear in mind the universe" (116). I assume that the name "Dunraven" is an allusion to the author of "The Raven," as the name "Unwin" is to the unwinnable game of trying to be one up on a double, assumptions supported by the fact that Dunraven is a poet and Unwin a mathematician. These occupations recall as well the discussion of the dual character of the Minister D—— in "The Purloined Letter." Thinking that they have confused the Minister with his brother who has also "attained reputation in letters," the narrator identifies D—— as "a mathematician, and no poet." To which Dupin replies, "You are mistaken; I know him well; he is both. As poet and mathematician, he would reason well; as mere mathematician, he could not have reasoned at all, and thus would have been at the mercy of the Prefect" (986). As we noted earlier, the Minister's dual character as poet and mathematician mirrors that "double Dupin" whose reciprocal powers ("the creative and the resolvent") reminded the narrator in "The Murders in the Rue Morgue" of "the old philosophy of the Bi-Part Soul" (533). Borges echoes this reciprocal relationship between the creative and the resolvent when he has the poet Dunraven suggest a mathematical solution to the mystery of the labyrinth and the mathematician Unwin counter with a poetic one. Dunraven asks whether, in trying to solve the mystery, Unwin has considered "the theory of series" or "a fourth dimension of space," and Unwin replies, "No . . . I thought about the labyrinth of Crete. The labyrinth whose center was a man with the head of a bull" (123). Borges adds that Dunraven, "steeped in detective stories, thought that the solution of a mystery is always less impressive than the mystery itself. Mystery has something of the supernatural about it, and even of the divine; its solution, however, is always tainted by sleight of hand" (123).

Since the mininum number needed to constitute a series is three (even if there are only two items in a series, the idea of their serial relationship is already a third thing), Dunraven's question about whether the solution might involve "the theory of series" or "a fourth dimension of space" suggests, in effect, that the key to the mystery turns upon choosing between the numbers three and four. And this implied oscillation between three and four, combined with the image of the labyrinth, returns us to the triangular/quadrangular maze of "Death and the Compass" and to its origin in the numerical/geometrical structure of "The Purloined Letter"—in much the same way that Borges's remark about the solution always being less impressive than the mystery itself returns us to the simple-minded question that began this inquiry.[5] For by now it should be clear that that question was, in the spirit of the genre, framed so as to contain a clue, in reverse, to its answer. Which is to say, the question about how one writes the analytic detective story as a rereadable form was, like Scharlach's maze, a device to focus attention in one direction while leading us in the opposite, leading us to the point where that simple-minded question about the unlimited repeatability of a form becomes an endlessly repeatable because constantly reformulated question about the simplicity of mind, a question always about to be answered because it requires only one more step to complete the analysis.

Poe's genius in the invention of the genre was precisely to understand that the analytic solution of a mystery always leaves us at the end with the mystery of an analytic solution, the mystery of that solving power that catches a partial glimpse of itself in the achievement of a deductive conclusion but that, maddeningly enough, cannot gain a complete view of itself no matter how often it repeats the analytic moment, cannot totally comprehend itself, simply because in doubling back to effect an absolute coincidence of the self with itself it finds that it is based on an original noncoincidence. This paradox of a (non) self-including self—that if the process of thinking and the content of thought ever absolutely coincided, they would vanish in a condition of no-difference, taking with them the differential entity that is the self—lies at the heart of the detective genre that Poe invented. And within the dynamics of the text, this ultimate condition of no-difference (the imaginatively projected goal of the self's attempt to be absolutely even with itself) makes its presence felt in that ceaseless oscillation of differential poles associated with specular doubling, that continual reversal of a signifying term into its opposite which, in its fluctuating equation of opposing terms, produces a differentiation that seems to make no difference.

Notes

An earlier version of this essay appeared as "Mysteries We Reread, Mysteries of Rereading: Poe, Borges, and the Analytic Detective Story; also Lacan, Derrida and Johnson" in *Modern Language Notes* 101, 5 (1986): 1168–1215, subsequently reprinted and expanded in my book, *The Mystery to a Solution: Poe, Borges, and the Analytic Detective Story* (Baltimore: Johns Hopkins University Press, 1994). Reprinted with permission of Johns Hopkins University Press.

1. The earlier version of this essay goes on to discuss Johnson's summary of Derrida on the uncanny effects of doubling in Poe's story.

2. The original essay proceeds to analyze Johnson's rhetorical strategies in detail.

3. See the definition of "simple" in *Webster's New World Dictionary* (1359). The etymologies of "even" and "odd" are also taken from this edition.

4. All subsequent quotations referring to Fludd's diagram are cited from Heninger. This diagram was brought to my attention by my student James Boylan.

5. In the original version, this essay goes on to discuss the geometrical figure implied by Poe's story in terms of its three/four oscillation and its similarity to the quadrangular maze in Borges's tale. That Borges deciphered the game of simple/odd, even/odd in "The Purloined Letter" and then reencrypted it in "Death and the Compass" seems beyond doubt. What still remains to be noted

in closing the circle of this essay is the distinct possibility that it was Borges's tale which originally directed Lacan's attention to the numerical/geometrical dimension of the story, and thus suggested "The Purloined Letter" as an ideal text for an analysis of psychoanalysis that would project the structure of the Oedipal triangle onto the reciprocity of blindness and insight in the psychoanalytic encounter. The evidence of this influence is circumstantial, but certainly no psychoanalyst should object to that. One of the first promoters of Borges's work in France was Roger Caillois, the noted critic and sociologist whose writings influenced Lacan. In 1951 Caillois published in Paris a translation (by P. Verdevoye and Nestor Ibarra) of Borges's *Ficciones*, the collection that contains both "The Garden of Forking Paths" and "Death and the Compass" (Rodríguez Monegal 420). There was, then, a translation of "Death and the Compass" widely available in France under the aegis of Caillois some five years before the publication of Lacan's "Seminar on 'The Purloined Letter.'" And given Caillois's interest in the detective story and his ongoing promotion of one of the genre's most distinguished modern practitioners, and given the influence of Caillois's writings on Lacan and the psychoanalyst's natural interest in analytic detection, it seems hard to believe that Lacan had not read "Death and the Compass" sometime in the early 1950s. Such a knowledge of the story on Lacan's part would at least go a long way toward explaining the extremely odd reference he makes to Borges in a footnote [which alludes obliquely to Borges's 1941 "The Analytical Language of John Wilkins"] to the "Seminar on 'The Purloined Letter'" (53). The earlier version of this essay analyzes more fully the implications of Borges's influence on Lacan's reading of Poe.

Works Cited

Borges, Jorge Luis. *The Aleph and Other Stories, 1933–1969.* Trans. Norman Thomas di Giovanni. New York: Dutton, 1978.
———. "An Autobiographical Essay." [1970]. *Aleph* 203–60.
———. "Commentaries." *Aleph* 263–83.
———. "Death and the Compass." ["La Muerte y la brújula," 1942]. *Aleph* 65–72.
———. "From Someone to Nobody." ["De Alguien a nadie," 1950]. *Other* 146–48.
———. "The Garden of Forking Paths." ["El Jardín de senderos que se bifurcan," 1941]. Trans. Helen Temple and Ruthven Todd. *Ficciones*, ed. Anthony Kerrigan. New York: Grove, 1962. 89–101.
———. "Ibn Hakkan al-Bokhari, Dead in his Labyrinth." ["Abenjácan el Bojarí, muerto en su Laberinto," 1951]. *Aleph* 115–21.
———. "Note on Walt Whitman." ["Nota sobre W," 1947]. *Other* 66–72.
———. *Other Inquisitions, 1937–1952.* [*Otras inquisiciones*, 1952]. Trans. Ruth L. C. Simms. New York: Simon and Schuster, 1965.
Chandler, Raymond. "The Simple Art of Murder." [1950]. In *Detective Fiction: Crime and Compromise,* ed. Dick Allen and David Chacko. New York: Harcourt, 1974. 387–99.
Derrida, Jacques. "The Purveyor of Truth." Trans. W. Domingo, J. Hulbert, M. Ron, and M.-R. Logan. *Yale French Studies* 52 (1975): 31–113.
Emerson, Ralph Waldo. "Brahma." *The Complete Works of Ralph Waldo Emerson,* ed. E. W. Emerson. 12 vols. Boston: Houghton Mifflin, 1903–4. 9: 195.

The Encyclopaedia Britannica. 11th ed. 29 vols. New York: Encyclopaedia Britannica, 1911.

Haycraft, Howard. *Murder for Pleasure: The Life and Times of the Detective Story.* [1941]. New York: Carroll and Graf, 1984.

Heninger, S. K., Jr. *The Cosmographical Glass: Renaissance Diagrams of the Universe.* San Marino, Calif.: Huntington Library, 1977.

Johnson, Barbara. "The Frame of Reference: Poe, Lacan, Derrida." *The Critical Difference: Essays in the Contemporary Rhetoric of Reading.* Baltimore: Johns Hopkins University Press, 1980. 110–46.

Lacan, Jacques. "Seminar on 'The Purloined Letter.'" [1956]. Trans. Jeffrey Mehlman. *Yale French Studies* 48 (1972): 38–72.

Poe, Edgar Allan. *Collected Works of Edgar Allan Poe,* ed. Thomas Ollive Mabbott. 3 vols. Cambridge, Mass.: Harvard University Press, 1969–78.

———. "Epigram for Wall Street." [1845]. *Collected* 1: 378.

———. "The Fall of the House of Usher." [1839]. *Collected* 2: 392–422.

———. "Morella." [1835]. *Collected* 2: 221–37.

———. "The Murders in the Rue Morgue." [1841]. *Collected* 2: 521–74.

———. "The Mystery of Marie Rogêt." [1842–43]. *Collected* 3: 715–88.

———. "The Purloined Letter." [1844]. *Collected* 3: 972–96.

Rodríguez Monegal, Emir. *Jorge Luis Borges: A Literary Biography.* New York: E. P. Dutton, 1978.

Simpson, D. P. *Cassell's Latin Dictionary.* New York: Macmillan, 1978.

Webster's New World Dictionary of the American Language. College ed. Cleveland: World Publishing, 1964.

Chapter 2
Borges's Library of Forking Paths
Robert L. Chibka

> Alors je rentrai dans la maison, et j'écrivis, Il est minuit. La pluie
> fouette les vitres. Il n'était pas minuit. Il ne pleuvait pas.
> —Samuel Beckett, *Molloy* [1951] (239)[1]

I begin this essay about Jorge Luis Borges's "The Garden of Forking Paths" (1942), appropriately enough, with a small confession. I am here engaged in a practice of which I generally disapprove: writing professionally on a text in whose language of composition I am illiterate. That a trivial discrepancy between two English translations of "El Jardín de senderos que se bifurcan" started me down this path is a paltry excuse.[2] Yu Tsun, whose sworn confession constitutes all but the first paragraph of "The Garden of Forking Paths," has this advice for the "soldiers and bandits" he sees inheriting the world: "*Whosoever would undertake some atrocious enterprise should act as if it were already accomplished, should impose upon himself a future as irrevocable as the past*" (*F* 92–93). Typically, Yu places his emphasis squarely on the individual will (in this case, will masquerading as destiny), as if we deliberately chose both our atrocious enterprises and the means of pursuing them. I, on the contrary, seem to have been led by the world's most brilliant (and devious) librarian through certain half-lit stacks without regard to (if not precisely against) my will. I have watched this enterprise gradually come to appear less atrocious and less revocable. Like spying for foreign powers, the scholarly mission can take on a compulsive tinge.

I have something of a bibliographical detective story to tell, one that disrupts common assumptions about the nature of texts and their relation to the world they both constitute a part of and purport to document. The burden of my story is that, in reading "The Garden of Forking Paths," we can become characters in another story that is incited and "scripted," if not precisely written, by Borges. Reading this tale (and reading around it), we are encouraged simultaneously, disconcertingly, to replicate and to question Borges's story, the stories of spy-narrator-murderer Yu Tsun and sinologist-metaphysician-corpse Stephen Albert, and the story we inhabit and habitually, blithely, call "history." As readers, we seek the source of a crime; as critic, I have sought the source of a citation.

Generically, "The Garden of Forking Paths" is multiply suggestive.[3] As a spy thriller, it depends on the forward momentum toward a mysterious but univocal climax that such stories generally exploit; Yu Tsun's narrative emphasizes linear time pressure—a conscious deadline, a short headstart, the maddeningly implacable Richard Madden hot on the trail—with dozens of temporal markers. Borges, in his prologue to *Ficciones*, called it "a detective story; its readers," he continued, "will assist at the execution, and all the preliminaries, of a crime, a crime whose purpose will not be unknown to them, but which they will not understand—it seems to me—until the last paragraph" (*F* 15). This story partakes of the subgenre sometimes referred to as "metaphysical" or "analytic" detective stories. Readers of detective stories, from metaphysical to pulp, may always be in some sense accomplices (to mystery, at least, if not to mayhem), but this story is unusual in its inversions of typical mystery form: the murder occurs at the end, we seek not perpetrator but rationale, and we "solve" the crime a couple of sentences after it takes place. Further, the reader-as-accomplice has a conflict of interest, since, as Stephen Rudy notes, the reader is also "the real 'detective' in the story" (142n15).[4] Ironically, the character who "plays detective" (deciphering past actions and motives, solving the mystery of Yu's great-grandfather Ts'ui Pên's apparently unaccountable literary behavior) is the victim, Stephen Albert. But "The Garden of Forking Paths" bears in its opening paragraph the trappings of another genre that interprets, or "solves," the past in a different way: it presents itself as a footnote to a history book, purporting to document a causal chain of specific, knowable, more or less explicable events. This is where my detective story will begin, in the bibliographical and pseudohistorical opening paragraph of Borges's story; or, more precisely, of two English translations thereof.

I

> In still another, I utter these same words, but I am a mistake, a ghost.
>
> —Jorge Luis Borges, "The Garden of Forking Paths"
> (*Labyrinths* [henceforth *L*] 28)

In yet another, I say these very same words, but am an error, a phantom.

—Jorge Luis Borges, "The Garden of Forking Paths" (*F* 100)

Reading a memorable text in two translations can incite a touch of the uncanny, like meeting a friend's close relatives. The conjunction of near congruence with nonidentity allows an unnerving intuition: *déjà-lu*. Even without verbatim recall, one senses that memory has shifted— broken into pieces and recombined—while one was looking the other way. Phrases, images, tonalities, narrative gestures, stored in the same organ as recollections of childhood, can induce a dreamlike feeling of revisiting a familiar house whose furniture has been rearranged in some imponderable way, a feeling perhaps not unlike Yu Tsun's when he revisits his ancestor's "shapeless mass of contradictory rough drafts," "translated" by Stephen Albert not only into English but into a work of philosophical genius (*F* 96, 100).

Reading a memorable text in two translations, one can also feel betrayed, not only with regard to an unexamined faith in the efficacy or transparency of translation, but also by personal memory, private lectorial history. Even when translations appear compatible, their differences explicable, one can feel betrayed, as I do by that "Garden of Forking Paths" whose final sentence refers to Yu's "innumerable contrition and weariness" (*L* 29) rather than his "infinite penitence and sickness of the heart" (*F* 101). The idea of enumerating contrition or weariness is certainly (in English) gauche, but offends me more than it ought to because it vies with a preferred phrase.[5] The reader in translation is at the mercy of both authorial representations and an intermediary's interpretive *re*presentation. If translations differ not only in matters of taste ("contrition" versus "penitence"), but on the simplest, least disputable facts, one feels obliged to take sides, to get to the bottom of a presumably not bottomless mystery.

My Grove Evergreen edition of *Ficciones* contains a story called "The Garden of Forking Paths" (translated by Helen Temple and Ruthven Todd) that begins:

In his *A History of the World War* (page 212), Captain Liddell Hart reports that a planned offensive by thirteen British divisions, supported by fourteen hundred artillery pieces, against the German line at Serre-Montauban, scheduled for July 24, 1916, had to be postponed until the morning of the 29th. He comments that torrential rain caused this delay—which lacked any special significance. (*F* 89)

My New Directions edition of *Labyrinths* contains a similar story, also called "The Garden of Forking Paths" (translated by Donald A. Yates), that begins:

On page 22 of Liddell Hart's *History of World War I* you will read that an attack against the Serre-Montauban line by thirteen British divisions (supported by 1,400 artillery pieces), planned for the 24th of July, 1916, had to be postponed until the morning of the 29th. The torrential rains, Captain Liddell Hart comments, caused this delay, an insignificant one, to be sure. (*L* 19)

The text that follows, both translations agree, will cast "unsuspected light" on this delay.

We note first, in both passages, the typically Borgesian urge to pin down a new explanation for something whose insignificance all versions of the story wryly stipulate. We may suppose the difference in titles (*A History of the World War* versus *History of World War I*) to be a function of Borges's translation of an English title into Spanish and its subsequent retranslation into the language where it started. The discrepancy in page references (212 versus 22) looks like a simple typographical error in one edition or the other. So far, so good; we scholars are all too familiar with the everyday perils of transcription and typesetting.[6]

We are also notorious, though, for being easily upset by details—however significant or trivial—that refuse to cohere, such as the asymmetry of these numeric palindromes. Were it not for this discrepancy, I might have shared John Sturrock's aggressively breezy attitude toward Borges's reference to Liddell Hart: "I have not checked this quotation because it does not matter in the least whether it is accurate" (191). Personally, I might favor *in*accuracy; Borges, after all, has the uncanny ability (even in translation) to create the illusion that he invented not only Kafka and Pierre Menard, but the very idea of the encyclopedia or the tiger. I would prefer, for instance, to be allowed the conviction that Borges invented "Liddell Hart" in homage to Lewis Carroll. Instead, knowing that actuality provided this name before Borges could conjure it up, I am forced to view this nominal bit of history as something like a "found poem," a delicious morsel of linguistic nature that Borges dressed to advantage. Likewise, in a text concerned with the supposition that we inhabit not a universe but a multiverse, a polyverse, I feel obliged to seek a rationale for the appearance of two incompatible page numbers. Borges, most fantastical of writers, often chastens his readers' predilection for fantasy.

Dialing up mainframes or riffling through obsolete paper card catalogs to determine which translation got title and page reference right (and by the bye, since we know Borges was a tricky devil, what the historian "historically" wrote), we learn that Captain Basil Henry Liddell Hart produced at least two histories of that world war generally designated, without fear of inaccuracy (without fear, that is, of discovering multiple, proliferating First World Wars), "I." His titles, by emphasizing unitary, bedrock actuality, tend to belie their own multiplicity: *The Real War, 1914–1918* appeared in 1930; *A History of the World War, 1914–1918,* a revised, expanded edition of *The Real* (the surreal, the ultrareal?) in 1934. We find in *The Real War* a paragraph on the insignificant delay of an attack against the Serre-Montauban line: "The bombardment began on June 24; the attack was intended for June 29, but was later postponed until July 1, owing to a momentary break in the weather . . . the assaulting troops, . . . after being keyed up for the effort, had to remain another forty-eight hours in cramped trenches under the exhausting noise of their own gunfire and the enemy's retaliation—conditions made worse by torrential rain which flooded the trenches." This paragraph appears not on page 22, not on page 212, but on pages 233–34. *A History of the World War* includes an identical paragraph, postponed some eighty pages to 314–15.

Critics who notice such discrepancies usually dismiss them as simple irony—"La référence est, en effet, très précise mais, en fait, inexacte" ("The reference is, in effect, very precise but, in fact, inexact" [Berveiller 281n113; my trans.])—or typical Borgesian playfulness. But vigorous play can evoke serious vertigo, and those critics who attend to the Liddell Hart citation tend to show symptoms of the disorientation that labyrinths traditionally produce. Mary Lusky Friedman, who notes that the tale is presented "as a sort of corrective footnote to Liddell Hart's standard history," requires a corrective footnote of her own. "The narrator of the story's first paragraph," she writes, "recalls Germany's bombardment of a British artillery park during World War I and promises that what we are about to read will shed light on events surrounding the surprise attack" (17). The narrator of the various first paragraphs I have read recalls no such thing; Friedman conflates the Allied offensive with the German attack that, according to Yu Tsun, postponed it. Gene Bell-Villada contends that "the report of a postponed British attack on Serre-Montauban . . . is mostly 'Borgesian' invention. Hart does allude to a battle in 1916 near Montauban, in which the same number of British divisions (thirteen) were involved, but there is no mention of a postponement; and the heavy rains took place in November, not July, as Borges indicates" (93). Does the corresponding paragraph in Bell-Villada's copy of Liddell Hart mention the battle, then, but omit the two-day delay and the torrential rains?

Stephen Rudy's more meticulous reading remarks several discrepancies: that "the action on the Somme took place a month earlier than Borges quotes Liddell Hart, falsely, as having stated"; that "Borges refers in various places to Liddell Hart's book under [three different] titles"; that Liddell Hart published two versions of what Friedman calls the "standard history." Finally, he notes that "the page references to Liddell

Hart given in the two English translations differ: p. 22 according to *Ficciones*; p. 212 according to *Labyrinths*. Neither has anything to do with the Battle of the Somme," he concludes, and leaves it at that; a later note, however, mentions "p. 315 of *A History*," making it clear that Rudy tracked down the appropriate reference to the Somme (133, 141n6, 141n8). Thus, in the footnotes to his illuminating analysis of plot elements, Rudy points to virtually all the incongruities I have mentioned so far—without seeming to notice that they make "The Garden of Forking Paths" (taken as the sum of its printed versions) enact something similar to what Albert's theory of repetitive divergence describes. As if Borges's labyrinth allows no one safe passage, Rudy rechristens the London publisher "Faber and Facer" (141n6), although this error, like the delay of the British offensive, is "an insignificant one, to be sure."

I would be surprised to learn that I have emerged unscathed, have not gotten some big or little thing wrong. Part of Borges's game consists in misleading and confounding readers; with reference to the sometimes atrocious enterprise of criticism, he seems to have played this game with remarkable success. Professional readers, in this regard, are ironically more vulnerable than amateurs; like martial artists who exploit opponents' weight and momentum, Borges's story lets our own aggressive impulses toward textual mastery throw us off balance. The gremlins that affect translators do not spare critics, and discussing "The Garden of Forking Paths," like hooking a Persian rug, seems to require a flaw.

The page of a particular volume on which a particular sequence of words appears ought not to mean a thing. Excepting a couple of Laurence Sterne's typographical quips, pagination is an accident of layout and leading, formatting and font. To seek numerological patterns in, say, *The Faerie Queene*, one examines verbal echoes, poetic subdivisions—stanzas, cantos, books—not edition-specific ordinals. The latter are dead twigs on the tree of causality, with no purpose more intriguing than idiotically predictable sequencing. If we found the word "armadillo" on all pages divisible by seventeen, but no other pages, of some contemporary novel, we might think it worthy of cocktail chat but not of *Notes and Queries*. In fact, we would never discern that pattern, because we would not be looking for it or anything like it. We cast pariah page references out of syntax, marking them as untext with the stigmata of parentheses. Because they are as dumb and devoid of significance as they are necessary and useful, they are the last place we should expect to find any intimation of the labyrinth. By incorporating the inconsequential sequentiality that all books display—the very emblem of linear textuality—as a problematic feature of his story, Borges points obliquely to Liddell Hart's question about the weather, Yu Tsun's question at the instant of pulling the trigger, the question that the best fiction always poses more complicatedly than it can answer: What weighs, what matters, what signifies?

II

> No book is ever published without some variant in each copy. Scribes take a secret oath to omit, interpolate, vary.
> —Jorge Luis Borges, "The Babylon Lottery" (*F* 71)

Ignoring the discrepancy in dates (which echoes and reinforces the page-number puzzle but would entail a distracting bifurcation), we sally into musty stacks to determine which page of which work Borges's narrator actually cited.[7] Our willingness to ignore certain "facts" (the dates) makes us resemble Yu after the commission of his crime: "What remains [that is, his arrest and condemnation to death—not to mention the upshot of a world war] is unreal and unimportant" (*F* 101). Our obsession with precision, our library research, our conviction that one page in one book will give us what we need, make us more closely resemble Yu planning his crime, searching the telephone directory for "the name of the one person capable of passing on the information" (*F* 91). Both American editions claim (*F* 4; *L* iv) to translate the same Spanish *Ficciones*—published in 1956 as volume 5 of Emecé's ten-volume *Obras completas (1953-60)*—in which "El Jardín de senderos que se bifurcan" begins: "En la página 22 de la *Historia de la Guerra Europea* de Liddell Hart" (*Ficciones, Obras* 5: 97; thus also Emecé's 1956 two-volume *Obras completas* 2: 97). This might have been the end of the story: no mystery at all, but a garden-variety mistranscription by a compound culprit, the suggestively named translating team of Temple and Todd.

Borges rarely affords such easy egress. Nor, in this case, do his publishers, who counterintuitively managed eighteen years later to condense the still-growing "Complete Works" into one volume. Perhaps Emecé took to heart the suggestion in the brilliant final footnote of "The Library of Babel" (1944): "Strictly speaking, *one single volume* should suffice: a single volume of ordinary format, printed in nine or ten type body, and consisting of an infinite number of infinitely thin pages" (*F* 88; trans. Anthony Kerrigan). In any case, one needn't have Spanish to see that the narrator of "El Jardín" in *Obras completas, 1923-1972* (1974) turns over a new leaf to keep our story interesting: "En la página 242 de la *Historia de la Guerra Europea* de Liddell Hart" (472; thus also a 1980 Barcelona compilation of Borges's *Prosa completa* 396).

Another country heard from, and mystery reinstated. Clearly, the *Obras* were no more "completas" in 1974 than in 1956, and not only because Borges would live another dozen years; a truly complete edition (even ignoring translations)—an *Obras completas completa*, if you will—would apparently include at least two (trivially different) "El Jardín"s. This new and thoroughly Argentine discrepancy shows, at least, that translation is not the source of the problem, but merely one of several sites where citations can proliferate. Compilation may be another; if so, we need to consult the *in*complete works. In the original story, then—the one *Borges* wrote, the one we might wish, following Liddell Hart, to call the *real* story—what page is cited? This desire to know what something really was or first was—this fetishizing of the origin—is the futile wish for "history" *an sich*, the "actual" offensive, the "actual" delay, of which Liddell Hart's reports are, as it were, only later editions. Clever postmodernist theories of representation notwithstanding, however, we seem to have a right to ask, in so simply numerical a case, what the blind librarian himself cited.

Working backward toward an elusive origin, I recall Borges's analysis, in "Kafka and His Precursors" (1951), of the way that a prior past can be irreversibly redefined by subsequent developments in a more recent past. He is quite convincing on the slippery, intuitive issue of literary "influence"; but such an argument ought not to apply to something so finite and (unmeta)physical as a page number. Because no matter how much we enjoy playing Borgesian games, no one finally believes that the planet we live on follows their rules. No idealist's "proof" of immateriality makes anyone (even the idealist) sit less heavily, chew less thoroughly, or feel less rotten about being trapped in a cramped trench flooded by torrential rains. And so we can't stop short of first editions: lovers of fiction, we seek fact; like historians, we desire the original, crave the truth.

The truth: the first edition of *El Jardín de senderos que se bifurcan* (1942) and the first edition of *Ficciones* (1944) both cite page 252 (*El Jardín* 107; *Ficciones* 109).[8]

This (historically) first page number is the sixth one on my list. Through what combination of errata, corrections, hypermetropia, and/or disinformation were these bifurcating, trifurcating, hexafurcating variants introduced? Is there in our libraries a book to reconcile or, at least, explain them? Perhaps a Spanish translation of Liddell Hart (of *which* Liddell Hart? we wonder in passing): the book Borges's narrator refers to, entitled *Historia de la Guerra Europea*. This *History of the European* (not the World, not the Real) *War* may provide the clue we bibliographical detectives crave. Such a volume could contain a paragraph describing an insignificant delay on page 212, 22, 233, 314, 242, or 252. More likely, it would add a seventh number to my list. And an eighth, a ninth: revised, expanded editions of this work might in their turn present incompatible paginations. But this path seems to be, as some forks must be, a cul-de-sac; I have tried, and failed, to ascertain that Liddell Hart's work ever found a Spanish translator.[9] There may be a relatively sensible explanation—of the sort that Captain Liddell Hart would favor—for this history of proliferative, hence indeterminate citations, this bibliotechnical version of the Stephen Albert/Ts'ui Pên phenomenon, whereby simple facts become trembling constellations of possibilities. If so, life has only accidentally imitated art, giving our Boolean searches a suspiciously Borgesian plot. Whether accidentally or conspiratorially, though, what happens, in short, is this: "The Garden of Forking Paths" breaks the binding of any book that seeks to contain it, sending us through stacks that begin eerily to resemble the Library of Babel, full of possibly insignificant variants on indeterminately significant texts. Recalling the volume of *The Anglo-American Cyclopaedia* described in "Tlön, Uqbar, Orbis Tertius" (1940)—the single copy that differs from others in a single crucial detail—we may begin to wonder whether each volume we consult accurately represents the edition of which it is an example. I located one of my Spanish "originals," for instance, in the collection of Wellesley College, and received a photocopy of the other from Middlebury College; if I happened to live in Chicago and had examined midwestern copies instead, might this essay now be headed in a different direction?

Generally impervious to the charms of mysticism, I find the direction it *has* taken quite disconcerting. "The Garden of Forking Paths" makes me ask strange questions whose answers generate stranger ones. The story (taken, again, as the sum of its versions) presents not the familiar musical format of theme and variations but variants with a theme. Differences one would otherwise deem "insignificant" (in "El Jardín de senderos que se bifurcan," in "The Garden of Forking Paths," and in the histories to which they ostensibly refer) become thematically charged when one of the story's explicit themes is, precisely, that of proliferant variations.

Given Liddell Hart's oddly redundant publishing history and Borges's oddly *non*redundant citations, we may view Stephen Albert's theory of forking time in a new light. Our libraries become themselves gardens of forking paths—in space, not time—labyrinths that problematize the unitary status of Liddell Hart, of Borges, and (of course) of the story itself. Like the fragment of a letter that affords Albert the clue he needs to decipher Ts'ui Pên's life, like Yu Tsun's fragmentary deposition that constitutes nearly all of this story, all texts and explanatory impulses begin to appear incomplete, elusive, teasing.[10] We rely implicitly on the idea that any text—Yu's deposition, Albert's scrap of a letter, Ts'ui Pên's chaotically fragmentary "novel," Liddell Hart's history, our own scholarly article—can cast light ("unsuspected" or otherwise) on its subject; here, in contrast, we find arresting intimations that texts offer only shadowy glimpses of mutating, more or less irrelevant, necessarily indefinitive possibilities—"a shapeless mass of contradictory rough drafts," as Yu calls Ts'ui's manuscript (*F* 96). Between these opposing ideas an insoluble tension arises. It recreates in readers' experiences the tension in the story's structure between the illusion of precise, linear, forward momentum in Yu's singleminded plot and the illusion of infinitely branching, looping movements (both experiential and narrative) in Albert's reading of Ts'ui Pên's theory of the universe. The unlikely publishing histories of a British military historian ("external to" this story) and an Argentine librarian (its creator) combine to reinforce a British sinologist's notion of radical contingency.

But Borges's characteristically metaphysical undercutting of metaphysics ought to remind us that Albert's, like all other "theories of the universe," is far more theoretical than universal. "The universe, the sum of all things," Borges wrote in "A New Refutation of Time" (1947), "is a collection no less ideal than that of all the horses Shakespeare dreamt of—one, many, none?—between 1592 and 1594. I add: if time is a mental process, how can thousands of men—or even two different men— share it?" (*L* 223; trans. James E. Irby). He made the same point more bluntly in "The Analytic Language of John Wilkins" (1941): "there is no classification of the universe that is not arbitrary and conjectural. The reason is very simple: we do not know what the universe is" (*Other* 104; trans. Ruth L. C. Simms). Such idealist sentiments may place an extravagant theory like Albert's on the same plane as our everyday understandings, but only by throwing common sense into crisis, not by giving the extravagant theory a leg to stand on. Truly radical uncertainty leaves no stone undoubted, and its theorists may find themselves hobbling on toes stubbed against the actual.

Albert, whose name makes him a useful corpse in the same "accidental" way that Liddell Hart's name recalls the imponderable conundrums of Carroll's *Alice* books, ironically facilitates his own death by proposing a theory in which personal responsibility is muted (even mooted) by multiple realities. Yu's pulling of the trigger is made easier, more likely, by the idea that this encounter has alternative, indeed innumerable, upshots. Yu's method for convincing himself of his own courage— "*impos[ing] upon himself a future as irrevocable as the past*" (*F* 93)—suggests the linear inevitability of traditional notions of fate. But Albert's precisely opposite idea of a temporal labyrinth serves Yu's purpose even better by reducing every future, if not to revocability, then at least to inconsequentiality, to the status of one among many.

Yu never considers the mind-boggling ramifications of Albert's theory of ramification (I cite just one: that in "other branches of time," Ts'ui Pên did no such thing as what Albert, in his univocally explanatory reading of a labyrinthine manuscript, claims he did). Nevertheless, Yu allows this theory to mitigate the horror of what he is about: the irrevocable murder of a man who is singular in two senses. Since the telephone directory contains only one Albert, this *one* must be killed in order to transmit a municipal name to Yu's hateful German Chief (some people will do anything for the sake of a pun). But of all human beings, Albert is precisely the *one* Yu is least inclined to kill: "an Englishman—a modest man—who, for me, is as great as Goethe" (*F* 91). The entire story, in terms of plot, is built on this tension between Yu's goal-oriented mission and the notion of infinitely meandering possibilities. In terms of character, it is built on the tension between Yu's unequivocal adoption of his mission and the equivocations inevitably introduced by Albert's theory—which, by redeeming the honor of Yu's ancestor, makes Albert both a latterday version of Ts'ui and a personal hero for Yu. Whatever equivocations he feels, however, Yu relates to the wavering, multiplying "pullulation" (*F* 100) he senses at the brink of the atrocious act, the "swarming sensation" (*L* 28) that seems to confirm Albert's theory and thus, paradoxically, to minimize moral equivocation.

Yu, who calls himself "a timorous man" (*F* 91), must welcome a theory that can mitigate his inexcusable act; but he sees in the image of "Albert and myself, secretive, busy, and multiform in other dimensions of time" (*F* 100–101) a "tenuous nightmare" (*L* 28), and this vision of multiplicity quickly yields to one indivisible fact: "In the black and yellow garden there was only a single man" (*F* 101). The deposition returns at its climactic moment to the figure with which it began: the implacable Madden who takes Yu as his singular target, just as Yu has taken Albert. Of course, Yu's mission is more complex than Madden's. If, by killing Albert, he proves to his hated Chief "that a yellow man could [temporarily] save his armies" (*F* 91), he also (permanently) destroys the source of his rehabilitated family honor. Albert stands in for Ts'ui by translating his humiliating work into an instance of familial, if not racial, pride; insofar as he regenerates and "embodies" Ts'ui, he not only makes a long-deceased ancestor killable but authorizes, with a stroke of Ts'ui's own pen as it were, Yu's annihilation of his own great-grandfather.

Albert thus participates in a highly personal, hyper-Oedipal drama whereby Yu proves his "manhood" (and, he fancies, redeems his race) by eliminating his most formidable male ancestor.[11] Borges's story does not entail, as Rudy asserts, a consistent "negation of the concept of 'individuality,'" in "characters [who] act as 'functions' (much as they do in the folk tale)," by a thorough "suppression of the psychological element" (137, 138); such a claim locates only one of the opposing forces that structure the story. The other is suggested by Bell-Villada: "Yu's nar-rative is held together by an underlying unity of tone and sentiment— a combination of fear, sadness, and guilt. Yu Tsun is neither the hard-boiled nor the coldly rational operative. Indeed, for a spy he is oddly sensitive and conscience-ridden" (96). Yu's conscience is visible not only in the way he ends his confession, with an implied wish for absolution, but in his touching, if hopeless, attempt to mitigate his report of the crime: "I swear his death was instantaneous, as if he had been struck by lightning." To the extent that "instantaneous" suggests removal from the temporal realm of cause, effect, and personal responsibility, this sen-tence states a wish, not a fact; Albert is struck not by lightning, but by a bullet Yu inscribed with his name and "fired with the utmost care" into his back. The astonishing detachment of Yu's act works its finest effect only in concert with our full belief in his "infinite penitence and sick-ness of the heart" (*F* 101).

Borges's genially bewildering experiments often lead critics to em-phasize their more surprising, metaphysical extremes and understate the counterpoint of their more conventional, almost "realist" aspects.[12] Thus, for instance, Rudy claims that "history, chronological time, has no place in Borges's universe," that Borges "correct[s] Liddell Hart (os-tensibly in the interests of historical truth), outdoing the very concept of cause and effect to the point that it turns on itself, and all notions of history, causal time, and truth are overthrown by the 'unfathomable'" (133, 134). Rudy's reading of "two parallel yet incompatible plots, one of a detective, the other of a metaphysical, nature" (135) is both sensi-tive and insightful, but "The Garden of Forking Paths" has only a single, relentlessly chronological plot, in the course of which a character pro-pounds a *theory* of plot that, while perhaps problematizing the story we read, does not govern it. Rudy's "metaphysical plot" exists only by im-plication, and then only if we (temporarily) accept Albert's theory as accurately describing not only Ts'ui Pên's fictional *Garden of Forking Paths* but also our world. Albert writes up a one-way ticket to a startling and seductive destination, but the story in which he appears sends us on a round trip. For the momentary sake of argument, we may entertain Albert's entertaining theory; but even before we emerge from the story to resume our extra-Borgesian lives, Yu Tsun's contrite coda restores something like our "usual" understandings of causality, psychology, and history. Only against the always implicit ground of such understandings, in fact, would the contrary theory appear so seductive. Even the once crimson slip of paper that gives Albert his crucial clue to the meaning of Ts'ui Pên's work is "faded with the passage of time" (*F* 97).

No single version of "The Garden of Forking Paths" bears any struc-tural similarities whatsoever to Ts'ui's *Garden of Forking Paths*. Borges's plot does not pretend to enact infinity; it contains within it a discussion of infinity, but its shape relentlessly enforces temporal finitude. Even Ts'ui Pên's work makes only the most transparent pretense of enacting infinity, merely alluding indirectly to the idea—just as a couple of (re)quoted sentences can deftly establish the idea of Pierre Menard's (re)writing of the *Quixote* by gesturing toward it, not (re)presenting it, in Borges's 1939 story. Albert claims that each character in *The Garden of Forking Paths* "chooses—simultaneously—all" imaginable alternatives, that "in the work of Ts'ui Pên, all possible outcomes occur" (*L* 26). This is not true by a long, an infinite, shot. All the alternatives Albert cites from Ts'ui's work are perfectly conventional, drawn from a stagnant pool of plot components collected from epic, tragic, and detective traditions. They embrace armies marching into battle and murderers knocking at doors, but no broken shoelaces or mediocre stir-fries, no ingrown hairs or wrong numbers, nary a single subepic inconsequentiality. In the "two versions of the same epic chapter" (*F* 98) Albert reads to Yu, "all possible outcomes" comprise, with trenchant irony, winning a battle and winning it again. To judge from Albert's samples, this version of infinity is poor indeed, its complexity and novelty entirely conceptual, its notion of cause-and-effect far closer to Liddell Hart's than to Borges's.

Albert's speculations about the ways in which a book might approach infinity include mental gymnastics familiar from other Borges stories—circularity, infinite regress—but conclude with the idea of "a Platonic hereditary work, passed on from father to son, to which each individual would add a new chapter or correct, with pious care, the work of his elders" (*F* 97). This concept of infinity as lineage is not even remotely labyrinthine; on the contrary, it is as unidirectional as Borges's plot (or Liddell Hart's, for that matter) and scarcely distinguishable from what the vernacular calls "family history." [13]

The broad counterpoint between singular and plural (or, if you will, between plot and theory) is echoed, on smaller scales, in many internal reflections duly noted by critics. But if Borges, like Ts'ui, struggles (or chafes, at least) against the linear and the finite, he does so in a medium that is incontrovertibly finite and unremittingly linear, both temporally and spatially. Only in such a medium can he work his particular brand of narrative magic (as, for instance, only an audience that implicitly owns the notion of a unified self is fit to hear the lovely, disconcerting ironies of the 1960 prose poem "Borges and I"). In the case of "The Garden of Forking Paths," however, Borges manages to break the mold of his medium and press into service the world outside the story. Albert's theory could be safely contained—as a fine and ephemeral fancy—within the very finite limits of Yu's deposition, if only our libraries did not teem with wrong page numbers, intimating an invasive, mutating Albert-virus that infects readers with Yu's "swarming sensation." Liddell Hart's works, like his name, function in the manner of "found poems"; their iterativity plants a germ of the uncanny in the most unlikely spot.[14] The pullulating variants of the Borgesian text spread the contagion, so that we find *outside the bounds of the story* what we expect to have left between the closed covers of a single volume. Like "the victim within" a "strong labyrinth" in one critic's description, we "experience a bending of apparently straight lines, a perplexing of space, even while [we], in playing back, attempt[ ] to straighten them" (Wilson 18); and this perplexity is visited upon us in libraries, our bastions of order and precision, if not necessarily or exclusively of truth.

III

> It seems probable that if we were never bewildered there would never be a story to tell about us; we should partake of the superior nature of the all-knowing immortals whose annals are dreadfully dull so long as flurried humans are not, for the positive relief of bored Olympians, mixed up with them.
> —Henry James, preface to *The Princess Casamassima* (xxxi)

Finally, we in our libraries, like Yu in his prison cell, occupy an impossible, an untenable position. Regardless of theories of the universe, we live the lives we live, consult the volumes we have at our disposal— variants, discrepancies, fragmentarity, and all; like Yu, faced with odd echoes and unexpected twists, we do what little we can. Yu has a thought, early in his journey to Ashgrove, that reverberates later as a counterweight to the Ts'ui Pên/Albert theory: "Then I reflected that all things happen, happen to one, precisely *now*. Century follows century, and things happen only in the present. There are countless men in the air, on land and at sea, and all that really happens happens to me" (*F* 90). That Yu negates, even as he alludes to them, the "countless men" suffering and dying in a war more real than anything Liddell Hart ever wrote is, I hope, chilling to us. What disturbs him at the story's end is something quite different, however: his "*now*" in which "all things happen" comprises more than time; the "me" to whom "all that really happens happens" is constructed and defined by a horribly singular past, the story's ending insists. "What remains"—the attestable, publishable account of an event—"is unreal and unimportant" to Yu not in an absolute sense but by contrast to the *subjective* aftermath of an irrevocable action. His "infinite penitence and sickness of the heart," which the Chief "does not know, for no one can" (F 101), announce a different kind of infinity: selfsame, unvarying through time, "innumerable" because it represents the final victory of singular over plural. Liddell Hart's delay is "insignificant" not to a soldier trapped in a flooded trench, but to the scholar whose magisterial view cannot afford to accommodate either the emotional bewilderment that comes to Yu as "sickness of the heart" or the intellectual bewilderment that can affect a critic like a fever of the brain. With the (unwitting, I presume) assistance of publishers and translators, Borges reinstates such bewilderment as the most genuine response to the nightmare of history.

The excruciatingly coincidental encounter of Yu Tsun and Stephen Albert underscores singularity in both senses. It emerges from an infinity of possible stories as the one worth telling, the one told; at the same time, this singular coincidence constitutes a merging of people and ideas, the opposite of a forking path. The story counterbalances the striking "theory" of bifurcation with the even more striking (and, for Yu, heartbreaking) "fact" of convergence. Let us stipulate, although no one believes it for a second, that time "actually" resembles the labyrinth Albert finds in Ts'ui's work; even so, for any given mortal, situated instantaneously at a given spot on a given branch, no labyrinth will exist. Borges said of his own "A New Refutation of Time": "I believe in the argument logically, and I think that if you accept the premises, the argument may stand—though at the same time, alas, time also stands" (di Giovanni et al. 63).[15] Language may win a battle, but time wins the war. In a fight to the death between time and a theory, it would be simply foolish to put one's money on the theory.[16]

Within "The Garden of Forking Paths," Yu stands in for time, killing the beautiful theory (or, at least, the theorist); in doing so, he collaborates with narrative's linear form. If Albert, Liddell Hart, far-sighted copyeditors, errant translators, and who knows what printer's devils have conspired to provide an intimation of the labyrinth, narrative form nevertheless enforces the irrevocable, heartbreakingly finite nature of life "as we know it." We are left with the effect that Borges described in reviewing Liddell Hart's meditation on war psychology and the dangers of military gigantism, *Europe in Arms*, for the April 30, 1937, issue of *El Hogar*: "Goce desengañado, goce lúcido, goce pesimista" (*Textos* 125). Disillusioned pleasure, lucid pleasure, pessimistic pleasure. One imagines that this is exactly the sort of pleasure the historical Borges derived from concocting—in the midst of a war that would retroactively transform The Great War, The Real War, the War to End Them All, into the first of a series—a story of repetition, divergence, and wishful escape from the inescapably vectored movement of time. Albert's hope that he might retreat from worldly (and World War) concerns into a placid scholarly contemplation—as Ts'ui did in another place and time by retiring to the Pavilion of the Limpid Solitude—is unequivocally dashed:

"The reality of the war conquers. It's sad, but it must be so."[17] The "un-suspected light" that Yu's narrative casts on history is dark indeed.

Notes

An earlier version of this essay appeared as "The Library of Forking Paths" in *Representations* 56 (1996): 106–22. Reprinted with permission of the Regents of the University of California.

1. "Then I went back into the house and wrote, It is midnight. The rain is beating on the windows. It was not midnight. It was not raining" (Beckett, *Molloy* [1955] 241).

2. That a "former teacher of English at the Tsingtao Hochschule" would presumably have "dictated" (*Ficciones* [1962; henceforth *F*] 89) a deposition to his British captors *in English* affords neither excuse nor solace.

3. Here is a skeletal version of Borges's plot: Yu Tsun, a Chinese spy for the Germans in England during World War I, has been found out. Before he is captured or killed, he must somehow transmit to his chief in Berlin the secret location of a new British artillery park: the city of Albert. He will do so by murdering a stranger named Stephen Albert; his chief, poring over newspapers for word of his minions' activities, will find the name Yu Tsun linked with the name Albert and solve the riddle. Before he can kill Albert, Yu discovers that the latter, once a missionary in China, has devoted his energies to solving another riddle: that of Yu's great-grandfather, Ts'ui Pên, who "gave up temporal power to write a novel . . . and to create a maze in which all men would lose themselves. . . . His novel had no sense to it and nobody ever found his labyrinth" (*F* 93). Albert has concluded that book and maze are one and the same, that Ts'ui's novel, *The Garden of Forking Paths*, portrays a temporal labyrinth: "Your ancestor," Albert tells Yu, "did not think of time as absolute and uniform. He believed in an infinite series of times, in a dizzily growing, ever spreading network of diverging, converging and parallel times. This web of time—the strands of which approach one another, bifurcate, intersect or ignore each other through the centuries—embraces *every* possibility" (*F* 100). The former missionary is now proselytizing to redeem the metaphysical theory and reputation of Yu's ancestor, who died in disgrace under suspicion of luncacy; Albert proclaims Ts'ui's *The Garden of Forking Paths* not a senseless jumble but a work of genius. Yu murders Albert anyway, is arrested, and dictates, under a sentence of death, the deposition that we read.

4. Rudy goes on to differ with Borges about the story's secret, saying that the reader-detective "should be able to anticipate the 'solution' offered in the last paragraph" (142n15). Borges, I think, gauges the prescience of his typical reader more accurately.

5. Borges's word is "innumerable," which Shaw (1976) quite rightly links to the "innumerables futuros" Albert sees in Ts'ui Pên's work (44).

6. In a 1971 seminar at Columbia University, Norman di Giovanni, who collaborated with Borges on numerous translations, quoted two versions of the sentence about torrential rain as his "whole textbook on translation." He severely criticized Yates's version in *Labyrinths*: "It should be obvious that the elements of the . . . sentence are put together all wrong" (di Giovanni et al. 134, 135). Borges, who was at his elbow, did not disagree. The alternative that di Giovanni praised, however, was not Temple and Todd's; in any case, his critique concerned effective English syntax rather than accuracy.

7. For a discussion of the story's historicity that makes much of the discrepancy in dates between Borges and Liddell Hart, see Balderston 39–55.

8. Balderston reveals that the first British edition of *The Real War* (as opposed to the first American edition cited above) contains the passage in question on page 252 (Balderston 151n5). It appears, then, that once upon a prelapsarian time, page numbers in "El Jardín" and one version of *The Real War* corresponded neatly. But seeds of discrepancy, already sown in Liddell Hart's multiple editions of history, eventually sprouted to full-blown inconsistency in various versions of Borges's "Garden."

9. "BORGES: . . . I've done most of my reading in English" (di Giovanni et al. 137). But see Irby's footnote to a similar statement: "Bien que Borges soit systématiquement anglophile et surtout saxophile il prononcerait un jugement très différent selon la nationalité de son interlocuteur: à un Italien il parlerait de Dante; à un Français de Hugo, Baudelaire ou Toulet. C'est là un trait essentiel de son comportement social" (Although Borges is systematically an Anglophile and above all a Saxophile, he would pronounce a very different judgment depending on the nationality of his interlocutor: to an Italian he would speak of Dante; to a Frenchman of Hugo, Baudelaire or Toulet. That is an essential trait of his social deportment) (Borges, "Entretiens" 401; my trans.).

10. Friedman notes that "the compromising letter Yu pulls from his pocket, a letter whose contents the reader never learns, has a double in the exquisitely penned fragment of a letter, key to interpreting Ts'ui Pên's chaotic novel, that Albert will later take from a lacquered drawer" (19). Yu's never-explained letter, "which I decided to destroy at once (and which I did not destroy)" (*F* 91), is unusual among the story's texts in not being described explicitly as a fragment; but it is the ultimate fragment in the sense that one can make absolutely nothing of it.

11. Borges, who would undoubtedly dislike my Freudian lingo, nevertheless saw Albert as a parent figure for Yu: "Il est plus pathétique que Yu Tsun tue un homme ayant su comprendre l'énigme de son propre ancêtre, un homme devenant ainsi presque son parent" ("It is more moving that Yu Tsun kill a man who has solved the riddle of his own ancestor, a man who thus becomes almost his parent") ("Entretiens" 394; my trans.).

12. Balderston, who believes that Borges's historical references push this story "much closer to the realistic than to the fantastic," expresses surprise at "how often Stephen Albert's theory of parallel universes has been taken as an explanation of the text"; "critics [who] speak of games with time," he argues, repeat "Albert's position in the story, deprived of its dialectical punch" (51, 6, 40).

13. This progressive work, ever subject to revision and expansion but infinite only in the very limited sense of remaining unfinished, is not only more commonplace but infinitely more practicable than the others that Borges and Albert enjoy dreaming about. The single all-encompassing volume posited at the conclusion of "The Library of Babel" would simplify reference protocols but, by the same token, render citation useless; the distress of a scholar attempting to verify a quotation from "p. ∞" could properly be characterized as boundless.

14. Borges listed Liddell Hart's work at least twice among the most reread and annotated books in his library; his transmigrational phrasing adumbrates a problematic of uncanny repetition and incompatible variation by now familiar to my reader. His review of Liddell Hart's *Europe in Arms* begins: "Revisando mi biblioteca, veo con admiración que las obras que más he releído y abrumado de notas manuscritas son el *Diccionario de la Filosofía* de Mauthner, *El mundo como*

voluntad y representación de Schopenhauer, y la *Historia de la guerra mundial* de B. H. Liddell Hart" (*Textos* 125). His review of Edward Kasner and James Newman's *Mathematics and the Imagination* begins: "Revisando la biblioteca, veo con admiración que las obras que más he releído y abrumado de notas manuscritas son el *Diccionario de la Filosofía* de Mauthner, la *Historia biográfica de la filosofía* de Lewes, la *Historia de la guerra de 1914–1918* de Liddell Hart, la *Vida de Samuel Johnson* de Boswell y la psicología de Gustav Spiller: *The Mind of Man*, 1902" (*Obras completas, 1923–1972* 276). The former review appeared in *El Hogar* (April 30, 1937); the latter first appeared in *Sur* (October 1940) and was collected with other "Notas" in a 1957 revision of the 1932 *Discusión* (see de Roux and de Milleret 448; Becco 49). Both reviews foresee the addition of the volume under review to their respective lists.

15. Rimmon-Kenan, arguing that "the same phenomenon of repetition which disintegrates the autonomy of the individual also defines it," quotes, from the text of "A New Refutation of Time," a longer and more beautiful but tonally similar passage, which concludes, with piercing resignation: "The world, unfortunately, is real; I, unfortunately, am Borges" (192).

16. The romantic dichotomy between concrete human constructions (gilded monuments, hard copy) and their intellectual or aesthetic counterparts (powerful rhymes, theories of the universe) is deconstructed by the recognition that the latter are transmissible only by concrete means: mortal tongues (like Albert's, forever silenced), physical texts (like Yu's, its opening pages irretrievably lost), diskettes and drives (like mine, subject to surges and crashes). The nature of language as continually mediating between abstraction and concretion collapses the pretty notion that writing (a sonnet, a military history, a short story, an e-mail flame) is less susceptible to sluttish time's besmearments, less inherently finite, than any material medium (a stone tablet, a bound volume, a snippet of paper faded from crimson to sickly pink, a fiber optic cable). These days, when information seems to depend less on dimensionality (what would Borges have made of the Internet and World Wide Web?), access relies more than ever on hardware. I may have more memory than I'll ever use, but I can no longer work in the absence of a grounded outlet. All the world's knowledge in CD-ROM format becomes a mere source of frustration when the system goes down. Our only route to the "virtual" is by way of the actual: the material and temporal. (Even thoughts we keep to ourselves depend for processing, storage, and retrieval on hard-wired nervous systems.)

17. This is my translation of the final two sentences of Borges's response when asked why, after discovering in Albert a soulmate ("frère spirituel"), Yu pursues his murderous plan anyway: "La réalité de la guerre vainc. C'est triste, mais cela doit être ainsi" ("Entretiens" 394, 395). (Shaw [1986] quotes the answer to this question in Spanish: "La realidad de la guerra vence. Es triste, pero tiene que ser así" [116]. The entire Spanish interview may be found in Irby et al., *Encuentro.*) Borges seems to have meant that "cela doit être ainsi" for aesthetic reasons: "pour que l'effet soit bouleversant, pathétique" ("Entretiens" 394). I would say that his decision to show Albert and Yu both destroyed by the brutal reality of war makes the story not only more surprising and moving, but also truer.

Works Cited

Balderston, Daniel. *Out of Context: Historical Reference and the Representation of Reality in Borges.* Durham, N.C.: Duke University Press, 1993. 39–55.

Becco, Horacio Jorge. *Jorge Luis Borges: Bibliografía total 1923–1973.* Buenos Aires: Casa Pardo, 1973.

Beckett, Samuel. *Molloy.* [Paris: Minuit, 1951]. Trans. Samuel Beckett and Patrick Bowles. New York: Grove, 1955.

Bell-Villada, Gene H. *Borges and His Fiction: A Guide to His Mind and Art.* Chapel Hill: University of North Carolina Press, 1981.

Berveiller, Michel. *Le Cosmopolitisme de Jorge Luis Borges.* Paris: Didier, 1973.

Borges, Jorge Luis. *El Jardín de senderos que se bifurcan.* Buenos Aires: Sur, 1942.

———. "Entretiens." Interview with James E. Irby. De Roux and de Milleret 388–403.

———. *Ficciones.* Buenos Aires: Sur, 1944.

———. *Ficciones,* ed. Anthony Kerrigan. New York: Grove, 1962.

———. *Ficciones. Obras completas (1953–60).* 10 vols. Vol. 5. Buenos Aires: Emecé, 1956.

———. *Labyrinths: Selected Stories and Other Writings.* Ed. Donald A. Yates and James E. Irby. New York: New Directions, 1964.

———. *Obras completas.* 2 vols. Buenos Aires: Emecé, 1956.

———. *Obras completas, 1923–1972.* Buenos Aires: Emecé, 1974.

———. *Other Inquisitions, 1937–1952.* Austin: University of Texas Press, 1964.

———. *Prosa completa.* Vol. 1. Barcelona: Bruguera, 1980.

———. *Textos cautivos: Ensayos y reseñas en "El Hogar."* Ed. Enrique Sacerio-Garí and Emir Rodríguez Monegal. Barcelona: Tusquets, 1986.

De Roux, Dominique and Jean de Milleret, eds. *Jorge Luis Borges.* [1964]. Paris: L'Herne, 1981.

Di Giovanni, Norman Thomas, Daniel Halperin, and Frank MacShane, eds. *Borges on Writing.* New York: Dutton, 1973.

Friedman, Mary Lusky. *The Emperor's Kites: A Morphology of Borges's Tales.* Durham, N.C.: Duke University Press, 1987.

Irby, James E., Napoleón Murat, and Carlos Peralta. *Encuentro con Borges.* Buenos Aires: Galerna, 1968.

James, Henry. *The Princess Casamassima.* [1886]. New York: Knopf, 1991.

Liddell Hart, B. H. [Basil Henry]. *A History of the World War, 1914–1918.* London: Faber and Faber, 1934.

———. *The Real War, 1914–1918.* Boston: Little Brown, 1930.

Rimmon-Kenan, Shlomith. "Doubles and Counterparts: Patterns of Interchangeability in Borges's 'The Garden of Forking Paths.'" *Critical Inquiry* 6 (1980): 639–47. Reprinted in *Modern Critical Views: Jorge Luis Borges,* ed. Harold Bloom. New York: Chelsea, 1986. 185–92.

Rudy, Stephen. "The Garden *of* and *in* Borges's 'Garden of Forking Paths.'" In *The Structural Analysis of Narrative Texts: Conference Papers,* New York University Slavic Papers, ed. Andrej Kodjak, Michael J. Connolly, and Krystyna Pomorska. Columbus, Oh.: Slavica, 1980. 132–44.

Shaw, Donald L. *Borges: Ficciones.* Critical Guides to Spanish Texts 14. London: Grant and Cutler, 1976.

———. *Jorge Luis Borges: Ficciones.* Guías Laia de Literatura II. Barcelona: Laia, 1986.

Sturrock, John. *Paper Tigers: The Ideal Fictions of Jorge Luis Borges.* Oxford: Clarendon Press, 1977.

Wilson, Robert Rawdon. "Godgames and Labyrinths: The Logic of Entrapment." *Mosaic* 15, 4 (1982): 1–22.

Chapter 3
(De)feats of Detection
The Spurious Key Text from Poe to Eco

Joel Black

> "Why . . . is everybody so interested in texts?"
> —Thomas Pynchon, *The Crying of Lot 49* (78)

Interpretation and Detection

It's customary to credit Poe with elaborating all the conventions of detective fiction that subsequent practitioners of the genre have followed to a greater or lesser degree.[1] Yet Poe's privileged role as founder or father of a literary genre—a role perhaps unique in literary history—has obscured the fact that he marks what can now be recognized as a first phase of the genre's development. Key works of detective fiction in the twentieth century, especially in its latter half, represent a distinct departure from Poe's "tales of ratiocination" and, indeed, from traditional hermeneutics.[2] Before we can delineate this later phase, however, we need to review the tradition inaugurated by Poe.

The mental activity of analysis extolled by Poe's detective Dupin is distinct from mere mathematical calculation, in that it entails empathetic understanding through identification with another. In "The Purloined Letter" (1844), Dupin finds the place where the Minister has "hidden" the letter by identifying himself with the thief—a relatively easy matter for Dupin since the Minister is an analytic genius like himself, a poet as well as a mathematician. Dupin's analytic powers are called on, however, not to interpret a text but to find one. The mystery of the purloined letter concerns only its location—in plain view in the Minister's card rack—which the story ultimately reveals. The mystery has nothing to do with the letter's content, which is not disclosed in the story, remains unknown to the reader, and must therefore be assumed to be irrelevant to the tale. It was precisely this reticence about what the letter said or signified that aroused Jacques Lacan's interest in this story, and prompted his analysis of the letter's function as a "pure signifier" (32), "a signifier of the repressed" (Felman 146).[3] In the absence of the text of the purloined letter, Lacan—and later Jacques Derrida, Barbara Johnson, and others— have been compelled to seize on a *second* letter in the story whose text *is* disclosed. This, of course, is the substitute letter that Dupin places in the Minister's card rack after he retrieves the original. The text of this substitute letter consists of a couplet from Crébillon's revenge play *Atrée et Thyeste* that Dupin has copied out and left as a literary signature, a personal message of retribution to the Minister for some unspecified past offense.

At the conclusion of Poe's tale, the stolen letter is retrieved and returned to its rightful owner, the Queen, while its contents are made known to everyone except the reader (and, of course, the King). The substitute letter is left in the Minister's card rack where it will remain for an indefinite time, its contents known to all the principal characters in the story (as well as to the reader) except the Minister, on whom the final joke is played. We may imagine the Minister's situation after the end of the story, at that hypothetical moment when, out of idle curiosity or misguided revenge, he finally discovers the substitute letter. In finding that he has been duped by Dupin, the Minister will no longer be in the role of poet-analyst, but of critic-interpreter, teasing out the meanings of Dupin's art of allusion.

I have said that because the contents of the stolen and retrieved letter are not revealed in the story, Poe's commentators have had to turn much of their own analytical powers to offering ingenious interpretations of the substitute letter and its significance. It is almost as if, having withheld from his readers the textual contents of the purloined letter, Poe tossed his future interpreters—as Dupin tossed the Minister—the sop of the substitute letter with its quotation from Crébillon as an object on which they can exercise their hermeneutic ingenuity and industry. The business of interpreting texts is left to the Minister and the poststructuralists (despite their disingenuous claims to the contrary); it has nothing to do with Dupin or, for that matter, with Poe, who are concerned instead with detecting texts—with seeing where texts are, and with seeing texts for what they are. Yet, in the future development of the genre, the detective's abilities will be increasingly taken up with the interpretation of texts, with determining what texts *mean*; as a result, his chances of success will be increasingly compromised by the likely possibility of misinterpretation.

Unread and Unreadable Texts

"The Purloined Letter" has to do, on the one hand, with a text that is undiscovered because, although readily available, it remains "hidden"; and, on the other hand, with texts that are potentially available but that go unread because their message is either withheld (the contents of the purloined letter are not made known to the reader) or ignored (it will presumably be some time before the Minister thinks to check the letter in his card rack). Yet although all these texts go unread, there is nothing inherently unreadable about them, nothing intrinsically opaque about their contents. If Poe were a bit more prolix, Dupin a bit less discreet, or the Minister a bit less self-assured, the letters would prove readily readable. For that matter, had Poe's tale belonged to the more conventional genre of historical romance, the letter's text, and its surrounding sexual-political context, would have been the story's central concern, while Dupin's skill in foiling the Minister's plans would have been of only peripheral interest.

Poe's narratives abound in mysterious documents or texts that are hard to read in the sense that it isn't easy to see (or hear) them, but easy to read in the sense that once they *are* seen (or heard) their meaning is more or less clear. The stolen document in "The Purloined Letter" eludes detection because, although it is in plain view where it is least expected, it has been disguised: it has been "soiled and crumpled," "torn nearly in two" (995), "turned, as a glove, inside out" (996), and readdressed, "in a diminutive female hand, to D——, the Minister, himself." Despite the fact that the letter in the Minister's card rack "was, to all appearance, radically different from the one" stolen from the Queen, Dupin readily identifies it as the same letter; its "excessive" physical disfigurement does not extend to the message itself, which has been left intact (995). Similarly, the unintelligible utterances of the unseen killer-orangutan in "The Murders in the Rue Morgue" (1841) elicit conflicting interpretations from various witnesses that baffle the police, until Dupin, learning about the case in a newspaper, recognizes that the speaker's very unintelligibility is the key to its identity. For several pages in *The Narrative of Arthur Gordon Pym* (1838), Arthur struggles to make out Augustus's desperate note in the dark hold of a ship; he later tries to make sense of runes that he finds in a cave. Poe and his readers were intrigued by cryptic texts that resist interpretation (Wimsatt; Irwin, *American*); in "The Gold-Bug" (1843)—written a year before "The Purloined Letter"—a scrap of paper picked up on the shore turns out to conceal an invisible, encoded message detailing the precise whereabouts of Captain Kidd's buried treasure. All of these narratives are centered on the problem of a text that is illegible but not unintelligible. For one contrived circumstantial reason or another, the texts presented in these stories are difficult to read (because of bad lighting, or human error that mistakes animal sounds for speech), or even difficult to recognize *as* texts (the letter crumpled in the Minister's card rack, the parchment strewn on the beach, the caves that not only contain runes but are themselves a form of writing). If these purely logistical difficulties can be overcome and the message can be made out or deciphered, then understanding the message (or decoding it, finding its appropriate code) is a relatively simple, straightforward matter.[4] The challenge facing the detective in these cases is the phenomenological problem of identifying the text (and even recognizing it *as* text), not the hermeneutic problem of interpreting it. Prior to the emergence of a truly hermeneutic type of detective fiction, and prior to detective fiction's being dubbed "the hermeneutic genre *par excellence*" (Holdheim 2), Poe's tales of ratiocination actually had little to do with the detective's interpretation of texts.

   Now that the popular "art" form of detective fiction has become a serious object of academic study, and now that it is common for the detective in contemporary fiction (often written by academics themselves) to resort to interpretive strategies, it's tempting for critics and scholars to allegorize the genre as a reflection of their own activities as textual interpreters. When this happens, the detective becomes a romantic projection of the critic qua analyst or of the analyst qua critic. Lacan's emphasis on the stolen letter's illegibility, which he conflates with its unintelligibility (cf. Felman 149), is telling in this respect. Such illegibility/unintelligibility is only a problem for the reader of "The Purloined Letter,"[5] not for the detective, Dupin, whose only concern is to find the letter and retrieve it. As we shall see, later practitioners of the genre make both the legibility and the intelligibility of the text a central problem for the detective as well as the reader.

   A fresh look at "The Purloined Letter" and Poe's other narratives may perhaps reveal what the French critics (like the Paris police in the story) have overlooked in their search for the letter qua signifier— namely, the difference between the analytical activities of the detective and the critic; the difference between a text's legibility and its intelligibility; the fact that the analytical skills of the detective are focused on the *pre*hermeneutic task of detecting and deciphering documents, rather than on the problem of interpreting and understanding texts. The kinds of writing that challenge the traditional detective's analytical skills are not texts that are readable or unreadable, intelligible or unintelligible, but "simply" documents that are legible or illegible, read or unread.

Key and Prize Texts

The rest of this essay will trace a lineage in detective fiction consisting of works that develop Poe's prehermeneutic orientation into a hermeneutic mode that nevertheless reveals anti- or even posthermeneutic features. We may begin with a few general observations about stories, like "The Purloined Letter," in which the sleuth's attention and the reader's interest are directed to a document that plays a crucial role in the narrative. As important as such a "key text" may be, it is not itself the ultimate object of the detective's quest. The detective uses the information supplied by the key text to achieve his final goal, which is to discover or recover a prized object that may well be *another* text. The detective's success in finding the prize will depend on his prior ability to find and read the key text that specifies its whereabouts, and even its identity.

Thus, in "The Gold-Bug," Kidd's parchment is a key text that designates the location of the prized treasure. In "The Purloined Letter," the "hidden" letter could be considered either a key text or a prize text: it is a key text that Dupin must recover in order to get his reward (or his revenge), but it can also be viewed as the ultimate object of Dupin's quest, and in this sense would be a prize text.[6] Indeed, the fact that the key and prize text are ultimately not distinguishable in "The Purloined Letter" is chiefly responsible for the seminal role commentators have accorded this story in the genre of detective fiction. "The Purloined Letter" represents a limit case; most works of detective fiction in which texts play a crucial role make a fairly clear distinction between the key and the prize text.

As the object of the detective's quest, the prize text is clearly of greater intrinsic value than the key text. But detective stories are about finding something (out), and in this respect the key text is of greater interest and importance. When we say that the problem with the key text is that it is illegible or unrecognizable, we often mean that its *value* in relation to the prize text is not evident. In "The Purloined Letter," the Minister knew what he was doing when he disguised the valuable letter as a piece of ordinary crumpled paper: with their eyes on the prize, the police investigators were sure to overlook it. In "The Gold-Bug," Legrand utterly fails at first to value Kidd's key text; he uses it to wrap up the bug that he believes to be of value, but which, compared with Kidd's treasure, is worthless.

In *The Maltese Falcon* (1930), Dashiell Hammett develops the motif whereby a devalued key text is wrapped around a false prize: Spade's statuette turns out to be as worthless as the "husk of coarse grey paper" and "egg-shaped mass of pale excelsior" that covers it (183). The gold bug of Poe, the black bird of Hammett—in the end, all are red herrings.

Much of the suspense in detective fiction is generated by the detective's (and the reader's) misrecognition of textual value—either by overvaluing the prize (text) at the expense of the key text (as the police do in "The Purloined Letter"), or by valuing as a key text some discourse that proves to be unreliable (such as the history of the statue that Gutman tells Spade in *The Maltese Falcon*, or, as we shall see, the Templar document in Eco's *Foucault's Pendulum*), and that leads the detective to a false prize or a dead end.

What has been called "metaphysical detective fiction" (Merivale, Holquist) addresses this issue of value, and reveals the worth of the prize text to be contingent on a proper assessment of the key text. Before the detective and the reader can make an accurate interpretation of signs and events that will lead them to the prize, they must have the necessary information provided by the key text, which itself becomes the desired object. Metaphysical detective stories often take this situation to its logical conclusion. Very little is finally revealed about the object of the detective's quest, or about why it should be so valuable; to do so would diminish the reader's interest in the quest, as well as the reader's sense of the object's prestige, and would ultimately lead the reader to a reexamination of *all* values. The prize object appears invaluable precisely because it is inaccessible and unintelligible. The fact that we never learn the contents of the purloined letter exponentially enhances our sense of its worth. The enduring value of the letter in Poe's story, or the falcon in Hammett's tale,[7] lies in the fact that even when the precious object is revealed, we know precious little about it: who its sender or rightful owner is, or what it means.

The reader of metaphysical detective fiction—and increasingly, as the genre develops, the detective himself—never learns much at all about the signified object of supposedly priceless value and tremendous power that has caused such torment. In its place, the reader's and the detective's interest is focused on the substitute object of the key text—the Crébillon quotation, Gutman's history of the falcon, or even Spade's own narrative about Flitcraft, which seems altogether irrelevant to the detective plot. One is reminded of what Shoshana Felman, following Lacan, has described as a shift in the reader's and detective's respective analyses from the signified to the signifier as the present sign of an absence (148). But by the end of the metaphysical detective story (if we can indeed speak of an "end"), both reader and detective learn that the key text is less a signifier of the prize text than a substitute for it, and often a spurious one at that. As the aged narrator Adso wearily observes at the end of Umberto Eco's first novel, it is not the rose itself that we are left holding, but only its name.[8]

Wrong Shapes

> In whodunits, murder, being a pretext for a logical puzzle, is hardly
> ever an irrational act.
> —Thomas Pynchon, "Is it O.K. to Be a Luddite?" (41)

The first writer to work a significant variation on the theme of the
problem-text introduced by Poe is G. K. Chesterton. In the 1911 tale
"The Wrong Shape," the problem is no longer one of finding a text, as
in "The Purloined Letter," but of reading it. This is not as simple as it
sounds, because what the text appears to say is not necessarily what its
author intended. Before the detective, in his role as reader, can take a
message at its face value, he must be sure there is nothing *wrong* with
the message. In "The Wrong Shape," it is not the message per se that
presents an interpretive problem, but the very medium or "shape" of the
message that renders what it appears to say misleading or irrelevant.[9]

An apparent suicide note is found on the desk of a writer who has
died in his study from a dagger thrust. The note, written in the deceased
man's handwriting, reads "I die by my own hand; yet I die murdered!"
The suspicions of Chesterton's sleuth, Father Brown, are aroused by the
odd shape of the paper, the edge of which has been sheared off at an
angle. The paper's strange shape is a sign that the text is not what it appears to be, and Father Brown quickly realizes that the supposed suicide
note is actually a quotation from a story that the writer was composing
at the time of his death. It turns out that the writer's personal physician
had entered his patient's study, noticed the quotation written across the
top of a sheet of paper, and saw his opportunity to do away with his
patient—making the death seem a suicide so that he could pursue an
affair with the writer's wife. All that was needed to make a fictional character's textual exclamation appear to be the author's was the removal
of the telltale set of quotation marks with a scissors. But Father Brown,
noticing the paper's strange shape, sees through the doctor's treachery.

In this play of quotation, substitution, and recognition, we hear echoes
of "The Purloined Letter," especially the altered appearance of the
stolen letter in the Minister's card rack and the second, substituted letter with the couplet copied from Crébillon which will reveal Dupin's triumph to the Minister. Noting "the play of quotation marks" at the end
of Poe's story, Derrida observes that Dupin signs his name with a literary
quotation, in effect putting his name in quotation marks (494–95). In
"The Wrong Shape," Chesterton uses the same device of a "quotation-
signature" (Irwin, *Mystery* 29) for a very different purpose. Dupin uses a
literary quotation to reveal his identity (and his poetic-analytical genius)

to his criminal adversary; in contrast, Chesterton's nefarious doctor attempts to conceal his criminal identity by passing off a literary quotation as the author-victim's own suicidal signature.

Whereas Poe uses the "quotation-signature" to frame (that is, to close) his narrative, Chesterton's doctor employs the same device to frame (that is, to incriminate) his victim as the agent of his own death. Father Brown is able to discern the doctor's deceit by attending, not to the message (which is false), but to the medium of transmission—the curious shape of the paper on which the message is written. Dupin, too, had noticed how the Minister had tampered with the letter addressed to the Queen, but in that case only the letter's appearance, and not its contents, had been altered. In Chesterton's story, the odd shape of the paper indicates that the text itself has been changed—a quotation mark has been excised that would have revealed the message to be a fictional text. The extratextual feature of the paper's shape is a signal to the alert detective that the key text, in this case, is a spurious message that has been dislocated from its proper context.

While Father Brown has little difficulty in determining what is wrong with the note "left" by the dead author, Agatha Christie's detective, Hercule Poirot, is for a time genuinely baffled by a spurious key text in *The ABC Murders* (1936). Each month he receives a letter, signed "A.B.C.," that specifies the date of a murder and the town in which it will occur. After receiving the third such letter, Poirot confesses to his sidekick, Captain Hastings, that "I felt from the first, when I read the original letter, that there was something wrong—*misshapen*" (101; my emphasis). Despite his hunch, however, Poirot is unable to put his finger on what is wrong. Only at the end of the story does Poirot realize that it had not been the original letter that seemed odd, but the third letter which had been "*wrongly addressed*" to him (228; Christie's emphasis). Poirot had noticed the error at the time, but had attached no importance to it, believing it only a mistake on the writer's part. It takes Hastings, Poirot's plodding companion, to recognize what Poirot can't—namely, that the faulty address was not an accident, but a ruse planned by the malefactor, as in "The Purloined Letter." But in that story, the Minister readdressed the letter he had stolen to conceal it from the police; in Christie's novel, the killer wrongly addressed the letter in order to delay its arrival, thereby preventing the police from arriving at Churston in time to prevent the third—and, it turns out, crucial—murder.

Poirot is guilty of the hermeneutic fallacy: in contrast to Dupin and Father Brown, he has allowed himself to be distracted by the killer's message, and thereby neglected the significance of the message's medium of transmission, its faulty context, the false address.[10] As we shall see, Poirot's fallacy is repeated by a host of other detective figures—often with dire results.

Jorge Luis Borges's debt to—and departure from—Poe is most evident in "Death and the Compass" (1942), a story that, as John T. Irwin has shown, "rewrites [the] numerical/geometrical structure" of "The Purloined Letter" and "antedates the earliest of the three analyses [of Poe's tale—that is, those of Lacan, Derrida, and Johnson] by some fifteen years" (p. 41 above). While this is very much to the point, an important intermediary in the Poe-Borges connection and an important aspect of that connection—namely, the role of the spurious key text—is overlooked if we neglect the figure of Chesterton. (Whereas Irwin introduces Borges into the quadrangular configuration of Poe-Lacan-Derrida-Johnson, I want to elaborate a different configuration: Poe-Chesterton-Borges-Eco.) An enthusiastic admirer of Chesterton, Borges adopted his mentor's idea of the spurious key text (the literary quotation misrepresented as suicide note). In presenting the detective's fatal failure to recognize what is wrong with the spurious key text, however, Borges seems less to be following Chesterton in "The Wrong Shape" than Christie in *The ABC Murders*.

"Death and the Compass" opens with virtually the identical scene of the crime described in "The Wrong Shape." A writer, in this case a scholar named Yarmolinsky who is a delegate to the Third Talmudic Congress, is found stabbed to death in his hotel room. As in Chesterton's story, moreover, a "message" is found near the body: the words, "The first letter of the Name has been uttered," appear on a sheet of paper in the dead man's typewriter (78). But Borges's protagonist, Erik Lönnrot—who views himself as "an Auguste Dupin" (76)—is more of a reader, and less of a detective, than his precursors in Poe or Chesterton. He seizes on the "clue" presented by the typed page, sensing that a diabolical plot lies behind the "unfinished sentence" (78). In contrast, his practical colleague Treviranus maintains that the typed statement is a red herring, and that Yarmolinsky was mistakenly stabbed to death in a bungled attempt to steal the precious sapphires of the Tetrarch of Galilee from an adjacent hotel room. Lönnrot ignores this obvious (and, it turns out, true) explanation, and proceeds to look for the key to Yarmolinsky's death in his writings. He is convinced—especially after two other murders take place, each accompanied by messages similar to the first—that Yarmolinsky was sacrificed by a Hasidic sect in search of the secret name of God.

As Lönnrot and the reader learn at the story's conclusion, the note in the typewriter was not written by Yarmolinsky's assassins, but—as in

Chesterton's story—by the victim himself, who had been "working on some notes, apparently, for an article on the Name of God." But when Lönnrot's nemesis (and double) Red Scharlach, eager to avenge the arrest of his brother by Lönnrot in a shootout three years before, got wind of the detective's erroneous hunch, he set himself "the task of justifying that conjecture" (85). Scharlach planned the other "murders" (one of the accomplice who inadvertently killed Yarmolinsky while attempting to steal the Tetrarch's sapphires for himself, the other a fake killing in which Scharlach himself played the victim) and left the accompanying messages in order to confirm Lönnrot's fantastic conspiracy theory. Scharlach even provided Lönnrot with a map showing that the locations of the murders formed a triangle, marked in red ink. On the basis of this map and other clues, Lönnrot mistakenly concludes, in Irwin's words, "that the series of murders is not threefold but fourfold and that the *shape* which the location of the crimes describes on the map is not a triangle but a diamond" (p. 44 above; my emphasis). What is left unsaid, but goes without saying, is that Lönnrot—no Father Brown, he— has misread the map and identified "the wrong shape." The dazzled detective proceeds to the fourth point of the diamond, where he walks into Scharlach's trap and becomes the third murder victim.

Bipartite Texts

Umberto Eco's allusion to Borgesian themes and motifs in his fiction is especially evident in his first novel, *The Name of the Rose* (1980). Besides the labyrinthine library, and the memorable villain (Jorge of Burgos) who is based on the aged, blind Argentine writer, the novel's title recalls the key text of "Death and the Compass"—"The first letter of the Name has been uttered."[11] But it is the particular device of the spurious key text, derived by Borges from Chesterton and employed so effectively in "Death and the Compass," that Eco elaborates on an unprecedented scale in both *The Name of the Rose* and his second novel, *Foucault's Pendulum* (1988). Early in each narrative, the detective figure receives a cryptic message which he attempts to decipher in order to gain access to a priceless secret, in pursuit of which others have already perished. Most of the ensuing narrative in both novels is concerned with the investigator's efforts, first to decipher, and then to decode this mysterious key text.

Even the structure of the key text in both novels is remarkably similar. At the top of a sheet of paper, a short message is written in code; beneath this is a longer text in a recognizable language, the meaning of which is nevertheless obscure and requires interpretation. These key texts thus reproduce quite literally Saussure's semiotic schema of $\frac{\text{Signified}}{\text{Signifier}}$, in which a cryptic (or more cryptic) expression is inscribed over a decrypted (or less cryptic) one. When the upper and lower levels are combined into a "whole," the resulting bipartite key text itself becomes a signifier with respect to the elusive prize text, the transcendental Signified that is the detective's ultimate goal.

In *The Name of the Rose*, the key text is a page of "notes" written by Venantius, a young monk murdered in 1327 because of a valuable book, hidden in the monastery's library, that he managed to locate. Before his death, Venantius used "a zodiacal alphabet," invisible ink, and a code to record the book's hiding place; underneath this short message he copied out some notes from the book in Greek, writing "in a disorderly way" that was difficult to read (165, 162). Investigating Venantius's death, William of Baskerville and his young protégé, Adso, the novel's narrator, are hot on the trail of the secret book; but just as they are about to retrieve it from the dead monk's desk, it is snatched away—along with William's state-of-the-art spectacles. All they have left to go on is the parchment with Venantius's cryptic writing, which slipped out of the prize text of the purloined book.

Reading Venantius's text is the crucial task that William must accomplish if he is to solve the mystery of its author's death—which turns out to be one of a series of murders at the monastery—and if he is to locate the prize text. No simple matter, this task occupies him intermittently for the rest of the novel. Having to wait for new glasses to be made, William cannot study the (lower) Greek portion of the text for two days, during which time another murder takes place. Even when he eventually succeeds in deciphering the Greek text, he must still interpret its meaning, which is very obscure, consisting of enigmatic phrases like "The venerable figs" and "To them the cicadas will sing from the ground" (284). William is sure these phrases are notes copied by Venantius from the mysterious book, and although they make no sense to William, he has an uncanny feeling that he has come across them elsewhere. Maddeningly, the reference eludes him until the novel's end.

As for the (upper) message in zodiacal alphabet, although William handily deciphers it into Latin as "Secretum finis Africae manus supra idolum age primum et septimum de quatuor," its meaning remains obscure for hundreds of pages. William knows that the mysterious phrase it contains, "the end of Africa," is a cataloging reference used by the librarian, but its meaning only becomes clear when he visits the forbidden library (recalling the library of Babel in Borges's famous eponymous story of 1944) and realizes that its many chambers are alphabetically organized on a model of the known world. The "finis Africae" is the central chamber in the library's south tower, where "texts by infidel authors"—which include the sought-after book—are to be found. Unfortunately, this chamber is walled off, and it is impossible to gain access to it. William suspects that part of Venantius's decoded message explains how to enter the "finis Africae," but he can't figure out what this key element of the key text means until near the novel's end, when Adso's idle chatter provides him with the needed clue. "Why, of course, suppo-sitio materialis, the discourse is presumed de dicto and not de re. . . . 'primum et septimum de quatuor' does not mean the first and seventh of four, but of *the* four, the word 'four'!" (457–58). When William places his fingers above the letters *q* and *r* of the seven-letter word "quatuor" (a word which baffled him for so long because of the absence of quotation marks, as in the stories by Chesterton and Borges) in the inscription on the sealed chamber, the wall is broached, the villain unmasked, and the identity of the secret book revealed.

In *Foucault's Pendulum*, the narrative again hinges on a key text con-sisting of two parts: an upper, shorter, coded section that must be deci-phered, and a lower, longer, uncoded (but ambiguous) section that must be interpreted. The text in this case transcribes what the retired colonel Ardenti believes to be a genuine Templar document from the four-teenth century. According to Ardenti, the document was discovered by a Russian dragoon named Ingolf in Provins at the end of the nineteenth century.[12] The only trace of the original document—which has since dis-appeared—is a copy that Ardenti claims Ingolf made and that Ardenti now possesses. He presents a copy of this copy to Casaubon, Belbo, and Diotallevi—editors at Garamond Press, a Milan publishing house spe-cializing in occult works—whom he hopes will publish the book that he has written on his findings.

The upper part of the document is a meaningless "demoniacal litany" (132) that Ardenti, using Trithemius's treatise on cryptography, has de-ciphered to read "Les 36 inuisibles separez en six bandes"—"a kind of headline announcing the establishment of a group" (134–35). The lower part of the document, written in fourteenth-century French, ap-parently outlines the suppressed Templars' plan to transmit a secret wis-dom, learned from their infidel enemies during the Crusades, to their successors. Eventually—in the year 2000, once the necessary scientific and technological innovations had been developed—this secret wisdom would enable the Templars to avenge their persecution nearly seven hundred years earlier by Philip the Fair, and achieve world domination. Immediately after offering this bizarre interpretation to the skeptical but intrigued editors, Ardenti himself vanishes. For the next several hundred pages, the copy of the alleged Templar document that Ardenti has left behind functions as a key text to which the editors return, at first intermittently, then obsessively. They corroborate the colonel's story with dubious information from a host of different sources, including Garamond's own stable of hermetic crackpot authors, the Diabolicals.

At one point Casaubon, the novel's narrator, suggests to his two associates that they use Belbo's computer program to scramble the database provided by the Diabolicals, thereby generating their own secret history:

What if . . . you fed it a few dozen notions taken from the works of the Diabolicals—for example, the Templars fled to Scotland, or the Corpus Hermeticum arrived in Florence in 1460—and threw in a few connective phrases like "It's obvious that" and "This proves that"? We might end up with something revelatory. Then we fill in the gaps, call the repetitions prophecies, and—voilà—a hitherto unpublished chapter of the history of magic, at the very least! (375)

Through this random method of generating a fictive history, the editors authenticate and supplement Ardenti's key text, producing their own revelation of the "Plan" in which they find themselves fatally implicated. The narrative's climax occurs when Casaubon witnesses what appears to be Belbo's execution by a group of Diabolicals, who suspect him of withholding vital information about the Plan that he himself created. At the novel's conclusion, Casaubon searches through Belbo's computer files for some explanation of his friend's mysterious fate. He finds what he calls "the Key Text" (625)—a file in which Belbo recounts an epiphanic primal scene in his youth that Casaubon believes may explain his friend's obsessive interest and investment in the Plan, to the point where he actually sacrifices his life for it in a kind of repetition compulsion.

This is hardly the only key text in the novel, however. In fact, many of these key texts are not *in* the text of *Foucault's Pendulum* at all, but outside it or in the margins: namely, as numerous epigraphs taken from (apparently) actual hermetic and heretical works in Eco's own library (another Borgesian convention) that head each of the novel's 120 chapters.[13] But the principal key text in the novel is Ardenti's Templar document. This text plays the same role in *Foucault's Pendulum* that Venantius's notes played in *The Name of the Rose*: they are ambiguous, two-part texts that provoke inquisitorial monks and scholarly editors into undertaking outrageous feats of detection. These feats are the main source of interest in Eco's first two novels, and the principal activity described therein.

Yet aren't these tours de force of detection really *de-*feats? After all, Eco's detectives fail in the end to recover the prize texts that are the object of their respective searches: the second volume of Aristotle's *Poetics* and the Templars' secret. The detectives' failures to retrieve these prize texts are a direct result of their misreading the key texts that are their principal—indeed, their only—leads.

William of Baskerville has no trouble decoding the upper portion of Venantius's parchment, but he misunderstands it by reading it "de re" rather than "de dicto," with reference to a signified rather than as referring to another signifier. And once his spectacles are restored and he can read the lower part of the parchment, his inability to identify the *Poetics* as the subject of Venantius's notes causes a further, fatal delay in reaching a solution. Misreading the key text is even more crucial in *Foucault's Pendulum*. Here the editors distort Ingolf's original text, first by assenting to Ardenti's farfetched interpretation of the meager, fragmentary "message," and then by outdoing him—using their own encyclopedic knowledge of the occult, and the resources of a computer's prodigious memory bank, to generate a voluminous secret history with its own compelling "truth." It is as if the detectives in this novel are governed by the principle that the wilder the interpretation, the more valid the description of events. Actually, though, it is the editors' present act of interpretation that creates these "events," which supposedly took place in the distant historical past.

Just how strange this hermeneutic alchemy is becomes especially evident when we consider that the cryptic message, upon which the three editors base their idea of global conspiracy, may be entirely spurious. Instead of a messianic message, the supposed Templar document may be nothing more than a "laundry list" (534), to use the apt phrase of Lia, Casaubon's female companion. According to her decipherment, which is at least as credible as that of the Garamond editors, the second part of Ardenti's text is not a plan for passing a Templar secret down through the ages, but merely a fourteenth-century Provins rose-merchant's delivery schedule. The cryptic first part of the text was not added until the nineteenth century, when Ingolf, "an enthusiast of hermetic messages [and] cryptography" (537), devised it as a lark. Ardenti, the "imbecile colonel," had taken the message to be a genuine Templar document; after he had offered his interpretation to Casaubon and his colleagues and then mysteriously disappeared, the editors first playfully, and later seriously, began to devise a Templar conspiracy that gradually acquired an objective reality of its own. If Lia's commonsense version of events is correct, then the entire Plan is an instance of scholarly interpretation gone mad, the discovery of messianic, and even apocalyptic, meaning in a laundry list.

Even if Ardenti's text is genuine—something neither the narrator nor the reader can ever know—then the very nature of its message renders it hopelessly obscure. For the document neither describes nor refers to the Templar's secret in the way that Venantius's parchment locates, and even quotes, Aristotle's treatise on comedy. The most that Ardenti's text does is to relate an *itinerary*, the stages through which the secret—whatever that may be—will pass. The document is not a signified, or even a signifier, but a signifying chain without any objective reference. The detective must become an analyst: his task, in Felman's words, "is not to read the letter's hidden referential content, but to situate the superficial indication of its textual movement, to analyze the paradoxically invisible symbolic evidence of its displacement, its structural insistence, in a signifying chain" (148).

The treasure-hunting editors in *Foucault's Pendulum* will never find the object of their quest because, supposing that the Templar document is "authentic," their interpretation of it can only have the effect of indefinitely extending the chain of signifiers, the way stations of the Plan, without ever penetrating to the Plan itself. Such is the document's diabolical structure that its signifying links fatally inscribe/enchain Ardenti, Belbo, and anyone else who sets out to give it a serious reading.

Justifying the Detective's Conjecture

In their misreadings of key texts and, more precisely, in their mistaking spurious texts *for* key texts, Eco's investigators echo Lönnrot, Borges's detective in "Death and the Compass." Lönnrot's dream was to match the analytical brilliance of Poe's Dupin, but he belonged to a new generation of detectives and a different genre of detection. As we have seen, the problem was no longer to find a text but to read it. And so as Lönnrot tried to live up to his acknowledged precursor, Dupin, he fell far short of his *un*acknowledged precursor, Father Brown, who knew how to read texts for what they were by recognizing their proper shape.

Chesterton devised the scenario in which a writer unwittingly contributes to his own murder by leaving behind a stray text; his killer wrenches that text from its original context and inscribes it in another of his own making, thereby constructing a false version of events to deceive his pursuers. In Borges's and Eco's treatment of this scenario, it is the detective rather than the killer who (albeit unintentionally) uses the text of a writer-victim (Yarmolinsky, Venantius, Ingolf/Ardenti) to create a fictional (if not altogether false) version of events. Thus, in "Death and the Compass," Lönnrot wrongly attributes Yarmolinsky's text to the killer whom he assumes is seeking the Tetragrammaton. In making this assumption, he inadvertently provides the killer, Scharlach, with a cabalistic pattern for a series of murders that culminates in Lönnrot's own death. Like Lönnrot, Eco's detectives also fall short of Father Brown by going too far; they don't exercise sufficient tact in their dealings with texts. Some deeply entrenched hermeneutic code (Jewish mysticism, Christian revelation) determines their deductions and interpretations, and motivates their misreading, and even their misidentification, of key texts.

In *The Name of the Rose*, the series of murders is engineered by Jorge of Burgos to conceal an ancient text that threatens the social order— Aristotle's treatise on comedy. But the *pattern* of the murders (and, in-

deed, the arrangement of the library itself) is modeled on another ancient text, St. John's Apocalypse. This pattern has not been devised by
the killer, but discerned by the detective. A senile monk's remark led
William to believe that the series of murders "followed the sequence
of the seven trumpets of the Apocalypse" (469)—the first victim per-
ishes amidst hail, the second in a vat of blood, the third in water, and
the fourth after being struck by an armillary sphere (the third part of
the sky). In fact, this pattern was coincidental at first, until Jorge played
along with William's hypothesis by making the fifth murder appear to
result from exposure to a book with "the power of a thousand scorpi-
ons." As a "disconcerted" William admits at the novel's end, "I conceived
a false pattern to interpret the moves of the guilty man, and the guilty
man fell in with it" (470). Like Red Scharlach in Borges's story, Jorge of
Burgos merely justifies the detective's conjecture.

By adopting a millenarian concept of history as their code, the editor-
detectives in *Foucault's Pendulum* not only force their bizarre reading on
Ardenti's text, but literally create a murderous adversary. Belbo transforms his romantic rival, Agliè, into his spiritual nemesis, thereby vali-
dating the ingenious conspiracy theory that he and his colleagues have
evolved on the basis of Ardenti's (mis)information. In the process, moreover, Belbo unwittingly transcends his role as would-be detective, becoming himself a part of the conspiracy he has created. This is Casaubon's belated realization:

> It's the old story of spies: they infiltrate the secret service of the enemy, they
> develop the habit of thinking like the enemy, and if they survive, it's because
> they've succeeded. And before long, predictably, they go over to the other side,
> because it has become theirs. Or take those who live alone with a dog. They
> speak to him all day long . . . until they're sure he's become just like them,
> human, and they're proud of it, but the fact is that they have become just like
> him: they have become canine. (467)

In postmodernist works of detective fiction in which detective and criminal simulate one another, it's typically the hyperanalytic detective, not
the criminal, who proves to be too smart for his own good.[14]

Since "The Purloined Letter," the detective has often assumed the
role of the analyst who tries to solve a mystery by outwitting his opponent. For Poe's Dupin and Christie's Poirot, the absence or presence of
a letter presents an intellectual challenge posed by a criminal adversary.
With Borges (by way of Chesterton), the detective evolved into a reader
of texts whose chief task was to decipher and interpret an inscrutable
document. The adversary's role in such cases becomes a good deal more
ambiguous; whatever antagonist the investigator-protagonist suspects is
likely to be a figment of his imagination, and may distract him from—

or even become—his actual enemy. The postmodernist detective's perception of an adversary may be based on nothing more than the fact that a key text resists interpretation; the adversary's only "crime" may be his supposed attempt to baffle the detective. It is no longer a case of the investigator beating his artful adversary at his own game, by stealing back a purloined letter and substituting a literary signature-quotation in its place. For the postmodernist detective to beat his adversary, he must either hatch a plot *before* his opponent does, or conceive a more *elegant* scheme than his nemesis is capable of by willfully misinterpreting his rival's all too banal intention. The quest for such an aesthetic triumph, however, ultimately leads to hermeneutic defeat, since the detective cannot be content with simple solutions, and perhaps can't countenance any solution at all. As Lönnrot replies to Treviranus's obviously correct explanation of Yarmolinsky's murder, "Possible, but not interesting" (77). In his futile quest for an absolute order, the postmodernist detective is likely to find his only source of satisfaction in the paranoid or diabolical order provided by the Plan.

Missed Messages

> Perhaps, after all, America never has been discovered . . . I myself
> would say that it had merely been detected.
> —Oscar Wilde, *Complete Works* (43)

If, as I have suggested, the protagonist's principal activity in postmodernist detective fiction is no longer detection (that is, seeking answers to the traditional questions, "Whodunit?" or "Where is it?"), but the reading and interpretation of texts, then is it really accurate to continue to speak of detectives? Eco's novels point up a feature borne out in other works of the genre—namely, that the person or persons engaged in the detective quest are not professional or even amateur detectives. Whether they are medieval inquisitors or modern editors, these characters are investigators only in a metaphorical sense. When professional detectives do appear as protagonists in postmodernist fiction, as in the work of Borges, Alain Robbe-Grillet, or Paul Auster, it is hard to take their pretense of being criminal investigators seriously. Such characters, vestiges of the traditional detective, are out of place in an updated genre in which the paramount problem is interpreting texts rather than solving crimes.[15]

We may briefly consider, in this regard, two postmodernist novels that, while technically not detective stories, nevertheless thematize the activity of interpreting texts as a central intellectual and metaphysical problem. In Thomas Pynchon's *The Crying of Lot 49* (1966), Oedipa Maas is thrust into an investigative role when she is unexpectedly named executor of the will of her former lover, real estate tycoon Pierce Inverarity. The novel is strewn with potential key texts: Inverarity's will, his stamp collection that had "something to tell her" (45), letters (indeed, the entire postal system), the variants of a Jacobean revenge tragedy, ominous restroom graffiti, even the suburban sprawl of L.A., which resembles a printed circuit and conveys "a hieroglyphic sense of concealed meaning, of an intent to communicate" (24). At first these texts fascinate Oedipa, but as their references to a secret global network known as the Tristero multiply and become clearer, they torment her to the point that she would rather know that she was crazy than that such a network exists. The novel's ending leaves unclear whether Oedipa has encountered an actual historical conspiracy, or whether it was Inverarity himself who "discovered the Tristero, and encrypted that in the will, buying into just enough to be sure she'd find it" (178). Then again, there is the possibility, made explicit by Borges and Eco, that Oedipa's paranoid suspicions have retroactively created the Tristero, and that her suspicions have been reinforced by some unknown adversarial demon—possibly some part or projection of herself—through a plethora of spurious texts.

The strangest instances of detection/interpretation involve texts of nonhuman provenance, such as the molecular configurations "explicated" by the "coal-tar Kabbalists" (590) in Pynchon's *Gravity's Rainbow* (1973), or the "atmospheric radio disturbances," or "sferics" (213), studied by engineering student Kurt Mondaugen in Pynchon's *V.* (1963).[16] (Mondaugen "detected a regularity or patterning which might almost have been a kind of code. But it took him weeks even to decide that the only way to see if it were a code was to try to break it" [228].)[17] Even more baffling is the self-fulfilling (as well as self-defeating) detective quest presented in Don DeLillo's 1976 novel *Ratner's Star*. A fourteen-year-old, Nobel-prize-winning mathematician named Billy Twillig is conscripted into a supersecret research project at a remote outpost called Field Experiment Number One. Eventually he learns that the purpose of the project, which involves a host of fellow researchers specializing in fields as arcane as his own, is to interpret a set of extraterrestrial signals that has been picked up by the "synthesis telescope" from the region of Ratner's star. Billy's job is to interpret this "message"—a task that Space Brain, the Field Experiment's supercomputer, has been unable to do. As the project's "last hope" (48), Billy applies himself for the remainder of this long novel to the task of discovering a mathematical principle behind the signals, which might make their message (assuming there is one) intelligible.

At first he is lackadaisical about his work, but as he warms to the seductive spell of numerical analysis, he proceeds with growing intensity and determination. Ironically, as Billy becomes more involved in the project and closer to finding a "solution," new information about the source of the signal makes it less important (or desirable) that a solution be found. First it's learned that there is no planetary object that could support intelligent life in the vicinity of Ratner's star; then it seems that Ratner's star is not generating the transmission, but merely reflecting it from some other unknown location. When Billy is informed by one of the project's directors that his efforts are no longer necessary, he states:

> "You want to find out who sent it and from where but not what it says."
> "It would only beg the question."
> "An answer."
> "Exactly. . . ." (185–86)

Having first been asked to analyze the message "to know what it says," Billy is then told that the mission of Field Experiment One has changed, and that the project is no longer one of interpretation but of detection: to find out where the message came from—a task that appeals far less to Billy's riddle-solving mind.

Midway through the novel, then, the reader suspects that the content of the message is as irrelevant to *Ratner's Star* as the content of the pur-loined letter was to Poe's story. But whereas the letter's destination was of crucial importance in "The Purloined Letter," as Lacan observed, it is the message's source that becomes the new object of investigation in DeLillo's novel. Ultimately, destination and source prove indistinguish-able: in a surprising final revelation, the earth itself is identified as the place where the message originated. This finding is corroborated by a Chinese archaeologist who discovers traces of an ancient civilization, more advanced than our own, that could have sent eons ago the mes-sage that is now being reflected back from Ratner's star (402).

If this is what has happened, then history seems to be repeating itself, because in the second part of the novel Billy's mentor, Robert Softly, organizes an elite group of researchers from Field Experiment One to devise "a transgalactic language," based on "pure and perfect mathe-matical logic," that will be "a means of speaking to the universe" (274). Softly tries to persuade his protégé to apply his mathematical expertise to Logicon Project Minus-One, as the new mission is called, but Billy can't seem to stop working on the message. "It seems to me if I remem-ber correctly," he tells Softly, "they got me here to explain a message from outer space. Do I keep on doing that too or do I just work on this other stuff?" To which Softly responds, "You can play with the code in your spare time" (285). This is precisely what Billy does, eventually de-ciphering the message—"not through mathematics as much as through junk mail" (385)—which turns out to be, according to his interpretation, the particular time of an unspecified day. Billy assumes that the unknown initiators of the transmission "wanted us to know that something might happen at twenty-eight minutes and fifty-seven seconds after two p.m. on a day yet to be determined" (385). In contrast to this apocalyptic interpretation, the reader is left with the impression that the meaning of the message is absurdly trivial, like Lia's explanation that the supposed Templar text in *Foucault's Pendulum* is nothing more than a laundry list. (Similarly, the decoded message of the sferics in *V.*—the Wittgensteinian tag "DIEWELTISTALLESWASDERFALLIST" [258]—is both/either profound and/or banal.) The entire enterprise of interpretation and detection described in *Ratner's Star* may well be an enormous joke—far greater than the "grand practical joke" that Oedipa Maas suspects her dead ex-lover may have played on her (Pynchon, *Crying* 170)— that none of the hilariously earnest characters in the novel seems to appreciate: the human species is engaged in an enormous endeavor, across vast reaches of space and history, to tell itself the time of day.

The interstellar transmissions in DeLillo's and Pynchon's fiction are the most spurious of all the key texts encountered in the works discussed in this essay. For while more may have been read into the parchment in *Foucault's Pendulum* and the Jacobean tragedy in *The Crying of Lot 49* than was warranted or reasonable, there was never any doubt that those texts meant *something*. This cannot be said with any certainty in the case of the "atmospheric radio disturbances" in *V.* (213), or the signal from the "artificial radio extants" in *Ratner's Star* (274). Even if it were known in the latter case that the signal was indeed a message, and even if its meaning were known to be a particular time of day, it would still be impossible to know the context of that message, and thus to know whether its meaning was trivial or apocalyptic. We would not even know whether the message was sent by extraterrestrial beings or by our own human ancestors, by the Other or by ourselves. As one researcher on the Logicon project observes, extraterrestrials "would probably have less trouble understanding a message from Earth than we ourselves experience every time we try to decipher fragments of an ancient language found buried somewhere on our own planet" (289). DeLillo, of course, is pointing up the absurdity of any scientific attempt to communicate with aliens or ancestors, when characters themselves are repeatedly foiled in their everyday speech by what Pynchon calls "their inabilities to communicate" (*Crying* 46). In the postmodern era, simple acts of verbal communication, let alone of textual interpretation, prove a good deal more daunting than Dupin's stupendous feats of detection. But the only nonhuman adversary Dupin had to face was an orangutan, while postmodernist cryptographers are haunted by the possibility that the texts they endeavor to decipher have been sent by nonhuman beings whose intelligence is vastly superior to their own.

Notes

1. Thus, according to Richard, Poe "invented and exhausted the so-called genre of the detective story in 'The Murders in the Rue Morgue' "; in "The Purloined Letter," he wrote "a meta-detective story about the theft of that letter which enables one to write detective stories" (2).

2. Holdheim remarks that "the detectory effort [in Poe] has a psychologistic emphasis that lies in the line of an older, pre-phenomenological, romantic conception of hermeneutics" (5). For a detailed phenomenological account of Poe, see Halliburton.

3. For Lacan, the letter's importance consists in the "symbolic circuits" it establishes between different characters in the story, rather than in its signified content. In his celebrated critique of Lacan's "Seminar," Derrida argues that the letter's content (meaning) is not a mystery for the reader ("In fact, we know what is in the note" [438]). He contests Lacan's implication that the letter's meaning is irrelevant to Poe's story, and declares as blatantly "*false*" Lacan's "allegation that in this affair everything occurs 'without anyone ever having to be concerned with what it [the letter] meant' " (490n66).

4. Thus, in "The Gold-Bug" there is nothing ambiguous about the meaning of Kidd's message that requires great interpretive or investigative skill. Even the code in which the message was written is "of a simple species" (835) that presents no real challenge to Legrand: "having once established connected and legible characters, I scarcely gave a thought to the mere difficulty of developing their import" (835). Legrand's real feat is establishing the message *as* a message, which he accomplishes through a "*very* extraordinary" "series of accidents and coincidences" (833). As in "The Purloined Letter," the paper on which the message was written is out in the open where anyone can see (and overlook) it. Like the purloined letter, Kidd's parchment is less an unreadable text than a text that has simply gone unread.

5. Lacan writes that "the tale leaves *us* in virtually total ignorance of the sender, no less than of the contents, of the letter" (41; my emphasis).

6. If the purloined letter is a prize text, the question arises as to what the key text in the story would be. I've already suggested one possibility: namely, the Crébillon quotation in the letter substituted by Dupin; by treating the substitute letter as a key text, Poe's commentators—would-be detectives themselves—claim to have gained access to the prize text of the story of "The Purloined Letter" itself. As an alternative key text, Susan Elizabeth Sweeney has suggested to me the map in Dupin's analogy of a "game of puzzles" in which participants have "to find a given word . . . upon the motley and perplexed surface of the chart." Such a childish game may have prepared Dupin for the serious task of finding the prize text of the letter; the map would itself be a "legend" that made the letter legible.

7. Or, for that matter, the prophecy about the Elector's fate in Kleist's *Michael Kohlhaas* (1810). Although not a work of detective fiction, this novella anticipates Poe's "Purloined Letter" in the way that it both displays and conceals a text (the gypsy woman's prophecy) of crucial political importance. For a Lacanian analysis of Kleist's story that parallels Lacan's own reading of "The Purloined Letter," see Gallas.

8. "Stat rosa pristina nomine, nomina nuda tenemus" (*Name* 502). Pepin translates the verse as "The rose of old stands in name; we hold mere names," and traces it to the twelfth-century work *De Contemptu mundi* by Bernard of Morval (151). Moreover, he raises the possibility that Eco's allusion is a misreading caused by a typographical error—literally, a purloined letter—in Bernard's text. Noting that the quotation's "original context clearly favors the reading *Stat Roma* for *Stat Rosa*," Pepin argues that "Adso's closing line should be "The Rome of old stands in name; we hold mere names" (152).

9. It might be objected that Poe subverts the hermeneutic tradition with his first detective story, "The Murders in the Rue Morgue." Dupin must identify a killer—an orangutan—with whom any identification is impossible, and whose "speech," as reported by several witnesses, defies interpretation. Yet, as I suggest below, the beast's otherness is not so extreme as to present Dupin with any real difficulty in solving the crime; in fact, it is precisely this otherness that provides Dupin with the solution.

10. Poirot also errs in the contradictory assumptions that he makes about the letters' author. First, because the letters are addressed to him, he assumes that the author is a worthy intellectual adversary who has set out to match wits with him, as was the case in "The Purloined Letter" with the rivalry between the Minister and Dupin. Secondly, because the killings seem to have no motive and reveal no pattern, other than that the victims' last names and the towns where they are killed follow an alphabetical sequence, Poirot initially assumes that the author is insane.

11. We might also note that the key text of Chesterton's "The Wrong Shape"— "I die by my own hand; yet I die murdered!"—aptly applies to Adelmo, the first monk to die at the abbey, who hurls himself from the Aedificium's window in despair after confessing his sins to Jorge. For further parallels, see Lailhacar, Parker, and Smith.

12. Susan Elizabeth Sweeney has pointed out to me the similarity between the trail of the Templar document and the history of the Maltese falcon in Hammett's novel. Dating from the time of the Crusades, the falcon was owned by another religious military order and last possessed by a "Russian general" (Hammett 145), the counterpart of Eco's Russian dragoon.

13. These epigraphs produce an uncanny effect in the novel. When in chapter 19 we first come upon the Provins key text which specifies that the Templars' secret message be relayed to a new location every 120 years, we assume that "120" is an arbitrary number. As we read on, however, we are inundated with more and more information about the numerological beliefs of cabalists, Rosicrucians, and Masons, and by the time we reach chapter 70, we find the following epigraph, ostensibly from a 1614 text called *Fama Fraternitatis*: "Let us remember well, however, the secret references to a period of 120 years that brother A . . . , the successor of D and last of the second line of succession—who lived among many of us—addressed to us, we of the third line of succession" (394). Similarly, when we first read the "headline"—itself a kind of epigram—of the Provins key text, "Les 36 inuisibles separez en six bandes," we may assume that these numbers are also arbitrary. Yet chapter 72 provides this epigraph from a 1623 French work called *Effroyables pactions faictes entre le diable & les pretendus Inuisibles*: "Nos inuisibles pretendus sont (à ce que l'on dit) au nombre de 36, separez en six bandes" (402). What we took to be an arbitrary line of Eco's own invention appears 53 chapters later as an actual fragment of hermetic wisdom. The novel's preposterous notion of a secret Plan transmitted down through the ages begins

to acquire a kind of authority and apparent authenticity when we encounter epigraphs taken from seventeenth-century works that seem to validate the arbitrary assertions of the novel's "key" text. As the skeptical narrator Casaubon and his fellow editors come to believe in the objective existence of the Plan that they themselves are plotting, so the reader of *Foucault's Pendulum*, on the basis of the novel's numerous epigraphs, discovers that Eco is not inventing a puzzle out of whole cloth, but following the logic of his actual sources.

14. A good example is David Fincher's 1995 film *Seven*.

15. Indeed, in both fiction and real life, solving crimes is often a matter of interpreting a text: in Caleb Carr's 1994 novel *The Alienist* and in the Unabomber's manifesto, the key clue that leads to the alleged killer's identification and apprehension is a text he has written.

16. My thanks to Susan Elizabeth Sweeney for suggesting the relevance of both *V.* and *The Crying of Lot 49* to this essay.

Works Cited

Borges, Jorge Luis. "Death and the Compass." ["La Muerte y la brújula," 1942]. Trans. Donald A. Yates. *Labyrinths: Selected Stories and Other Writings*. Ed. Donald A. Yates and James E. Irby. New York: New Directions, 1964. 76–87.

Carr, Caleb. *The Alienist*. New York: Random, 1994.

Chesterton, G. K. "The Wrong Shape" [1911]. *The Annotated Innocence of Father Brown*, ed. Martin Gardner. New York: Oxford University Press, 1988. 138–59.

Christie, Agatha. *The ABC Murders*. [1936]. New York: Simon and Schuster, 1963.

DeLillo, Don. *Ratner's Star*. New York: Random, 1976.

Derrida, Jacques. "The Purveyor of Truth." ["Le Facteur de la vérité," 1975]. *The Post Card: From Socrates to Freud and Beyond*. Trans. Alan Bass. Chicago: University of Chicago Press, 1987.

Eco, Umberto. *Foucault's Pendulum*. [*Il Pendolo di Foucault*, 1988]. Trans. William Weaver. San Diego: Harcourt, 1989.

———. *The Name of the Rose*. [*Il Nome della rosa*, 1980]. Trans. William Weaver. San Diego: Harcourt, 1983.

Felman, Shoshana. "On Reading Poetry: Reflections on the Limits and Possibilities of Psychoanalytic Approaches." Muller and Richardson 133–56.

Gallas, Helga. *Das Textbegehren des "Michael Kohlhaas": Die Sprache des Unbewussten und der Sinn der Literatur*. Reinbek bei Hamburg: Rowohlt, 1981.

Halliburton, David. *Edgar Allan Poe: A Phenomenological View*. Princeton, N.J.: Princeton University Press, 1973.

Hammett, Dashiell. *The Maltese Falcon*. [1930]. New York: Vintage, 1984.

Holdheim, W. Wolfgang. "The Hermeneutic Genre." Unpublished paper.

Holquist, Michael. "Whodunit and Other Questions: Metaphysical Detective Stories in Post-War Fiction." *New Literary History* 3 (1971–72): 135–56. Reprinted in *The Poetics of Murder: Detective Fiction and Literary Theory*, ed. Glenn W. Most and William W. Stowe. New York: Harcourt, 1983. 149–74.

Irwin, John T. *American Hieroglyphics: The Symbol of the Egyptian Hieroglyphics in the American Renaissance*. New Haven, Conn.: Yale University Press, 1980.

———. *The Mystery to a Solution: Poe, Borges, and the Analytic Detective Story*. Baltimore: Johns Hopkins University Press, 1994.

Johnson, Barbara. "The Frame of Reference: Poe, Lacan, Derrida." [1977]. Muller and Richardson 213–51.

Kleist, Heinrich von. *Michael Kohlhaas.* [1810]. *Sämtliche Werke.* Munich: Winkler Verlag, 1967. 7–85.

Lacan, Jacques. "Seminar on 'The Purloined Letter.'" [1956]. Trans. Jeffrey Mehlman. Muller and Richardson 28–54.

Lailhacar, Christine de. "The Mirror and the Encyclopedia: Borgesian Codes in Umberto Eco's *The Name of the Rose.*" In *Borges and His Successors: The Borgesian Impact on Literature and the Arts,* ed. Edna Aizenberg. Columbia: University of Missouri Press, 1990. 155–79.

Muller, John P. and William J. Richardson, eds. *The Purloined Poe: Lacan, Derrida and Psychoanalytic Reading.* Baltimore: Johns Hopkins University Press, 1988.

Parker, Deborah. "The Literature of Appropriation: Eco's Use of Borges in *Il nome della rosa.*" *Modern Language Review* 85, 4 (1990): 842–49.

Pepin, Ronald E. "Adso's Closing Line in *The Name of the Rose.*" *American Notes and Queries* 24, 9–10 (1986): 151–52.

Poe, Edgar Allan. *Collected Works of Edgar Allan Poe.* Ed. Thomas Ollive Mabbott. 3 vols. Cambridge, Mass.: Harvard University Press, 1978.

———. "The Gold-Bug." [1843]. *Collected* 3: 799–847.

———. "The Murders in the Rue Morgue." [1841]. *Collected* 2: 521–74.

———. *The Narrative of Arthur Gordon Pym of Nantucket.* [1838]. Ed. Harold Beaver. New York: Penguin, 1975.

———. "The Purloined Letter." [1844]. *Collected* 3: 972–97.

Pynchon, Thomas. *The Crying of Lot 49.* Philadelphia: Lippincott, 1966.

———. *Gravity's Rainbow.* New York: Viking, 1973.

———. "Is It O.K. to Be a Luddite?" *New York Times Book Review* 28 Oct. 1984: 1, 40–41.

———. *V.* [1963]. New York: Bantam, 1964.

Richard, Claude. "Destin, Design, Dasein: Lacan, Derrida and 'The Purloined Letter.'" *Iowa Review* 12, 4 (1981): 1–11.

Seven. Dir. David Fincher. Perf. Brad Pitt, Morgan Freeman, Kevin Spacey, and Gwyneth Paltrow. 1995.

Smith, April Kendziora. "The 'Other' in Borges, Borges in Others." *Perspectives on Contemporary Literature* 12 (1986): 104–12.

Wilde, Oscar. *Complete Works,* intro. Vyvyan Holland. New York: Perennial Library, 1989.

Wimsatt, William K. "What Poe Knew About Cryptography." *PMLA* 58 (1943): 754–79.

Hard-Boiling
Metaphysics

Chapter 4
Gumshoe Gothics
Poe's "The Man of the Crowd" and His
Followers
Patricia Merivale

> We, reading the detective novel, are an invention of Edgar Allan
> Poe.
> —Jorge Luis Borges, "The Detective Story" (21)

"An excellent idea, I think, to start from a dead body," said Kobo
Abe (*Inter* 47), and Hubert Aquin, similarly, "L'investigation délirante
de Sherlock Holmes débute immanquablement à partir d'un cadavre"
("Sherlock Holmes's dizzying investigation unfailingly starts off from a
corpse" [*Trou* 82]). About how the classical detective story starts they
were both right. But, of course, quite often there isn't a corpse in the
postmodernist library. "There is no body in the house at all," said Sylvia
Plath, in an inscrutable poem called "The Detective" (1962), which I
suspect is, like most of the texts I am discussing, about Missing Persons rather than Dead Bodies. There is, however, always a book there,
or rather a corpus of many books, for the "metaphysical" (otherwise
known as the "postmodernist" or the "anti-") detective story is inherently the most intertextual of genres (Sweeney 14). And one book invariably found in that library is *Tales of Mystery and Imagination*, by Edgar
Allan Poe. "Poe projected multiple shadows," said Borges, one of his
most notable followers. "How many things begin with Poe?" he asked
rhetorically ("Detective" 16). I would like to add a couple of "things" to
an already long and familiar list.

One work of detective-story criticism, Martin Priestman's *The Detective
Story and Literature: The Figure on the Carpet*, plays punningly in its sub-

title with the hermeneutics of the (Henry) Jamesian title "The Figure in the Carpet," that inaccessible pattern which, if only it could be discovered, would explain everything about a work of art by catching its radiant essence. The figure on the carpet is of course that very "body in the library" that stands, by synecdoche, for the classical detective story, especially in its "soft-boiled" variant (Arthur Conan Doyle, Agatha Christie, Ellery Queen).

The Body is to be found in the Library, where the closed world of the country house limits the number of suspects; the classical detective will reason, ingeniously, from the clues to the solution, revealing the criminal from among the pool of available suspects. Logical deduction (or perhaps, courtesy of C. S. Peirce and Umberto Eco, "abduction" [Eco and Sebeok]) leads to a solution, which equals the restoring, through the power of reasoning, of a criminally disrupted but inherently viable Order, which equals Narrative Closure. "Closure" is, to simplify, the sort of conclusion by which the preceding narrative comes, in hindsight, to "make sense," and thus, reciprocally, to make the conclusion itself seem inevitable.

You can imagine how unattractive—and yet tempting—that scenario is to your average postmodernist, Donald Barthelme for instance, who asks, even more rhetorically: "Where is the figure in the carpet? Or is it just . . . carpet?" (*Snow White* 129). Being a parodist, a filching underminer of traditional forms, an eviscerator of the formulaic to its very marrow, said postmodernist will write a story looking very like a soft-boiled classical detective story or its "hard-boiled" variant, as written by Raymond Chandler, Dashiell Hammett, or Ross Macdonald. It could also be a crime story, spy story, or conspiracy novel, or, to use the umbrella term, "mystery story"—but it will, in all these modes, suffer from a surfeit of clues, a shortage of solutions, and thus a distinct lack of narrative closure.

The current use of the term "metaphysical" for such stories takes a lot of explaining. In one sense, the term, like many other critical designations, is used because it has been used; it would be more trouble than obtaining some inexact precision is worth, to try to replace a term already so familiar. In another sense, it is explicable in terms of its origins. It was first used by Howard Haycraft (1941), speaking of the theological detective stories that G. K. Chesterton wrote about that eminently rational yet splendidly visionary perceiver of the miraculous in the mundane, the priest-detective, Father Brown. He is a detective who finds solutions, but ones that happen to be allegories of God's own theologically necessary solutions, perceived, however dimly, mysteriously, and paradoxically, by the God-given reasoning powers of Man. Chesterton himself said, in "How to Write a Detective Story," "The secret must be simple; and in this also it is a symbol of higher mysteries. . . . [It is] the belated realisation that two and two make four" (113). And, in the 1913 Father Brown story, "The Head of Caesar": "What we all dread most . . . is a maze with *no* centre. That is why atheism is only a nightmare" (235). The term "metaphysical" thus seems to retain, in the case of Chesterton at least, some vestige of its normative philosophical meaning.

Then, by Michael Holquist and myself among others, the term "metaphysical detective story" was used to describe the detective stories of Borges, Vladimir Nabokov, and the early Alain Robbe-Grillet, where, since the allegory is by now a secular and largely aesthetic one, what I have called "the flaunting of artifice" yields, among other things, self-reflexive postmodernist artist-parables. While the solutions are surprising and paradoxical, there is still, emphatically, closure (although it may be, as often in Borges, only the "closure" of an apparently infinitely recursive Möbius strip). The cases are solved. But, especially in the early Robbe-Grillet, ambiguity and indeterminacy enter: closed cases are beginning to turn into Open Texts. The secular allegory becomes negatively hermeneutic: the lack of solutions stands for the lack of answers to any question of essence, knowledge, or meaning. What the world "really" is, or who "I" really am, are questions not only unanswerable, but essentially not even formulatable. And the story of the detective trying to follow "clues" until he reaches the "solution" of a "mystery" is the perfect postmodernist vehicle for such an allegory, as John T. Irwin's title, *The Mystery to a Solution*, makes brilliantly clear. The postmodernist detective story makes its first order of business to restore that very "nightmare" of the centerless maze that Chesterton was so eager to dispel. Epiphanies (solutions) become "anti-epiphanies"; detectives now find that their inquiries have become "epistemological" and their tangled case reports "metafictional," causing the inherent "voyeurism of the detective . . . to boomerang into self-inspection" (Saltzman 63). "In a very Poesque way," says Stefano Tani, "the confrontation [in the metaphysical detective story] is no longer between a detective and a murderer, but between . . . the detective's mind and his sense of identity, which is falling apart, between the detective and the 'murderer' in his own self" (76). A model liminal case is Samuel Beckett's *Molloy*, where detective Moran shadows Molloy until his own identity breaks down, until, indeed, the detective becomes essentially indistinguishable from the man he was sent in search of (Saltzman 59); Beckett's high modernism begins, by the same token, to become essentially indistinguishable from postmodernism.

When this by now negatively hermeneutic allegory joins up with the postmodernist rejection of closure, what results is the "postmodernist" detective story: that is, the contemporary inheritor of the Chestertonian metaphysical detective story, as secularized by Borges. A formal subversion or undermining of the highly formulaic patterns of the detective story is its *modus operandi*; thus the term "anti-detective story" (coined by William V. Spanos) becomes appropriate whenever the subversive relationship of the postmodernist detective story to its classical model is emphasized. Hence the attractiveness of that model to the postmodernist writer: it is obvious when the rules are being broken because every reader knows, at least subliminally, what the rules of the detective story are.

If I may provide a speedy genealogy to accompany this sketchy taxonomy (see the diagram in this volume's introduction, p. 18), the metaphysical detective story, like the classical detective story (though by a slightly different route), derives from Poe's three great originating detective tales: "The Murders in the Rue Morgue" (1841), "The Mystery of Marie Rogêt" (1842–43), and "The Purloined Letter" (1844). "The Purloined Letter" is, notoriously, a key text for the psycho-deconstructive branch of contemporary critical theory (Jacques Lacan-Jacques Derrida-Barbara Johnson-John Irwin, to mention just the major players), wherein casebook after casebook is being built up on the interlocking interpretations of the theoretical implications of the story. "The Murders in the Rue Morgue" serves a similar though less brain-twisting function in the critical history of the classical soft-boiled detective story, contributing such elements as the locked room, the least likely suspect, traces of the criminal left in tiny material clues, and the armchair detective. Even the ugly stepsister of the trio, "Marie Rogêt," is at last beginning to be appreciated (for example, by Priestman [51] and Saltzman, who sees the detection as "entirely textual" [238]) as a proto-postmodernist detective story, made up only of the inevitably inconclusive interpretations of variant texts—the newspaper accounts that Dupin collates and mulls over en route to his uncharacteristically tentative hypothesis, one never to be confirmed within the text of the story itself.

At least one other Poe story, however, one not usually considered to be a detective story at all, has analogous affinities with the hard-boiled or "gumshoe" detective story, and thus also with its metaphysical descendant, which I call the "metaphysical gumshoe story," or "Gumshoe Gothic," for short. "The Man of the Crowd" (1840) has been sidelined partly because, although not without a detective surrogate, it lacks Dupin; but more fundamentally because—like Nathaniel Hawthorne's "Wakefield" (1835) and Gertrude Stein's "Blood on the Dining-Room Floor" (1935), postmodernist *avant la lettre*—it enacts a definitively insoluble mystery. Poe "never," Borges, for one, complains, "invoked the help of the sedentary French gentleman Auguste Dupin to determine the precise crime of 'The Man of the Crowd' " ("Modes" 89), in whose heart lurked, as we shall see, a text of such horror that, like the "impenetrability" of "Wakefield," "es lässt sich nicht lesen" (it does not allow itself to be read [Poe, "Man" 107]). But it does allow itself to be written. Parts of my argument have been anticipated and confirmed by Patrick Quinn, who as early as 1954 saw the title character, the Man of the Crowd, as the future double of the narrator: "Dr. Jekyll foresees the Mr. Hyde he will become" (229); by David Lehman, who sees the narrator, usefully, as a "gumshoe" detective interpreting clues (119); by Jonathan Auerbach, who through the window, which is also a mirror (30), connects the Crowd and the Man sections of the story into a coherent reading (whereas most critics choose one or the other); and especially by Gerald Kennedy, who sees the structural details implicit in the Man of the Crowd's "mirror[ing of] the narrator's compulsive behavior" in his attempts to escape his pursuer ("Limits" 191). Quinn, Auerbach, and Kennedy rebut, in different ways, the majority of commentators (for example, Priestman, Lehman, Gavin Lambert, and Arnold Weinstein) who seek, unsuccessfully, to figure out the "precise crime" of the Man of the Crowd.

The other substantial group of critics, those who, like Dana Brand, Robert Byer, and Monica Elbert, follow the line of thought originated by Baudelaire and Walter Benjamin, see the Baudelairean flâneur in the narrator and the problem of urban modernity—the City of Dreadful Night—in the Crowd.[1] This quasi-sociological view is undoubtedly the major contribution of "The Man of the Crowd" to contemporary critical theory, one analogous, on a smaller scale, to the contribution made by "The Purloined Letter."

We, clued in to the unreliability of Poe's narrators, may be left to wonder, on the other hand, if the supposed criminal can be shown to have committed any crime at all. But if he hasn't, then what sort of a detective story can it be? In all probability, a metaphysical one. Rather than dealing with a Body on the Carpet and another (clearly "other") character who put it there, a metaphysical detective story is likelier to deal with a Wakefield, a Missing Person, a person sought for, glimpsed, and shadowed, gumshoe style, through endless, labyrinthine city streets, but never really Found—because he was never really There, because he was, and remains, missing. One was, as postmodernist detective after postmodernist detective discovers, only following one's own self. In Kobo Abe's earthier formulation, "No matter how I follow myself around, I will never see anything but my own backside" (*Secret* 37). Perhaps "The Man of the Crowd" can be read as a prototype or paradigm of such a story, not only of Gumshoe Gothics in general, but also, as we shall see, as an explicit source for several specific stories, the textual "followers" of "The Man of the Crowd."

Poe's story opens with the first-person narrator's reflections on the hideous, untellable mysteries of the human heart, a proposition which the story that follows seems designed to illustrate through the eponymous persona, the title character, of the Man of the Crowd. The narrator's observations "through the smoky panes" of a London coffee house, "into the [crowded] street" (108), begin with Dupinesque deductions about the general social groupings of the members of the crowds which pass his vantage point. The gamblers, for instance, are recognizable from their "guarded lowness of tone in conversation, and a more than ordinary extension of the thumb" (neither of which are likely to be perceptible through a closed window). "Descending in the scale . . . I found darker and deeper themes for speculation . . . feeble and ghastly invalids . . . women of the town . . . putting one in mind of the statue . . . with the surface of Parian marble, and the interior filled with filth . . . the late hour brought forth every species of infamy from its den" (109–10).

Unlike the sociological critics, who tend to stop at this point, the literary imitators of the story tend to start here, largely omitting the Crowd in favor of the "I, Him, and Me" pattern of the rest of the story. "Suddenly there came into view a countenance (that of a decrepit old man, some sixty-five or seventy years of age)." Then, forming the hinge between the Crowd story and the Man story, "came a craving desire to keep the man in view—to know more of him" (112). So the narrator turns from observation and rumination to obsessive action. He begins to follow the Man of the Crowd, who "having made the circuit of the square . . . turned and retraced his steps . . . [and] rushed with an activity I could not have dreamed of seeing in one so aged, and which put me to much trouble in pursuit" (113). And so on.

In this short story, for perhaps the first time in fiction, a man shod in "caoutchouc over-shoes" (that is, rubber galoshes ca. 1840), "tying a handkerchief about [his] mouth," inaudibly and obsessively pursues another man—seemingly the "type and genius of deep crime," whose secret he, detective-like, wishes to discover—through the mean streets of a labyrinthine modern city (114, 113, 116). The primacy of this story among Gumshoe Gothics has been little noted, however, for the narrator catches up to the Man of the Crowd only to realize that his utterly guilty secret, perhaps mercifully, "lässt sich nicht lesen" ("does not allow itself to be read"). He turns away, having failed in his quest (that is, having in both senses come to no conclusion), and tells us, Poe's characteristic implied auditors, his story, one seemingly without point or closure. If we read "beyond the ending" (in Rachel Blau DuPlessis's phrase), however, it becomes apparent that the narrator has projected his sense of his own (literally) un-utterable wickedness upon the Man of the Crowd, who, for any evidence we are given about him, may be no more than the quite innocent and wholly terrified victim of the narrator's sinisterly silent, masked, seemingly motiveless pursuit. If we are to "refract the detective's investigation from the mystery outside to the mystery inside his own person," as Tani invites us to do (77), then we must indeed read beyond the ending: to take over, on behalf of the narrator, the function of supplying the very point that "does not allow itself to be read" at and as the ending.

In the narrative structure of "The Man of the Crowd," "my" (that is, the detective-narrator's) silent pursuit of the Other, who turns out to be "Me," exemplifies the reductionist form of the metaphysical detective story, in which the triadic multiplicity of detective, criminal, and victim is reduced to a solipsistic unity. From the narrator's point of view, I, the detective, am following the criminal, to discover more about him. From the Man of the Crowd's point of view, I, the victim, am being followed by a masked and ominously silent criminal. In this situation, it is hardly to be wondered at if he seeks out safety in the places where the crowd of relatively ordinary humanity is still lingering. The narrator mimics the Man's obsessive search for crowds; the very title of the story can be read ambiguously, for in the "elegiac romance" structure (I'm telling you a story about him which is really a story about Me), it is the narrator who is "really" the Man of the Crowd.[2] From the reader's point of view, I am following (as I read), and mirroring, as I follow, the movement of a man who is detective, criminal, and victim in one. Poe invented not only detective fiction but also the "reader of detective fiction," Borges declared ("Detective" 16). The exercise of following oneself following Poe's narrator, while one reads "The Man of the Crowd," tends to confirm his observation.[3] As Umberto Eco puts it, "Any true detection should prove that we are the guilty party" (*Postscript* 81).

But now the contemporary metaphysical (or postmodernist) detective story flaunts its lack of closure, the failure of the detecting process, and makes explicit that synonymity of detective, criminal, and even victim which is always at least potential in the hard-boiled detective story, if not in the detective story as a whole. Perhaps it is time to elevate Poe's "The Man of the Crowd" to join his three far better-known detective stories (the Dupin series) among the ancestral texts of metaphysical detective fiction. I shall illustrate these propositions in terms of some explicit adaptations of "The Man of the Crowd." It has been closely imitated in stories by Chesterton and by that other mildly heretical Catholic, Graham Greene. It has been brilliantly "postmodernized," in the service of a hermeneutic at once gloomier and more playful, in metaphysical detective novels by Kobo Abe and Paul Auster.

Chesterton, in his magnificent metaphysical conspiracy novel, *The Man Who Was Thursday* (1908), narrates the eerie pursuit of the hero, Thursday, through snowy London streets, by the crippled old Anarchist—who turns out not to be an aged and unutterably wicked enemy (like the Man of the Crowd), but a youthful friend and ally in disguise. There are some scenes of gumshoe pursuit in the Father Brown stories: for example, in "The Blue Cross" (1911) and "The Pursuit of Mr. Blue" (1935).[4] The latter hinges upon a characteristic Chestertonian paradox: an observer inside a sealed but transparent container (for example, an old-style telephone booth), around which one person is chasing another, may well mistake the pursued for the pursuer. But most explicitly based on Poe is the relatively lighthearted story, "The Painful Fall of a Great Reputation" (1903), in *The Club of Queer Trades*, which anticipates, although in a lighter key, Sunday's, or Father Brown's, paradox (like that found in the "Hound of Heaven") of God's loving pursuit of the human soul. What at first suggests evil and terror turns out to be not unlike Sunday's godgame jokes on his much-loved children.

In this story, the narrator and his friend come across "The wickedest man in London . . . [who is] passing quickly among the quickly passing crowd." His hair is "largely gray," and he seems to have "adopted some imposture" or deceitful disguise ("Painful" 58–59). The friend, who "never saw [this old man] before in [his] life" (60), nevertheless insists on jumping from a tram car to follow him. The man, in an odd part of London to begin with, takes an odd turning; the two friends follow him "through a labyrinth of London lanes" from gaslight to gaslight through the intervening darkness. When they almost run into him, he, like the Man of the Crowd, "did not [seem to] realize that we were there" (64). As this "criminal" finally shakes off his pursuers—by entering, to their shocked astonishment, "the house of a very good man" (65)—Chesterton's narrator at last defies his friend. He also speaks, perhaps, for the reader of "The Man of the Crowd," who might well wish to address Poe's narrator thus: "You see a total stranger in a public street; you choose to start certain theories about [the wickedness of] his eyebrows. You then treat him as a burglar because he enters an honest man's door. The thing is too monstrous. Admit . . . it" ("Painful" 67). Chesterton's solution, however, unlike Poe's nonsolution, is that of a rather anticlimactic quasi-godgame, designed to bring "adventure" into the characters' lives with the (paradoxical) aid of the "queer trade" of an artificial, imaginative, and collusive imposture.

Graham Greene, in his 1935 short story "A Day Saved," on the other hand, writes in what is, for him, an uncharacteristically Poe-like Gumshoe Gothic mode. His narrator, a certain "Robinson," tells the curious little story of his following "like a shadow" a randomly ordinary man, who remains nameless (although "I [Robinson] might guess at his name, calling him . . . Wales, Canby, Fotheringay" [528]), in order to get possession of something, he doesn't know what, that the other is carrying, perhaps "even closer to his heart than the outer skin" (528). Something like, it may be, the dagger and the diamond which Poe's narrator glimpses in the bosom of the Man of the Crowd (112). Robinson is prepared to kill the stranger to find out what it is: "All I want in the world is to know," he tells us, stressing the detective's epistemological quest. Then he adds, ambiguously, "I should have to kill him *before* I knew all" (530; my emphasis). But, as in Poe, and later in Auster, the impassioned, apparently pointless quest for an unspecified but certainly unattainable certainty fades into an identification of the pursuer with the pursued, by way of Robinson's anticlimactic (and syntactically ambiguous) curse upon him: "[Someday], when he is following another as I followed him, closely as people say like a shadow, so that he has to stop, as I have had to stop, to reassure himself [as, the syntactical pattern implies, 'I have had to reassure myself']: you can smell me, you can touch me, you can hear me, I am not a shadow: I am Fotheringay, Wales, Canby, I am Robinson" (533).

The curse is self-reflexive; the two men are, by the end, interchangeable, at least from the narrator's shattered perspective. "Like a shadow": as with our other shadowers, the process of shadowing—detective-story terminology, reified and taken literally—takes the form of repeating the movements and actions of the man pursued, thus turning the detective into a shadow, or mirror image, of him. And, I would add, putting the reader into the same place in the sequence as Poe does, making him into a "follower" of the detective, who is "following . . . ," and so on. Robinson (like the others) is a supposedly unobserved observer, who can only infer the name and nature of the man he is shadowing, even though at times he is led to feel a sympathy, an affinity, bordering upon identity with him, by way of a blending of affection and curiosity. As a thwarted "outsider," a "voyeur," watching "the impenetrable solidity of the Other," Robinson has himself become, more literally than he expected, "a shadow—a mere reflection" of the (substantial) being of Canby, Wales, Fotheringay, and so on (Colburn 384). Greene, whose narrator becomes merely the anxious shadow of the pursued, seems to be inverting Poe's schema, in which the pursued becomes merely the emanation, the psychological projection, of the fluidly hysterical consciousness of the narrator.

Although the metaphysical detective story at large has overlapped with conspiracy fiction, from Chesterton's *The Man Who Was Thursday* to Thomas Pynchon's *The Crying of Lot 49* (1966) and beyond (in Don DeLillo, for instance), a somewhat Kafkaesque sense of amorphous conspiracy sets the terms of the contemporary narrator-investigator's inquiry, including its failure, and presides over the detective-criminal's reidentification of himself as victim. Consider the contemporary Japanese novelist Kobo Abe, who is sometimes called "the Japanese Kafka" but is, nevertheless, notably eclectic in his deployment of Western influences. The "Man of the Crowd" pattern is fascinatingly and with great originality grafted onto a science-fiction plot of thwarted apocalypse in *Inter Ice Age 4* (1968), and onto an amalgam of mask stories from both East and West in *The Face of Another* (1964).

In these two stories, minor episodes provide remarkably explicit Poe-like inner duplications of the more generally Poe-like main action. In *Inter Ice Age 4*, an utterly typical and ordinary person must be chosen as the subject of the preliminary trials of a science-fictional "forecasting machine." The search for such an experimental subject involves the scientists in choosing and shadowing through city streets a superlatively ordinary man whose fate nevertheless, in the end, forms a predictive and sinister microcosm of the narrator's own fate (see chapters 6–10, especially pp. 31–35). In *The Face of Another*, a similar sifting through the innumerable possibilities of the crowd takes place to select a man whose face can be "borrowed" to serve as a model for the narrator's mask (58–83). Both pursuers are Poe-like in their surreptitiousness, in their weaving through crowds to keep the subjects in view, and in the gumshoe silence of their rubber jump shoes. And in both cases, as in Poe, the eventual doubling of the subject chosen and the narrator constitutes the significance of the episodes, just as, in Abe's macroplots, Abe's detective inevitably becomes the missing man for whom he, like all his fellow gumshoes, is searching.[5]

The penultimate line of *The Face of Another*, "The footsteps are coming closer" (237), is, anywhere in Abe, as in Poe (and in the Gothic generally), a signal for the murderous reduction of identities. The narrator of another Abe novel, *Secret Rendezvous* (1977), is, by trade, a salesman for rubber "jump shoes [which] make almost no noise" (34). They supply only the most conspicuous examples of the Abean obsession with either the echoing, rhythmic sound of footsteps as synecdochal for the progress of the pursuer or the arrival of the killer/victim, or its converse, the nonsound of footsteps negated, concealed, by rubber soles (like the "boots with very soft soles" that are worn in Margaret Atwood's "Murder in the Dark" [29]). *Inter Ice Age 4* likewise ends with the words "Outside the door the footsteps stopped" (225), and we are left, once again (as in "The Man of the Crowd"), to read beyond the ending. We remember that in Poe, "caoutchouc over-shoes" silenced the tread of the pursuing narrator; thus "The Man of the Crowd" can be seen as the first metaphysical gumshoe story.

The postmodernist private eye, who is the contemporary follower of "The Man of the Crowd," could be described thus: "Possessing all of the marginality, but none of the self-confidence of the classic detective, he spends much of his time walking in circles through streets that look alike, adopting roles for himself to boost his confidence or stepping into roles suggested for him by others, acting a suspect before he is one, excusing his guilt before he becomes guilty," says Jeanne Ewert, writing on Patrick Modiano's investigators (168). Her comments are equally applicable to Greene's, Beckett's, Abe's, or Auster's protagonists.

The most complex and profound reworking of Poe along these lines is found in Auster's brilliant metaphysical detective-story sequence, *City of Glass* (1985), *Ghosts* (1986), and *The Locked Room* (1986), published collectively as *The New York Trilogy*. In these books, indeed, all the ghosts of the American Renaissance—Thoreau, Bronson Alcott, Melville, Whitman, as well as Poe and Hawthorne—come back to haunt his detective-authors and their self-reflexive texts. Auster's protagonists find the stories that they themselves write interesting "not [for] their relation to the world, but [for] their relation to other stories" (8). Hawthorne's "Wakefield," for instance, that paradigmatic metaphysical Missing Persons story, is as notable an intertext for Auster as it was earlier for Abe. It is explicitly cited and retold (*Ghosts* 209–10), lest one miss the paralleling of its storyline in each volume of the trilogy. It is even truer of the *New York Trilogy* than of Abe's novels that "The Man of the Crowd" episodes are a *mise en abyme* of the main action (recast, like the "Wakefield" analogues, but on a diminishing scale, in each successive book of the trilogy). I shall concentrate on the most extended and explicit Poe-like episode, which is professional detective-story writer and amateur detective Daniel Quinn's[6] stalking of the old man (Peter Stillman Sr.) in the first volume of the trilogy, *City of Glass* (chapters 7–9).

Auster refers explicitly to Poe with the "strange hieroglyphs" in "the concluding pages of *A. Gordon Pym*" (*City* 85); and with "Riverside Park . . . at 84th Street [from which,] in . . . 1843 and 1844, Edgar Allan Poe gaz[ed] out at the Hudson," as both Quinn and Stillman are doing now (*City* 100). More obliquely, the identification of detective Dupin's reasoning intellect with that of his (criminal) opponent foreshadows the identification, on very different terms, of Quinn, supposedly the pursuer, with Stillman, supposedly the pursued. In *The Locked Room*, it is Fanshawe who pursues this same Quinn. Fanshawe declares, "[Quinn] thought he was following me, but in fact I was following him . . . I led him along [like Shelley's Monster leading on Frankenstein], leaving clues for him everywhere . . . watching him the whole time" (362). In this way, the reader is continually invited to read back the later works in the trilogy onto the earlier ones: the trilogy thus constitutes a kind of double palimpsest.

Quinn first picks up Stillman's trail in the "rush-hour crowd" at Grand Central, a crowd in which "each [person, unlike those in Poe's "crowd,"] is irreducibly himself" (*City* 61, 66). He follows Stillman, careful not to be seen—"even if he stood directly in front of him, he doubted that Stillman would be able to see him" (69). Yet the "broken down and disconnected" shabby old man, "moving with effort," forces Quinn into "slowing his pace to match the old man's" (67).

The writing process is explicitly thematized throughout the trilogy, just as it is in Abe's novels. Auster's protagonists are, like Abe's, author-investigators, keeping in colored notebooks the record of their largely ineffectual, even counterproductive, search among a surfeit of clues leading to a shortage of solutions. Quinn found quite early on in his "tailing" that "walking and writing were not easily compatible" (76). He fails to draw the moral from this miniature artist-parable, however, and turns the maps he has made of Stillman's labyrinthine daily path among the streets of New York into as many letters, spelling out his version of Stillman's monomania: "- - - - O W E R O F B A B - -." Though the message could be "a hoax [a key word in Poe] he had perpetrated on himself," he still, at the end of *City of Glass*, wonders what word the map of all the walking of his own life would spell out (155).

"He had lived Stillman's life, walked at his pace, seen what he had seen, and the only thing he felt now was the man's impenetrability. . . . [H]e had seen the old man slip away from him, even as he remained before his eyes" (80). Stillman, formerly, and now again, the Missing Person of this disembodied story, "had become part of the city . . . a brick in an endless wall of bricks. [Quinn] had followed the old man for two weeks. What, then, could he conclude? Not much" (109). "Tied by an invisible thread to the old man" (110), Quinn appropriates his wandering, his notetaking, his avoidance of people; he takes up Beckettian residence in an ash can, doing a futile stakeout on characters long since departed. Quinn becomes, in short, the same sort of "disconnected" bag-man-as-Missing Person as Stillman; and, indeed, like Stillman, he too finally "melted into the walls of the city" (139). As the darkness grows and the empty pages in his notebook dwindle, this seems to be the end, also, of Quinn's fragile textual life.[7]

A finely crafted fugue on Missing Persons, written in a lucidly self-deconstructing style with Beckettian subtones (cf. Stephen Bernstein's essay in Chapter 6 of this volume), the episode constitutes a deliberate critique-cum-interpretation of "The Man of the Crowd." And the moral of this adapted parable is a recasting, as I see it, of the "es lässt sich nicht lesen" of Poe's story. As Auster puts it, near the end of the *Trilogy*, "No one can cross the boundary into another—for the simple reason that no one can gain access to himself" (292). His *Trilogy* is a fugue on the collapsing of personalities into identities, of identities into a single uncertain, shifting identity base, and of that, in turn, into the game or play of the postmodernist text, a process first adumbrated a century and a half ago in Poe's always-already postmodernist hermeneutic allegory of the inaccessibility of the dark secrets in our hearts.

Notes

An earlier version of this essay appeared in *Narrative Ironies*, ed. Raymond A. Prier and Gerald Gillespie (Amsterdam and Atlanta: Rodopi, 1997), 163–79. Reprinted with permission of Editions Rodopi.

1. Ross Macdonald, with help from Doyle and T. S. Eliot (but not Poe), finds the "inferno" of the Baudelairean city to be part of the matrix for the "mean streets" of the hard-boiled detective story (115–16).

2. Such Poe stories as "The Fall of the House of Usher" ("my story about him") and "The Cask of Amontillado" ("my story about me") approach this narrative structure, but "The Man of the Crowd" is, in my view, the earliest successful example of it. (A nearly flawless successor is Melville's "Bartleby, the Scrivener.") Compare the narrative structure of *The Locked Room*, the third volume of Auster's *New York Trilogy*. The narrator's "biography" of his friendship with Fanshawe could be, as the wife he inherits from the Wakefield-like Fanshawe puts it, "as much about you as about him" (290), and thus a type of elegiac romance. See Bruffee for a fuller explanation of this term, which he originated. Kennedy ("Limits") makes similar points about such matters as the victimization of the Old Man and the ambiguity of the title, while Weinstein has written eloquently about Hawthorne's story "Wakefield," which I see as yet another ancestor of the metaphysical detective story to be found among the parables of the American Renaissance. See also Swope on the "Wakefield" topos.

3. Compare Sweeney's interpretation of Poe's "locked room" stories, which elucidates the parallels between their architectural enclosures and their narrative structures.

4. I am unable to account for this chromatic coincidence.

5. For a fuller account of the Poe-like elements (as well as the "Wakefield" series) in Abe's four major metaphysical detective novels (the three discussed briefly here, plus *The Ruined Map* [1967; trans. 1980]), see my essay "Gumshoes: Kobo Abe and Poe."

6. There seems to be an actual (or perhaps pseudonymous) "Daniel Quinn" whose books can sometimes be found on the pulpier airport detective-novel shelves, in addition to (or the same as?) Daniel Quinn, author of the novels *Ishmael* (1992), *Providence* (1994), and *My Ishmael* (1997), in addition to (or the same as?) the Daniel Quinn whom Auster cites in his *Red Notebook*. So overdetermined is this name already that "Daniel Quinn," the narrator-hero of William Kennedy's *Quinn's Book* (1988), can be left out of account entirely. Or, as Stillman Sr. himself puts it, "I like your name enormously, Mr. Quinn. It goes off in so many little directions at once" (*City* 90). The merely autobiographical echo is of Auster's using the name "Paul Quinn" to sign some very early book reviews: "Seeing that the magazine wasn't going to add up to much, I signed my articles [sic] with a pseudonym, just to keep things interesting. Quinn was the name I chose for myself, Paul Quinn" (*Hand* 48). I would not dare to hazard a guess as to the relevance of these observations. But they suggest that Austerian "levels of artifice," like the books in Borges's "Tlön, Uqbar, Orbis Tertius" (1940), can make an imprint on the "real world." See also my essay "The Austerized Version."

7. Here the gothic-romantic motif seems to be that of Balzac's fatal chiasmus in "La Peau de chagrin," where to "live" shrinks the possibility of life. Auster deploys it again in the story of the iced-in explorer who diminishes his supply of air each time he exhales, because the condensation of his breath freezes on the inside of his igloo (300–301).

Works Cited

Abe, Kobo. *The Face of Another.* [*Tanin no kao,* 1964]. Trans. E. Dale Saunders. New York: Knopf, 1966.
———. *Inter Ice Age 4.* [*Dai yon Kampyo-ki,* 1968]. Trans. E. Dale Saunders. New York: Knopf, 1970.
———. *Secret Rendezvous.* [*Mikkai,* 1977]. Trans. Juliet W. Carpenter. New York: Knopf, 1979.
Aquin, Hubert. *Trou de mémoire.* Montreal: Cercle du Livre de France, 1968.
Atwood, Margaret. "Murder in the Dark." *Murder in the Dark: Short Fictions and Prose Poems.* Toronto: Coach House Press, 1983. 29–30.
Auerbach, Jonathan. *The Romance of Failure: First-Person Fictions of Poe, Hawthorne, and James.* New York: Oxford University Press, 1989.
Auster, Paul. *City of Glass.* [1985]. *New* 1–158.
———. *Ghosts.* [1986]. *New* 159–232.
———. *Hand to Mouth.* New York: Viking, 1997.
———. *The Locked Room.* [1986]. *New* 235–71.
———. *The New York Trilogy.* New York: Penguin, 1990.
———. *The Red Notebook and Other Writings.* [1993]. London: Faber, 1995.
Balzac, Honoré de. *La Peau de Chagrin.* [1831]. *Oeuvres complètes.* Paris: Conard, 1925. 27: 1–316.
Barthelme, Donald. *Snow White.* New York: Atheneum, 1967.
Baudelaire, Charles. "Le Peintre de la vie moderne." *Ecrits ésthetiques,* ed. Jean-Christophe Bailly. Paris: Union Générale d'Editions, 1986. 360–404.
Benjamin, Walter. "On Some Motifs in Baudelaire." *Illuminations.* [1955]. Ed. Hannah Arendt, trans. Harry Zohn. New York: Schocken, 1988. 155–200.
Borges, Jorge Luis. *Borges: A Reader,* ed. Emir Rodríguez Monegal and Alastair Reid. New York: Dutton, 1981.
———. "The Detective Story." Trans. Alberto Manguel. *Descant* 16, 4 (1985): 15–24.
———. "Modes of G. K. Chesterton." [1936]. Trans. Karen Stolley. *Borges* 87–91.
———. "Tlön, Uqbar, Orbis Tertius." [1940]. Trans. Alastair Reid. *Borges* 111–22.
Brand, Dana. "From the Flâneur to the Detective: Interpreting the City of Poe." In *Popular Fiction: Technology, Ideology, Production, Reading,* ed. Tony Bennett. London: Routledge, 1990. 220–37.
Bruffee, Kenneth. *Elegiac Romance.* Ithaca, N.Y.: Cornell University Press, 1983.
Byer, Robert H. "Mysteries of the City: A Reading of Poe's 'The Man of the Crowd.'" In *Ideology and Classic American Literature,* ed. Sacvan Bercovitch and Myra Jehlen. Cambridge: Cambridge University Press, 1986. 221–46.
Chesterton, G. K. "The Blue Cross." [1911]. *Complete* 3–23.
———. *The Complete Father Brown.* New York: Penguin, 1988.
———. "The Head of Caesar." [1913]. *Complete* 232–44.
———. "How to Write a Detective Story" [1925]. *Chesterton Review* 10, 2 (1984): 111–18.
———. "The Painful Fall of a Great Reputation." [1903]. *The Club of Queer Trades.* New York: Harpers, 1905. 59–67.
———. "The Pursuit of Mr. Blue." [1935]. *Complete* 894–913.
Colburn, Steven E. "Graham Greene's 'A Day Saved': A Modern Fable of Time and Identity." *Studies in Short Fiction* 29, 3 (1992): 377–84.
DuPlessis, Rachel Blau. *Writing Beyond the Ending.* Bloomington: Indiana University Press, 1985.

Eco, Umberto. *Postscript to* The Name of the Rose. [*Postille a* Il Nome della Rosa, 1983]. Trans. William Weaver. London: Secker and Warburg, 1985.

Eco, Umberto and Thomas A. Sebeok, eds. *The Sign of Three: Dupin, Holmes, Peirce.* Bloomington: Indiana University Press, 1983.

Elbert, Monika M. " 'The Man of the Crowd' and the Man Outside the Crowd: Poe's Narrator and the Democratic Reader." *Modern Language Studies* 21, 4 (1991): 16–30.

Ewert, Jeanne C. "Lost in the Hermeneutic Funhouse." Walker and Frazer 166–73.

Greene, Graham. "A Day Saved." [1935]. *Collected Stories.* New York: Viking, 1973. 528–33.

Hawthorne, Nathaniel. "Wakefield." [1835]. *Tales and Sketches,* ed. Roy Harvey Pearce. New York: Library of America, 1982. 290–98.

Irwin, John T. *The Mystery to a Solution: Poe, Borges, and the Analytic Detective Story.* Baltimore: Johns Hopkins University Press, 1994.

Kennedy, J. Gerald. "The Limits of Reason: Poe's Deluded Detectives." *American Literature* 47 (1975): 184–96.

———. *Poe, Death, and the Life of Writing.* New Haven, Conn.: Yale University Press, 1987.

Kennedy, William. *Quinn's Book.* New York: Viking, 1988.

Lambert, Gavin. *The Dangerous Edge.* London: Barrie and Jenkins, 1975.

Lehman, David. *The Perfect Murder: A Study in Detection.* New York: Free Press, 1989.

Macdonald, Ross. "The Writer as Detective Hero." *Self-Portrait: Ceaselessly into the Past.* Santa Barbara, Calif.: Capra Press, 1981. 113–22.

Merivale, Patricia. "The Austerized Version." Review of *Beyond the Red Notebook,* ed. Dennis Barone; *Review of Contemporary Fiction* Paul Auster issue, ed. Dennis Barone; and *L'Oeuvre de Paul Auster,* ed. Annick Duperray. *Contemporary Literature* 38, 1 (1997): 185–97.

———. "The Flaunting of Artifice in Vladimir Nabokov and Jorge Luis Borges." In *Nabokov: The Man and His Work,* ed. L. S. Dembo. Madison: University of Wisconsin Press, 1967. 290–324. Reprinted in *Critical Essays on Jorge Luis Borges,* ed. Jaime Alazraki. Boston: G. K. Hall, 1987. 141–53.

———. "Gumshoes: Kobo Abe and Poe." In *Proceedings of the XIIIth International Comparative Literature Association Meeting,* Tokyo, 1991, ed. Gerald Gillespie. Tokyo: Tokyo University Press, 1995. 100–106.

Plath, Sylvia. "The Detective." *Collected Poems,* ed. Ted Hughes. London: Faber, 1981. 209.

Poe, Edgar Allan. "The Cask of Amontillado." [1846]. *Tales* 224–30.

———. "The Fall of the House of Usher." [1839]. *Tales* 137–55.

———. "The Man of the Crowd." [1840]. *Tales* 107–16.

———. "The Murders in the Rue Morgue." [1841]. *Tales* 411–44.

———. "The Mystery of Marie Rogêt." [1842–43]. *Tales* 445–93.

———. "The Purloined Letter." [1844]. *Tales* 493–511.

———. *Tales of Mystery and Imagination.* Ed. Graham Clarke. London: Dent, 1984.

Priestman, Martin. *Detective Fiction and Literature: The Figure on the Carpet.* New York: St. Martin's Press, 1990.

Quinn, Daniel. *Ishmael.* New York: Bantam, 1992.

———. *My Ishmael.* New York: Bantam, 1997.

———. *Providence.* New York: Bantam, 1994.

Quinn, Patrick F. *The French Face of Edgar Poe*. [1954]. Carbondale: Southern Illinois University Press, 1957.

Saltzman, Arthur. *Designs of Darkness in Contemporary American Fiction*. Philadelphia: University of Pennsylvania Press, 1990.

Spanos, William V. "The Detective and the Boundary: Some Notes on the Postmodern Literary Imagination." *Boundary 2* 1, 1 (1972): 147–60. Reprinted in *Repetitions: The Postmodern Occasion in Literature and Culture*. Baton Rouge: Louisiana State University Press, 1990. 322–42.

Sweeney, Susan Elizabeth. "Locked Rooms: Detective Fiction, Narrative Theory, and Self-Reflexivity." Walker and Frazer 1–14.

Swope, Richard. "Approaching the Threshold(s) in Postmodern Detective Fiction: Hawthorne's 'Wakefield' and Other Missing Persons." *Critique* 39, 3 (1998): 207–27.

Tani, Stefano. *The Doomed Detective: The Contribution of the Detective Novel to Postmodern American and Italian Fiction*. Carbondale: Southern Illinois University Press, 1984.

Walker, Ronald G. and June M. Frazer, eds. *The Cunning Craft: Original Essays on Detective Fiction and Contemporary Literary Theory*. Macomb: Western Illinois University Press, 1990.

Weinstein, Arnold. *"Nobody's Home": Speech, Self and Place in American Fiction from Hawthorne to DeLillo*. New York: Oxford University Press, 1993.

Chapter 5
Work of the Detective, Work of the Writer
Auster's *City of Glass*

Jeffrey T. Nealon

> Quinn was nowhere now. He had nothing, he knew nothing, he knew that he knew nothing. Not only had he been sent back to the beginning, he was now before the beginning, and so far before the beginning that it was worse than any end he could imagine.
> —Paul Auster, *City of Glass* (124)

> The writer's solitude, then, this condition that is his risk, arises from the fact that in the work he belongs to what is always before the work. Through him the work arrives, is the firmness of a beginning, but he himself belongs to a time dominated by the indecision of beginning again.
> —Maurice Blanchot, *The Space of Literature* (261)

The detective novel is often analyzed in terms of its metafictional and metaphysical appeal. Whether consciously or unconsciously, the genre comments upon the process of sifting through signs, and ultimately upon the possibility of deriving order from the seeming chaos of conflicting signals and motives. The unraveling work of the detective within the story mirrors and assists the work of the reader, as both try to piece together the disparate signs that might eventually solve the mystery. The reader of the detective novel comes, metafictionally, to identify with the detective, because both reader and detective are bound up in the metaphysical or epistemological work of interpretation, the work of reading clues and writing a solution or end (see, for example, Hühn and Porter).

Within this strongly metafictional and metaphysical genre, perhaps no detective story foregrounds these aspects more than Paul Auster's *City of Glass* (1985), a detective story about a writer of detective stories, and the first book of Auster's *New York Trilogy*.[1] Daniel Quinn, the protagonist of *City of Glass*, writes detective stories under the name "William Wilson"; in turn, the detective-protagonist of the Wilson mysteries is named "Max Work."[2] Quinn is himself the perfect metafictional character; like most mystery writers, he has little or no actual experience of the crime-ridden underworld of the detective story: "What interested him about the stories he wrote was not their relation to the world but their relation to other stories" (8). Early in the book, Quinn muses on his own interest in reading and writing detective fiction:

> In the good mystery there is nothing wasted, no sentence, no word that is not significant. And even if it is not significant, it has the potential to be so—which amounts to the same thing. . . . Since everything seen or said, even the slightest, most trivial thing, can bear a connection to the outcome of the story, nothing must be overlooked. Everything becomes essence; the center of the book shifts with each event that propels it forward. The center, then, is everywhere, and no circumference can be drawn until the book has come to its end.
> The detective is the one who looks, who listens, who moves through this morass of objects and events in search of the thought, the idea that will pull all these things together and make sense of them. In effect, the writer and the detective are interchangeable. (9)

This quotation reflexively explains much of the detective story's appeal: the work of the detective mirrors not only the work of reading (where "each event . . . propels [the story] forward . . . and no circumference can be drawn until the book has come to its end"), but also—and more importantly for Quinn—the work of writing. The writer is the one who initially creates the disparate world of ruses and clues that is the mystery, but also the one who searches—perhaps more desperately than the reader—for its end, for "the idea that will pull all these things together and make sense of them."

In fact, writing seems *more* closely tied to the work of the detective than reading, insofar as the writer and the detective—unlike the reader—embark on a journey that has no guaranteed destination. For the reader, the mystery always ends, regardless of whether it is solved. Even if the detective is thwarted or killed, the book eventually does come to a conclusion (however satisfying or unsatisfying the reader may find it). No such luxury, however, is available to the writer or the detective. Once they enter the space of the mystery, there is no guarantee of an ordered conclusion—no guarantee even of the closure afforded the reader by the final period placed after the final sentence. For the writer and the detective, as the narrator says about *City of Glass*, "The question is the story itself, and whether or not it means something is not for the story to tell" (3). After the story's end, the reader has the luxury of deciding "whether or not it means something," but from within the space of the story itself—from the tenuous place of the writer or the detective—such certainty is never easily attainable.

Quinn strongly feels this bond between writer and detective in his relationship to the hard-boiled Max Work, a bond mediated through his nom de plume "William Wilson": "In the triad of selves that Quinn had become, Wilson served as a kind of ventriloquist, Quinn himself was the dummy, and Work was the animated voice that gave purpose to the enterprise" (6). For Quinn, Max Work's ability always to lift himself out of the uncertainty that is the writer/detective's plight gives purpose to the entire enterprise of writing. Quinn is fascinated by Work's unfailing ability to order and thus escape from chaos. Work allows Quinn to make sense of the myriad meaningful (or meaning*less*) clues that make up Quinn's own writing process; in fact, "it reassured him to pretend to be Work as he was writing his books" (10). In short, Work (as a character) allows Quinn's writing to perform work (as a concept): Max Work allows Quinn's literary works to perform a properly philosophical brand of work.

Work allows Quinn's texts to accomplish an end, to create order, to solve the mystery by building a satisfying solution; and this is precisely the comfort that Quinn takes in his character, Work, through the writing persona of Wilson: "If Wilson did not exist, he nevertheless was the bridge that allowed Quinn to pass from himself into Work. And little by little, Work had become a presence in Quinn's life, his interior brother, his comrade in solitude" (6–7). For Quinn, this curious phrase "pass from himself into Work" carries a dual meaning: first, writing under the pen name "Wilson" allows the writer, Quinn, to take on the active persona of the detective, Work; but, and perhaps more important, this relationship also allows Quinn's writing to pass from the always idling stages of composition into a meaningful metaphysical realm. Quinn's passing from himself into Work allows his writing to pass from the literally limitless realm of composition (where confusion reigns because anything and everything is possible and meaningful) into the limited realm of work.

This understanding of the work of the detective and the work of the writer circumscribes Quinn's initial relation to (his) writing in *City of Glass*—and constitutes the beginnings of what could be called a metafictional reading of the novel, wherein the reading and writing processes are themselves among the novel's themes.[3] One could track the ways in which this initial unproblematic relation of writer to work becomes increasingly complicated in the course of the story, to the point that it no longer holds by the novel's end. It is precisely in this frustration of work that Auster's novel could be seen as the sort of postmodernist anti-detective novel that William Spanos calls for when he writes that the postmodernist writer's "most immediate task" is "undermining the detectivelike expectations of the positivistic mind" (48). Indeed, the destruction of Quinn's initial "positivistic" relation to (his) writing arises when he allows himself to be caught up in the difficulties of a "real" story. When Quinn takes on the Stillman case (after he is mistaken for the detective "Paul Auster"), he can no longer withdraw from the unsure place of the writer into the safety of Work.

But, as Spanos points out, such a postmodernist "de-composition or de-struction [of traditional plot forms] is not, as is too often protested, a purely negative one" (28). Rather, "de-struction" can unleash plural possibilities, insofar as such a postmodernist undermining "becomes the agency not just of despair but also and simultaneously of hope, that is of *freedom, the infinite possibility of free play*" (28; my emphasis). As Alison Russell writes in a similar vein, concerning the structure of frustrated endings throughout Auster's *New York Trilogy*, one could certainly argue that "The lack of any one solution leaves the narrator, and the implied author, of the trilogy free to choose any or none of the potential solutions available to him; he is free to begin another quest in the new world full of possibilities" (83). And just as the narrator is freed to consider "infinite possibility" in the postmodernist anti-detective novel, so too is the reader "free to begin another quest in the new world full of possibilities."

While such a reading of *City of Glass* is compelling, I will argue a slightly different thesis concerning Auster's metaphysical detective story. Although I spin out a kind of Spanos-inspired Heideggerian reading of *City of Glass*, I am finally interested in taking up the limitations of a reading that emphasizes the plurality of subjective possibilities. In the end, I want to suggest that *City of Glass* offers a confrontation not so much with a *reading* space of play and possibility—the dominant concepts in American postmodernism of the 1970s—but rather with a *writing* space of (im)possibility, hesitation, and response to alterity, those crucial watchwords for the second wave of artistic and critical postmodernist inquiry. If, as Spanos argues, the detective-as-reader is a privileged site for understanding the first wave of destructuring postmodernism, I will argue that Auster's detective-as-writer constitutes a privileged site for understanding a slightly different impulse within postmodernist American fiction.[4]

I

In the beginning, Quinn's job as detective in *City of Glass* is to protect the victimized Peter Stillman from his mad father—Peter Stillman Sr.—and find out why the elder Stillman has returned to New York after his release from the mental hospital where he was placed years earlier for abusing his son. Quinn's investigation quickly takes on the look and feel of a detective story. However, this particular story does not seem to allow Quinn to pass from his own uncertainty to the confidence of Work; rather, it is a story that ceaselessly throws Quinn back to the uncertain place of the writer: "Little by little, Quinn began to feel cut off from his original intentions, and he wondered now if he had not embarked on a meaningless project" (73). Quinn's "original intentions" had been to have a Work-like experience for himself—to give some concrete meaning to his stories, to have an extratextual adventure that would supplement and enhance his fascination with writing about detectives. However, Quinn's detective work and his writing soon become one and the same thing. As he monotonously trails Stillman, Quinn becomes bored—a part of detective work rarely thematized in detective fiction—and looks for something to pass the time: "Quinn realized that he needed something more to keep himself occupied, some little task to accompany him as he went about his work. In the end, it was the red notebook that offered him salvation" (75). Quinn purchases a notebook and begins to take down everything obsessively, writing as he trails Stillman. Soon his surveillance—the work that he had hoped would bring him out of the indecisive realm of writing and into contact with Work—collapses back into writing, into a realm characterized by "seeing the thing and writing about it in the same fluid gesture" (77).

Here we see Quinn's conception of Work collapsing: his extratextual job or quest becomes text; his attempt to withdraw from the uncertain space of the artistic work into the productive economy of metaphysical work fails. And it is likewise here that his initial unproblematic analogy between the writer and the detective seems to fall apart:

It was all a question of method. . . . He had always imagined that the key to good detective work was a close observation of details. The more accurate the scrutiny, the more successful the results. The implication was that human behavior could be understood, that beneath the infinite facade of gestures, tics, and silences, there was finally a coherence, an order, a source of motivation. But after struggling to take in all these surface effects, Quinn felt no closer to Stillman than when he first started following him. He had lived Stillman's life, walked at his pace, seen what he had seen, and the only thing he felt now was the man's impenetrability. Instead of narrowing the distance that lay between him and Stillman, he had seen the old man slip away from him, even as he remained before his eyes. (80)

Here the story, while it should progress for Quinn—should allow him to pass into Work—instead stubbornly reverts back to the time of writing, to the predicament of the writer at the time of writing, a time characterized by an "infinite facade of gestures, tics, and silences," a time bereft of "coherence, an order, a source of motivation." The mystery slips back from work as an assured interpretive process to a jumble of "surface effects"—indeterminate words and images that, like Stillman, "slip away from him, even as [they] remained before his eyes."

But why is it that Quinn finds it so difficult to pass into Work? Why does a writer find it so hard to make his or her literary work pass into the realm of metaphysical work? As Maurice Blanchot notes, "If we see work as the force of history, the force that transforms man while it transforms the world, then a writer's activity must be recognized as the highest form of work" (*Gaze* 33).[5] Blanchot here follows a scrupulous philosophical analysis of work.[6] He uses the example of a stove: if a person wants to get warm, she builds a stove; she negates merely disparate elements by casting them together in a higher unity. By performing this work, she affirms something new and brings it into the world by denying or negating the old elements. Blanchot suggests that this conception of work is also a conception of historical or philosophical progress: "The idea of heat is nothing, but actual heat will make my life a different kind of life, and every new thing I am able to do from now on because of this heat will also make me someone different. Thus is history formed, say Hegel and Marx—by work which realizes being in denying it, and reveals it at the end of the negation" (33). Blanchot here gives a concise summary of the work of dialectic, which negates in order to bring elements into a higher transformation or synthesis within the teleological economy of history. The idea of heat is realized in the work that builds the stove; the end product of heat is brought about and mastered in the negation of the disconnected elements—steel, rivets, pipe, rock, cement—that form the final unity of the usable stove. In turn, the stove's heat provides the conditions for further transformations—allows other ideas to be mastered, allows other ends to be attained, allows history to progress. For Blanchot, the writer *seems* to do precisely this kind of work when she brings a transformation of ink and paper into the world. Insofar as the writer negates language in its present form and offers it a new form, her work allows the progress of further artistic transformations, thereby performing what would seem to be philosophical work par excellence.

But is it? Is there a difference—and a difference that unmakes difference as negation—that characterizes the work of the writer? Blanchot suggests that the writer's work is different from the philosophical work of mastery insofar as the thing produced by the writer remains unmasterable, refuses to pass into work. Words—writing's "raw material"—refuse to be negated within a higher unity; they are always there to attest to what should have been destroyed in the limiting negation that brings about the work of meaning. They attest to a time other than the time of philosophical progress. Blanchot writes that the literary work "negates the negation of time, it negates the negation of limits. This is why this negation negates nothing, in the end, why the work in which it is realized is not a truly negative, destructive act of transformation, but rather the realization of the inability to negate anything" (35). For Blanchot, the literary work is characterized not by its negation of words before the inevitable ends and limits of meaning, but rather by the work's inability to be limited, to mean something univocally, "the inability to negate anything" at all. This strange inability at the heart of the artistic work is what disrupts writing's status as properly philosophical work. For him, the literary work is not simply another limited context which allows continued progress or mastery, but rather the constant disruption of an end-oriented economy of meaning. The artistic work does not allow the mastery of philosophical work because it refuses to be limited by an end; and "one cannot accomplish anything in the unlimited" (35).

And this is exactly Quinn's dilemma in *City of Glass*. He enters a story, a time or place where the reassurance of limits or ends is withdrawn, where the economy of work is disrupted, where circumference becomes center and no distance can be drawn from the facts of the case, no principle can draw the case to an end. When Quinn falls into the time of the story, he finds not the revelation of an end, but rather the revelation of a dissembling endlessness that disrupts his initial understanding of the detective story's economy. This disruption occurs precisely by drawing this dominant economy out of work. It becomes impossible for Quinn to pass confidently into Work, to think of himself as the detective, "the man who looks out from himself into the world and demands that the world reveal itself to him" (10). This drama of revelation, mastery, and self is impossible for the writer; words refuse her mastery. The work remains unlimited—remains other—because of its ties to language, which Blanchot argues is not simply a functional entity that can unproblematically be exchanged for meaning. The writer is the one who most fully encounters this afunctionality in the time of composition—when all she has, so to speak, is a heap of broken images rather than a reassuring meaning and an end.

But, as we have seen, such an unproblematic economy of meaning characterizes Quinn's initial understanding of writing the detective story. Initially, his is an economy where the language of the story itself is unproblematic; it is transparent, simply there to describe the action and propel the story along, to allow the literary work to pass into Work. Quinn's increasing inability to pass into Work, then, is somehow tied to his strange relationship with the Stillman case, and, more specifically, with the problem of language vis-à-vis that case. Coincidentally enough, "the process of inventing a new language" (92) is *precisely* Stillman's project, carried out while Quinn follows him through the streets of New York. Stillman has been engaged in this project, it seems, for some time, and his interest in the possibility of a natural or Edenic language helps to explain why he abused his son by confining him without outside contact. Quinn traces Stillman's interest in language back to his doctoral dissertation, where Stillman argues—in classic Miltonic terms—that things are no longer whole, so we cannot express them properly with an "old" language. The post-Babel language of the Fall cannot hope to express adequately the everyday reality in which we live, much less the divine reality to which we aspire. As Stillman tells Quinn, "our words no longer correspond to the world" (92).

In his discussion with Quinn, Stillman uses the example of a broken umbrella to make his point about the fall of language; he says, "every object is similar to the umbrella, in that it serves a function. A pencil is for writing, a shoe is for wearing, a car is for driving. Now, my question is this. What happens when a thing no longer performs its function? Is it still the thing, or has it become something else?" (93). He goes on to answer his own question: "Because it can no longer perform its function, the umbrella has ceased to be an umbrella. . . . The word, however, has remained the same. Therefore, it can no longer express the thing. It is imprecise; it is false; it hides the thing that it is supposed to reveal" (93–94). Stillman puts forth here a classically onto-theological view of language as a fallen, corrupt system that cannot hope to lead to the ends of purity in rational inquiry; and, in the process, he reinforces Blanchot's sense of language's radical inability to perform metaphysical work (though for Blanchot this is not—as it is for Stillman and metaphysicians like him—a lamentable situation). For Stillman, the language of the fallen world hides rather than reveals the true functions of things.

In this reading of *City of Glass*, however, what particularly interests me is not Stillman's analysis of language per se, but rather his analysis of objects and their relationship to language. For Stillman, a thing *is* its function; when a thing (like an umbrella) ceases to perform its function, it is no longer that thing, no longer that word. Stillman's analysis of the world, then, bases itself on instrumentality—as does, for example, Heidegger's famous analysis of worldhood in *Being and Time*, where he analyzes the work of the hammer. Heidegger writes, "where something is put to use, our concern subordinates itself to the 'in-order-to' which is constitutive for the equipment we are employing at the time; the less we just stare at the hammer thing, and the more we just seize hold of it and use it, the more primordial does our relationship to it become, and the more unveiledly it is encountered as that which it is—equipment" (98). Stillman's analysis would seem to mime quite closely parts of Heidegger's analysis here: the thing reveals itself only in its use or function; we authentically relate to the object in its use, when "we just seize hold of it." But we must note that in the Heideggerian text, this "more primordial" relationship is profoundly atheoretical. In fact, one can never understand the hammer theoretically; one cannot "stare at the hammer" and hope to have its essence revealed. Rather, the hammer reveals itself in its uses. Using the hammer reveals the essence of equipment as *zuhanden* (ready-to-hand, able to be taken up for various usages) rather than as *vorhanden* (present-to-hand, theoretically [pre]determined for only one use). In other words, the primordial relation to the thing for Heidegger is not *simply* in its use (insofar as use remains a theoretical category), but rather in the nonteleological flux of *Zuhandenheit* which precedes any particular use. For Heidegger, then, the theoretical end of work or use is always derived from a prior state of multiple availability. Merely staring at the thing (theoretical consciousness) will never reveal this essence; rather, we must use the thing if we are to see that its essence lies in its multiple potentials for other uses.

In fact, for Heidegger, there is no quicker route to revealing the multiple essence of equipment than if the thing breaks, and therefore falls out of a strictly theoretical relation with an end (as present-to-hand) and back into its primordial relation (as ready-to-hand). As he writes, "When its unusability is thus discovered, equipment becomes conspicuous" (102). He goes on: "The ready-to-hand is not grasped theoretically at all, nor is it itself the sort of thing that circumspection [*Umsicht*, literally 'around-sight'] takes proximally as a circumspective theme. The peculiarity of what is proximally ready-to-hand is that, in its readiness to hand, it must, as it were, withdraw in order to be ready-to-hand quite authentically" (99). In other words, if what is proper to objects is the multiple possibilities of their readiness-to-hand, then readiness-to-hand "must, as it were, withdraw" in the theoretical (or present-to-hand) activity of end-oriented work. In short, what is proper to objects in an economy of work is their withdrawal. The essence of objects lies not in their ability to be used for a specific predetermined end, but rather in the primordial state of flux that precisely allows them to be taken up for this or that use. For Heidegger, then, the drama of hiding or withdrawing is part and parcel of the drama of instrumentality or work. We can forget the ready-to-hand that grounds the present-to-hand, but the multiple possibilities of the ready-to-hand remain and haunt all our end-oriented work.

Strangely enough, the primordial flux of the ready-to-hand especially haunts the work of signs. As Heidegger writes, "A sign is not a thing which stands to another thing in the relation of indicating; it is rather *an item of equipment which explicitly raises a totality of equipment into our circumspection* [again, *Umsicht*] *so that together with it the worldly character of the ready-to-hand announces itself*" (110; Heidegger's emphasis). One can, in other words, move from signs (as potential meaning ready-to-hand) to interpretation (as *a* meaning present-to-hand), but the signs themselves stubbornly remain, insistent and multiple, pointing to other possibilities. Signs, in fact, do nothing other than point beyond themselves, and this comprises their "ontological" character as ready-to-hand. The unsurpassable readiness-to-hand of signs or language is nothing other than the highest manifestation of equipment's pointing always outside itself, to ontological potential rather than to ontic ends. The upshot of all this is that the presence of the present-to-hand is predicated on a prior state of flux; rather than being the primary state of (things in) the world, presence is always *derived* from a realm of multiple possibility.

What, the weary reader may ask at this point, has all this to do with *City of Glass*? Well, first of all, Heidegger's analysis here helps explain the odd problem of Stillman's project: if the essence of objects is a kind of primordial flux rather than a kind of metaphysical unity, then the flux of language rather precisely names the essence of objects. Stillman's project is, in some sense, already complete: language does indeed in some way correspond to the essence of the world; it's just that Stillman has misunderstood the world's essence by conceiving of it univocally. Also, Heidegger's analysis suggests that even if Stillman completes his new language, this language itself will be subject to the same law of reference, of pointing always outside itself. Likewise, Heidegger's analysis suggests much about the nature of the detective story—a genre that depends upon the functionality of signs. What happens when one realizes that the clue in the detective story is grounded in the ready-to-hand, always pointing beyond itself toward myriad other things and many possible conclusions? One could, in fact, perform a Heideggerian analysis of the clue: theoretical reflection in the detective story has the power to forget the priority of the ready-to-hand's multiplicity. However, this would mean that the power of positivistic thinking is enabled by a flux that nags any conclusion with uncertainty; and, as Spanos argues, one can see this very clearly in the anti-detective genre, where one is never sure if the clues really add up.

Indeed, the surveillance that is the ground of the detective story can be thematized as the kind of sight that Heidegger analyzes in his discussion of instrumentality: a *Sicht* that is always an *Umsicht*—a sight that cannot see *into* things, but rather sees *around* them to their multiple possibilities. And this seems to be the kind of sight that Quinn increasingly directs toward the clues of the Stillman case: "Quinn looked at a picture of Stillman's face, hoping for a sudden epiphany, some sudden rush of subterranean knowledge that would help him to understand the man. But the picture told him nothing. It was no more than a picture of a man. He studied it for a moment longer and concluded that it could just as easily have been anyone" (37). For Quinn, Stillman's picture does not offer the detective's "subterranean knowledge" of the present-to-hand;

rather, it only returns him to the flux of the ready-to-hand: a flux in which Stillman's face leads not to knowledge, but only to ever more possibilities.

II

Perhaps Stillman's anonymity—this face which "could just as easily have been anyone"—returns us to Blanchot, who poses a serious question to the postmodernist Heideggerian reading sketched above. Such a reading, for all its radicalness, still seems to hold out the potential for something like a completion of Stillman's project, a new conception of language that could express the flux of the ready-to-hand. As Stillman says to Quinn, "Unless we can begin to embody the notion of change in the words we use, we will continue to be lost" (94). I have in fact been attempting to lay out the neo-Heideggerian assumptions behind such a postmodernist reading of *City of Glass*, one that emphasizes the potential multiplicity of the sign's references, and hence the plurality of possibility in the world.[7] Blanchot's question to language, however, is a more difficult one. For Heidegger, the sign's flux points to many potential uses; for Blanchot, however, the "image" or sign points *not* to the plurality of potential ends, but to the impossibility of *any* end, to the necessary *foundering* of theoretical thinking rather than its power to emerge from or describe a flux. In Blanchot, the circumspective gaze of Heidegger's *Umsicht* leads not to the revelation of many potential uses, but to the radical anonymity of Quinn's gaze at Stillman's picture, the radical interruption of any potential usage:

. . . in the very thing that makes it possible, the gaze finds the power that neutralizes it—that does not suspend it or arrest it, but on the contrary prevents it from ever finishing, cuts it off from all beginning, makes it into a neutral, wandering glimmer that is not extinguished, that does not illuminate: the circle of the gaze, closed on itself. . . . Fascination is the gaze of solitude, the gaze of what is incessant and interminable, in which blindness is still vision, vision that is no longer the possibility of seeing, but the impossibility of not seeing. (*Gaze* 75)

For Blanchot, the writer's encounter with language leaves her in this state of fascination, where "objects sink when they become separated from their meaning, when they subside into their image" (76). This fascinated gaze does not uncover the possibility of multiple personal ends; rather, it interrupts personhood or ends as such. The gaze of fascination is a kind of eternal vigilance which has no guarantee of an end, but rather consists of a constant interruption of ends. It is perhaps the gaze characteristic of a city of glass, where everything can be seen, stared at; however, because in a city of glass there is no longer the drama of the thing's being hidden or uncovered, "the thing we stare at has foundered, sunk into its image" (Blanchot, *Space* 255). A city of glass, in other words, would be characterized not by myriad perspectives and possibilities of seeing things, but by "the impossibility of not seeing" things. This sight is characterized by the interruption of what Blanchot calls the "neutral," the anonymous gaze that idles work rather than passing into it.

It is crucial to recall, however, that for Blanchot this radical neutrality is not merely a spoiling move or a simple frustration of the self that leaves the subject bereft and without knowledge or agency. The necessity of carrying on and responding in the face of this neutrality is intimately coupled with this ruinous difficulty. In other words, thinking and action are not merely stifled by such a radical interruption; their urgency is, in fact, heightened. As Paul Davies writes about Blanchot's interruptions of metaphysical thinking, "in being ruined as a totalizing discourse, philosophy *continues* in and as a responding discourse." Thinking and action do not end with their interruption, but they take on a different structure—not a mere recognition or revelation of impossibility, but what Davies calls a "continuing as response" (213). For Blanchot, the upshot of this distinction between "originary" possibility and (im)possibility is an ethical one. Heideggerian possibility accrues to—and therefore reinforces the privilege of—the subject. Subjective response, however, accrues to the other.

The *différend* spelled out here between Heidegger and Blanchot resonates with a larger debate about American postmodernist fiction. One could take, for example, Thomas Pynchon's *The Crying of Lot 49* to be the paradigmatic detective text for understanding postmodernism in the Heideggerian mode of possibility. Oedipa Maas realizes, at the end of the novel, the inadequacy of a constricting "either/or" modernist view of the world:

Behind the hieroglyphic streets there would *either* be a transcendent meaning, *or* only the earth. In the songs Miles, Dean, Serge and Leonard sang was *either* some fraction of the truth's numinous beauty . . . *or* only a power spectrum. Tremaine the Swastika Salesman's reprieve from holocaust was *either* an injustice, *or* the absence of a wind; the bones of the GI's at the bottom of Lake Inverarity were there *either* for a reason that mattered to the world *or* for skin divers and cigarette smokers. Ones and zeroes. So did the couples arrange themselves. . . . Another mode of meaning behind the obvious, or none. (181–82; my emphasis)

In learning to consider the excluded middles that lie between such limiting "ones and zeroes," Oedipa comes to see the possibilities that rest between the binary poles of certainty and chaos, and in the process articulates a certain understanding of postmodernism as opening subjective possibility: not the constricting "either/or," but the liberating "both/and."

Auster, however, allows no such rosy conclusion: certainly, *City of Glass* shows us the inadequacy of an "either/or" modernist worldview, but it does not open a clearing of subjective possibility or imperial subjective empowerment. Rather, it opens a space of hesitation and response to alterity. Near the end of *The Locked Room*, the final book of the *Trilogy*, Auster's narrator muses over Fanshawe's notebook: "everything remained open, unfinished, to be started again. I lost my way after the first word, and from then on I could only grope ahead, faltering in the darkness" (370). Here, while there certainly is openness and incompleteness, it does not seem to translate easily into a sense of increased subjective possibility. On the contrary, the "unfinished" notebook calls forth a different kind of response from the narrator, a hesitation wherein, even in the act of reading, one can "only grope ahead, faltering in the darkness." And this perhaps puts a sharper edge on the distinction between the work of the reader and the work of the writer: there is a *jouissance* to reading, even rereading. Starting again on a different adventure—or rereading particularly meaty texts—is a subjectively enriching experience. No such economy obtains for the writer, however: starting or restarting an "unfinished" story is a painful but oddly necessary process. Finally, one writes or rewrites out of a cathexis or fascination that cannot properly or simply be called subjectively enriching. In cryptic Blanchotian fashion, perhaps we could say that one reads for the self, while one writes for the others. Unlike the joyful fascinations of reading and the enriching gaze of the *Umsicht*, the interruptive fascinations of the writer are not so easily recuperable as, or in, a sense of increasing possibility.

In *City of Glass*, Quinn becomes fascinated by or in a kind of radical neutrality. Near the end of the novel, he drops out of all traditional economies of work and becomes a street person—obsessed with the interminable gaze he directs at Peter Stillman Jr.'s residence. His life becomes characterized not by myriad possibilities, but by a radically neutral ambivalence that nevertheless calls for constant vigilance and response. Even in the opening pages of the novel, Quinn seems open to this neutrality: "He was alive, and the stubbornness of this fact had little by little begun to fascinate him—as if he had managed to outlive himself, as if he were somehow living a posthumous life" (6). By the end of the novel, however, Quinn lives squarely in this neutral, fascinated time, the time of the gaze which carries no guarantee of end. It reveals only the impossibility of passing from himself into Work, the neutrality of his fate as a writer of detective stories:

Fate in the sense of what was, of what happened to be. It was something like the word "it" in the phrase "it is raining" or "it is night." What that "it" referred to Quinn had never known. A generalized condition of things as they were, perhaps; the state of is-ness that was the ground on which the happenings of the world took place. He could not be any more definite than that. But perhaps he was not really searching for anything definite. (133)

Once the writer passes into this fascinating time of the image, there is no withdrawal into a safe realm of possibility and work. The writer's obsession is sometimes her brilliance, but likewise her downfall: as Blanchot notes, the writer's obsession is "sometimes truth's elaboration in the world and sometimes the perpetuity of that which admits neither beginning nor end" (*Space* 261). The writer belongs to the frozen, fascinated time of the image, not the active time of "Work." As Blanchot writes,

The writer seems to be master of his pen, he can become capable of great mastery over words, over what he wants to make them express. But this mastery only manages to put him in contact, keep him in contact, with a fundamental passivity in which the word, no longer anything beyond its own appearance, the shadow of a word, can never be mastered or even grasped; it remains impossible to grasp, impossible to relinquish, the unsettled moment of fascination. (*Gaze* 67)

As Blanchot says of Kafka, literature begins in the slippage from the first person to the neutral, anonymous third person of writing; and for the writer, there is no going back, no moment of escape from the "fundamental passivity in which the work, no longer anything but its own appearance, the shadow of a word, can never be mastered." There is, in other words, no return to the self and its myriad possibilities, but rather a necessary exteriorizing of the self and a turn toward the other.[8] There is no end, as there is to a reading; rather, there is the hesitating, interminable response of writing.

This seems especially true of the writer of detective stories who finds he can no longer slip from himself into the comforting realm of Work, and it adds an ominous resonance to the final sentence in Quinn's red notebook: "What will happen when there are no more pages in the red notebook?" (157). Insofar as the world is the story for Quinn—the story of the slippage of the world into the time of the word—Quinn in some sense ceases to exist when the notebook runs out, when the writing ends. But his—and this novel's—is not a simple end; rather, this (missing) end only increases the tension of the question of ends. The question of ends in *City of Glass* is akin to the question of food on Quinn's final obsessive stakeout: for Quinn, "Food itself could never answer the question of food; it only delayed the moment when the question would have to be asked in earnest" (136). The end of *City of Glass*, insofar as it is not an end, does not satisfy like a meal, as the consumable ends of many detective novels do.[9] Instead, it brings the question of end ever closer, tries to ask that question in earnest. Whether or not that question has an answer, however, is not for the story—or its writer—to tell.[10]

Notes

An earlier version of this essay appeared in *Modern Fiction Studies* 42, 1 (1996): 91–110. Reprinted with permission of Johns Hopkins University Press.

1. Here I treat only *City of Glass* due to space constraints. While all three books should be read together—as each comments and expands on the others—*City of Glass* was originally published as a separate book, and holds together, in a manner of speaking, on its own.

2. Of course, "William Wilson" is a metafictional pen name, taken from the eponymous Poe story, which begins: "Let me call myself, for the present, William Wilson. The fair page now lying before me need not be sullied with my real appellation" (422).

3. For an exploration of *City* and reader-response theory, see Lavender.

4. Perhaps one could take Kathy Acker's comments as exemplary of this impulse. She argues that in the early to mid 1970s, an art of de-structuring critique was necessary and efficacious, and here she has much in common with Spanos's 1972 essay. But by the late 1980s—when, in Leonard Cohen's words, "everybody knows that the dice are loaded"—such a project, according to Acker, had played itself out. Acker writes about her 1988 novel, *Empire of the Senseless*: "Perhaps our society is now in a 'post-cynical' phase. Certainly, I thought as I started *Empire*, there's no more need [simply] to deconstruct, to take apart perceptual habits, to reveal the frauds which our society's living. We now have to find somewhere to go" (35).

5. We could, of course, investigate our own little textual mystery here concerning Blanchot's influence on Auster. This much we know: Auster has translated some of Blanchot's early fiction and the essay "After the Fact," and Blanchot's work is a recurring concern in Auster's memoir "Portrait of an Invisible Man." Also, Lydia Davis writes in her introduction to *The Gaze of Orpheus*: "Paul Auster deserves special thanks for his constant encouragement and thoughtful advice, and for first pointing the way to the works of Maurice Blanchot" (xv).

6. I should note that I am taking advantage of a slippage in the English word "work" that does not inhere in quite the same way in Blanchot's French. Here and elsewhere when Blanchot refers to the metaphysical work of building or progress, he uses a form of *le travail*; when he writes of (the) literary work, however, he tends to use a form of *l'oeuvre* or, more straightforwardly, *le livre*. This usage is further complicated by the recent translation of Blanchot's *La Part du feu* (1949) as *The Work of Fire*.

7. See Russell, who argues for just such a reading, which she calls a deconstruction. While I do not have space to work it out here, I would argue that such a pluralist reading seriously distorts Derrida's texts, where undecidability is *not* the consequence of semantic fertility or a freedom to choose among alternatives. As Derrida writes, "I set down here as an axiom and as that which is to be proved that the reconstitution cannot be finished. This is my starting point: no meaning can be determined out of context, but no context permits saturation. *What I am referring to here is not richness of substance, semantic fertility, but rather struc-*

ture: the structure of the remnant or of iteration" (81; my emphasis). For more detailed discussion of this point, see my essay "The Discipline of Deconstruction."

8. See, for example, the narrator's sentiments in *The Locked Room*: "By belonging to Sophie, I began to feel as though I belonged to everyone else as well. My true place in the world, it turned out, was somewhere beyond myself, and if that place was inside me, it was also unlocatable. This was the tiny hole between self and not-self, and for the first time in my life I saw this nowhere as the exact center of the world" (274–75).

9. On hunger and stories, see also Auster's "The Art of Hunger."

10. This essay, of course, has its own story—a story of debts impossible to repay. Thanks to Paul Davies and Tom Sheehan for their insights into Blanchot and Heidegger—though, of course, no philosophical warranty is implied. Also, special thanks to Ed Kern, who first gave me the "gift without presence" of Paul Auster.

Works Cited

Acker, Kathy. "A Few Notes on Two of My Books." *Review of Contemporary Fiction* 9, 3 (1989): 31–36.

Auster, Paul. "The Art of Hunger." *The Art of Hunger and Other Essays.* London: Menard Press, 1982. 9–22.

———. *City of Glass.* [1985]. *New* 1–158.

———. *The Locked Room.* [1986]. *New* 235–71.

———. *The New York Trilogy.* New York: Penguin, 1990.

———. "Portrait of an Invisible Man." *The Invention of Solitude.* New York: Sun, 1982. 1–70.

Blanchot, Maurice. *The Gaze of Orpheus.* Ed. P. Adams Sitney, trans. Lydia Davis. Barrytown, N.Y.: Station Hill Press, 1981.

———. *The Space of Literature.* [*L'Espace littéraire*, 1955]. Trans. Ann Smock. Lincoln: University of Nebraska Press, 1982.

———. *The Work of Fire.* [*La Part du feu*, 1949]. Trans. Charlotte Mandell. Stanford, Calif.: Stanford University Press, 1995.

Davies, Paul. "A Fine Risk: Reading Blanchot Reading Levinas." In *Re-Reading Levinas*, ed. Robert Bernasconi and Simon Critchley. Bloomington: Indiana University Press, 1991. 201–28.

Davis, Lydia. "A Note on the Translation." Blanchot, *Gaze* xiii–xv.

Derrida, Jacques. "Living On—Border Lines." Trans. James Hulbert. In *Deconstruction and Criticism*, ed. Harold Bloom et al. New York: Seabury Press, 1979. 75–176.

Heidegger, Martin. *Being and Time.* Trans. John Macquarrie and Edward Robinson. New York: Harper, 1962.

Hühn, Peter. "The Detective as Reader: Narrativity and Reading Concepts in Detective Fiction." *Modern Fiction Studies* 33 (1987): 451–66.

Lavender, William. "The Novel of Critical Engagement: Paul Auster's *City of Glass.*" *Contemporary Literature* 34, 3 (1993): 219–39.

Nealon, Jeffrey T. "The Discipline of Deconstruction." *PMLA* 107, 5 (1992): 1266–79.

Poe, Edgar Allan. "William Wilson." [1839]. *Collected Works of Edgar Allan Poe*, ed. Thomas Ollive Mabbott. 3 vols. Cambridge, Mass.: Harvard University Press, 1978. 2: 422–51.

Porter, Dennis. "Backward Construction and the Art of Suspense." In *The Poetics of Murder: Detective Fiction and Literary Theory*, ed. Glenn W. Most and William Stowe. New York: Harcourt, 1983. 327–40.

Pynchon, Thomas. *The Crying of Lot 49.* [1966]. New York: Harper, 1986.

Russell, Alison. "Deconstructing *The New York Trilogy*: Paul Auster's Anti-Detective Fiction." *Critique* 31, 2 (1990): 71–84.

Spanos, William V. "The Detective and the Boundary: Some Notes on the Postmodern Literary Imagination." *Boundary 2* 1, 1 (1972): 147–60. Reprinted in *Repetitions: The Postmodern Occasion in Literature and Culture.* Baton Rouge: Lousiana State University Press, 1987. 13–50.

Chapter 6
"The Question Is the Story Itself"
Postmodernism and Intertextuality in Auster's
New York Trilogy

Stephen Bernstein

> Traces of the letters are still discernable; but the writer's many ef-
> forts could never discover a connected meaning.
> —Nathaniel Hawthorne, *Fanshawe* (108)

> If there may not be no more questions let there at least be no more
> answers.
> —Samuel Beckett, *Ill Seen Ill Said* (43)

Paul Auster's *New York Trilogy* of metaphysical detective novels— *City of
Glass* (1985), *Ghosts* (1986), and *The Locked Room* (1986)[1]—clearly fulfills
Fredric Jameson's definition of those "postmodernisms" that are "fascinated precisely by this whole 'degraded' landscape of schlock and kitsch
. . . of so-called paraliterature with its airport paperback categories of
the gothic and the romance, the popular biography, the murder mystery and science-fiction or fantasy novel: materials they no longer simply
'quote'. . . but incorporate into their very substance" (55). This fascination ultimately confirms Tzvetan Todorov's comment that "at a certain
point detective fiction experiences as an unjustified burden the constraints of this or that genre and gets rid of them in order to constitute
a new code" (52). Thus in numerous ways Auster's trilogy attempts to
sever its ties with all but the exoskeletal form of detective fiction. The
closural epistemological certainty that long characterized the genre is
just one code dispensed with as Auster places his mystery novels within
several other important textual traditions. By deftly mixing the American Renaissance's literature of darkness with the postmodern instability

and fragmentation of Samuel Beckett's trilogy *Molloy* (1951), *Malone Dies* (1951), and *The Unnamable* (1953)—a trio Auster has called "masterpieces" (*Hunger* 50)—he raises his detective fiction to the metaphysical level.

Auster manipulates intertextuality in two ways. Compositionally, intertextuality works as a way of constructing new texts, as when we are told of Daniel Quinn, the mystery writer of *City of Glass*, that "Whatever he knew about [crime], he had learned from books, films, and newspapers. . . . What interested him about the stories he wrote was not their relation to the world but their relation to other stories" (8). Psychologically, Auster foregrounds intertextuality as a determinant of existence and experience, as when Blue, the detective protagonist of *Ghosts*, thinks: "This is strange enough—to be only half alive at best, seeing the world only through words, living only through the lives of others" (202).

This dual conception of intertextuality informs the trilogy's version of detection, which (through the isolation central to the stakeout or the search) focuses the detective's attention on the intensely problematic nature of unitary subjectivity. At the same time, Auster poses such a slippage as the condition of the novel itself, so that these novels become more like works of literary criticism than fictional depictions of crime and detection. Hence the metafictional intrusions of authorial figures in all three works: an exploding system of *Doppelgängers* finally collapses into a number of closural scenes of reading, with reader-writer confrontations that manifest textual instability. The trilogy ultimately dramatizes detection as an unworkable confrontation with a reality whose dubious significance cannot be credibly decoded.

Indeed, Auster frames the trilogy with comments that cast doubt on the project of detection. The first paragraph of *City of Glass* offers the caveat, "The question is the story itself, and whether or not it means something is not for the story to tell" (3), while late in *The Locked Room* the anonymous narrator (seemingly a version of Auster himself) announces:

The entire story comes down to what happened at the end, and without that end inside me now, I could not have started this book. The same holds for the two books that come before it, *City of Glass* and *Ghosts*. These three stories are finally the same story, but each one represents a different stage in my awareness of what it is about. I don't claim to have solved any problems. . . . I have been struggling to say goodbye to something for a long time now, and this struggle is all that really matters. The story is not in the words; it's in the struggle. (346)

These statements pose the trilogy's central question: whether meaning inheres in the details and clues traditional to the detective genre, or whether meaning is itself a quixotic dream akin to the novels' other recursions to Cervantes. The first quote warns the reader that this story abdicates any responsibility to clarify meaning; the second baldly states that whatever story actually exists is more agonistic than linguistic. Such remarks initially place Auster's reader in a role similar to that of the detectives themselves: we search for clues to some pattern of meaning, but the text under our scrutiny (like the New York of the trilogy) rigorously resists any such hermeneutic recuperation.[2] By examining several of the trilogy's intertexts, we can better see from what nexus Auster's texts communicate if not that of the traditional detective novel. The trilogy, in this light, is "meta-" detective fiction: the case which it actually poses for the reader is ultimately unlike the cases of its individual novels, with their collective culmination in ambiguity and instability rather than knowledge. As a metaphysician, Auster takes the ironic byway, pointing to the fragmentation of the subject through what turns out to be strikingly cohesive fiction. In order to understand how Auster's commentary is constructed, we will first examine how he posits postmodernist experience as a textual issue, and then how he implicates the resultant textuality in an intertextual relationship with *Don Quixote*. We can then probe the interrelationships of Auster's metafictionality with the classic texts of the American Renaissance and Samuel Beckett, until Auster's goal—the refutation of meaning through meaning—becomes abundantly clear.

From *City of Glass* to *City of Words*

Reality's surface, so resistant to interpretation, is figured in the trilogy through references to glass and mirrors. In *Ghosts* the narrator etymologizes Blue's habit of "speculation": "To speculate, from the Latin speculatus, meaning to spy out, to observe, and linked to the word speculum, meaning mirror or looking glass" (171–72). The trilogy portrays detection itself as a look in the mirror, any gaze outward becoming instead a focused inwardness. At the same time, the "looking glass" reference brings to mind the work of Lewis Carroll and sets the stage for the trilogy's mirror games and logic problems. New York, the city of glass, presents many reflections and problematizes the understanding of depths; the novels' protagonists are never sure whether anything actually exists behind the mirror, through the looking glass.

Quinn spends a good deal of time "watching the glass door" of the hotel where *City of Glass*'s Peter Stillman Sr. (who speaks admiringly of Carroll's Humpty Dumpty as linguistic theorist) is staying (71); the mystery, however, lurks uncomprehended within and eventually vanishes under Quinn's nose. After Stillman's disappearance Quinn suffers a breakdown, living in the streets for months, finally seeing his reflection in a storefront: "He had no feeling about it at all, for the fact was that he did not recognize the person he saw there as himself" (142). This is the greatest and most constant threat which detection holds in the trilogy, the promise that too long a consideration of pointless clues, too intense a search for an impossible coherence, finally unhinges the stability of personality. As Blue thinks early in *Ghosts*, "I'm changing. . . . Little by little I'm no longer the same" (173–74). This emphasis on the metaphysical consequences of detection highlights the problematic of postmodern subjectivity, wherein "the subject has lost its capacity actively to extend its pro-tensions and re-tensions across the temporal manifold, and to organize its past and future into coherent experience" (Jameson 71). Auster's detectives devolve into fragmentation and madness precisely because they can make no holistic response (whether as a model of past, present, or future) to a reality that has no coherent structure.

Detectives respond through reports; speech and writing are central to *City of Glass*'s surface/depth and subjectivity problems. Alison Russell sees the novel's quest as a "search for transparent language" (72). Stillman, Quinn reflects at his disappearance, "was gone now. The old man had become part of the city. He was a speck, a punctuation mark" (109)—a metaphor which suggests that the city is a text. Auster's subject, then, is not unlike what the critic Tony Tanner terms the "city of words," a place inhabited by "a general self-consciousness about the strange relationship between the provinces of words and things, and the problematical position of man, who participates in both" (21). The writing protagonists of Auster's trilogy clearly live in such a place: although Fanshawe achieves a level of artistic prowess characterized by "a new availability of words inside him, as though the distance between seeing and writing had been narrowed, the two acts now almost identical, part of a single, unbroken gesture" (*LR* 326); although Blue's method of composing reports "is to stick to outward facts, describing events as though each word tallied exactly with the thing described" (*G* 174); and although Quinn reaches a point where he can "divide his attention almost equally between Stillman and his writing, glancing up now at the one, now down at the other, seeing the thing and writing about it in the same fluid gesture" (*CG* 76–77)—such correspondence eventually gives way, nevertheless, to an intense subject/object confusion. This breakdown gives rise in turn to the contemporary literary preoccupation with "an abiding dream . . . that an unpatterned, unconditioned life is possible, in which your movements are all your own; and . . . an abiding American dread that someone else is patterning your life, that there are all sorts of invisible plots afoot to rob you of your autonomy of thought and action, that conditioning is ubiquitous" (Tanner 15). When language no longer describes outer reality, that is, reality itself becomes a battleground of differing interpretations—and freedom may be as illusory a concept as any of the others occluded by linguistic expression.

While Thomas Pynchon articulates such paranoia most astutely, Auster's works are not without a similar anxiety. Detective fiction is fertile ground for interpretive anxiety, as it offers a generic expectation that patterns *do* cohere behind the confusing surface of reality, and that there exists a specialized group, detectives, who can read them. The detective, argues Patrick Brantlinger, "expresses a wish fulfillment shared by all of us, to be able to know or to read just a few things very well, like clues, but through reading them very well to penetrate the deepest mysteries of life" (17). We see such a conviction in Quinn, who "always imagined that the key to good detective work was a close observation of details. . . . The implication was that human behavior could be understood, that beneath the infinite facade of gestures, tics, and silences, there was finally a coherence, an order, a source of motivation" (*CG* 80).

Detective fiction—and its concern with reading social detail—arose at the time of massive urban growth in the nineteenth century; as Walter Benjamin remarks, "The original content of the detective story was the obliteration of the individual's traces in the big-city crowd" (43). The title of Auster's trilogy signifies his entry into the urban-detective generic tradition, but the entry is subversive: his trilogy consistently defers the expectation that the city can be read, or the individual recovered from the crowd. As Julian Hurtsfield notes, Auster's "particular concern is that staple of detective fiction, the missing person. But his narrators and his detectives do not discover very much, except how little they know about themselves" (176). Auster's urban milieu also resembles Jameson's conception of "postmodern hyperspace," that site which shows up "the incapacity of our minds, at least at present, to map the great global multinational and decentered communicational network in which we find ourselves caught as individual subjects" (84). A meaningful totality, urban or global, is impossible to grasp; when Quinn suspects that Stillman's walking routes through New York might be patterned after letters of the alphabet, they seem to spell out "THE TOWER OF BABEL" (*CG* 85)—yet another suggestion of the fragmentation, the unrecoverability, of reality as text.

In *The Invention of Solitude* (1982), a book of memoirs that precedes the trilogy, Auster meditates on the possibilities that meaning may inhere in reality. Considering a number of surprising coincidences in his life, Auster (writing about himself in the third person as "A.") concludes that there is a

temptation to look at the world as though it were an extension of the imaginary. . . . Like everyone else, he craves a meaning. Like everyone else, his life is
so fragmented that each time he sees a connection between two fragments he
is tempted to look for a meaning in that connection. The connection exists. But
to give it a meaning, to look beyond the bare fact of its existence, would be to
build an imaginary world inside the real world, and he knows it would not stand.
At his bravest moments, he embraces meaninglessness as the first principle. . . .
There is the world, and the things one encounters in the world, and to speak of
them is to be in the world. . . . It means only what it is. (148–49)

This is the governing hermeneutic philosophy of the trilogy; or rather,
the trilogy utilizes such a philosophy to refute hermeneutics. The literary embodiment of this metaphysical dilemma is *Don Quixote*, called
by Auster "consciousness gone haywire in a realm of the imaginary" (*IS*
148)—a good model for the problems of Auster's protagonists in the
trilogy. Their "haywire consciousnesses" result from attempts to create
imaginary models that might describe reality. Once this situation begins,
it proceeds inevitably until each protagonist breaks down completely.
"Something happens, Blue thinks, and then it goes on happening forever" (*G* 193): the hall of mirrors is the analogue of the self-generating
cycles of false hypotheses which destroy each of Auster's detectives.

Quixote and the *Doppelgänger*

The reference to *Don Quixote* is essential, because that is a central metafictional intertext in the trilogy. Not only does the narrator of *The Locked
Room* consider himself "an adolescent Sancho astride my donkey" to
Fanshawe's Quixote (254), but the plot of *City of Glass* is significantly
motivated by several references to Cervantes's novel of quests gone mad.
The Auster Detective Agency is recommended to Virginia Stillman by
a retired policeman, Michael Saavedra (35); Quinn ponders late in the
novel "why Don Quixote had not simply wanted to write books like the
ones he loved—instead of living out their adventures . . . [and] why he
had the same initials as Don Quixote" (155). The answer to these questions appears earlier in the novel, when a woman in Grand Central Station reading one of his novels tells Quinn that "there's a part where the
detective gets lost that's kind of scary," a textual analogy to Quinn's fate
which nevertheless fails to keep him from "nurturing the chivalric hope
of solving the case . . . brilliantly" (65, 77).

The most important of the *Quixote* references, however, is Quinn's
metafictional discussion with "Paul Auster" in chapter 10, which focuses
not on the quest romance but on the fiction/reality paradox. "Auster"
theorizes that Cervantes's novel is actually narrated by Sancho, put in

literary form by the barber and the priest—just as Stillman Sr.'s depre-
dations on his son are narrativized as testimony by a Miss Barber (*CG*
31)—translated into Arabic by Samson Carrasco, and then translated
back into Spanish by Quixote himself. As Russell points out, "This analysis, when applied to *City of Glass*, raises a number of questions about the
book's authorship, and results in endless doublings and mirror images,"
with Quinn "a paper-Auster" (74, 73).

"Auster's" *Quixote* theory does indeed suggest Quinn as Auster's double. "Auster" states that "In some sense, Don Quixote was just a stand-in
for [Cervantes] himself"; as Stillman Sr. asks when he hears the detective's name, "Rhymes with twin, does it not?" (117, 89). Quinn is the
only witness to all of the novel's events, which he writes down in a red
notebook so that at certain points there are "two or even three lines
on top of each other, producing a jumbled, illegible palimpsest" (76).
This manuscript is prepared for publication by the narrator who, toward
the end of the novel, relates "Auster"'s account of Quinn's involvement
with him, and his inability to track him down. "Somehow," the narrator
states, "I had an intuition . . . where Quinn had wound up"; Quinn, he
decides on the next page, "will be with me always" (157, 158). Indication of this doubling relationship actually appears much earlier in *City of
Glass*, when we are told that Quinn's pseudonym is "William Wilson" (we
might remember that both of Poe's Wilsons share their author's birthday of January 19 [Poe 342]). As Russell suggests, doubles are pervasive
in Auster's novels; not only can we see Quinn as a version of the narrator
of *City of Glass*, who must be, in realistic terms, a version of Paul Auster,
but numerous other possibilities emerge throughout the trilogy.

At the end of *The Locked Room* the narrator reads a red notebook that
has been written for him by Fanshawe, the figure he has sought throughout the latter part of the narrative. About this piece of writing we are
told that "Each sentence erased the sentence before it, each paragraph
made the next paragraph impossible. . . . I came to the last page just as
the train was pulling out" (370–71). Not only does this scene of notebook reading link the narrators of *City of Glass* and *The Locked Room*, it
also ties the ending of the latter novel to a scene early in the former,
in which Quinn begins writing in *his* notebook after Stillman Sr.'s train
pulls *into* Grand Central Station (68). The notebook thus seems to be
the entire *New York Trilogy* (between *City of Glass* and *The Locked Room* it
expands from one hundred to two hundred pages in length); but, as we
will see below, its recurrence produces a hermeneutic problem like that
experienced by *The Locked Room*'s narrator.

Ghosts raises similar problems of metafictional self-reflexivity. Late in
the novel Blue goes to the apartment of Black, the man he has been
hired by White to watch; Black answers "with an uncapped fountain pen

in his right hand, as though interrupted in his work" (218), a description related to one in *City of Glass*, where "Auster" comes to the door when Quinn calls on him: "In his right hand, fixed between his thumb and first two fingers, he held an uncapped fountain pen, still poised in a writing position" (111). Auster further identifies Black as himself through setting. Black's "austere" apartment (219) registers through its onomastic pun the starkness of the showdown between writer and character. Both scenes, significantly, find their author figures in the act of writing; they reflect a textual incompleteness which Auster's narratives only efface at the moment of closure when, in each novel, someone reads the writing that has amassed during the course of the narrative.[3]

Other relationships among the three novels are significant at this point. One arises through the fact that both Fanshawe and Stillman Sr. are nicknamed "the Professor" (*LR* 321, *CG* 106), which in turn recalls the protoanarchist bomb expert of Conrad's *The Secret Agent*, who, at the close of that dead-end detective story (a novel concerned more with the metaphysics of entropy than with crime-solving), disappears threateningly into the London crowd. But another, more important, parallel occurs through the appearances of the character Peter Stillman Jr. In *City of Glass* he is Quinn's tormented employer, a man locked in a dark room by his father between the ages of two and eleven. In the year in which the novel is set, 1982, Peter is twenty-four. "Everything about Peter Stillman was white," we are told at his first appearance (17); during his odd and rambling monologue he tells Quinn that "In the winter I am Mr. White" (21). This would appear to connect Peter Stillman Jr. with White in *Ghosts*, a disguised man who hires Blue in February 1947 (162).[4] Peter Stillman also reappears in *The Locked Room*, where the narrator describes him in Paris, in 1979, as "obviously American . . . tall, athletically built, with sandy hair and an open, somewhat boyish manner. I guessed his age at twenty-six or twenty-seven. . . . I had never seen this man before, and yet there was something familiar about him" (347–48). Not only does the age of this Peter Stillman pose a problem; his athletic build is equally incommensurate with the character in *City of Glass*, who moves in a way "machine-like, fitful, alternating between slow and rapid gestures, rigid and yet expressive, as if the operation were out of control, not quite corresponding to the will that lay behind it" (17). Of course it is possible that Peter Stillman Jr. is one of the trilogy's numerous disguise artists—White; Blue, who is "no amateur in the art of disguise" (*G* 162); Quixote, whom "Auster" describes as one "skilled in the art of disguise" (*CG* 119); or Fanshawe, who claims, "I think I'm unrecognizable" (*LR* 365)—but the confusion here suggests a more complex point. It is one of many odd onomastic interrelationships that problematize the traditional mode of realistic reading, which would see the novels not only as in some sense reflections of reality, but also as connected works giving unified, consistent meaning to such signifiers as proper names. There are many other examples of this phenomenon. In *Ghosts*, White also appears to be Black; when Blue and Black meet undisguised they drink "Black and White on the rocks" (212). Their relationship not only points out the illogic of this fictional universe (where black is white) but alludes also to the mixture of the colors, Gray (a missing person in one of Blue's earlier cases [166], and a reference to another work of doubling and aesthetic reflection, Wilde's *Picture of Dorian Gray*), and to writing itself: Blue's reports are "spelled out in black and white" (*G* 224), while Quinn is told by the clerk at the Hotel Harmony that Stillman Sr.'s checkout is "down here in black and white" (*CG* 106). Fanshawe states that he is using the alias of "Henry Dark" (*LR* 366), a figure invented by *City of Glass*'s Stillman Sr. to put forward his own insane linguistic theories, and adopted by Quinn during a discussion with him (95; Quinn later uses the name Peter Stillman). Fanshawe speaks of crossing paths with Quinn (who is hired by Fanshawe's wife Sophie to find him), and claims "I scared him to death. . . . He thought he was following me, but in fact I was following him" (362). Yet the entire action of *The Locked Room* transpires before that of *City of Glass*, so either this is a different Quinn (the Quinn of *City* has never before taken a case), or yet another reminder that this universe has no realistic connecting logic. Like the narrative of Fanshawe's notebook, the elements here seem "to have been put together strangely, as though their final purpose was to cancel each other out" (*LR* 370). And Fanshawe's notebook, we should recall, is recovered and read on April Fool's Day (*LR* 356).

Auster further blurs the boundaries of characterization and fictiveness by peppering the trilogy with autobiographical information. This data appears furtively in all the novels, and seems to be governed less by a structural plan than by a metafictional aesthetic which requires that characters double not only one another, but the author as well. *City of Glass* finds Quinn walking by 6 Varick Street, "where he had once lived" (127); this is the address at which Auster writes one of the memoirs in *Invention*. Quinn's parents' anniversary (11) appears from further information in the memoirs to be that of Auster's parents, just as the date on which *Ghosts* begins—February 3, 1947—is Auster's birthday. The narrator of *The Locked Room* and Fanshawe share birthdays in February 1947, and both have significantly parallel careers with Auster: the narrator as census worker, critic, and translator; Fanshawe as merchant seaman, poet, Parisian screenwriter and ghostwriter, and brother to a schizophrenic sister. A Dr. Wyshnegradsky in *City of Glass* (26) has become Ivan Wyshnegradsky, an aging Russian composer, in *The Locked Room* (332); the latter has his analogue as "S." in the memoirs (140). Fanshawe inherits an overcoat from a suicide who lived in a sixth floor maid's room in Paris (*LR* 325); the memoirs identify this apartment as Auster's (63). Finally, *The Locked Room*'s film producer lives in a "monumental apartment on the Avenue Henri Martin" (340), and it is to just such an address, to see just such a man, that Auster and his father go in *Invention* (64). The importance of such niggling points should be clear: the characters of the trilogy collapse into one another through their own labyrinthine (but illogical) interrelationships and then, finally, into multiple images of the author himself. The interior space of the novels becomes the locked room of the psyche: as the narrator of *The Locked Room* says of Fanshawe, "From the moment his letter arrived, I had been struggling to imagine him, to see him as he might have been—but my mind had always conjured a blank. At best, there was one impoverished image: the door of a locked room. That was the extent of it: Fanshawe alone in that room, condemned to a mythical solitude—living perhaps, breathing perhaps, dreaming God knows what. This room, I now discovered, was located inside my skull" (344–45). This locked room, then, must be considered as the epistemological and textual terminus of the city of glass.[5]

Thresholds and Locked Rooms

Like other themes in the trilogy, psychic isolation is foregrounded through a system of intertextual references. The idea of the room or house as a model for the mind is an old one, but Auster looks to nineteenth-century American literature for his preferred versions. Thoreau's *Walden* (1847), for example, compares the cabin to the self, demonstrating how psychic changes can be mirrored through setting, so that "Though the view from my door was still more contracted I did not feel crowded or confined in the least. There was pasture enough for my imagination. . . . I dwelt nearer to those parts of the universe and to those eras in history which had most attracted me" (392). It is *Walden*, then, that Blue begins to read in *Ghosts*, and about which the narrator comments: "What he does not know is that were he to find the patience to read the book in the spirit in which it asks to be read, his entire life would begin to change, and little by little he would come to a full understanding of his situation—that is to say, of Black, of White, of the case, of everything that concerns him" (194). Blue does not find this patience, however, and therefore never learns that Thoreau was, in Auster's words, "exiling himself in order to find out where he was" (*IS* 16). All the trilogy's locked rooms bear a similar meaning, whether they echo Thoreau's cabin or something more sinister—the mazelike school where Poe's "William Wilson" first encounters his double. They are places where the deepest understanding of the self is possible, but where one might just as easily (or as a result) slip beyond unitary subjectivity entirely.

This last observation brings up the relevance of a passage from Hawthorne's "Wakefield," a work that Black mentions in *Ghosts* (209–10). "Amid the seeming confusion of our mysterious world," Hawthorne writes, "individuals are so nicely adjusted to a system, and systems to one another, and to a whole, that, by stepping aside for a moment, a man exposes himself to a fearful risk of losing his place forever" (298). "Wakefield" not only suggests that abandoning the reliable quotidian systems of life may make one "the Outcast of the Universe" (298), as happens with several characters in the trilogy, but it also points out the impossibility of traversing certain thresholds. This impossibility is underlined in Black's account of the tale in a conversation with Blue:

> And so, without giving it any more thought than that, he walks up the steps of the house and knocks on the door.
> And then?
> That's it. That's the end of the story. The last thing we see is the door opening and Wakefield going inside with a crafty smile on his face.
> And we never know what he says to his wife?
> No. That's the end. Not another word. But he moved in again, we know that much, and remained a loving spouse until death. (209–10)

This less than thorough account of Hawthorne's ending exemplifies the closure of each novel in the trilogy: *City of Glass* ends with Quinn leaving the Stillmans' old apartment, having crossed a threshold beyond which he cannot be found; *Ghosts* closes on Blue (who, through his case, has effected a Wakefield-like disappearance from his fiancée) walking out of Black's apartment as the narrator comments, "When Blue stands up from his chair, puts on his hat, and walks through the door, that will be the end of it" (232); and *The Locked Room* focuses on its eponymous setting, one into which the narrator is forbidden entry. Hawthorne, again, provides a model for these scenes. At the close of "Wakefield" the narrator announces that "We will not follow our friend across the threshold" (298).

It is significant that Tanner sees in "Wakefield" a model for the larger problematic that he discusses in *City of Words*. "Both tale and moral," he finds, "are profoundly American. The feeling that society is an arbitrary system or fiction which one might simply step out of is one which still motivates a large number of American heroes. Outside all systems and fictions, freedom and reality may yet be found. At the same time, there has always been the concomitant dread that 'by stepping aside for a moment,' one might simply step into a void" (30). Auster follows Tanner's lead in reading "Wakefield" as a master narrative for the experience of solitude and darkness surrounding individual subjectivity. "What sort of man was Wakefield?" Hawthorne's narrator asks on the second page of his story (thus originating his own project of metaphysical detection), and answers: "We are free to shape out our own idea, and call it by his name" (291). This freedom to rewrite what the narrator reports as a story from "some old magazine or newspaper . . . told as truth" (290) again redounds onto Auster's narrative, with its convoluted problematizing of the relationships among fictional works and between fiction and reality.

Auster further exploits Hawthorne, as a psychologically investigative precursor, by alluding to his early novel *Fanshawe*. The central but unseen character of *The Locked Room*, Fanshawe (neither has a first name), echoes his fictional forebear's qualities. Hawthorne's figure is one who

was possessed of a face and form, such as Nature bestows on none but her favorites . . . all his features were formed with a strength and boldness, of which the paleness, produced by study and confinement, could not deprive them. The expression of his countenance . . . was proud and high—perhaps triumphant—like one who was a ruler in a world of his own, and independent of the beings that surrounded him. But a blight, of which his thin, pale cheek and the brightness of his eye were alike proofs, seemed to have come over him ere his maturity. (15)

Similarly, Auster's Fanshawe

stood apart from us, and yet he was the one who held us together, the one we approached to arbitrate our disputes, the one we could count on to be fair and to cut through our petty quarrels. There was something so attractive about him that you always wanted him beside you, as if you could live within his sphere and be touched by what he was. He was there for you, and yet at the same time he was inaccessible. You felt there was a secret core in him that could never be penetrated, a mysterious center of hiddenness. (248)

Hawthorne's novel provides the hero, then, and a hero who features a locked room of sorts at the center of his existence. Just as the motives and desires of Hawthorne's character are never fully understood, just as he "seemed, to others and to himself, a solitary being upon whom the hopes and fears of ordinary men were ineffectual" (18), so does Auster's Fanshawe remain an enigma—"haunt[ing] the edges of things . . . shunning the spotlight for a stubborn marginality" (253, 255)—whose central purpose is to provide a pretext for other characters' actions. Hawthorne's Fanshawe refuses his claim on the affections of Ellen Langton, who eventually marries the rival Edward Walcott; Auster's character similarly deserts his marriage (à la Wakefield), leaving behind manuscripts and directions for literary executorship. "That was my excuse," he says to the narrator; "My real reason was to find a new husband for her" (364). Hawthorne's texts thus invade Auster's to the degree that they structure character and plot, focusing Auster's concerns in a way similar to Hawthorne's. Melville wrote of the earlier writer that a "black conceit pervades him, through and through" ("Hawthorne" 2060), and we might agree that such a conceit pervades Auster also. It is the blackness of the locked rooms that exist throughout the trilogy, locked rooms that are never merely architectural facts, but always psychological oubliettes, prisons of metaphysical gloom.

As noted above, black and white in the universe of the trilogy are interconnected in such a way as to exist in a strangely illogical gray area. Thus the letters that Stillman's walks might be outlining, in *City of Glass*, remind Quinn of "the concluding pages of *A. Gordon Pym* and . . . the discovery of the strange hieroglyphs on the inner wall of the chasm" (85). The letters in Poe's work, of course, are initially thought by Pym to be devoid of meaning, but are interpreted by the editor as denoting " 'To be shady'—whence all the inflections of shadow and darkness," and " 'To be white,' whence all the inflections of brilliancy and whiteness" (1181). John T. Irwin has shown that Poe draws on actual hieroglyphic forms, and confuses their points of origin, in an attempt to combine "the journey to the Abyssinian source of the Nile and the voyage to the polar abyss as reciprocal quests for the linguistic origin of the self" (200). Again, in other words, Auster's subtly planted intertextual clue yields another metaphysical detective story, revealing in turn Auster's own elusive formulation. Although to Quinn "on second thought this [comparison to *Pym*] did not seem apt" (85), it becomes remarkably apt to Auster's reader, who sees how this allusion, like numerous others, penetrates the very surface that Auster's protagonists cannot. Auster's detectives, however, can find no such apposite supplement to their reading projects.

The blending of light and dark is also important to Auster in other ways. As Ishmael remarks of the color white in *Moby-Dick*,

there yet lurks an elusive something in the innermost idea of this hue, which strikes more of panic to the soul than that redness which affrights the blood. This elusive quality it is, which causes the thought of whiteness, when divorced from more kindly associations, and coupled with any object terrible in itself, to heighten that terror to the furthest bounds. (185)

Is it by its indefiniteness it shadows forth the heartless voids and immensities of the universe, and thus stabs us from behind with the thought of annihilation, when beholding the white depths of the milky way? . . . pondering all this, the palsied universe lies before us a leper. (192)

The universe of the trilogy is similarly palsied, as Auster shows that white and black, light and darkness, are at bottom the same. Thus Peter Stillman Jr., who calls himself "Mr. White," and White himself motivate investigations which in truth only thrust the detective further into the depths of personal darkness. "Henry Dark" in *City of Glass* and *The Locked Room*, and "Black" in *Ghosts*, heighten the overwhelming presence of darkness around these characters, a darkness that intensifies, rather than dissipates, upon illumination. "I clung to the doorknob for support, my head going black inside," the narrator of *The Locked Room* says after his meeting with Fanshawe (369); similarly, Blue, "the moment he sets foot in Black's room, . . . feels everything go dark inside him" (*G* 223). One of Fanshawe's ostensibly posthumous works is entitled *Blackouts*, a nice metaphor for the displacement of consciousness by an oppressive epistemological darkness at the center of each of the trilogy's novels. "There is something nice about being in the dark," Blue decides early on in *Ghosts*, in a pun that links epistemological clarity and illumination while rejecting both; there is "something thrilling about not knowing what is going to happen next" (182).

The thrill of ignorance is always replaced by the *frisson* of occlusion for Auster's characters, however, and this enveloping anxiety in the various narratives finally surrounds, as it emanates from, the locked rooms. The detective's necessary isolation undoes these characters; unlike Thoreau, they cannot see seclusion as a route to self-knowledge. Instead, although solitude becomes, as the narrator of *The Locked Room* terms it, "a passageway into the self, an instrument of discovery" (327) for each of them, it is not a discovery they wish to make, and it is never a salutary or liberating one. The problem which emerges, as stated regarding Blue, is "How to get out of the room that is the book that will go on being written for as long as he stays in the room" (*G* 202).

In Auster's trilogy, the "inexhaustible space" of New York City (*CG* 4)—described early in each novel as a place for wide-ranging walks, a place where Blue considers himself "essentially free" (*G* 200)—collapses, like so many of the other standard categories of realistic fiction, into the narrow space of the individual mind. As Jean-François Lyotard argues, in postmodernism "the grand narrative has lost its credibility, regardless of what mode of unification it uses" (37). That all individuals in these novels can be viewed as versions of the author thus becomes of central importance. Russell terms the trilogy "the selves of Paul Auster" (79); its reader, like its detectives, finally arrives at the locked room of Auster's mind, a place where the author, like Blue, has discovered that "More than just helping to pass the time . . . making up stories can be a pleasure in itself" (*G* 172).

At the close the reader, like the narrator of the final novel, is outside the writer's locked room, a room which, the trilogy now completed, affords no passage whatsoever over its threshold. Although the classic "locked-room" detective story poses "the puzzle of a dead body found in a room which seems to be effectively sealed" (Symons 36), Auster is not interested in such problems or their solutions. The result is that his trilogy—for all its self-conscious immersion in nineteenth-century American literature, in *Don Quixote*, and in literary theory—is tied more strongly to its postmodernist predecessor, Samuel Beckett's trilogy *Molloy*, *Malone Dies*, and *The Unnamable*, than to any other of its numerous intertexts.

"I can't go on, I'll go on."

Arthur Saltzman points to the fact that "the absurd dance of detective and detected in *City of Glass* parallels that of Beckett's *Molloy*" (59), but in a broader sense Beckett's trilogy provides an excellent model for the literary text as the wandering ruminations of the intensely limited psyche. Nowhere is there a better example of this narrative approach for Auster to appropriate than that of Malone, who decides, early in his tale, "I shall not answer any more questions. I shall even try not to ask myself any more. While waiting I shall tell myself stories, if I can. They will not be the same kind of stories as hitherto, that is all. They will be neither beautiful nor ugly, they will be calm, there will be no ugliness or beauty or fever in them any more, they will be almost lifeless, like the teller" (180). These stories are recorded, Malone goes on to relate, in a "thick exercise-book": "It is ruled in squares. The first pages are covered with ciphers and other symbols and diagrams, with here and there a brief phrase. Calculations, I reckon. They seem to stop suddenly, prematurely at all events. As though discouraged" (209). It is from such a strategy—and scene—of writing that Auster's trilogy is ultimately generated. There is, as in Beckett, an obsessive concern with where the story is located: on what paper, in what room, at what point in literary history. There is the same focus on breakdown, on the insufficiency of a name or comparable linguistic icon in the struggle to delineate the personality: Fanshawe screams, "Not Fanshawe—ever again!" to an unnamed narrator only a few pages from the end of Auster's trilogy (*LR* 361), just as Beckett ends his with a novel named for—and narrated by—the "unnamable." And there is the self-negating nature of the entire project: Fanshawe's text, the elements of which "cancel each other out" (*LR* 370); Blue's conclusion that "what happened is not really what happened" (*G* 176); Quinn's lying assertion that he is "Paul Auster," because "anything else, even the truth, would be an invention" (*CG* 89)—such remarks extend Beckett's closural strategy in *Molloy* ("Then I went back into the house and wrote, It is midnight. The rain is beating on the windows. It was not midnight. It was not raining" [176]) and *The Unnamable* (". . . I can't go on, I'll go on" [414]). Such commitment to Beckett's strategies may be signaled in Quinn's deliberations about fate: "It was something like the word 'it' in the phrase 'it is raining' or 'it is night' " (*CG* 133); indeed, Beckett mentions characters named "Quin" in *Malone Dies* and in *Mercier and Camier*.[6]

As Saltzman notes, Beckett's trilogy also provides Auster with a specific model of the metaphysical detective genre, *Molloy*. In that novel Moran, the second narrator, comments that once he has been charged to find Molloy, "the color and weight of the world were changing already;" "soon," he continues, "I would have to admit I was anxious" (96). By the novel's end, Moran—who, like Auster's detectives, never fully closes in on his quarry—states that "physically speaking it seemed to me I was now becoming rapidly unrecognizable" (170), demonstrating the outward manifestation of inner dissolution so common to Auster's central figures. Auster has written of Beckett, "the movement in each of his works is toward a kind of unburdening, by which he leads us to the limits of experience" (*Hunger* 53); set down ten years before *City of Glass*, these words have obvious application to the later trilogy. The issue of the *Doppelgänger* is here for Auster's attentive eye as well, since it is never entirely clear whether Molloy and Moran are separate entities, or another of what the unnamable terms "pseudocouples" (297), or á confirmation of Hugh Kenner's speculation that perhaps "a Molloy is simply what a Moran turns into when he goes looking for a Molloy" (65)—just as a Stillman seems to be what a Quinn turns into when he goes looking for a Stillman in *City of Glass*. In the course of *The Unnamable* it becomes possible to see all the narrators of the trilogy as various forms of Beckett himself. Thus *Molloy*, and Beckett's trilogy in general, may provide the clearest formal model for what Auster attempts in his own trilogy. Auster also adopts (and adapts) Beckett's postmodernist tonality, however, with the result that his trilogy amounts to nothing less than a wholesale revision of Beckett's.

With the trilogy viewed as such a revision, not only does Auster infuse his American tradition with a distinctly European angst but, as a result, he takes a step past towering precursors such as Poe, Melville, and Hawthorne. He reiterates the metaphysical darkness that these writers so rigorously confirm at the heart of subjectivity, but makes it even blacker through allegiance to Beckett's relentless depiction of the lone psyche, isolated in the darkness, telling itself stories because narration is all that is left, and because (despite narrative's fictiveness) the refusal to narrate would be monstrous. If Thoreau's form of isolation is one which can help locate the individual, then Beckett's presence in Auster's fiction shows that such spirited, individualistic self-improvement is no longer possible, and that this location, this locked room, is the site of a blank interiority.

Detection in Auster's work is, through the trilogy's immense intertextual debt, cleansed of hermeneutic promise. Quinn tries, perhaps too successfully, to reason like Poe's Dupin, but questions the efficacy of such a strategy (*CG* 48); "I'm not the Sherlock Holmes type," Blue says quite early in *Ghosts* (166); and *The Locked Room*'s narrator winds up "feeling like a down-and-out private eye, a buffoon clutching at straws" (343).[7] These characters intuit the trilogy's insistent premises: that reality is not the storehouse of signification that literature is, that coherent patterns of meaning do not leap out from beneath quotidian surfaces, and that too persistent a search for such patterns ends in the dissolution of a centered, socially interactive, "logical" personality.

Yet Auster's novels *are* literary, so that as a writer he is able finally to utilize the very repository of hermeneutic plenitude that he repeatedly demonstrates as unworkable. The pursuit of the intertextual clues woven into the fabric of the trilogy does yield a coherent pattern—even if that very pattern insists even more strenuously, through its unique mixture of a brooding nineteenth-century American pessimism and a brooding postmodernist French solipsism, that looking for meanings is, and will remain, a fool's errand. Auster emerges, like the Beckett who asserts in *Watt* that there are "no symbols where none intended" (254), as a master ironist, a practitioner in the absurd who wants to communicate nothing so much as that communication is impossible. He is thus able to ask the questions that Hayden White ascribes to the generation of critics whom he terms absurdists: "When the world is denied all substance and perception is blind, who is to say who are the chosen and who the damned? On what grounds can we assert that the insane, the criminal, and the barbarian are wrong? And why should literature be accorded a privileged position among all the things created by man? Why should reading matter?" (282). Despite himself, Auster answers that reading does matter: that reading is about other reading, writing about other writing, and that even the most predictable and formulaic of genres can be resuscitated to give urgent new voice to the postmodern condition.[8]

Notes

1. In parenthetical citations Auster's works will henceforth be abbreviated as follows: *CG* (*City of Glass*), *G* (*Ghosts*), *LR* (*The Locked Room*), *IS* (*The Invention of Solitude*).

2. It is telling that Blue is the only actual detective in Auster's trilogy. Quinn, in *City of Glass*, gets his case through a wrong number; the narrator of *The Locked Room* functions as Fanshawe's literary executor and biographer. Writing and reading are central activities in the lives of all three protagonists, another way in which Auster foregrounds linguistic practice and connects it to the author/reader relationship.

3. The parallel here with García Márquez's *One Hundred Years of Solitude* is unmistakable. In García Márquez's 1967 novel, Aureliano finally reads the manuscripts which are both the history of his family and the text of the novel: "he

began to decipher the instant that he was living, deciphering it as he lived it, prophesying himself in the act of deciphering the last page of the parchments, as if he were looking into a speaking mirror. . . . Before reaching the final line, however, he had already understood that he would never leave that room, for it was foreseen that the city of mirrors (or mirages) would be wiped out by the wind and exiled from the memory of men" (383). Like Auster's novels, García Márquez's employs the image of the mirror as an overt commentary on the meta-fictionality and surface orientation of its own structure. Auster's Latin American precursors also include Borges, although with present space I can only suggest this relationship.

4. This bond between characters who hire detectives also relates to the trilogy's author figures. *Pinocchio* is significant to Peter Stillman Jr.'s depiction in *City of Glass*; seeing him walk into a room is, for Quinn, "like watching a mario-nette trying to walk without strings" (17), while Peter himself says "I know I am still the puppet boy. . . . But sometimes I think I will at last grow up and become real" (26). All this is relevant to Auster's lengthy meditations on Collodi's story in *The Invention of Solitude*, especially his observation that "Collodi leaves little doubt that he conceived of himself as the puppet's double" (164).

5. Auster explores this architectural model elsewhere. "The Death of Sir Walter Raleigh" (1975) begins with the statement, "The Tower is stone and the solitude of stone. It is the skull of a man around the body of a man—and its quick is thought. But no thought will ever reach the other side of the wall. . . . The man is a stone that breathes, and he will die" (*White Spaces* 7). The House of Usher-like wealth of architectural-psychological connections which Auster later explores in the trilogy is already present here—as is an attraction to Raleigh's story, which turns up again in *The Invention of Solitude* (97), as one of many examples of problematic father-son relationships (another of Auster's frequent themes, and one which links him to detection's Ur-myth, *Oedipus*), and in *The Locked Room*, where Raleigh's *History of the World* constitutes part of Fanshawe's formative reading (325).

6. I am indebted to Patricia Merivale for pointing out the relevant passage in *City of Glass*.

7. In *A Study in Scarlet*, when Watson tells Holmes "You remind me of Edgar Allan Poe's Dupin," Holmes responds contemptuously, "in my opinion, Dupin was a very inferior fellow. . . . He had some analytical genius, no doubt; but he was by no means such a phenomenon as Poe appeared to imagine" (24). Although the remark chiefly reveals Doyle's own anxiety of influence, it also demonstrates that the metafictional aspect of detective fiction is not postmodernist in origin. Indeed, one can take the street Audley Court—where Holmes and Watson find Constable John Rance (*Scarlet* 34)—and trace it to its namesake, an ancestral manse in Mary Elizabeth Braddon's mid-Victorian shocker *Lady Audley's Secret*, wherein the detective hero proclaims that he hasn't read "Wilkie Collins for nothing" (263). The wealth of such intertextuality in the detective genre would be of great attraction to a writer like Auster, fascinated as he is by connections whose intentionality and significance are often dubious.

8. The research for this project was supported in part by a fellowship from the Faculty Research Initiative Program of the University of Michigan, Flint.

Works Cited

Auster, Paul. *The Art of Hunger and Other Essays.* London: Menard Press, 1982.
————. *City of Glass.* [1985]. *New* 1–158.
————. *Ghosts.* [1986]. *New* 159–232.
————. *The Invention of Solitude.* New York: Sun, 1982.
————. *The Locked Room.* [1986]. *New* 235–71.
————. *The New York Trilogy.* New York: Penguin, 1990.
————. *White Spaces.* Barrytown, N.Y.: Station Hill Press, 1980.
Beckett, Samuel. *Ill Seen Ill Said.* [*Mal vu mal dit*]. Trans. Samuel Beckett. New York: Grove, 1981.
————. *Molloy, Malone Dies, The Unnamable.* [*Molloy,* 1951; *Malone meurt,* 1951; *L'Innomable,* 1953]. Trans. Samuel Beckett and Patrick Bowles. New York: Grove, 1965.
————. *Watt.* [1958]. New York: Grove, 1959.
Benjamin, Walter. *Charles Baudelaire: A Lyric Poet in the Era of High Capitalism.* Trans. Harry Zohn. London: New Left Books, 1973.
Braddon, Mary Elizabeth. *Lady Audley's Secret.* [1862]. New York: Dover, 1974.
Brantlinger, Patrick. "What Is 'Sensational' About the 'Sensation Novel'?" *Nineteenth Century Fiction* 37 (1982): 1–28.
Doyle, Arthur Conan. *A Study in Scarlet.* [1887]. *The Complete Sherlock Holmes.* 2 vols. New York: Doubleday, 1988. 1: 15–86.
García Márquez, Gabriel. *One Hundred Years of Solitude.* [*Cien años de soledad,* 1967]. Trans. Gregory Rabassa. New York: Avon, 1971.
Hawthorne, Nathaniel. *Fanshawe.* [1828]. *Novels,* ed. Millicent Bell. New York: Library of America, 1983. 1–114.
————. "Wakefield." [1835]. *Tales and Sketches.* Ed. Roy Harvey Pearce. New York: Library of America, 1982. 290–98.
Hurstfield, Julian G. "Mean Streets, Mystery Plays: The New Pathology of Recent American Crime Fiction." In *The New American Writing: Essays on American Literature Since 1970,* ed. Graham Clarke. New York: St. Martin's Press, 1990. 165–81.
Irwin, John T. *American Hieroglyphics: The Symbol of the Egyptian Hieroglyphics in the American Renaissance.* New Haven, Conn.: Yale University Press, 1980.
Jameson, Fredric. "Postmodernism, or the Cultural Logic of Late Capitalism." *New Left Review* 146 (1984): 53–92.
Kenner, Hugh. *Samuel Beckett: A Critical Study.* New York: Grove, 1961.
Lyotard, Jean-François. *The Postmodern Condition: A Report on Knowledge.* Trans. Geoff Bennington and Brian Massumi. Minneapolis: University of Minnesota Press, 1984.
Melville, Herman. "Hawthorne and His Mosses." [1850]. In *The Norton Anthology of American Literature,* ed. Ronald Gottesman et al. 2 vols. New York: Norton, 1979. 1: 2056–70.
————. *Moby Dick.* [1851]. New York: Holt, 1957.
Poe, Edgar Allan. *Poetry and Tales,* ed. Patrick F. Quinn. New York: Library of America, 1984.
Russell, Alison. "Deconstructing *The New York Trilogy*: Paul Auster's Anti-Detective Fiction." *Critique* 31, 2 (1990): 71–84.
Saltzman, Arthur M. *Designs of Darkness in Contemporary American Fiction.* Philadelphia: University of Pennsylvania Press, 1990.

Symons, Julian. *Bloody Murder: From the Detective Story to the Crime Novel: A History.* 2nd rev. ed. New York: Penguin, 1985.

Tanner, Tony. *City of Words: American Fiction, 1950–1970.* New York: Harper, 1971.

Thoreau, Henry. *A Week on the Concord and Merrimack Rivers; Walden; or, Life in the Woods; The Maine Woods; Cape Cod.* Ed. Robert F. Sayre. New York: Library of America, 1985.

Todorov, Tzvetan. "The Typology of Detective Fiction." *The Poetics of Prose.* [*Poétique de la prose,* 1971]. Trans. Richard Howard. Ithaca, N.Y.: Cornell University Press, 1977. 42–52.

White, Hayden. "The Absurdist Moment in Contemporary Literary Theory." *Tropics of Discourse: Essays in Cultural Criticism.* Baltimore: Johns Hopkins University Press, 1985. 261–82.

Postmortem: Modern and Postmodern

Chapter 7
Reader-Investigators in the Post-*Nouveau Roman*
Lahougue, Peeters, and Perec

Michel Sirvent

It is not impossible to imagine . . . a novel whose fiction would be
exciting enough so that the reader intensely felt the desire to know
its last word which precisely, at the last minute, would be denied to
him, the text pointing to itself and toward a rereading. The book
would be thus, a second time, given to the reader who could then,
while rereading it, discover everything in it which in his first mad
fever he had been unable to find.
—Benoît Peeters, "Agatha Christie: Une écriture de la lecture" (177)

Toward a Post-*Nouveau Roman* Detective Novel

A trend that I will characterize as the "post-*nouveau roman* detective
novel" may be distinguished in the current French literary scene.[1] A
new narrative hybrid form is being developed which partakes of both
the mystery story and the early *nouveau roman*. Novels of the first phase
of the *nouveau roman*, particularly Alain Robbe-Grillet's *The Erasers* (*Les
Gommes*, 1953), Michel Butor's *L'Emploi du temps* (1957), and Claude Ollier's *La Mise en scène* (1958), as well as a *nouveau nouveau roman* like
Jean Ricardou's *Les Lieux-dits* (1969), used detective-story structures.[2]
Although they played with some traits of mystery fiction, they did not
fully belong to the detective genre. They were parodies, metafictions,
or anti-detective novels, but not traditional detective stories. Likewise,
thirty years later, a significant number of novels by authors as different
as Patrick Modiano, Jean Echenoz, René Belletto, or Jacques Roubaud
draw from the detective model without entirely following the rules of the
game.[3] As opposed to current representatives of the genre,[4] the *nouveau*

roman detective novel and post-*nouveau roman* detective novel recycle generic characteristics by means of innovative textual strategies.[5] Georges Perec calls his *"53 jours"* a "literary *thriller*" (Bellos 710) and, to use an expression from the text, Jean Lahougue's *La Doublure de Magrite* can be defined as a "feuilleton avant-gardiste" (186).

It is well known that the *nouveau roman* calls into question most of our expectations of what a narrative should be—in terms of plot, psychology, characters, logical and chronological series of sequences. However, its "anti-representational" or "auto-representational" effects, as Ricardou analyzed them at the time, are now fairly familiar to the postmodern reader: what used to be *scriptible* (writable) has since become a little more *lisible* (readable).[6] Today, whether such narrative strategies are called "self-reflexive," "metatextual," "metafictional" or, preferably, "metarepresentational,"[7] post-*nouveau roman* detective novels use *nouveau roman* textual devices while returning to what may appear to be a more conventional way of storytelling.[8] They offer the pleasures of reading (it is a clear return to the *romanesque*, or novelistic) and do not obviously subvert our expectations. Beneath their innocent surface, however, what supports these puzzles may be a very sophisticated network of infra-textual as well as intertextual correspondences. Briefly, in these novels metarepresentional strategies are no longer deliberately antirepresentational. Contemporary with the *nouveau roman* but distinct from it, Perec's versatile work—which shifts constantly from playful Oulipian mechanical exercises (performed also by Italo Calvino and Roubaud, among others) to autobiographical and extraordinarily imaginative, often humorous, novels—has certainly anticipated this significant evolution, one that blends intricate *specific* formal constraints with a more representational narrative format.

Although I would not agree with Stefano Tani that *any* interesting contemporary fiction takes more or less advantage of detective-story techniques (149, 151), I don't deny that there may be a fundamental mystery or suspense in any non-detective novel per se ("une forme fondamentale": see Boyer 74). There must be a structural reason, as well as several cultural factors, that explain why some contemporary French novels innovate (from a narrative or textual standpoint) while drawing material, substance, patterns, and elements from the detective genre.[9] The reason is the reader's assigned role in the construction of these fictional universes, as related to underlying textual strategies. Beyond the various analogies that facilitate this parallel between two stages of the French novel—from the early *nouveau roman* in the 1950s, via Perec's original itinerary, to the post-*nouveau roman* of the 1980s, a time when most former *nouveaux romanciers* turned to autobiography—the mystery structure provides a crucial place for the reader to participate in the very intrigue she is expected to complete.

And Then There Were . . . Three

> I rarely feel like reading what it is possible for me to live outside of novels. From this stems my interest in Agatha Christie.
> —Jean Lahougue, "Ecrire à partir d'Agatha Christie" (5)

It is no coincidence that three French detective novels—Benoît Peeters's *La Bibliothèque de Villers* (1980), Lahougue's *Comptine des Height* (1980), and Perec's *"53 jours"* (1989)—all draw, in different ways, from one of the most classic detective novelists: Agatha Christie. In his afterword to the first edition of *La Bibliothèque*, Peeters recalls Christie's principles of composition, as inferred from her "romans à énigme," and correlates the formalized structures that organize her mysteries with Ricardou's textual principles, as developed through his theory and practice of the *nouveau roman*. Peeters focuses on the generative role of nursery rhymes in such Christie plots as *Ten Little Indians* (1939): "Very few books correspond better than Agatha Christie's to Jean Ricardou's phrase: 'composing a novel does not mean having an idea, and then giving it a form; rather, it means having the idea of a form from which a story may be deduced'" ("Tombeau" 121–22).

Lahougue explains "how to write from Agatha Christie," analyzing the composition of *Ten Little Indians* and referring to Ricardou's concept of "générateur" to define the nursery-rhyme device as "the most demanding of all constraints chosen by Agatha Christie," since "it supplies the number of characters, a symbolism, the modalities, and even the name and form of place" ("Ecrire à" 6). Not only does Lahougue's title *Comptine des Height* also suggest nursery-rhyme technique, but his foreword announces: "I am one of those who learned to read with Agatha Christie." Indeed, the structure of *Comptine des Height* borrows its plot from *Ten Little Indians*: "Ten characters in a closed place die one by one according to the mechanisms of the nursery rhyme and the implicit rules of the 'puzzle type' of detective novel" ("Ecrire à" 8). Like Peeters, then, Lahougue not only recognizes his debt to Christie's generative nursery-rhyme formula, but emphasizes writing principles very similar to the ones defended by Ricardou in *Problèmes du nouveau roman*. Both authors renounce any extratextual point of departure in composing a novel, focusing instead on the determination of fictional matter by narrative and writerly constraints derived from the peculiarities of the medium, material context, or specific genres chosen: "We must impose the most formal constraints upon ourselves. Problems of writing that must be resolved will be born from these constraints and it is essentially the resolution of these problems that will produce the organization of the book, its landscape, its intrigue and its heroes" (Lahougue, "Ecrire à" 5).

So it is no surprise that Annie Combes points out the "modernity" of the author of *The Murder of Roger Ackroyd* (1926), and specifies that some of Christie's narrative devices may be very close to what has been radicalized in the writing techniques of some *nouveaux romanciers*—and Perec (10, 249). She compares Christie's use of generative schemes (based on phrases, numbers, or letters) to organize the plot, as well as the order of chapters, with Raymond Roussel's way of creating a story by playing on the linguistic dimension of a given proverb (102–12).[10] Just as Christie "constructs a book around a nursery rhyme, basing the progression of the narrative on the order of the stanzas," building "a plot on a number, and using the alphabet to establish a series of crimes" (Combes 10), so Perec proceeds in a Roussellian manner. For example, Combes shows how the series of deaths in Christie's *The ABC Murders* (1936) is determined by the alphabet: the victims' names and the names of the places where they are killed suggest "alphabetical murders"; "the whole story derives from the letters A, B, C" (219). The structure of Perec's *A Void (La Disparition*, 1969) is also determined by the alphabet: it omits the letter *E* so that the missing letter becomes an enigma, both unsaid—unnameable—and evoked allegorically. Furthermore, there is a missing chapter (number five, which corresponds to the position of *E* in the alphabet) in this novel composed of twenty-six chapters. Although Perec's lipogrammatic novel does not explicitly belong to the mystery genre, it can thus be read as a mystery. As in a "classical detective story" (Combes 220), the disappearance of the letter *E* is constantly signified, yet never declared: it constitutes the "crime" to be unveiled by the reader (see my "Lettres volées" 14–15).

Along with these writing constraints, which Christie and Perec have in common with *nouveaux romanciers* and with Roussel, Perec's novels also refer to Christie's stories, although not as overtly and systematically as Lahougue's *Comptine des Height* and Peeters's *La Bibliothèque de Villers*. In *"53 jours"*, one of the characters, Wargrave, clearly borrows his name from *Ten Little Indians*. In *Life: A User's Manual* (1978), there is also a "Lawrence Wargrave," author of the detective story "The Judge Is the Assassin"; and the synopsis of this detective story provides an intertextual clue to *"53 jours"*: "X killed A in such a way that Justice, who knows it, cannot accuse him. The committing magistrate kills B in such a way that X is suspected, arrested, judged, condemned and executed without having ever been able to prove his innocence" (*Life* 334). But more generally, when Perec declared his interest in mysteries, long before he decided to write a detective novel, he mentioned Hercule Poirot in a passage that summarizes many of the novelistic traits in question:

> I hardly read detective novels any more, except some old Hercule Poirot. But as a producer of fiction, the detective novel continues to interest me and concern me in the sense that it explicitly works as a game between the author and the reader; a game whose intricacies of plot, the mechanism of the murder, the victim, the criminal, the detective, the motive, and so on, are obviously pawns: this match that is played between a writer and his reader, and whose characters, settings, sentiments, happenings are but fictions which drive one to the sole pleasure of reading (of being puzzled, moved, delighted, etc.), is for me one of the most efficient models of novelistic functioning. ("Entretien" 10)

First, the mystery genre's stereotypical pattern makes it a convenient narrative model for Perec. Second, what it narrates is overtly fictitious: the game relationship displaces the referential background. This does not mean, however, that detective fiction is not representational. It refers less to "the real world" than to an intertextual—or infratextual—set of rules. Third, Perec takes the detective genre as a model because he finds its paradigmatic plot structure "one of the most efficient models of novelistic functioning" as a whole. This detective model can thus be a paradigm for any novelistic plot structure, whether it reads as an explicit detective story or not. Last, the detective narrative paradigm underlies any fiction, insofar as the plot becomes a pretext for a writer-reader game. Perec emphasizes that most classic mysteries are games. Conventionally, the reader loses the match against the author "if s/he fails to discover who is guilty before the final explanation scene" (Combes 36). S. S. Van Dine set out the famous detective-story rule that the reader, as well as the detective, should be given the opportunity to solve the enigma. While Perec's last unfinished work, *"53 jours"*, Benoît Peeters's *La Bibliothèque de Villers*, and Lahougue's stories adhere more closely to the mystery genre than do *nouveaux romans*, one might wonder how the reader's role in these recent fictions differs from that induced by "tales of pure puzzle" written by Van Dine, Christie, G. K. Chesterton, and Dorothy Sayers around the time of the Detective Club. The "pragmatic situation" has changed: the reader's role is transformed insofar as narrative strategies are no longer simply representational.

In the classic mystery, enabling the reader to solve the puzzle demands specific narrative strategies that imply a "fair" distribution of relevant information. "Writing (organization of anecdote as well as textual arrangement) is directly conceived in relation to the deciphering process that follows" (Peeters, "Agatha" 166).[11] It is because the subsequent reading of the text determines its writing that we can speak, as

Peeters says, about "écriture de la lecture" ("writing the reading"). By means of a careful distribution of lures and clues, which Combes calls a "writing contract," "the secret of the narrative will be shown by meticulously chosen details that will suggest the mystery *without betraying it*" too soon (17; my emphasis). A practical condition of mystery writing, its "double imperative," is "to hide the criminal as well as possible and distribute the signs of his guilt" (18). This is also the role of the writer for Lahougue: "Through convention I will show a crime (insert signs in my narrative which will permit reconstruction, its place, time, author and cause) and at the same time conceal it (thereby exploiting all the ambiguities of these signs)" ("Ecrire à" 5). Combes calls this strategy "écriture indicielle" (68, 229–45). In this sense, the writer is certainly the author of the crime, and the reader the detective of the text: "the author's relationship with the reader parallels that of the detective with the criminal." Peeters summarizes this correspondence in the following equation: "criminal = author: detective = reader" ("Agatha" 167).

However, although Christie "inscribes the solution to the puzzle between the lines" (Combes 9), it has often been pointed out that the mystery reader is rarely capable of solving the puzzle before the conclusive explanation scene (Eisenzweig 49–77; Combes 245, 264). For instance, Lahougue insists that practically any of the protagonists could have committed the crimes in *Ten Little Indians*: "although there are no arbitrary details, this does not mean that we can find revealing details either. Unlike Poirot, Wargrave does not tell us at the end of the book: 'Here is what you should have noticed.' And for a good reason: no contradiction, no clue (in spite of this implicit rule and formal constraint, according to which the narrative should show the murder before concealing it) denounces the murderer before his own confession" ("Ecrire à" 8). On the one hand, the textual possibility of discovering the solution is often doubtful. On the other, Peeters points out that since the investigator generally "carries out his investigation to the end," the anticipated explanation scene discourages the reader "from doing as much" ("Agatha" 176). As Peeters puts it, "what's the use of reading since the text will end up reading itself?" This is why the author of *La Bibliothèque de Villers* would prefer *Ten Little Indians* without Judge Wargrave's final confession of his crimes and his suicide: "*Ten Little Indians*, abandoned to themselves, leaving the text literally without voice, would be a book ten times more exciting" (176). Toward the end of his study, Peeters quotes Borges's 1941 story "An Examination of the Work of Herbert Quain": "The reader of this singular book is thus more discerning than the *detective*" (176; Peeters's emphasis)—implying that, to whatever degree a mystery might be left unsolved by its fictional agents, the actual reader might still be able to carry on the investigation.

The consequences of this narrative strategy are that one is led to formulate two complementary constraints. First, instead of being able to rely on a final explanation delivered by an omniscient detective, or carefully prepared by a manipulative narrator, the reader is confronted with a textual construct that deliberately *omits* this conventional elucidation scene, as in *La Bibliothèque*.[12] Hence the reader must complete the *incomplete structure*, because it is deprived of its unraveling phase, the one characterized by a "final nomination" (Barthes 216). In a sense, such metarepresentational detective novels radicalize only one provisional condition of the mystery: the temporary incompleteness that defines the "hermeneutical code" (215). In Barthes's terms, "Le lisible a horreur du vide" ("what is readerly hates emptiness") (112), whereas the *nouveau roman* accumulates, as Robbe-Grillet recalls, "lacunae and contradictions."[13] Second, and more important, what is questioned is the existence of sufficient textual means to enable the reader to find the solution of an unresolved mystery.

Various Cases of Intertextuality

Following the *nouveau roman* theory and practice of generators (Ricardou, "Révolution" 930), these three novels call attention to two problems. First, they question the "lecturabilité" (readability) of the detective text (Ricardou, "Eléments" 17). I will call *readability* (and, in this context, *detectability*) *the mystery text's construction which, despite its incompleteness, virtually enables the reader to pursue*—that is, *to complete—its unsolved or unresolved aspects through a precise strategy of clue distribution*. In the analyses that follow, I will emphasize the reader's complementary response to the structure of the text in Perec's and Peeters's novels.

But—here is my second focus—these three novels make us question how fiction is intertextually determined. The three novels help us better distinguish between a variety of intertextual productions. The first level of intertextual relations is *generic*, since all three texts refer to a particular genre—or subgenre—and, more specifically, to a particular representative of the mystery genre (Agatha Christie or Georges Simenon). They actually combine two generic traits, since these novels also relate to another novelistic form, the one that characterizes the *nouveau roman*. Indeed, at the second level of intertextual relations, these three different novels also share the *generative* principle underlying some of Roussel's, Christie's, and the *nouveaux romanciers'* compositions.

However, on a third level, post-*nouveau roman* intertextual practice differs from the *nouveau roman* in that each novel *overtly* relates to a *particular* mystery classic. In the *nouveau roman*, the relation to the detective genre is mostly paradigmatic: it refers to an abstract pattern that is inverted or subverted (see *The Erasers*, with its underlying reference to the Oedipus narrative). Whereas post-*nouveaux romans* are specific transformations (*récrits*, literally "re-writes") of anterior texts, the major difference between the earlier "deconstruction" of the detective genre in the *nouveau roman*, and that in the post-*nouveau roman*, is that the relation in the latter is overtly *hypertextual* (Genette, *Palimpsestes* 14). To take the example of Lahougue—who is, in this regard, the most representative of the three writers—each of his latest stories is an experiment in various types of hypertextual relations. As *Comptine des Height* develops and goes beyond the writing constraints of *Ten Little Indians*, so "La Ressemblance" (1989), from his recent collection of the same title, takes up many elements from Vladimir Nabokov's *Despair* (1934), while complicating its ambiguous ending.[14] In a similar way, *La Doublure de Magrite* (1987) partly rewrites Simenon's *La Première enquête de Maigret* (1948).

Furthermore, I will distinguish—and this explains the progression I see from Lahougue to Perec via Peeters—between Lahougue's deliberate hypertextual strategy and a fourth level of intertextual relationship. This level not only involves a single model or text—the canonical model, or a particular story by Christie or Simenon—but several specific texts at the same time. To qualify this type of *(poly)hypertextual* integration—as opposed to Lahougue's *(mono)hypertextual* practice—I borrow Ricardou's concept of "syntext" (*Nouveaux problèmes* 304). I argue, then, that Peeters's and Perec's practice is *syntextual*, as opposed to Lahougue's hypertextual strategy. For example, Peeters's novel not only relates to *Ten Little Indians* but also, as we shall see, draws on two or three other texts which seem to have been selected because they share a similar plot (see Baetens 225–26). Finally, with Perec, the syntextual connection is far more diversified, although still very discernable, because he borrows his pre-texts from Stendhal, Flaubert, and Balzac, or from his own earlier fictions—as is the case for most of his novels, from *W, or the Memory of Childhood* (1975) to *Life: A User's Manual* (see Magné). The relation of *"53 jours"* to Christie's fictions, if not loose, is certainly less systematic than in *Comptine des Height* and *La Bibliothèque de Villers*. However, we will see that the structure of this last novel reflects the intertextual strategy itself, making the textual puzzle *detectable*.

La Doublure de Magrite

> Please do not think, Mademoiselle, that I am inventing. I am only pilfering here and there various details which I will use to organize my story. Everyone does the same, by the way, not only the authors of detective stories!
>
> —Georges Perec, *"53 jours"* (91)

The ties are so close between Lahougue's *La Doublure de Magrite* and Simenon's *La Première enquête de Maigret* that we can speak of hypertextual transformation—which is my third level of intertextual relation. Instead of syntextually transforming and merging *more than one* text, as Peeters and Perec do, Lahougue is literally and explicitly concerned with *one* specific pre-text. For instance, the epilogue of Lahougue's novel rewrites the prologue of Simenon's story.[15] Lahougue explains in his essay "Ecrire vers Simenon" how he cited, modified, and elaborated the original text, just as Maigret sympathizes with his targets by absorbing their social milieu. In other words, Maigret's very method of investigation inspires and motivates the rewriting technique: "Georges Simenon's Maigret . . . unlike his elders, Holmes and Poirot, who are pure logicians of the novel's time and space, as we know, proceeds through 'sympathy' or by identification with the other. In *La Première enquête de Maigret*, Simenon said of him: 'He was capable of living the life of all men, of putting himself in the place of all men' " (12). *La Doublure* deals with an actor's performance in a play adapted from a book by "Georges Simon [sic]." Because he has the same name as "Simon" 's famous character, Magrite, the actor involuntarily becomes the detective he represents on stage, Inspector Magrite (*Doublure* 12, 129). The psychological identification between detective and criminal that defines Maigret's method of investigation (81, 134) translates into the actor's *actual* identification with the role he plays. The hero's acting out of the character he represents on stage is thus a *mise en abyme* of how the writer models his own principle of composition according to Maigret's notorious fictional method of investigation. In a Borgesian way, it is the very process of hypertextual rewriting that is fictionalized and shaped accordingly: "And because my hero identified with Maigret, and since one of the major themes of the novel was the identification with the other, how could I fail to identify myself with Georges Simenon? Hence the idea of a pastiche" ("Ecrire vers" 12–13).

In addition to frequently quoting Simenon's classic detective novel (from the epigraph to scattered citations throughout the text), *La Doublure* also borrows from Robbe-Grillet's *The Erasers*.[16] In both novels, a character's role can be transformed into its own opposite through identification. While Robbe-Grillet's detective, Wallas, becomes in spite of himself the criminal he seeks, in *La Doublure* the amateur actor, like Proteus, acts out his fictional role to the point where he will "successively assume all the roles of the characters he encounters": "Let us imagine a murder scene with four characters: an assassin, a victim, an active witness, a passive witness. Let us imagine that such a scene is repeated four times in the course of the narrative in identical conditions, and that the hero becomes in turn the active witness, the assassin, the passive witness and the victim" ("Ecrire vers" 11). In *The Erasers*, it is the investigation that motivates the crime. In other words, the crime is less a cause than a consequence. In *La Doublure*, however, Magrite is the product of his own performance: the identification motivates first the investigation and finally the acting out of the most characteristic detective functions. In short, acting determines action. These character functions (detective, suspect, criminal, and so on) are not only reversible, in the manner of Oedipus (the detective/criminal), but this reversibility (which was only *virtual*, that is, psychological, in Simenon's fictions) happens to be *actualized*. To generalize this pattern, *subjects become the object* of their quest — which metaphorically defines the process of reading.

While *La Doublure* uses materials from detective classics, it also draws from the poetics of the *nouveaux romanciers*. One example is the Robbe-Grilletian theatrical staging of the original realist description of Maigret's office (219–21). Robbe-Grillet's theatrical detective universe is well known: his characters give the impression of playing a role, like Mathias in the 1955 *Le Voyeur* (Boyer, "Double" 65); the ensemble of literal and fictional elements find themselves in a labyrinthine mirror game, in a general system of duplication, in short in the poetics of "auto-representation" (Ricardou, *Nouveaux problèmes* 140–78). But while in *The Erasers'* world of variations, doubles, reflections, and simulations, the investigator and criminal end up identifying with each other, in *La Doublure*, Robbe-Grilletian parodic theatricality is literally acted out: actors perform in reality the parts that they happen to represent in fiction. This situation not only re-presents the writer-reader interactive relationship, but also points out a Borgesian communication between the two "logically" separate universes—the one in which we narrate or read, the one which is narrated or represented ("extradiegetic" and "diegetic," in narratological terms: see Genette, *Narrative* 228–31).

While on one level *La Doublure* concerns the way in which fiction transforms reality, on another, it calls into question any clear borderline between one's own identity and that of one's double (45–49). The novel, for instance, stresses the themes of the "I," the "mirror," "the loss of and quest for identity," and the "role of memory" in this quest for identification with the other (Lahougue, "Ecrire vers" 12). The very concept of "identity" (not simply the characters' identity) is challenged by the hero's functional metamorphosis. In this sense, the novel appears as a fable about the power of re-presentation as well as a fable about novelistic characterization. Lahougue's ambition was to "make [his] reader become a real character in the plot," while including "three essential acts, namely: the opening of the book, its reading, the closing of the book in the story. The third act, which actually consists in making the narrator disappear, seemed to me comparable to a murder or a kidnapping" (11).[17] The actor, Magrite, as a multifunctional character (one name stands for various characters, each with different perspectives), represents the reader—the one who acts, or rather, who activates written fiction and replays the scenes as described from different angles. As the heterodiegetic narrator who is "killed" by the closing of the book, Magrite stages his own disappearance: in the final act, he "pretends to be dead" (215). We might surmise that the actual reader may be led, by identifying with this process of shifting between fiction and reality, to become the producer of fiction as well as the murderer of the text—just as the actual writer, Lahougue, who rewrites the "master narrative" (Simenon's text), is thus a reader (the Oedipal murderous "son") who becomes the detective writer of a new hypertextual story. As it is reactivated in *The Erasers*, the Oedipus pattern, which recurs throughout the detective genre, becomes the allegory of hypertextual rewriting.[18]

La Bibliothèque de Villers

> They must have been convinced that the missing chapter would appeal to me.
> —Georges Perec, *"53 jours"* (158)

La Doublure combines at least two intertextual relations besides the fact that it pertains to the detective genre: first, a *generic* relation—mostly mediated by the Oedipus narrative—which concerns the parodic strategy, more than the text itself, of *The Erasers*; second, a *hypertextual* relation that consists of literally rewriting specific passages—borrowing specific metaphors and traits from Simenon's text. Whereas this first relation is mostly paradigmatic and covert—it refers to an abstract pattern much as *The Erasers* relates to the Oedipus narrative—the ties between *La Doublure* and *La Première enquête de Maigret* are, by contrast, overtly textual. But while Lahougue's hypertextual practice involves a single text model for each new story, Peeters's *La Bibliothèque de Villers* and Perec's *"53 jours"* specifically relate to several pre-texts at the same time; this level of intertextual relation is *syntextual*. *"53 jours"* multiplies allusions to several texts, including Stendhal's *La Chartreuse de Parme* (Magné 186), while Peeters's plot draws its material and principles from—besides Christie's *Ten Little Indians*—novels and short stories as different as Borges's "Death and the Compass," Butor's *L'Emploi du temps*, Ollier's *La Mise en scène*, Ricardou's *Les Lieux-dits*, or Maurice Leblanc's "La Dame à la hache" (in *Les Huit coups de l'horloge*). *La Bibliothèque de Villers*, on the one hand, mostly discovers and combines one structural pattern common to Borges's and Leblanc's short stories and, on the other, reuses the circular rereading pattern as developed in Ricardou's study of *La Mise en scène* (*Pour* 159–99). Both Christie and Leblanc made use of numerical generators to build up some of their stories (Combes 173–79), but in "La Dame à la hache," this type of textual organization is far more developed than in Christie, and closer to the *nouveau roman* and *La Bibliothèque de Villers*. I will focus on the structural resemblance of *La Bibliothèque* to Leblanc's story, which—although Peeters never mentions it, whereas he clearly acknowledges the connection with Borges and Christie in the novel's two editions—is particularly striking.

In Leblanc's short story, solving the puzzle amounts to discovering the logic of a series of crimes. As indicated by its title, Leblanc's collection *Les Huit coups de l'horloge* (1923) is composed of eight short stories. In "La Dame à la hache," the investigator, Prince Renine, alias Arsène Lupin, discovers that the female victims' names are all formed of eight letters and start with the letter *H* (like "Honorine"). Then another variable appears: for each crime, the murderer kills with an axe. Since in French the word *hache*, or axe, is pronounced the same way as the letter *H*, which is the eighth letter in the alphabet, one surmises a kind of numerical and literal solution. The logic of numbers and letters, once disclosed, suggests that there may be eight victims, all women whose names will begin with an *H* and be composed of eight letters. As these similarities unfold to disclose the pattern, the investigator is led to foresee and then prevent another murder in extremis: the seventh crime, whose victim was supposed to be his very own mistress, Hortense. Finally, we deduce that the murderer, Hermance, had planned to commit suicide, becoming the eighth victim and thus completing the series.

Peeters's story contains a similar structural investigation: hidden analogies must be found between crimes which at first seem unrelated. Furthermore, this investigation clearly amounts to a deciphering process: four murders, whose disclosed similarities enable the narrator-investigator to prevent the fifth crime. As *Les Huit coups de l'horloge* consists of eight stories, so *La Bibliothèque de Villers* is divided into five chapters. Furthermore, the recurring number (5), which is transposed through various details within the story, becomes a clue to the discovery of the assassin: his or her name should be composed of five letters. We are led to this solution by the peculiarity in the first four victims' names: their first and last names start with the same initial—Ivan Imbert, Virginie Verley, René Roussel, Edith Ervil.

Peeters's story is far more elliptical than Leblanc's. There are many fictional as well as narratological aspects setting up this organized yet incomplete structure. The narrator is not only a mystery reader, but an amateur detective who becomes the main investigator. While doing some research at the Villers library, where he is investigating five unsolved crimes that took place twenty-five years before, another series of five crimes occurs in which he becomes more and more involved. At one point, the narrator-detective is led to suspect his chess partner, Lessing (cf. Ollier's *La Mise en scène*), the librarian who invited him to investigate the old crimes and who turns out to be a detective novelist. Until the fourth crime is committed, Lessing represents the author-criminal of the present murders who competes with the narrator. But with the fifth crime, he suddenly becomes the victim—leaving narrator and reader without any plausible solution.

Like the special agent Wallas in *The Erasers*, Peeters's narrator takes on the two opposite character functions of detective and criminal. In Robbe-Grillet's novel, however, the detective is described in the third person; there is an invisible narrator as absent as possible from the narration, and no fictional investigator whose main occupation is reading. Peeters's narrator, on the other hand, is an anonymous character. He could be anyone. Indeed, he progressively takes on all possible roles (as in *La Doublure de Magrite*). He becomes witness, detective, accomplice, possible victim. Through a classical process of elimination, he is one of the last characters left alive and thus becomes one of the major suspects. When we realize that the reader completely relies on this ambivalent narrator-investigator's autodiegetic narrative, we then expect some comprehensive explanation in which the narrator turns out to be the murderer, as in Christie's *The Murder of Roger Ackroyd*. But, being deprived of it, one of the fundamental grounds of the narrative-reader contract is completely undermined: the narrative account as a whole becomes suspicious.

The second major break in the narrative-reader contract lies in the fact that the elliptical scene is, unconventionally, not the very "crime scene" that the investigator's discourse usually reconstructs, but this missing final explanation scene itself. Inasmuch as the narrative is totally unreliable, what is to be produced here is merely *another scenario*. If we have no choice but to put ourselves in the detective's place to finish the story, we end up *rereading* the text, thus assuming the narrator's role— but according to a different readerly frame. The correlation of variables —the distribution of black and white objects and descriptive details, constituting the metaphor of linguistic signs on the page; the recurring number 5, referring to the spatial organization of the text; the narrative construction—invites the reader to formulate the unsaid culprit's name: the "LIVRE" (that is, the "book" that we have been reading). This solution derives from the anagrammatic and acrostic rapport between the five victims' names, including Lessing, whose name allows us to supply the first missing letter (*L*). Also, each chapter starts with one of the victims' initals printed in bold, in this precise order: 1. "**Il** . . ."; 2. "**Vê**tu . . ."; 3. "**Re**lier . . . "; 4. "**Ed**ith . . . "; and 4. "**La** mort . . ." This reading is confirmed by the town's name, "VILLERS," which contains, except for one (the *S*), the same letters. What is perhaps more important than this infratextual solution is that the incomplete/substitutive structure of the narrative invites us to an infinite elliptical process—in the rhetorical as well as geometrical sense of the term (because the last letter, *L* for "Lessing," has to be placed at the beginning of the series, suggesting this circular rereading). Since the librarian/murderer/detective novelist's place is left *vacant*, the narrator or reader may take on Lessing's role and become the next librarian/murderer/detective novelist. Twenty-five years later, we may surmise that another reader or detective will be induced by a new Lessing to do some research in the Villers library and end up becoming still another Lessing, and so on ad infinitum. This interpretation is supported by an anagram of the library's name, "LIVRES" (as well as *en vrilles* ["in spiral form"], shall we add?)—that is, "books," this time in the plural, which is suggested by the extra letter (*S*) in the town's name—but also by the name "Lessing" (*"les signes"*), which offers an intertextual clue: the cyclic pattern forming the structure as well as the subject matter of Ollier's *La Mise en scène*. As a reader, the narrator is first of all our double. In the end, our role is to double the narrator: by being *the one who narrates the unsaid*.

"53 jours"

> "La Crypte" is a novel in two parts whose second part meticulously destroys all that which the first has tried to establish; a classic procedure of many mystery novels here pushed to an almost caricatural paroxysm.
>
> —Georges Perec, *"53 jours"* (42)

I will here focus on intertextual reading as investigation in Perec's last novel—in which, as Roubaud puts it, "the mystery of unaccomplishment is tied to the project of the book" (97). It is as if the unfinished state of the novel—interrupted by Perec's death in 1989—echoed the construction of the plot itself. There are structural reasons—not only biographical reasons—which may have led Perec to put elements of unaccomplishment into the fiction: the intricate construction of the novel composes the enigma (96). The book, decentered, was supposed to be in two parts, of thirteen (eleven more or less entirely written) and fifteen chapters, respectively (*"53 jours"* 191). It would have had the same title— *"53 jours"*—as its first part: " '53 jours' is the title of the story in the first part which the narrator of the second receives and about which he undertakes the exegesis" (194).

The text follows an embedded narrative pattern "whose center is the detective novel" (199), the author of which turns out to be both false victim and real criminal, and whose fictional reader-narrator becomes the investigator—only to be trapped, in the end, as the accused. A deciphering of "53 jours" constitutes the investigation in the second narrative by the second narrator—"Un R est un M qui se P le L de la R"—wherein we can recognize an abridged transcription of Stendhal's famous phrase, "Un Roman est un Miroir qui se Promène le Long de la Route" ("A novel is a mirror that strolls along the road"). Here, not only does investigating revert to reading a detective novel, but, since the text to be deciphered is constituted by a metadiegetic narrative, we find ourselves confronted by exactly the same material as the metafictional detective.

There are three *mises en abyme* of this overall structure in the first part, "53 jours." A detective novelist, Serval, mysteriously disappears; in order to resolve this puzzle, the anonymous narrator, given the role of temporary detective, is assigned to read the notes for Serval's novel, "La Crypte," whose main character (according to Ellery Queen's rule, which states that the "pseudonym and the hero must be confused"), is a homonym of the author, Serval. As does *"53 jours"* itself, "La Crypte" contains "a rather curious photograph in black and white" with the inscription "Tombouctou 52 jours," which allows us to suppose a count down of these embedded narratives. Of course, in this succession of internal duplications, the Serval of "La Crypte" must also read a detective novel to solve a puzzle—that is, the mysterious story "The Judge is the Assassin," whose author and narrator's name, Laurence Wargrave, recalls the apparent victim and assassin of *Ten Little Indians*. Internal analogies and intertextual links lead us to suspect that the accidental death of a certain Rouard, in "La Crypte," is nothing but the simulation of a false victim. According to the summary of "The Judge is the Assassin," a Mr. Tissier explains to Wargrave that "he was able to stage his own murder"—from which Rouard was able to draw "the organizing principle" thanks to which the victim of a simulated crime can be designated as the criminal. The composition of the novel is thus like that of a quadruple bottom box, the four levels being, within *"53 jours"* and retrospectively within "Un R est un M qui se P le L de la R," first, "53 jours"; second, "la Crypte"; third, "Le juge est l'assassin"; fourth, "K comme Kaola" (217). We learn that four models, working as self-reflexive clues, inspired "La Crypte": first, *Ten Little Indians*; second, a short story by Maurice Leblanc entitled "Edith au cou de cygne"; third, Bill Ballinger's *Une Dent contre lui*;[19] and fourth, the spy novel *K comme Kaola*, from which Serval borrows fourteen lines that he transcribes, with the exception of twelve words of twelve letters each (92–94). And, of course, each of these intra-/intertextual references could hide the key to the puzzle.

What gradually emerges from this imbroglio is the identification of the narrator-reader-detective with his model, who is the author of the detective novel and, at the same time, the director of his own kidnapping: Serval. In the last chapter completed by Perec (the twelfth!), the narrator searches—in "La Crypte"—for a solution to the case in which he is involved, not only as investigator and reader but also as victim of a kidnapping. Thus, while reading a "miniature plot that reflects our own," the unwilling investigator ends up through identification "in the ghostly skin of that murderer of himself." Thus, in respect to either the reader-detective or the narrative structure, the process—one of self-effacement—seems to evolve toward progressive dissolution. And the final explanation is infinite, first given and then refuted, indefinitely combinable and deferrable.

Like Perec's "fictional autobiography," *W, or the Memory of Childhood*, *"53 jours"* is composed around a typographical ellipsis. The diptych structure juxtaposing two separate narratives constitutes a major element in the enigma. Not only does the unresolved mystery of the first part turn out to be embedded in the second part, but it will serve, literally, as the very material to be deciphered in order to pursue the ongoing investigation. Furthermore, this dizzy embedding of overlapping narratives reflects the structure of labyrinthine investigation into one's own past. Biographical allusions abound in *"53 jours"*, thus linking the detective story to Perec's fantasy/autobiography. Undoubtedly, the common denominator between the detective plot, the autobiographical enterprise, and the puzzle game is the pattern of investigation as reconstruction from fragmentary elements. (For instance, *Life: A User's Manual*, which is organized like a jigsaw puzzle, offers multiple embedded, interlocking tales—like chapter 31, entitled "Beaumont 3"—that are parodic detective stories.) A simple look at the notes left by Perec, and published in the same posthumous volume, suggests that the writer was also searching for a solution to this unprecedented structure—to such an extent that in the last chapter of the novel, the next fictional writer-investigator, whom the unsuccessful preceding investigator-reader is to meet, is called "G. Perec" (186).

Instead of Ending . . .

> One dreams in vain of a final chapter which would be itself a bearer
> of new ambiguities and which would oblige one to reread the book.
> —Jean Lahougue, "Ecrire à partir d'Agatha Christie" (6)

Agatha Christie's best works combine two contradictory tendencies. On the one hand, she innovates: the occasional use of generative pretexts announces a literary practice in which "the laws that govern [her] novels have nothing to do with those that organize reality" (Peeters, "Tombeau"

100). In this sense, her writing anticipates the reader's investigation of the text. On the other hand, there was, at the time, another generic constraint: the laws of representation. She "had to continuously disguise the process which makes fiction come about," which could therefore threaten representational illusion (122). In short, this comes down to a poetics that, on the whole, *dissimulates* textual strategies, which is opposed to a poetics of metarepresentation: the pleasures of fiction should not necessarily entail the obfuscation of the mechanisms that produce it (Ricardou, "Innocence" 281–82). Thus, if for Christie "there is always a thought concerning the effect to be produced" (Peeters, "Tombeau" 128), it does not mean that her stories actually enable the reader to carry on the investigation beyond their representational ending.

In post-*nouveaux romans*, endings are always illusory, incomplete, and/or virtually infinite: they seem at least to propose a rereading of endings that never stop ending. Between chapters 4 and 5 of *"53 jours"*, a series of hypotheses follows the false final explanation in "La Crypte": "Once a solution is found, another one which is absolutely different is in turn given in a few lines; it's the basis of it, the case's final new development, its ultimate reversal, its last revelation, its anticlimax, which leaves the reader perplexed or delighted, facing two hypotheses which are both acceptable even though diametrically opposed" (70). After a period of deconstructing the detective genre in the *nouveau roman*, the strategy of the post-*nouveau roman* seems to be to *construct* the pragmatic conditions of an interactive rapport between text and reader. By eliminating the final explanation scene or multiplying cryptic versions of it, the plot leaves us no choice but to continuously reread and pursue the text. In *"53 jours"*, the core of the enigma is this virtually infinite, metadiegetic, digressive, and reflexive structure through which the narrative progresses. Each narrative, whether primary or secondary, proceeds by commenting on similar overlapping narratives. In this embedded structure of stories that mirror each other, we grasp that no story can explain the puzzle that initiates it *on its own level*. The overall principle seems to be that each puzzle resolves itself by shifting to another diegetic level, by a sort of leap—or metadiegetic transfer—in a series of abysses that become more and more minuscule up to the last, utterly cryptic point. The outcome of such a text remains unresolvable, unless it is referred to the next intertextual scene. In other words, the novel's intratextual structure is *the metaphor of its intertextually oriented solution.*

Also, this mystery, like those in Lahougue's or Peeters's detective stories, is both incomplete and *virtually* completable. The reader is given the opportunity to complete such unresolved texts because the mystery also lies, at the level of the signifier, among the textual traces to be disclosed. Clues are not only *diegetic*, addressed to a fictional investigator whom the reader tries to surpass, or to a fictional reader represented in the story, but they are also *likely to be textually detected*, in the same way that we could tentatively form the unsaid and improbable name of the culprit in *La Bibliothèque de Villers*. Reading thus becomes a multidimensional activity that takes into account all aspects of the text, narrative as well as linguistic, fictional as well as structural. Combes calls these clues "textual detectandes" (240–41); I will call them, more precisely, *extradiegetic detectandes*, insofar as they can only address the reader—not the characters. This is the case when detectandes lie in the narrating discourse, not the narrated fiction. They are, like clues at the diegetic level, both masked and traceable, hidden and "readable": they are simply *deferred*, left to the reader's perspicacity. Thus we better understand Peeters's formula: "to investigate is to detect the signs that have been distributed throughout the text" ("Ecriture" 169). We could thus define the *detectability* of the mystery as this *textual possibility* of finding a solution that is never made explicit.

By reformulating Ricardou's once famous phrase, let us provisionally sum up this evolution: from a time when fiction narrated the "adventures of writing" (*Problèmes* 111), to one in which narratives call forth "the adventure of reading."

Notes

An earlier version of this essay appeared in *Romanic Review* 88, 2 (1997): 315–35. Reprinted with permission of Columbia University.

1. My translations unless otherwise noted. For a preliminary study of the post-*nouveau roman* detective novel, see my "(Re)writing Considered as an Act of Murder" (255–59).

2. On the relationship between the *nouveau roman* and the detective genre, see Alter, Boyer, Charney, Combes, Janvier, Lits 60–61, and Vareille 191–203. The detective genre in question is more or less a *type* of the mystery genre, that is, the tale of detection, "the tale of pure puzzle, pure ratiocination" (Holquist 154). This model is not far from the one privileged by the early *nouveau roman*, as Eisenzweig points out (Robbe-Grillet, "Entretien" 18).

3. Along with the three writers studied here, this post-*nouveau roman* detective novel could include Modiano's *Rue des Boutiques Obscures* (1978); Echenoz's *Méridien de Greenwich* (1979) and *Cherokee* (1983); Belletto's *Film noir* (1980) and *Sur la terre comme au ciel* (1982); Roubaud's *La Belle Hortense* (1985), *L'Enlèvement d'Hortense* (1987), and *L'Exil d'Hortense* (1990), among others.

4. For example, Manchette's or Daenincks's sociopolitical crime stories are popular representatives of the genre. Like most novels published by Gallimard's *série noire*, they remain clearly bound within a representational strategy.

5. The borderline between, on the one hand, "the detective novel taken seriously"—to borrow the conclusive phrase from Janvier's inaugural study of the *nouveau roman* policier—and, on the other hand, a so-called typical detective story is certainly not always clear. Although Japrisot was published earlier and

is perceived as a "popular" writer, his *Piège pour Cendrillon* (1962) presents traits that can be found in Peeters's *La Bibliothèque de Villers* and Lahougue's "La Ressemblance," particularly the use of narrative voice (infra). Similarly, a widely read author such as Pennac is not only published in the prestigious "blanche" collection from Gallimard, but combines "low" and "high" art characteristics that explicitly recall Gadda's *That Awful Mess on the Via Merulana* (*Au bonheur* 137).

6. Although I think that Robbe-Grillet's *Le Voyeur* (1955), Ollier's *Le Maintien de l'ordre* (1961), or Pinget's *L'Inquisitoire* (1962) are not yet perceived as *textes lisibles* outside the academic world. I propose the term post-*nouveau roman* in reference to the textual/ narratological denominators conceptualized, in Ricardou's *Le Nouveau roman*, under the common strategy of a "*mise en cause du récit*" (231). See also Smyth, "*Nouveau*" 54–73. To make things clear, I never imply that there is only one *nouveau roman*: Sarraute, Ollier, or Pinget, and so on, are all "original" writers, and each experiments in many ways with uncommon narrative forms. What they share, however, whatever their differences are, is a common *metarepresentational* strategy (Ricardou, *Le Nouveau* 247).

7. See Ricardou, "How" 280–82. In short, written structures that bring about effects of meta-representation "exceed effects of representation" and "let transpire that which representation tends to obliterate within its mechanism" (281).

8. According to Renaud Camus, "Today's novelist inherits all the formal constraints of his predecessors as well as an extra constraint, which is that the text must be readable [*lisible*]" (quoted in Leclerc 67 and in Jullien and Polizzotti 337).

9. Obviously, the post-*nouveau roman* does not repeat the same parodic use of the detective genre as the early *nouveau roman*: Echenoz's first two books are clearly very different from Robbe-Grillet's *The Erasers*. However, for the *nouveau roman* detective novel, there remain "striking similarities which go beyond the whim of a particular inspiration, and we can wonder what they imply" (Charney 18). Vareille sees "an *internal necessity*" that explains the many borrowings from the detective genre (192–93; original emphasis).

10. Roussel became a major model for Robbe-Grillet, and Ricardou partly developed his theory of generators on the basis of Roussel's "procédés," as explained in *Comment j'ai écrit certains de mes livres*. For Roussel's connection to the *nouveau roman*, see Ricardou, "Le Nouveau Roman est-il roussellien?" and "L'Activité roussellienne" (*Pour* 91–117).

11. Ollier regards Leroux's *Le Mystère de la chambre jaune* as "a masterpiece of mystery fiction," producing a particularly complex "fictional dynamics" caused by the "discrepancy between the evidence acquired by the detective and the evidence made available to the reader." This discrepancy is the ground for every detective story ["le fondement de tout récit policier"], and in Leroux's book "it reaches the widest amplitude" ("La Double" 139).

12. If the *nouveau roman* "borrows countless techniques from the detective novel," that appropriation stands out for an essential reason: "The investigation is hardly ever resolved (it is perhaps Butor, in *Degrés*, who offers the most captivating model of total defeat). . . . In the detective novel, on the contrary, we are assured of reaching a solution, of attaining a complete reality that will join the various threads of the investigation and explain everything" (Charney 21).

13. "Someone investigates a case that he does not understand. Someone investigates a series of elements which seems to tell a story, but the story has many lacunae and contradictions" (Robbe-Grillet, "Entretien" 21).

14. Here the relation is still more complex, since we could say that Lahougue's

short story parodies and condenses, in Genette's sense of "serious transformation," a novel that is already a generic parody. In other words, we deal with a parody of a parody. In Nabokov's *Despair*, the narrator (Hermann) kills his assumed double (Felix) and takes his place. In Lahougue's "La Ressemblance," this scenario becomes a metaphor for his revision of Nabokov's novel (for an extensive study, see my essay "(Re)Writing Considered" 267–82).

15. In an earlier version, the epilogue transcribed the first pages word by word; but when Simenon complained, the published epilogue became a paraphrase of the original instead of a "collage." Indeed, the cover of *La Doublure de Magrite*—which was originally titled *La Doublure de Maigret*—quotes and parodies the original cover of Simenon's novel. It is an interesting case of what we may call, in Genette's terms, *peritextual hypertextuality* (*Seuils* 10).

16. The central café scene in *La Doublure*—repeated several times from a different actor's perspective, as each variation systematically drops one of its components, thus inscribing a different blank each time—recalls the already parodic (Simenonian) café scene in *The Erasers* ("Ecrire vers" 18).

17. Lahougue explains, "The detective becomes a victim. The reader becomes a detective. The assassin turns out to be the reader" ("Ecrire vers" 11).

18. "The detective novel enacts reading and thematizes the figure of the reader within its own narrative" (Felman 24). Felman sees *Oedipus Rex* as a "paradigm par excellence of the detective genre" (25n1).

19. The original title is *The Tooth and the Nail* (New York: Harper, 1955). For a bibliography of Perec's detective intertexts, see Bellos 121–22.

Works Cited

Alter, V. Jean. "L'Enquête policière dans le 'Nouveau Roman': *La Mise en scène* de Claude Ollier." In *Un Nouveau Roman? Recherches et tradition: La critique étrangère*, ed. J. H. Matthews. Paris: Minard, 1964. [*La Revue des Lettres Modernes* 94–99]. 83–104.

Baetens, Jan. "Qu'est-ce qu'un texte 'circulaire'?" *Poétique* 94 (1993): 215–28.

Barthes, Roland. *S/Z*. Paris: Seuil, 1970.

Belletto, René. *Film noir*. Paris: Hachette, 1980.

———. *Sur la terre comme au ciel*. Paris: Hachette, 1982.

Bellos, David. *Georges Perec: A Life in Words*. New York: HarperCollins, 1993.

Boyer, Alain-Michel. "Du Double à la doublure: L'image du détective dans les premiers romans de Robbe-Grillet." *L'Esprit Créateur* 26, 2 (1986): 60–70.

———. "L'Enigme, l'enquête et la quête du récit: La fiction policière dans *Les Gommes* et *Le Voyeur*." *French Forum* 6 (1981): 74–83.

Butor, Michel. *L'Emploi du temps*. [*Passing Time*]. Paris: Minuit, 1957.

Charney, Hanna. "Pourquoi le 'Nouveau Roman' policier?" *French Review* 46, 1 (1972): 17–23.

Christie, Agatha. *The ABC Murders*. New York: Pocket, 1936.

———. *The Murder of Roger Ackroyd*. New York: Pocket, 1926.

———. *Ten Little Indians*. [*And Then There Were None*]. New York: Pocket, 1939.

Combes, Annie. *Agatha Christie: L'écriture du crime*. Paris: Impressions Nouvelles, 1989.

Daeninckx, Didier. *Meurtres pour mémoire*. Paris: Gallimard, 1984.

Echenoz, Jean. *Cherokee*. [1983]. Trans. Mark Polizzotti. Boston: Godine, 1987.

———. *Le Méridien de Greenwich*. Paris: Minuit, 1979.

Eisenzweig, Uri. *Le Récit impossible: Forme et sens du roman policier.* Paris: Christian Bourgois, 1986.

Felman, Shoshana. "De Sophocle à Japrisot (via Freud)." *Littérature* 49 (1983): 23–42.

Gadda, Carlo Emilio. *That Awful Mess on the Via Merulana.* [*Quer pasticciaccio brutto de Via Merulana,* 1957]. Intro. Italo Calvino, trans. William Weaver. New York: George Braziller, 1984.

Genette, Gérard. *Narrative Discourse.* [*Figures III,* 1972]. Ithaca, N.Y.: Cornell University Press, 1980.

———. *Palimpsestes.* Paris: Seuil, 1982.

———. *Seuils.* Paris: Seuil, 1987.

Holquist, Michael. "Whodunit and Other Questions: Metaphysical Detective Stories in Post-War Fiction." *New Literary History* 3 (1971): 135–56. Reprinted in *The Poetics of Murder: Detective Fiction and Literary Theory,* ed. Glenn W. Most and William W. Stowe. New York: Harcourt, 1983. 150–74.

Janvier, Ludovic. "Le Point de vue du policier." *Une Parole exigeante.* Paris: Minuit, 1964. 37–49.

Japrisot, Sebastien. *Piège pour Cendrillon.* Paris: Denoël, 1962.

Jullien, Dominique and Mark Polizzotti. "Jean Echenoz." *Yale French Studies,* supplement (1988): 337–51.

Lahougue, Jean. *Comptine des Height.* Paris: Gallimard, 1980.

———. "Ecrire à partir d'Agatha Christie." *Texte en Main* 6 (1986): 5–10.

———. "Ecrire vers Simenon." *Texte en Main* 6 (1986): 11–29.

———. *La Doublure de Magrite.* Paris: Impressions Nouvelles, 1987.

———. "La Ressemblance." *La Ressemblance et autres abus de langage.* Paris: Impressions Nouvelles, 1989.

———. *Non-lieu dans un paysage.* Paris: Gallimard, 1977.

Leblanc, Maurice. *Les Huit coups de l'horloge.* [*Eight Strokes of the Clock*]. Paris: Le Livre de Poche, 1923.

Leclerc, Yvan. "Autour de minuit." *Dalhousie French Studies* 17 (1989): 63–74.

Leroux, Gaston. *Le Mystère de la chambre jaune.* [1907]. Paris: Le Livre de Poche, 1960.

Lits, Marc. *Pour lire le roman policier.* Paris: De Boeck-Duculot, 1989.

Magné, Bernard. "'*53 jours*'. Pour lecteurs chevronnés . . . ." *Etudes Littéraires* 23, 1–2 (1990): 185–201.

Manchette, Jean-Patrick. *Fatale.* Paris: Gallimard, 1977.

———. *La Position du tireur couché.* Paris: Gallimard, 1981.

———. *Le Petit bleu de la côte ouest.* Paris: Gallimard, 1976.

Modiano, Patrick. *Rue des Boutiques Obscures.* [*Missing Person*]. Paris: Gallimard, 1978.

Nabokov, Vladimir. *Despair.* [*Otchaianie,* 1934, 1936; rev. and trans. by the author, 1965]. New York: Putnam, 1966.

Ollier, Claude. "La Double logique de Gaston Leroux." *Nébules.* Paris: Flammarion, 1981. 139–40.

———. *La Mise en scène.* [*The Mise en Scène*]. Paris: Minuit, 1959.

———. *Le Maintien de l'ordre.* Paris: Gallimard, 1961.

Peeters, Benoît. "Agatha Christie: Une écriture de la lecture." In *Problèmes actuels de la lecture,* ed. Jean Ricardou and Lucien Dällenbach. Paris: Clancier-Guénaud, 1982. 165–177.

———. *La Bibliothèque de Villers.* [1980]. Paris: Impressions Nouvelles, 1990.

———. "Tombeau d'Agatha Christie." *La Bibliothèque* 97–136.

Pennac, Daniel. *Au Bonheur des ogres*. Paris: Gallimard, 1985.

Perec, Georges. *"53 jours"*. [*"53 Days"*]. Paris: P.O.L., 1989.

――――. "Entretien." Interview with Jean-Marie Le Sidaner. *L'Arc* 76 (1979): 3–10.

――――. *La Disparition*. [*A Void*]. Paris: Denoël, 1969.

――――. *Life: A User's Manual*. [*La Vie mode d'emploi*, 1978]. Boston: Godine, 1987.

――――. *W, or the Memory of Childhood*. [*W ou le souvenir d'enfance*, 1975]. Boston: Godine, 1988.

Pinget, Robert. *L'Inquisitoire*. Paris: Minuit, 1962.

Ricardou, Jean. "Eléments de textique (1)." *Conséquences* 10 (1987): 5–37.

――――. "How to Reduce Fallacious Representative Innocence, Word by Word." Interview with Michel Sirvent. *Studies in Twentieth Century Literature* 25, 2 (1991): 277–311.

――――. "La Révolution textuelle." *Esprit* 12 (1974): 927–45.

――――. *Le Nouveau Roman*. [1973]. Rev. ed. Paris: Seuil, 1990.

――――. "Le Nouveau Roman est-il roussellien?" *L'Arc* 68 (1977): 60–78.

――――. *Les Lieux-dits, petit guide d'un voyage dans le livre*. [1969]. Paris: Union Générale d'Editions, 1972.

――――. *Nouveaux problèmes du roman*. Paris: Seuil, 1978.

――――. *Pour une théorie du nouveau roman*. Paris: Seuil, 1971.

――――. *Problèmes du nouveau roman*. Paris: Seuil, 1967.

Robbe-Grillet, Alain. "Entretien." Interview with Uri Eisenzweig. *Littérature* 49 (1983): 16–22.

――――. *The Erasers*. [*Les Gommes*, 1953]. Trans. Richard Howard. New York: Grove, 1964.

――――. *Le Voyeur*. Paris: Minuit, 1955.

Roubaud, Jacques. "Entretien." Interview with Jacques Neefs. *Littérature* 80 (1990): 95–100.

――――. *La Belle Hortense*. [1985]. Paris: Seuil, 1990.

――――. *L'Enlèvement d'Hortense*. [1987]. Paris: Seuil, 1996.

――――. *L'Exil d'Hortense*. [1990]. Paris: Seuil, 1990.

Roussel, Raymond. *Comment j'ai écrit certains de mes livres*. Paris: Pauvert, 1963.

Simenon, Georges. *La Première enquête de Maigret*. Paris: Presses de la Cité, 1948.

Sirvent, Michel. "Lettres volées (métareprésentation et lipogramme chez E. A. Poe et G. Perec)." *Littérature* 83 (1991): 12–30.

――――. "(Re)Writing Considered as an Act of Murder: How to Rewrite Nabokov's *Despair* in a Post-Nouveau Roman Context." *Nabokov Studies* 2 (1995): 251–76.

Smyth, Edmunds J. "The *Nouveau Roman*: Modernity and Postmodernity." In *Postmodernism and Contemporary Fiction*, ed. Edmunds J. Smyth. London: Batsford, 1991. 54–73.

Tani, Stefano. *The Doomed Detective: The Contribution of the Detective Novel to Postmodern American and Italian Fiction*. Carbondale: Southern Illinois University Press, 1984.

Van Dine, S. S. "Twenty Rules for Writing Detective Stories." In *Writing Suspense and Mystery Fiction*, ed. A. S. Burack. Boston: The Writer, 1977. 267–72.

Vareille, Jean-Claude. *L'Homme masqué, le justicier et le détective*. Lyon: Presses Universitaires, 1989.

Chapter 8
"A Thousand Other Mysteries"
Metaphysical Detection, Ontological Quests
Jeanne C. Ewert

> Briefly, the story I have in mind opens as a very orthodox murder
> mystery in a rural district. The perplexed parties have recourse to
> the local barrack which, however, contains some very extraordinary
> policemen who do not confine their investigations or activities to
> this world or to any known planes or dimensions. Their most casual
> remarks create a thousand other mysteries.
> —Flann O'Brien, letter to Andy Gillette (quoted in Asbee 51)

Describing the novel that would become *The Third Policeman* (1967),
Flann O'Brien defines succinctly the postmodernist, or metaphysical,
detective story.[1] In this twentieth-century divergence from classic mysteries, apparently orthodox tales of detection are populated by extraordinary detectives subject to unexpected rules of behavior. Metaphysical
detection calls into question structures taken for granted after Edgar
Allan Poe's "Murders in the Rue Morgue" (1841): the hermeneutic
strategies of rendering meaningful those signs which are unintelligible
to others, and of divining the mind of an opponent; the epistemological
method of discovering truth by questioning sources of knowledge; and
the adept detective's triumph over the dangerous Other. Rather than
denying the viability of its predecessors, metaphysical detection carefully doubles its precursors—deliberately, flamboyantly, ironically—in
order to undermine them.

The Attack on Epistemology

> "You know," said Ratso, with something close to dismay in his voice, "sometimes I wonder, what fucking detective school did you go to, Sherlock?"
> "Elementary, my dear Ratso," I said, "Elementary."
> —Kinky Friedman, *Frequent Flyer* (226)
>
> Clues, legwork, investigative routine—none of this is going to matter anymore.
> —Paul Auster, *Ghosts* (175)

In *Postmodernist Fiction*, Brian McHale identifies metaphysical detection's greatest swerve away from classical models as a shift in the "dominants" characterizing modernist and postmodernist fiction. McHale addresses only classic detection, which he calls the "little sister" genre of modernism, citing their mutual dependence on epistemological concerns. He places science fiction and fantasy with postmodernism and the "ontological" (9). But McHale does not address metaphysical detection, which is also marked by an ontological dominant.

McHale borrows the term "dominant" from Roman Jakobson, who defines it as "the focusing component of a work of art: it rules, determines, and transforms the remaining components. It is the dominant which guarantees the integrity of the structure" (105). The shift in dominants that McHale identifies in postmodernist fiction corresponds to a change from questions of interpretation ("How can I know this world? What is there to be known? Who knows it? How do they know it and with what degree of certainty? How is knowledge transmitted and with what degree of reliability? What are the limits of the knowable?") to questions of "modes of being" ("Which world is this? What is a world? What kinds of worlds are there, how are they constituted? What happens when boundaries between worlds are violated?") (McHale 9–10).

He argues that science fiction and fantasy, which describe imaginary worlds, have always been ontological in emphasis, and that classic detective fiction, concerned with questions of interpretation, is essentially epistemological. Knowing is everything for Auguste Dupin and Sherlock Holmes, for Sam Spade and Philip Marlowe and their hard-boiled successors. Beyond mere problem solving, however, knowledge is life-giving for these detectives, a means of salvation when salvation means knowing more than and more about one's opponent. But when detective fiction of the postmodernist period makes the transition to an ontological dominant, it exceeds the simple category of the epistemological that McHale ascribes to it.[2] In the worlds of metaphysical detective fiction, created by writers like Jorge Luis Borges, Alain Robbe-Grillet, O'Brien, and Georges Perec, the bodies of dead detectives (and their victims) warn the reader away from the quest for knowledge.

Borges's short story, "An Examination of the Work of Herbert Quain" (1941), was perhaps the first to illustrate the shortcomings of classic detection methods in this new genre. The story describes a detective novel, written by the eponymous Quain, in which the detective arrives at a solution to the mystery but is contradicted by a comment from the narrator at the end of the novel. As Borges notes, "This phrase allows one to understand that the solution is erroneous. The unquiet reader rereads the pertinent chapters and discovers *another* solution, the true one. The reader of this singular book is thus forcibly more discerning than the detective" (74).

Borges again illustrated the inadequacies of classic detection in a later story, "Death and the Compass" (1942). Here the protagonist, Erik Lönnrot, models himself after Poe's master detective (he is "a pure reasoner, an Auguste Dupin" [129]), and the story is in many ways a commentary on Poe's detective fiction.[3] Lönnrot is called in to solve the mystery of a murdered rabbi in a local hotel. The police commissioner suggests that the motive for murder was the presence of the Tetrarch of Galilee's fine sapphires across the hall: a thief had entered the wrong room and murdered in a panic when he realized his mistake. But Lönnrot rejects this solution, which depends on chance and mistaken identity, preferring one which offers a complex pattern and scope for the epistemologically astute detective. He chooses, as he says, "a purely rabbinical explanation"—that is, one which involves obscure and recondite knowledge, "the immediate knowledge of all things that will be, which are, and which have been in the universe" (130, 131). Once he has announced his belief in a pattern, his archenemy, Red Scharlach, who commissioned the crime and knows that it was indeed a mistake, is able to create a trap for him based on the pattern that Lönnrot believes to exist. Borges emphasizes Scharlach's position as Lönnrot's double, pointing out in a note to the tale that the final syllable of "Lönnrot" means "red" in German, and that "Red Scharlach" is also translatable, in German, as "Red Scarlet." Lönnrot is doubled by a double red.

A look back at Poe's classic detective stories illustrates exactly where Lönnrot goes wrong. In Poe's stories, Dupin triumphs because he is able to identify so completely with his double as to be able to predict his next move. The narrator of "The Murders in the Rue Morgue" likens Dupin's skills to those demanded by the game of draughts. Chess he dismisses as demanding merely concentration, whereas draughts demands "superior acumen" of its winning player: "The analyst throws himself into the spirit of his opponent, identifies himself therewith, and not infrequently sees thus, at a glance, the sole methods (sometimes indeed absurdly simple ones) by which he may seduce into error or hurry into miscalculation" (3). The checker player must identify himself with his opponent, a process of doubling which the detective also performs when reconstructing a crime. Dupin models this process in "The Murders in the Rue Morgue" and again in "The Purloined Letter," the first time successfully enough to apprehend a sailor and an orangutan, and the second time so successfully that some readers have argued that Dupin and the Minister D——— are the same person (see Babener, and Blythe and Sweet). Lönnrot, on the other hand, fails—because mere identification with the double, with the Other, is an uncertain and problematic strategy in metaphysical detection. Or rather, Lönnrot fails because he has attempted to identify with the wrong adversary; the Other is not any human agent, but chance itself. The solution for which he searches is purely aleatory, and he fails to double his adversary because the aleatory cannot be mirrored.[4]

The fact that the police commissioner—who in classic detection is always astoundingly dense—is correct in his original solution to the crime only adds insult to injury. Scharlach steals the moment when the traditional detective explains the solution to his duped audience; this should alert the reader to the detective's inevitable downfall. Borges writes himself into the story as the thief and informer Azevedo, who breaks into the wrong room ("Azevedo" bears a variant of Borges's own name, Jorge Luis Borges Acevedo). In his position as thief, Borges has borrowed liberally from Poe; but as an informer, he tells us of Lönnrot's crime: this would-be Dupin has erred in believing that he still lives in an epistemologically oriented universe, where knowledge leads to successful detection and the detective invariably triumphs. He lives only long enough to discover that times have changed; knowledge means certain death, and detection is no longer a viable career.

Lönnrot is only the first detective to discover that the quest for knowledge is a mortal error. Georges Perec's *La Disparition* (1969, trans. as *A Void*, 1994), deals more destruction to truth seekers than perhaps any other metaphysical detective story. *A Void* is a detective story about a mysterious disappearance, a hole in the logic of the universe: the complete disappearance of the letter *E* from spoken and written language. The novel is a lipogram, a text which categorically excludes one or more letters of the alphabet; some 300 pages long, *A Void* is written entirely without *E*, the most common letter in the French language. The characters in the novel are aware of a loss, an absence, that they can describe but not name. In a retelling of the story of Oedipus and the Sphinx, for example, the sphinx poses this riddle:

Which animal do you know
That has a body curving as a bow
And draws back inwards straight as an arrow? (28)

The answer, of course, is "e."[5] *E* is also the grass growing in the shape of a "harpoon with 3 prongs or a hand with 3 digits" on the grave of one of the characters (90). The loss of the *E* creates havoc in the text: murder, mayhem, incest, infanticide, fratricide, and the disappearance of all who are marked with the fatal letter. What is left behind is a hole ("an omission, a blank, a void") into which it is fatal to look too closely, a "gradual invasion of words by margins" which will eventually leave all of us with nothing to say (13, 16).

Anton Voyl, whose own name points to the lost letter ("voyelle" without an *e*) and puns on "hidden" ("voile" means "veil"), spends the first four chapters of the novel looking into this abyss, trying to recall what is missing. Perec emphasizes the shortcomings of classic hermeneutic reasoning in an episode where Voyl reads a newspaper account of a stolen document of great importance, a document that the police are sure the thief has retained. The police have already searched the suspect's house twenty times when the great Dupin is called into the case. It is Dupin's opinion that the thief has not bothered to hide the fatal letter at all, that he would be subtle enough to leave it in plain sight. Dupin himself searches the house, but evidently doesn't identify closely enough with his opponent. He fails to find the missing letter, and leaves the police to their own devices in order to deal with the strange case of an orangutan which has committed some horrifying murders (39).

Voyl pursues his own mystery, then falls into the hole of chapter 5 and is gone. Or rather, he falls into the hole where chapter 5 should be; like the fifth letter of the alphabet, it has disappeared from the text (as has Part 2, representing the second vowel, and the fifth item in any collection of twenty-six objects—books, journals, photographs—which appears in the text). His friends assume that he has made a significant discovery; they read his journal, they exchange information, they track down his acquaintances. One by one, they themselves look into the awful blank and die. One succumbs while trying to explain to the others that the lipogram they have just read lacks not the *A* but the . . . (*E*). Another dies crying, "la Maldiction"—a complex pun which points to the missing letter, the curse associated with it, and the resulting truncation of language itself (195). The textual constraint is merciless. The letter is forbidden—to be marked by it, or to arrive at a knowledge of it, is to die and to disappear from the pages of the novel.

Even when classic epistemological methods are not fatal to the metaphysical detective, they are unsuccessful. William of Baskerville, investigating the murders of several Franciscan monks in a wealthy Italian abbey in Umberto Eco's *The Name of the Rose* (1980), makes a disastrous false conjecture—that there is a single murderer in the monastery who is following an apocalyptic pattern in his choice of methods. Preferring, like Borges's Lönnrot, a complex "rabbinical explanation" ("Death" 130), William falls neatly into the trap set for him by his antagonist, the appropriately named Jorge of Burgos, who understands William's conjecture and takes advantage of it.

Friedrich Dürrenmatt's detective in *The Pledge* (1958) also sets a trap that closes on the detective rather than the criminal. *The Pledge*, subtitled *Requiem for the Detective Story*, opens with a classically brilliant detective who is moved by a young girl's murder and anticipates a repetition of the crime. By reconstructing the criminal's methods and mentality, he is able to set a trap for him, and waits there with all the assurance of Holmes himself.[6] But whereas in the Holmesian world criminals never fail to act as expected, in Dürrenmatt's universe chance suddenly intervenes—unknown to the detective, the murderer is killed in an automobile accident on his way to commit the crime. Familiar only with a world where perfect logic leads to perfect solutions, the detective can envision no alternative but to wait, to wait his whole life, which is now as useless as the knowledge that has dictated his behavior.

In several metaphysical mysteries, the detective doesn't "fail" to solve the crime, but rather turns out to have committed it—perhaps the greatest failing of all in classical detection. This plot twist first appeared in Heimito von Doderer's *Every Man a Murderer* (1938). In this novel the protagonist becomes obsessed with solving the murder of his wife's sister, who was killed many years earlier in an apparent robbery on a train. His investigation reveals that he himself, in a childish prank perpetrated the first time he was allowed to take a train alone, caused the young woman's death without being aware of it. His growing sense of guilt fuels his obsession throughout the novel, forcing him to confront his own past even when all other investigators have given up the search.

Alain Robbe-Grillet's *The Erasers* (1953) is perhaps the best-known example of this motif in metaphysical detection.[7] His detective is sent to an unfamiliar Flemish city to solve one in a series of political assassinations, the work of a terrorist group trying to overthrow the government. Like Lönnrot, Special Agent Wallas refuses to account for chance and accidents, relying instead on the investigative strategies of his mentor in the department, a celebrated detective. For all his cunning, he ends up murdering the original victim himself. Professor Dupont, shot by the special agent who is trying to locate his "murderer," is a double victim—of the plot against his life, which left him wounded but not dead, and of the bungling detective, obsessed by an insoluble problem and a supposedly foolproof plan. Wallas spends much of his time walking in circles through city streets, adopting roles for himself to boost his confidence or stepping into roles suggested for him by others, acting like a suspect before he is one, excusing his guilt before he becomes guilty. He misses dozens of textual signs that intimate his role in the death of Professor Dupont: the representation of the Oedipus story in public statues, window curtains, paintings; the encounters with his stepmother, Dupont's wife; his own recollections of a previous visit to the city to see his father; the obvious conclusion that Dupont must have faked his own death after the first attack; and even the suggestion, by another investigator, that Dupont was killed by his own son.[8]

David Lehman tells us that "the most subversive thing that can happen in a detective novel is the recognition that . . . chaos is the norm and true detection impossible, and that the detective is therefore doomed to fail or die" (xiii). The quest for knowledge is fatal in metaphysical detection, but these narratives do not really constitute a requiem for the detective story. Rather, they are a requiem for a kind of detective story bound to the classic concerns of epistemology and hermeneutics. Metaphysical detection plays a different kind of game altogether.

The Failed Detective and the New Reader[9]

> What model reader did I want as I was writing? An accomplice, to be sure, one who would play my game.
> —Umberto Eco, *Postscript to* The Name of the Rose (50)

> As a producer of fiction, the detective novel continues to interest and concern me, to the extent that it functions explicitly as a game between author and reader.
> —Georges Perec, "Entretien" (10; my trans.)

Eco and Perec know as well as anyone that detective fiction has always been a game played between author and reader, and that the nature of the game has changed with the shift from classic to metaphysical detection. Eco, who described classic detective stories in an influential essay on Ian Fleming's James Bond novels,[10] spends the first hundred pages of *The Name of the Rose* preparing his reader for a new kind of detective fiction, a fiction "in which very little is discovered and the detective is defeated" (*Postscript* 54). Readers expecting conventional detective fiction will have to learn how to play the games of metaphysical detection:

What does it mean, to imagine a reader able to overcome the penitential obstacle of the first hundred pages? It means, precisely, writing one hundred pages for the purpose of constructing a reader suitable for what comes afterward. . . . Is there a writer who writes only for a handful of readers? Yes, if by this you mean that the model reader he imagines has slight chance of being made flesh in any number. But even this writer writes in the hope, not all that secret, that his book itself will create, and in great quantity, many new exemplars of this reader, desired and pursued with such craftsmanlike precision, and postulated, encouraged, by his text. (*Postscript* 48)

In order to survive Eco's first hundred pages, his new reader must first learn to play the game of detection by herself. She cannot wait for the detective to solve the text's problems.

Perec's *A Void* assaults the reader, however, with the message that other metaphysical detective fiction sends more subtly. It screams its detectives' incompetence from every page; it hurls the missing *E* in its reader's face. It quotes poetry every French schoolchild knows, but in lipogrammatic translation.[11] The novel's detectives are sure that something is not quite right, but they can't put a finger on what it is. Anton Voyl leaves behind a mysterious message—"Portons dix bons whiskys à l'avocat goujat qui fumait au zoo"—which is the French equivalent, sans *E*, of "The quick brown fox jumped over the lazy dog." His friends, unable to "read" the clue, run to the zoo, whisky in hand, to look for the boorish lawyer with a cigarette, and then to the track to watch a horse named "Whisky Dix" (the fifth horse of twenty-six), who disappears and forfeits the race. Only the reader understands—or rather, the reader should understand. Perec reports that some reviewers treated the novel as a conventional mystery without ever noticing its very unconventional exclusion of the *E* ("Un Roman" 96).

The example of Perec's reviewers suggests that if the reader of metaphysical detective fiction must give up her dependence on the detective, she must also give up her expectations of the methods of conventional detection, even though the novels deliberately invoke those expectations. Metaphysical detective novels often advertise themselves as classic mysteries: Robbe-Grillet writes in a *prière d'insérer* for *The Erasers*, for example, that "it is a detective story event—that is, there is a murder, a detective, a victim. In one sense their roles are conventional: the murderer shoots the victim, the detective solves the problem, the victim dies." Similarly, Eco's William of Baskerville is described, in the blurb for the Warner edition of *The Name of the Rose*, as a "uniquely deft" detective who "collects evidence, deciphers secret symbols and coded manuscripts, and digs into the eerie secret labyrinth of abbey life,"[12] while Borges characterizes *The God of the Labyrinth*, in "An Examination of the Work of Herbert Quain," as a novel in which "an indecipherable assassination takes place in the initial pages; a leisurely discussion takes place towards the middle; a solution appears in the end" (74).

Even inside the covers of these novels, the conventions tease the reader. William of Baskerville resembles Sherlock Holmes with his beaky nose, long thin face, indulgence in narcotics, and a certain tolerance for institutional incompetence, while the mystified Adso recalls Watson. Auguste Dupin is mentioned in several metaphysical detective stories, and makes a firsthand appearance in *A Void.* The naive reader expects the solutions that usually accompany such detective novel trappings, but the methods lead only to distraction and defeat; looking like Sherlock Holmes, walking the mean streets like Philip Marlowe, or employing versions of their methods, cannot guarantee their successes.

If the reader of metaphysical detection must cease to rely on detective conventions, she must also abandon her attempts to find order in the universes she is exploring. Adso, Eco's Watson in *The Name of the Rose*, illustrates the behavior of the reader of classic detection when first encountering metaphysical detection. Adso searches for a kind of ultimate history, a fundamental order in the universe. Eco's novel, however, illustrates a universe destined to frustrate, one that Eco describes in his *Postscript* with the metaphor of a net, a theory of conjectural thinking,[13] and an explanation of three kinds of labyrinths:

> At this point it is clear why my basic story (whodunit?) ramifies into so many other stories, all stories of other conjectures, all linked with the structure of conjecture as such.
>
> An abstract model of conjecturality is the labyrinth. But there are three kinds of labyrinth. One is the Greek, the labyrinth of Theseus. This kind does not allow anyone to get lost: you go in, arrive at the center, and then from the center you reach the exit. . . .
>
> [The second] is the mannerist maze: if you unravel it, you find in your hands a kind of tree, a structure with roots, with many blind alleys. There is only one exit, but you can get it wrong. You need an Ariadne's-thread to keep from getting lost. This labyrinth is a model of the trial-and-error process. (57)

Eco's metaphor of the mannerist maze is applicable to the problem-solving techniques of many classic detective novels: Agatha Christie's Poirot, Dorothy Sayers's Wimsey, or Raymond Chandler's Marlowe, for example, follow a series of misleading and dead-end clues before they discover the correct direction for their investigation. But problem solving (or the failure to solve problems) in *The Name of the Rose* is modeled on a third kind of labyrinth, which Eco goes on to describe:

> And finally there is the net, or, rather, what Deleuze and Guattari call "rhizome." The rhizome is so constructed that every path can be connected with every other one. It has no center, no periphery, no exit, because it is potentially infinite. The space of conjecture is a rhizome space. The labyrinth of my library is still a mannerist labyrinth, but the world in which William realizes he is living

already has a rhizome structure: that is, it can be structured, but is never structured definitively. (57–58)

Adso has tremendous difficulty, for example, reconciling the evidence of the world in which he finds himself with the world in which he thought he was living. It is William who finally recognizes that world's rhizome structure: "I behaved stubbornly, pursuing a semblance of order, when I should have known well that there is no order in the universe" (599). The reader of metaphysical detection must pattern herself after William rather than Adso.

If she survives the first hundred pages of *The Name of the Rose*, she can practice her new skills on Gilbert Sorrentino's *Odd Number* (1985). The novel's name is taken from Flann O'Brien's *At Swim-Two-Birds* (1951) — "Truth is an odd number" (149) — and depends fully on the pun in O'Brien's phrase. Several odd numbers, characters in the novel, attempt to describe the truth of a murder as they see it, but their accounts are so contradictory that the reader gradually understands that the truth must be even odder than they. The novel is set among the New York "cultural literati," the inbred, bored, and sophisticated members of a sleazy world of art, drugs, sex, and crime. The sections of the novel can be read as transcripts of interviews with different characters, conducted by a police detective. Each tells a different story of the murder itself, the victim's marital and sexual relations, the individuals present at the scene of the crime, and the motives of the characters involved. In this regard, the novel resembles the various firsthand accounts the detective must sort through in a classic detective story — except that in this case the stories contradict each other so blatantly, and the characters give so much obscure, irrelevant, and unnecessary information, that the detective himself becomes mired in their competing histories, and asks questions as irrelevant and obscure as the answers he gets. Nothing is resolved at the end of the novel; no history can be shown to supersede its competitors, and the witnesses' testimony builds a rhizomatic net of hypotheses and theories through which the detective wanders without coming to a conclusion.

The message for the reader of metaphysical detective fiction is clear: she must learn to read without relying on the detective's interpretations; she must also learn to read in a world that offers conjectures and structuring systems, but no single overriding structure. She must recognize that the labyrinth represents a radically different universe than the one she expected. For this, too, writers like Eco have been preparing her.

Ludics and Ontology

> We play with a plurality of make-believes, with the endless possibili-
> ties of existence in an infinite universe.
> — Umberto Eco, *Foucault's Pendulum* (62)

McHale takes his definition of literary ontology from Thomas Pavel:
an ontology is "a theoretical description of a universe" (Pavel 234).
McHale goes on to point out that this could refer to any universe: "In
other words, to 'do' ontology in this perspective is not necessarily to
seek some grounding for our universe; it might just as appropriately
involve describing *other* universes, including 'possible' or even 'impossible' universes—not least of all the other universe, or heterocosm, of
fiction" (27). The questions posed in and of ontological texts are posed
by the reader whenever unfamiliar universes (zones) are encountered,
and whenever the boundaries between universes are disturbed. McHale
identifies some potential causes of boundary disturbances: the appearance of real people and places in fictional universes; the intrusion of
the author into the text; transmigration of characters from one text to
another; the creation of alternative histories; self-consuming texts; excluded middles; multiple or circular endings; Chinese-box worlds; *mises
en abyme*; and self-referential texts.

Metaphysical detective fiction abounds with examples both of other,
unfamiliar universes and of the uneasiness produced when boundaries
between universes are violated, and it is for this reason that the term
"metaphysical" describes these works better than "anti-detective," which
indicates only what they deconstruct rather than what they construct.
Metaphysical detection plays its games in a different narrative (and narrated) world.[14]

O'Brien's *The Third Policeman* is a fine example of this unfamiliar realm.
His protagonist finds himself in a familiar yet strange universe when he
dies without being aware of his own death. The entire story is narrated
after this moment, and the reader, too, is unaware that the narrator is a
dead man describing the universe that he entered after death. Because
neither reader nor narrator is aware that the latter is dead, they are
together perplexed by this world, which looks like the narrator's native
Ireland but functions by different rules altogether—the transmigration
of atoms, for example, which allows people to turn into their bicycles
and bicycles to turn into people, if they are in contact for too long. In
this world, the narrator is convicted of a crime and hanged for it, despite the fact that he is already dead. He travels a circular path throughout the novel, always returning to the police station where he will once
again be accused of a crime, and once again be hanged. At the end of

the novel, the reader recognizes that this is the narrator's hell, and that what McHale would call the "strange loop"[15] of the text will keep him always returning there, while never remembering that he has traveled that road before.

Robbe-Grillet's Wallas (*The Erasers*) also finds himself in a universe with a different clock—his own watch stops when he enters it, and doesn't start again until he leaves. The novel's omniscient narrator describes what happens to time in this universe:

> Soon unfortunately time will no longer be master. Wrapped in their aura of doubt and error, this day's events, however insignificant they may be, will in a few seconds begin their task, gradually encroaching upon the ideal order, cunningly introducing an occasional inversion, a discrepancy, a confusion, a warp, in order to accomplish their work: a day in early winter without plan, without direction, incomprehensible and monstrous. (7)

Wallas discovers too late that he has stumbled into an extra twenty-four hours, an incomprehensible and fatal day, out of place in time, in which he will fire a bullet into a man who should have been dead the night before.

Sorrentino's *Odd Number* similarly uses the ontological convention of alternative histories. Each of the sections of the novel offers a unique history, and the detective loses himself in negotiating the maze that they form when added together. The plot is circular, ending with the description of a manuscript for a novel that is, of course, the series of transcripts that make up the novel itself.

The lipogrammatic *A Void* illustrates another kind of universe found in metaphysical detective fiction, one produced by textual constraints. The absence of the *E* regulates all levels of the text, not least of all the plot. The missing signifier de-structures—by its lack—the work of the detective: if the key to interpretation is absolutely, irreducibly missing, the interpretation can't (re)find it. Several of Perec's characters remark that they feel they are living in a strange kind of novel, in which "an author's imagination runs so wild, in which his writing is so stylistically outlandish, his plotting so absurd," that one would think him insane. The hypothetical author has

> an imagination aspiring to infinity, adding (or possibly subtracting) to (or from) its quasi-cosmic ambition a crucial factor, an astoundingly innovatory kind of linguistic originality running through it from start to finish. . . . such a work of fiction could not allow a solitary lazy or random or fortuitous word, no approximation, no passing and no nodding; that, contrarily, its author has rigorously to sift all his words—I say, all, from nouns down to lowly conjunctions—as if totally bound by a rigid, cast-iron law! (198–99)

His characters can't imagine what that law might be, although the paragraph above contains no *e*.

Other fictions employ similar kinds of constraints: Eco spends much of his *Postscript* explaining the historical restrictions governing the writing of *The Name of the Rose*; Borges's "Death and the Compass" depends on the content of the Jewish mystical texts Lönnrot interprets; and the plot of *The Erasers* must conform to the structure dictated by *Oedipus Rex*, the text on which it is patterned. The use of textual constraint directs the reader's attention to the artificiality of the text itself, and to the ontological status of the narrative it represents.

Other self-reflexive techniques include the intrusion of characters from other fictions (for example, Dupin's appearance in *A Void*); the manipulation of the work of real authors (Perec's misquotations of Mallarmé, Hugo, and Rimbaud, or O'Brien's positioning of an epigraph from the real Shakespeare next to one from the fictional DeSelby, suggesting that both may be fictional, or real); and at least one instance in which a novel (*A Void*) suggests itself as a fictional work that might illuminate the mystery confronting its own characters. Perec's *A Void* not only borrows characters and texts, but Perec writes himself into the novel on several occasions. It is Perec's voice, surely, that is the "Cri Vain," the vain cry whose curiosity must be sated by the text (201). The "cri vain" is the writer, the "écrivain," stripped of his *E*. Borges also writes himself into "Death and the Compass." One of the books studied by Lönnrot, *Vindication of the Kabbalah*, is by Borges himself, while Azevedo bears his name.

Two final examples of frame-breaking gestures are inspired by the classic hard-boiled detection of Raymond Chandler. Stephen King's *Umney's Last Case* (1993) is about a hack detective author writing in Chandler's style (the characters and locations all have names drawn from Chandler's novels), who, embittered and lonely after the death of his wife and son, decides to write himself into his fictional detective's world, and become himself the detective. The detective struggles to retain his fictional universe, but the author triumphs; and the detective finds himself in the "real" world, where he tries to learn to be the author. Hiber Conteris also recreates a Chandlerian universe in *Ten Percent of Life* (1985). It is set in Los Angeles in the 1950s, where both Chandler and his detective, Marlowe, exist in the same fictional universe, along with a slew of other people bearing the names of Chandler's characters. In Conteris's novel, Marlowe is the model for Chandler's detective, who is also named after him; but Marlowe is contemptous of Chandler's work, claiming that "the things Chandler thought up were impossible—his detective would never be able to solve a mystery in real life" (44). Marlowe is called upon to solve a murder in which Chandler is initially a suspect. Interviewing Chandler, Marlowe learns that he is disgusted with Hollywood and California, has given up writing detective fiction featuring his namesake, and is returning to England. From this moment on, Marlowe loses focus, and wonders if "a mysterious parallel might exist between Chandler's decision to write his last novel and the deadly apathy" which consumes him (192). Marlowe both is and is not Chandler's literary creation, existing in a netherworld where he can sit down for a drink with the author who made him famous, and yet can't survive in that world if his author leaves it.

Fatal Ludics and War Memoirs

These textual games, reminiscent of a popular children's series ("Where's Waldo?"), enable the reader to play "Where's Perec?" (or "King?" or "Borges?") with the text. Their pleasures are the reader's reward for learning the rules of metaphysical detection, and they allow her to congratulate herself for succeeding when the textual detectives fail. That is, if she wants to play the game at all. The worlds created in metaphysical detective stories are strange, uncanny . . . and dangerous. They are worlds without happy endings, where protagonists are lost in mazes without exits, destroyed by ruthless cabals, or simply doomed to impotence and incompetence. In them, neither brains nor brawn can save you if chance dictates otherwise—and chance has metastasized into malignant necessity.

Metaphysical detection is a genre predicated on the unpredictability of evil in a world where the rules are obscure and failure is fatal. Elliot L. Gilbert, in "The Detective as Metaphor in the Nineteenth Century," points to a moment when the most famous of the detective genre's players looked at the world and bowed out of the game. Arthur Conan Doyle, on the brink of World War I, recognized that even the combination of towering intellect and rabbinical solutions was doomed to fail:

The story called "His Last Bow" makes this point most incisively. Time and again in the early days, Holmes, by the simple expedient of discovering the hiding place of the top-secret plans or of revealing the activities of international spies, had single-handedly kept Europe from going to war. Now, however, it is August, 1914, and though the great man has come out of retirement to do battle once more with the forces of darkness, and though his mind seems as quick as ever, this time the darkness is not to be denied. To be sure, Holmes foils the German agent, but World War I, the ultimate symbol of irrationality, cannot so easily be put off. Can it be that in the end even Sherlock Holmes, whose creator—Conan Doyle—was himself to move from the realm of reason to the world of the occult, had come to doubt the efficacy of intellect? (292)

Detective fiction did survive the first world war, although Holmes did not; but Conan Doyle's move away from the positivism and epistemological solutions of the Holmes stories, on the brink of worldwide disaster, is significant when we consider the origins of its postmodernist successor.

Metaphysical detection, which also doubts the efficacy of intellect, dates from the brink of World War II, with many of its primary narratives written in the late 1930s and early to mid-'40s.[16] While two of the metaphysical detective stories I discuss here deal either implicitly or explicitly with the plight of European Jews during the war years, others betray the same feeling of impending disaster, of vague or shadowy evil, of tables being turned and the law-abiding being prosecuted as criminals. Running through these works is the sense that the detective, pledged to uphold the law, can suddenly find himself guilty of crimes he had no knowledge of committing, as well as the sense that the community has marked him, knows some secret about him. Doderer's *Every Man a Murderer* explores the anguish and growing sense of guilt of a man who had no motive to break the law and no reason to suspect himself guilty. In Robbe-Grillet's *The Erasers*, Special Agent Wallas is plagued by the notion that the city's inhabitants know some secret about him, causing him to lie when there is no need, and to act like a suspect when he has committed no crime. He cringes before the vague accusations of a drunk in a bar, and seems constantly to fear being found out by some shadowy organization of the law.

Patrick Modiano's *Rue des Boutiques Obscures* (1978) is narrated by the first detective protagonist we explicitly identify as Jewish and as a Holocaust survivor.[17] The amnesiac Guy Roland (a name he choose for himself because he cannot remember his own) is marked by some secret guilt that he fears others will see. Working for a detective agency in postwar Paris, he tries to reconstruct his past and his identity. Modiano strips away all illusions of the detective's authority from Roland in the novel's opening scene, as the detective explains his plans to his employer at the agency. Roland is not in a position of control (his own chair), but in the seat reserved for clients, and the glare from the desk lamp blinds him. The other man wears his coat belted, and keeps an open dossier on the desk. It is a scene of interrogation recognizable from hard-boiled detection and film noir, but in this case it is the detective who is under assault.

The motif is repeated at dinner with the detective's first contacts. Roland tells us, "The light from the fixture on the wall fell directly on me and blinded me. The others were in the shadow, but undoubtedly they placed me there in order to be better able to recognize me" (21). The two men question Roland, expressing disbelief when he claims to have no knowledge of his identity, and he comes hesitantly to concur with their assessment. At his next contact's apartment, the light is again directed onto Roland's face, silhouetting those of the others, which take on the appearance of mocking masks. If Modiano's use of light suggests scenes of interrogation, Roland's extreme shyness accentuates the impression that it is the detective who is being interrogated, and not his contacts. Like Robbe-Grillet's detective, he feels compelled to invent stories; he stutters, hesitates, often cannot work up the courage to ask the one question that might clarify everything, leaving the reader frustrated with his ineffectiveness.[18]

While Modiano's detective is recognizably Jewish, and his world recognizably postwar Paris, Perec's *A Void* deals with Holocaust themes on a more purely allegorical register. Perec was born in Paris in 1936, to Jewish parents who had recently emigrated to France. His father fought in the French army and was killed at the front in 1939. His mother was deported to the camps in 1942 and subsequently disappeared, presumably murdered at Auschwitz. Perec survived in the care of relatives (Bellos). The title of his novel, which loses some meaning in the English translation, is *La Disparition*, the disappearance. In French, it is also a term used for persons missing and presumed dead; indeed, the families of those Jews "relocated" to Germany during the Holocaust, who subsequently disappeared, were granted an *acte de disparition* by the French government after the war, which conferred on them certain legal rights in regard to pensions and property distribution.

The premise of Perec's novel is that certain of its inhabitants, all originally members of a single family, are marked with a secret sign, a sign which it is fatal to speak aloud, and which leads to sure destruction. It is not difficult to read this mark as one of absence—of a foreskin, of a place in the European social order after the war, of existence at all. Warren Motte estimates that "there are, at an absolute minimum, 1,000,789 murders in the 312 pages of *La Disparition*, for an average of 3,207 murders per page" (*Playtexts* 116): a novel-sized holocaust. The disappearance of those marked by the sign leaves a hole, a void, in the text, which its detectives cannot comprehend or explain. Perec, whose memoir of a childhood spent hiding from the Nazis is entitled *W ou le souvenir d'enfance*, dedicates that work "*pour E*"—which, as Motte points out, can be read "*pour eux*." For them, those that are marked by the letter *E* and disappear: "*mère, père, parents, famille, eux*" (*Playtexts* 122–25).

Elliot L. Gilbert suggests that Doyle, when faced with the destructiveness of the First World War, lost faith in the Holmesian tradition of inductive solutions in a positivist universe. Perec's novel suggests that the approaching shadow of the Holocaust may have had force enough to generate a new genre. His extended lipogram can be read as a threnody for the strategies and satisfactions of classic detection—which, confronted with madness and holocaust, simply, logically, fail. The disappeared *E* signals the hallmarks of a new detective fiction: a fiction without certainty, knowledge, sequence, cause, epistemology.

Notes

1. Merivale first applied the term "metaphysical detective story" to these fictions in her essay "The Flaunting of Artifice in Vladimir Nabokov and Jorge Luis Borges"; see also Holquist. Haycraft originally coined the term to describe the theological aspects of G. K. Chesterton's Father Brown mysteries.

2. While my argument is primarily that postmodernist detective fiction is ontological in emphasis, it should be noted that there is a subgenre which combines the epistemological and the ontological in ways that McHale (and I) might have difficulty classifying: the science-fiction detective story. Examples are Anthony's *Happy Policeman*, a detective novel set in a town taken over by aliens, and several works edited by Resnick, including *Sherlock Holmes in Orbit* and two volumes of *Whatdunits*, anthologies of alien detective stories.

3. Irwin treats Borges's rewriting of Poe's Dupin stories in detail in *The Mystery to a Solution: Poe, Borges, and the Analytic Detective Story.*

4. I am indebted to Terry Harpold for this observation.

5. The sphinx, intimately associated with that early disastrous detective enterprise, Oedipus's attempt to find the murderer of Laius, figures in more than one metaphysical detective story. See also *The Erasers* (225–26), where the riddle posed solves the mystery in much the same way that it does here.

6. *The Pledge* recalls several of Doyle's stories, including "The Adventure of the Speckled Band." In that story, Holmes lies in wait for a criminal who has murdered one young woman and plans to murder another. This is an effective maneuver in classic detective fiction: Doyle's murderer is in fact killed by the snake he planned to loose on the young woman.

7. I discussed *The Erasers* previously in "Lost in the Hermeneutic Funhouse."

8. Morrissette first identified and exhaustively studied the Oedipus structure and references in *The Erasers* (38–74).

9. This section of my essay owes much to Motte's study of authors, readers, and games, especially his discussion of ludic aspects of Perec's work (*Poetics* 22–23, 53).

10. "The criminal novel reduces redundancy; pretending to rouse the reader, it in fact reconfirms him in a sort of imaginative laziness and creates escape by narrating, not the Unknown, but the Already Known" (Eco, *Role* 160).

11. In Perec's original French, these include "Bris Marin" by Mallarmus, Hugo's "Booz Assoupi," and Rimbaud's "Vocalisations," with its famous first line: "A noir, [un blanc], I roux, U safran, O azur" (*La Disparition* 118–27). The non-lipogrammmatic sources are Mallarmé's "Brise marine," Hugo's "Booz endormi," and Rimbaud's "Voyelles": "A noir, E blanc, I rouge, U vert, O bleu." Adair's translation suggests appropriate English equivalents, including Shakspar's "Living, or not living" soliloquy, Milton's "On His Glaucoma," and Arthur Gordon Pym's "Black Bird."

12. Eco knows very well how to play on the naive reader's expectations: he devotes an entire essay, "Lector in Fabula," to an analysis of how Alphonse Allais's

Un drame bien parisien "carefully designs its naive reader as the typical consumer of adultery stories such as the market of *comédie de boulevard* had created," only to defy the expectations of that very reader (*Role* 207).

13. Eco's comments on conjectural thinking here build on his essay "Horns, Hooves, Insteps" (204–7); see also Cannon's discussion of Eco, conjecturalism, and reason (79–94).

14. Robert Harris's recent *Fatherland*, a more conventional thriller than most of the works discussed here, borrows from the techniques of his metaphysical precursors, creating an entirely new historical universe for his detective. *Fatherland* imagines Germany in the 1960s—after the Axis powers have won World War II. The novel depends on a compelling ontological device buried within an epistemological frame: the secret that drives the novel's action is clear to the reader early on, even as the detective struggles to discover it. But the reader knows the secret—the success of Hitler's "final solution to the Jewish problem"—only because she lives in a *different* universe, one where Hitler's forces lost the war and the horrors of the concentration camps were discovered. Harris's detective doesn't know the secret because, in his universe, Hitler succeeded in exterminating the Jews and hiding the evidence of their genocide.

15. McHale's allusion here to chaos theory and its relationship to the narrative structure of metaphysical detection is an avenue deserving further exploration.

16. In the introduction to this volume, Merivale and Sweeney trace the origins of metaphysical detection back to Poe; however, I agree with Sweeney's earlier claim, in "Aliens, Aliases, and Alibis," that its development as a self-conscious genre came in the 1930s with narratives by Borges, Felipe Alfau, Vladimir Nabokov, and O'Brien (208).

17. I discussed *Rue des Boutiques Obscures* extensively in "Lost in the Hermeneutic Funhouse."

18. The reader's frustration stems from the detective's move from the position of interrogator to interrogated. No longer able to pose questions, he ceases to aspire to the certain, saturated knowledge—or to the presentation of the grand narrative, in Lyotard's concept (34–37)—which was the birthright of his precursors.

Works Cited

Anthony, Patricia. *The Happy Policeman.* New York: Harcourt, 1994.

Asbee, Sue. *Flann O'Brien.* Boston: Twayne, 1991.

Auster, Paul. *Ghosts.* [1986]. *The New York Trilogy.* New York: Penguin, 1990. 159–232.

Babener, Lianha Klenman. "The Shadow's Shadow: The Motif of the Double in Edgar Allan Poe's 'The Purloined Letter.' " *Mystery and Detective Annual* (1972): 21–32.

Bellos, David. *Georges Perec: A Life in Words.* Boston: Godine, 1993.

Blythe, Hal and Charlie Sweet. "The Reader as Poe's Ultimate Dupe in 'The Purloined Letter.' " *Studies in Short Fiction* 26 (1989): 311–15.

Borges, Jorge Luis. "Death and the Compass." ["La Muerte y la brújula," 1942]. Trans. Anthony Kerrigan. *Ficciones* 129–41.

———. "An Examination of the Work of Herbert Quain." ["Examen de la obra de Herbert Quain," 1941]. Trans. Anthony Kerrigan. *Ficciones* 73–78.

———. *Ficciones.* Ed. Anthony Kerrigan. New York: Grove, 1962.

Cannon, JoAnn. *Postmodern Italian Fiction: The Crisis of Reason in Calvino, Eco, Sciascia, Malerba.* London: Associated University Press, 1989.

Conteris, Hiber. *Ten Percent of Life.* [*El Diez por cento de vida,* 1985]. New York: Simon and Schuster, 1987.

Doderer, Heimito von. *Every Man a Murderer.* [*Ein Mord den Jeder Begeht,* 1938]. Trans. Richard Winston and Clara Winston. New York: Knopf, 1964.

Doyle, Arthur Conan. "The Adventure of the Speckled Band." [1891]. *The Complete Novels and Stories.* 2 vols. New York: Bantam, 1986. 1: 346–69.

Dürrenmatt, Friedrich. *The Pledge: Requiem for the Detective Novel.* [*Das Versprechen: Requiem auf den Kriminalroman,* 1958]. Trans. Richard Winston and Clara Winston. New York: Knopf, 1959.

Eco, Umberto. *Foucault's Pendulum.* [*Il Pendolo di Foucault,* 1988]. Trans. William Weaver. New York: Ballantine, 1990.

———. "Hooves, Horns, Insteps: Some Hypotheses on Three Types of Abduction." In *The Sign of Three: Dupin, Holmes, Peirce,* ed. Umberto Eco and Thomas A. Sebeok. Bloomington: Indiana University Press, 1983. 198–220.

———. *The Name of the Rose.* [*Il Nome della Rosa,* 1980]. Trans. William Weaver. New York: Warner Books, 1983.

———. *Postscript to* The Name of the Rose. [*Postille a* Il Nome della Rosa, 1983]. Trans. William Weaver. New York: Harcourt, 1984.

———. *The Role of the Reader: Explorations in the Semiotics of Texts.* Trans. R. A. Downie. Bloomington: Indiana University Press, 1979.

Ewert, Jeanne C. "Lost in the Hermeneutic Funhouse: Patrick Modiano's Postmodern Detective." In *The Cunning Craft: Original Essays on Detective Fiction and Contemporary Literary Theory,* ed. Ronald Walker and June M. Frazer. Macomb: Western Illinois University Press, 1990. 166–73.

Friedman, Kinky. *Frequent Flyer.* New York: Berkeley, 1990.

Gilbert, Elliot L. "The Detective as Metaphor in the Nineteenth Century." *Journal of Popular Culture* 1 (1967): 256–62. Reprinted in *The Mystery Writer's Art,* ed. Francis M. Nevins, Jr. Bowling Green, Oh.: Bowling Green University Popular Press, 1970. 286–94.

Harris, Robert. *Fatherland.* New York: HarperCollins, 1992.

Haycraft, Howard. *The Art of the Mystery Story.* New York: Simon and Schuster, 1946.

Holquist, Michael. "Whodunit and Other Questions: Metaphysical Detective Stories in Postwar Fiction." *New Literary History* 3 (1971–72): 135–56. Reprinted in *The Poetics of Murder: Detective Fiction and Literary Theory,* ed. Glenn W. Most and William W. Stowe. New York: Harcourt, 1983. 150–74.

Irwin, John T. *The Mystery to a Solution: Poe, Borges, and the Analytic Detective Story.* Baltimore: Johns Hopkins University Press, 1994.

Jakobson, Roman. "The Dominant." In *Readings in Russian Poetics: Formalist and Structuralist Views,* ed. Ladislav Matjka and Krystyna Pomorska. Cambridge, Mass.: MIT Press, 1971. 105–10.

King, Stephen. *Umney's Last Case.* [1993]. New York: Penguin, 1995.

Lehman, David. *The Perfect Murder: A Study in Detection.* New York: Free Press, 1989.

Lyotard, Jean-François. *The Postmodern Condition: A Report on Knowledge.* Trans. Geoff Bennington and Brian Massumi. Minneapolis: University of Minnesota Press, 1984.

McHale, Brian. *Postmodernist Fiction.* New York: Methuen, 1987.

Merivale, Patricia. "The Flaunting of Artifice in Vladimir Nabokov and Jorge

Luis Borges." In *Nabokov: The Man and His Work*, ed. L. S. Dembo. Madison: University of Wisconsin Press, 1967. 290–324. Reprinted in *Critical Essays on Jorge Luis Borges*, ed. Jaime Alazraki. Boston: G. K. Hall, 1987. 141–53.

Modiano, Patrick. *Rue des Boutiques Obscures*. [*Missing Person*]. Paris: Gallimard, 1978.

Morrissette, Bruce. *The Novels of Robbe-Grillet*. Ithaca, N.Y.: Cornell University Press, 1975.

Motte, Warren F., Jr. *Playtexts*. Lincoln: University of Nebraska Press, 1995.

———. *The Poetics of Experiment: A Study of the Work of Georges Perec*. Lexington, Ky.: French Forum, 1984.

O'Brien, Flann. *At Swim-Two-Birds*. [1951]. New York: Plume, 1976.

———. *The Third Policeman*. [1967]. New York: Plume, 1976.

Pavel, Thomas. "Tragedy and the Sacred: Notes Towards a Semantic Characterization of a Fictional Genre." *Poetics* 10 (1981): 2–3.

Perec, Georges. *A Void*. [*La Disparition*. Paris: Denoël, 1962]. Trans. Gilbert Adair. New York: HarperCollins, 1994.

———. "Entretien." Interview with Jean-Marie Le Sidaner. *L'Arc* 76 (1979): 73–76.

———. "Un Roman lipogrammatique." *Oulipo: La littérature potentielle (Créations, re-créations, récréations)*. Paris: Gallimard, 1973. 94–96.

Poe, Edgar Allan. *The Complete Stories and Poems of Edgar Allan Poe*. New York: Doubleday, 1966.

———. "The Murders in the Rue Morgue." *Complete* 2–26.

———. "The Purloined Letter." *Complete* 125–38.

Resnick, Mike. *Whatdunits*. New York: Daw, 1992.

Resnick, Mike and Martin H. Greenberg, eds. *Sherlock Holmes in Orbit*. New York: Daw, 1995.

Robbe-Grillet, Alain. *The Erasers*. [*Les Gommes*, 1953]. Trans. Richard Howard. New York: Grove, 1964.

Sorrentino, Gilbert. *Odd Number*. San Francisco: North Point, 1985.

Sweeney, Susan Elizabeth. "Aliens, Aliases, and Alibis: Felipe Alfau's *Locos* as a Metaphysical Detective Story." *Review of Contemporary Fiction* 13, 1 (1993): 207–14.

Chapter 9
Postmodernism and the Monstrous Criminal
In Robbe-Grillet's Investigative Cell
Raylene Ramsay

Since the early 1950s, Alain Robbe-Grillet's writings and films have influenced that body of French literary investigative work which reflects the "suspicion" (in Nathalie Sarraute's sense) that the real world and natural language might be arbitrary constructions. Despite the metafictional character of his de-naturing of traditional narratives, his ex-posing of the ideologies concealed behind Western myths, and his interrogation of the hidden structures of thought and feeling (Logos and Eros) in which writer and reader are enmeshed, Robbe-Grillet's detecting project can itself be generated only from within the traditional frames of language, myth, and feeling.

In *Topologie d'une cité fantôme* (1976) and *Souvenirs du triangle d'or* (1978), Robbe-Grillet situates figures of the writer in a frame that is both a secret room and a prison. A geometrically precise description of the horizontal and vertical planes and parallel lines of this generating cell ("la cellule génératrice")[1] evokes the cross-ruled sheets of French writing paper; the symmetrical grids formed by its barred windows could be read as a literal manifestation of the prison house of language. As a place of imprisonment, a center of objective and scientific "detecting," and a locus of creation, this cell is both a privileged topos of Robbe-Grillet's metaphysical detective fiction and a metaphor of the postmodern.

There are other resonant figures around which objects and events gravitate in the texts of postmodernity (Jorge Luis Borges's "library" or Italo Calvino's "traveler," for example). Yet Robbe-Grillet's generating/prison cell and its monstrous occupant, the sinister "Dr. Morgan," is a significant material metaphor of both the sexual/textual impulse that produces the text, and the "complementary" character of this impulse. The cell—as "la chambre secrète" of Robbe-Grillet's eponymous short story, in which the female body is sacrificed, and as the prison for the criminal voyeur who stages such sacrificial rituals—is the hollow ("le creux") at the heart of the "I" under investigation in Robbe-Grillet's texts. It designates both the writer's room in general (for example, in *Dans le labyrinthe* [1959]) and Robbe-Grillet's personal study-bedroom in particular (in the "new autobiographies" *Le Miroir qui revient* [1985] and *Angélique ou l'enchantement* [1988]).

I

Robbe-Grillet's "project for a revolution" appeared to his early critics to be the objective, scientific observations and calibrations of an observer-detective. His first published novel, *Les Gommes* (1953), known in English as *The Erasers*, appropriates the structure of the detective novel as Wallas, a special investigator, walks the city streets, interrogating random, tenuous signs for clues to an uncertain crime. In *Le Voyeur* (1955), a traveler calculates his itinerary around an island, and his alibi, in terms of statistically probable watch sales, while an unidentified voyeur (Julien, Robbe-Grillet, the reader) constructs the possible concealed crime (the rape and murder of Violette) from clues suggested by objects and phrases and their transformations. In *La Jalousie* (1957), the investigative point of view measures, counts, and compares the regularities and irregularities in plots of banana plants on a tropical plantation, while searching for evidence of A . . .'s infidelity. In none of these detective fictions is there a resolution. The enigma (the sphinx's riddle in *Les Gommes*, Violette's death in *Le Voyeur*, the meaning of A . . .'s movements in *La Jalousie*) turns out either to be empty, or to offer a multiplicity of possible solutions that embed still other unanswered questions. Robbe-Grillet's own metacommentaries at once provide clues for the reader, and frustrate any clear solution to the numerous "little mysteries" that, according to Daniel Deneau, his texts put into play.

In the novels of Robbe-Grillet's second period, characterized by the writer and his critics as "subjective" rather than "objective," the detective project becomes less explicit, more complicated, and more self-conscious. The cell motif appears and begins to develop in these fictions. In *Dans le labyrinthe*, an anonymous narrator describes objects inside a room in which he is sheltered, invisible to us, up until his unexpected first-person emergence in the final line of the text ("all the town behind me" [221]). Such a narrator—confined by his contexts, comparing surfaces for sameness and difference, and seeking an always deferred meaning in the differential relationships between signs in a closed system—is a prototype of the de-centered self, constructed by the signs around it, that Derrida derives from Saussurian linguistics. Only through analogies between objects inside and outside his room, or by linguistic slippage, is this narrator able to move from the closed inside space to the outside of the narrative. He seeks in vain to establish coherence in his story of a soldier's death (suggested by the title of a military painting in his room, "La Défaite de Reichenfels"), through the traditional ordering of event and time in fiction by rationality and causality.

In the subsequent "assemblage" novels (texts characterized by intertextual collage), which no longer attempt to establish meaning through traditional ordering, the confining secret room at the center of the work becomes a prison cell. In *Topologie*, a land surveyor paces through the strata of the civilizations that feed into our own, recording the overlaying topologies of ancient and modern cities, all of which have a correctional institution or prison cell at their center. In *Souvenirs*, the narrator, attempting to construct a meticulous report, explicitly investigates a crime. The fictional autobiographies, *Le Miroir* and *Angélique*, subsequently stage the writer's self-investigation as he sifts through memories to construct a past from selected fragments, and discovers, in the "red hole" (designated in the subtitle of *Djinn* [1981]) or "hollow" of his own uncertain identity, a recursive primal scene of sexual violence. Doubt and dizziness surface in all these texts, despite Robbe-Grillet's insistence on recurrence, regularity, and patterning (mannerisms, as in Poe's fiction, that are evidently strategies for coping with vertigo). The precisely described objects; the soft, feminine, friable eraser with its rounded corners, and the masculine cube with its murderous sharp edges, in *Les Gommes*; the serial organization of generative objects; and the slow, insistent movement of the camera over baroque surfaces, which seeks ordering, prediction, and control—all simultaneously evoke hidden crime.

Robbe-Grillet's detective project has its origin in the subversive turning inside out of characters, of causality, of Cartesian rationality, of truth and self in the universal mimetic novel and, indeed, of the detective elements (enigma, investigation, and cathartic resolution) that shore up what in *Pour un nouveau roman* he called the "representational fallacy." In their place, Robbe-Grillet develops new literary forms better adapted to investigation and detection in a postmodern age (he prefers the more inclusive term *modernité*) which is also an age of new science. New scientific models move beyond traditional binary opposition to incorporate plurality, indeterminacy, and the breakdown of barriers between subject and object. Classical mechanics needed to know the exact state of a system in order to make accurate predictions, much as traditional detective fiction had to work from evidence. The fissures and flaws at the heart of Robbe-Grillet's fiction, however, make such classical detecting and prediction impossible. As in quantum physics, "uncertainty relations"—that is, the influence of the investigative process on the object under investigation—demonstrate virtuality and indeterminacy in our knowledge of the world around us and perhaps also in that world itself. "Complementarity"—that is, the dual nature of matter (particle or wave, continuous or discrete, according to the experimental frame)—permits nonexclusive contradictions. After Heisenberg, the writer-scientist can be both inside and outside the investigative cell simultaneously.

II

The slats of venetian blinds and the geometrical mazes that proliferate as metaphors of scientific investigation in Robbe-Grillet's early novels come to serve as metaphors of limitation and obsession. The prison bars of the assemblage novels no longer conceal the monsters of indeterminacy and the aleatory. Indeed, even as early as *Les Gommes*—in which the curve of the new geometries complicates the straight line of Wallas's Euclidean trajectory—imperfect symmetries and slight discrepancies transform the investigator (writer, character, reader) into the assassin; characters' functions and attributes are redistributed or reversed. Garinati, the hired killer, follows Wallas, the investigator, until the text points out "that it is impossible to confuse Garinati any longer with this fiction: another, this very evening, will replace him in his task" (99). The name "Wallas" reminds Inspector Laurent of the name of the replacement assassin, André V. S. (W. S./V. S), and Wallas is then twice mistaken for this shadowy second hired killer. Wallas (V. S.), in a telescoping of Freudian and detective stories, is the (Oedipal) detective who accidentally comes to kill and replace Dupont, the father figure and the murder victim. Similarly, at the end of the film *Glissements progressifs du plaisir* (1974), the detective arrives to affirm the nonexistence of the crime (Alice's murder of Nora), only to find another victim (Nora's double, the defense lawyer Maître David).

Fictional ghosts in search of an existence, mere doubles of their author—Wallas, whose identity card bears the photograph of an older individual with the dark moustache of "some Turk out of a light opera" (124–25), or Mathias, who feels a "hollow" developing within him—Robbe-Grillet's characters are also the victims of a deus ex machina. The perfectly regulated machinery, explicitly mentioned in *Projet pour une révolution à New York* (1970) and *Topologie*, is not only the machinery of the perfect crime and the detective genre. It is also, as Boyer suggests in his study of the detective figure in the early novels, a reference to the writer-criminal who turns detective-story conventions inside out. Manipulated by these textual machinations, the reader, too, becomes a victim-voyeur, reconstructing the clues to Mathias's torture and murder of Violette, or forced to occupy the position of the absent eye/I of the murderously jealous husband as he seeks to impose order on the threat of feminine disorder at the center of *La Jalousie*. In *Souvenirs*, and again in the film *La Belle Captive* (1976), the police inspector Francis V. Francisco turns out to be another version of the presumed villain Franck of *La Jalousie*, or his avatar, the traitor Franz of *L'Eden et après* (1970), or indeed of the nefarious Morgan in *Projet*.

Like the identities of assassin, victim, and detective, the functions of the crime are multiple and shifting. In *Trans-Europ-Express* (1966), a film about Robbe-Grillet making a film, Trintignant, alias Inspector Jean, pursues an organization that may be illegally smuggling diamonds, drugs, or guns; but it is this same detective who ties actress Marie-France Pisier, alias Eva, member of the secret Organization and/or prostitute, to an iron bedpost in a theatrical mise en scène, then rapes and strangles her to the ironic accompaniment of Verdi's *La Traviata*. This scene of sexual crime (after which the actress asks if she has given a good performance) obliges the filmmakers, within the film, to rescript the original detective-story and self-reflexive scenarios.

Such slidings of signifieds, and such rescriptings, are not a gratuitous game with the deconstructed fragments of the detective novel. According to Robbe-Grillet, they put into play the content of a "consciousness" whose stereotyped nature is the "constructed, insipid, everyday world," produced by our various censors—"morality, reason, logic, respect for the established order" (*Angélique* 182). Characters, for Robbe-Grillet, are effects of language and ideology, not beings of flesh; they function to reveal and thus destroy the traps constituted by ready-made, familiar, and completely understandable meanings. Yet, behind the narrative masks, just as behind the objective scrutiny of clues provided by the outside world, lurk unconscious sexual fantasies and violence. The most innocent and apparently objective description—such as that of the "quantum" beetles ("coléoptères") flying in "complementary" (both wave and corpuscle) and "chaotic" (unpredictable but intricately structured) configurations around the lamp in *La Jalousie*—carries a hidden metaphoric and subjective charge. The term *élytres*, used for the beetles' reddish V-shaped wing cases, is indeed entomological, but, significantly, it also refers to female genitals. The female beetle, described as a light-colored "stain" ("tache"), as a "little reddish beetle" ("petite coléoptère rougeâtre") "with closed wings" ("aux élytres fermés"), which strikes against the lamp "violently" and falls down on the table, is part of a series of small, reddish, V-shaped, curving, arousing or violently suppressed "feminine" objects, often seen as stains, fissures, or hollows ("taches," "creux"), which both conceal and reveal violence and sexual obsession even in the work's most apparently neutral descriptions (151).

Whose obsession? The proliferation of narrative orderings of the world introduces fissure into the author(ity). The decentered and multiple "I" is a "we." The author, however, is not dead; indeed, he, along with the mirror, "returns," if somewhat perversely, in the autobiographical fictions, where there is a more or less traditional identification among writer, narrator, and protagonist.

The constructions of the narrative voice(s) are themselves the object of critical investigation at various levels within Robbe-Grillet's text. In *Projet*, for example, the rule-bound voice of a public prosecutor (who will materialize as such in the film *Glissements*), protests inaccuracies in details of the New York scene as elaborated by the narrative. In *Souvenirs*, the narrator's choice of epithets to describe the "cruel" punishments inflicted on the "delicate" flesh of "charming" young girls is questioned by a narratee who claims that such epithets conceal and reveal suspect attitudes. Behind this interrogation of the text's pretended truth and innocence is the further metatextual questioning of what Bruce Morrissette sees as postmodernist "isolation," and "protection of the work of art" that "leads always back to the text" (10). But this questioning—whether by various "detective" readers in the text, or by the text's superego examining textual processes for traces of unspeakable id—emanates, in the final analysis, from the "complementary" (contradictory but not mutually exclusive) cell which the detective and the criminal cohabit.

III

The detective-criminal writer is necessarily a fissured subject. The following pages examine the relations between Morgan, Francis, and the "I": three alter egos of Robbe-Grillet, and "subjects" in the sense that they cannot be observed directly but only in the mirror (we cannot see ourselves directly) and in the movement of the text. The "illustrious" Dr. Morgan—an embodiment of the doctor-scientist as powerful and prestigious, but also as the object of considerable cultural anxiety, from Mary Shelley's Dr. Frankenstein to Hollywood's mad scientist—makes his appearance on the first page of *Projet*. Avatar of the early figures of the investigator-criminal (Wallas and the voyeur), or the criminal-doctor (Juard, who hides Dupont in what appears to be his abortionist's clinic in *Les Gommes*), Dr. Morgan makes subsequent appearances in many of Robbe-Grillet's texts, conjoining the "complementary" sexual/textual aspects of the self-investigation that characterizes Robbe-Grillet's detective fiction. On the first page of *Projet*, the white-coated doctor, syringe in hand, is leaning over a young woman who is naked, bound, and gagged. This scene of bondage and threatened sexual violence, more characteristic of the covers of cheap detective fiction than of horror novels or even pornography, turns out to be the cover art of a paperback novel that adolescent Laura is holding against the keyhole for the delectation of a peeping Tom. Another avatar of the sinister scientist, this bald, "short-sighted" voyeur is probably a homage to Freud, for whom the key and keyhole are sexual symbols and blindness a substitute for castration.[2] The bald, passive character, the opposite (and yet the double) of the all-too-active Morgan, returns in *Souvenirs*. From being an observer of the beautiful captive through the keyhole, he becomes himself a prisoner observed through the police spyhole. His "bald" head is, appropriately, now referred to as "shaven," and he is recognized by the narrator: "The man is alone, in the silence, in the middle of the cell. And little by little, as if with prudence, I observe that it is probably me" (41).

The voyeur thus observes the bald man with glasses (himself) observing the results of sadistic aggression against the body of the beautiful captive: "You can see the man with the bald head and the narrow dark glasses in the background, standing a little apart, watching the result of his abuse with a cruel smile" (106). If the voyeur himself also seems to pass "unnoticed," this is because "the bald-headed character with his narrow dark glasses is none other than his own reflection in a side mirror" (108). This bald sadist-voyeur, both a first-person "I" and a third-person "narrator" (115), simultaneously inside and outside the narrative and visible only in the play of mirrors, later appears in the "shop of dead dolls" (114), recalling both the dolls on the lining of Mathias's suitcase in *Le Voyeur* and the china dolls that were the victims of Robbe-Grillet's own sadistic childhood impulses, according to his "perverse" autobiographical "confessions" in *Angélique*. The reader begins to realize that this voyeur-sadist-prisoner does not coincide completely either with the character Morgan, or with the narrator, or with Robbe-Grillet. Meanings are created in the circulation between the different signs, but any definitive meaning is deferred.

Since *Topologie*, in which Morgan drugs and kidnaps a beautiful young woman from a beach café, that character (or sign) has been associated with a long, black-curtained automobile "recognized" by the narrator of *Souvenirs*: "I recognize it. It is the ambulance of the psychiatric hospital where in a few minutes I am going to find the sinister Doctor Morgan and his textual experiments once again" (155). The reference to "textual experiments" again suggests that Dr. Morgan is the writer's double (the writer himself); but who, then, is the "I" who speaks about the "sinister" psychiatrist? "Unable to stand it any longer, and at the risk of betraying without real necessity an identity cleverly kept secret until now, I run home and I open the drawer with its secret compartment. Everything is in order in the hiding place" (36). In this secret drawer are the needles and syringe and keys to the Cadillac which, since *Topologie*, have had a metonymical and metaphorical relation to the suspicious doctor. Only the fine blue slipper of the dead Angelica, with its symbolically broken heel—Robbe-Grillet's distinctive "sadistic" version of Cinderella's slipper—is missing from the suspect objects that have suggested sexual violence throughout his work. The narrator who possesses the secrets of this hidden drawer must then be a double of the "false" character Morgan and thus be, himself, the "true" sexual criminal—Robbe-Grillet? But true and false in Robbe-Grillet's work turn out to be another of those "complementary" pairs whose undecidability and even apparent interchangeability give classical logic such trouble.

Like non-mutually exclusive contradiction, the splitting of the character into coexisting "opposites" seems to be a proliferating, unstable process. "I call the office. It's Morgan who answers me" (156). Morgan, now a police medical expert, informs this "I" that the female victim did not in fact die from drowning, as had been believed. Suspect substances have been found in her blood. Who then is calling Morgan for information? The text identifies the caller and implies his guilt. At the recollection of "a false move" he has made, "Franck V. Francis feels a sudden hollow growing within his body" (37), the "hollow," experienced also by Mathias, that in Robbe-Grillet's works has come to connote the void, sexual violence, creative energy—the generative and criminal cell.

This "I"/"Franck V. Francis," policeman-criminal, has further variants. He is "Inspector Victor Francis" (223), the fascist "Francisco Franco" (224), and "le préfet de police Duchamp" (240). Linked to the photographer "E. Manroy" (327), he is also a humorous reference to the influence of the king ("roi")—Marcel Duchamp, Man Ray, or Manet, indeterminately—on Robbe-Grillet's work. But the law-enforcing investigator (like the artistic authority) is also a suspected law breaker. The text slips imperceptibly from evoking the inspector's uneasiness, as he hears the coroner's report on the young woman's death, to a dreamlike scene in which soldiers pound on the door of his "cell" and the prisoner "sinks into oblivion" (38).

Has the mystery of X (Morgan, Francis, the "I") been in any way resolved? The black car now merits its earlier only apparently contradictory ("complementary") designation as both "the disturbing and reassuring car" (51). It is "evidently," states the text, both the police car of Inspector F. V. Francis of the Vice Squad *and* the vehicle of the criminal machinations of Dr. W. M. Morgan. Robbe-Grillet's texts remain unclear about difference and sameness, about original truth and imitation, reality and invention. In a later passage from *Souvenirs*, we meet "the false Inspector Francis"/"I" (223), who appears to be interchangeable with "the false doctor"/"I" and to be generated by his relation to a "true" or "real" ("vrai") Inspector Francis/"I."

Angélique generates the Germanic variant "Morgen," the military doctor who has played a "determining role" in the capture of Carmina, a beautiful female spy who is escorted through the forest to her punishment by cavalry officer (Claude) Simon. The text asks the question: "What was a doctor doing in this story?" The answer is, as usual, "evident." In this forest peopled with stereotypes of medieval and operatic lore, Morgan/Morgen generates (or rather is generated by) another traditional version of false seeming and perversity, the fatal "Morgane-la-Faye": "In the heart of the lost forest, where the bird attempts in vain to warn him, innocent Siegfried gives himself up unawares to the fairy Morgane, that is, to the enchanter Klingsor, who is, moreover, soon going to reappear under the guise of a disturbing doctor" (81). The closed space of the forest takes over the functions of the earlier cell or secret room, stressing the "enchantments" to which even a self-conscious writer falls victim.

Morgan, Francis, and the "I" are detected only through "organic" and "morphological" knowledge, to use Barthes's expressions. For Barthes, the text is itself a dispossession which takes the writer beyond his "imaginary" person to "a kind of language without memory which is already that of the People, of the insubjective mass (or of the generalized subject)" (*Roland* 6). The character of William Morgan is a postmodernist play of Derridean "différance" (deferral and difference) that creates meaning out of limited sets of conventional linguistic elements and their displacements. It subverts traditional literary conventions of character, questioning their ontological status. If "Morgan" acquires continuity and solidity, it is due to the self-conscious repetition of identical semantic units that attach themselves repeatedly to the same name, according to the mechanisms of traditional literary character formation that Barthes analyzes in *S/Z*.[3] Yet "Morgan" is simultaneously dismantled by these mechanisms, as the "same" name attracts different epithets (professions, physical characteristics, clothing, character) and the "same" epithets come to define a different name altogether, making them discontinuous and unstable interacting particles. Onomastic play both bestows identity and essence, and destroys them, as it reveals that they are constructions from a limited set. Morgan's name, as Jean Ricardou has shown, is generated by/generates a series of phonemes and morphemes—such as "rogue," "orgue," "organe," "orgasme," "morgue"—as well as its own sememes, "mort" and "gants."

Morgan's "self," generated by his name, is the product of anagrammatic and anaphonic transformations. In the film *La Belle Captive*, a bilingual doubling of the semantic possibilities in the first syllable of his name transforms Morgan into Dr. Morgentodt, criminal psychiatrist and member of a secret society of sexual specialists. Many critics argue that such sadistic interrogations and penetrations are dislocations of a body that is textual rather than sexual; that the pleasure of Robbe-Grillet's criminal project inheres in textual slippages from sound to sense, and the subsequent bliss of sense's suppression. Crime in postmodernist literature is often presented as textual, deriving in many cases, like the characters themselves, from formal symmetries—much as Morgan's initials "W. M.," seen in a mirror, create the avatar "M. W."

Images of crime, bodily dismemberment, decapitation, or castration have all been used in postmodernist criticism as metaphors of reading and writing, as "cuts" in the body of the text. In *Glas*, Derrida establishes the simulacrum of castration as "the ruse of writing by which the text establishes its authority" in a repetition of the murder of the Father. Marguerite Duras's texts also valorize and aestheticize the criminal act as pointing toward the limits of narrativity and the unrepresentable or unsayable origins of desire. Crime, which Duras presents most often as self-immolation, and which Barthes calls the "disfiguration" of traditional (feminine) language/nature brought about by his new "masculine" text, is staged by Robbe-Grillet as an extreme, sustained, and apparently sustaining metaphor of the criminal rape and suppression of the female body.

In a study of Robbe-Grillet's use, in *Les Gommes*, of detective-story elements appropriated from Graham Greene, Robert Brock argues: "If he has borrowed from Greene, he has done so in the manner that an architect would borrow structural or ornamental elements from another respected architect. It is a case not of imitation but of initiation into the art of creating verbal architecture" (694). Yet the individuated choices among very different figures of criminality clearly implicate the reader (and writer) in more than mere "verbal architecture." Brock claims that whereas Greene, in *This Gun for Hire*, deals with the psychology of good and evil, "the sense of wrong that finally discourages Raven is totally missing in Juard, Garinati, the leader of the gang Bonaventure, and even Wallas" (693). I would suggest that although guilt may be rewritten in the figure of Morgan, it is not entirely absent. Morgan is also the vehicle for Robbe-Grillet's investigation of certain topoi of our time: our fascination with blood, death, bodily vulnerability, and sexual violence. The criminal project, like the detecting project, stalks all of Robbe-Grillet's cities; it is a project in which violence, sexuality, and power are recursively linked.

IV

The mysterious assassin "already on my own track," mentioned in a subtitle to *Topologie*, seems to imply a singular, solitary, and personal project.

Like the dreamer, the artist ultimately pursues those monsters within the self by which he is pursued. Again, like the dreamer, he is both inside the scene of pursuit and outside looking on; both inside language and outside it, examining its functioning. Inspector Francis seeks distance from and mastery of his objects of interrogation, but as the other side of Morgan's mask he shows the effects of countertransference and complicity. The detective reveals the illustrious scientist's double nature as an "I" who has powerful prelinguistic and prelogical relations with Angélique, victim and siren—even as he himself becomes suspect. According to Robbe-Grillet, any true creator becomes necessarily a criminal, at least in relation to the law, because "crime [is] the very driving force of his project" (*Angélique* 155). Like the protagonists in all Robbe-Grillet's works, Morgan is a "negative" hero. On one side of the mask, the reader sees the reassuring metatextual logic of linguistic and narrative structures, including those of detective fiction, and the connections between these narrative conventions and the structures of society and mind. On the other, the reader recognizes the imprisoning and limiting grids of this linguistic law and becomes involved in its transgression—an attempt to touch aspects of the unmediated chaotic real and the secret room, the void, of which this law can give little account.

It is the void, claims Robbe-Grillet, that throws one into the world hesitating between a becoming and a definitive absence to self (that is, being always already there, a product of discourse, as in Foucauldian postmodernism, or a product of the "misrecognition" that accompanies the self's entry into the symbolic/the other, as in Lacanian analysis). In such a context of absence to self occasioned by entry into ready-made language, art, for Robbe-Grillet, is the "collapse of the everyday," the writing "from the void" of an "imaginary" that would permit "escape from anguish" (*Angélique* 125).

But Morgan, I would argue, is *both* a figure of such an imaginary (that is, a figure "from the void" seeking a form of catharsis) and a figure of imprisonment in conventional discourses. An earlier version of Morgan roams the subway as a vampire in *Projet*. His avatars in "La Chambre," *Topologie,* and *Souvenirs* are assassin-rapists (of the slasher genre) who continue their slow climbing of the spiral stair where the female sacrificial victims (A . . . , Violette, Laura, Marie-Ange von Salomé, Caroline de Saxe) wait in fear in the secret bedroom-temple. As in a horror movie, the voyeur-assassin stalks his prey from room to room along endless corridors, while red blood pools beneath the doors and stains the virginal white. As in a classical metaphor, or a scene from a James Bond film pushed to its logical (sado-erotic) limit, young girls are hunted and devoured like does. As in Ingres's painting, *Roger Freeing Angelica,* the virgin chained to a rock twists gracefully to arouse the approaching sea monster. The "sea-monster who devours little girls" is also identified, however, as an ironic double of the narrator.

These images of sacrificing the virgin or punishing the seductive witch, derived from horror and slasher movies, mythologies, sadomasochistic fantasies, and detective stories, which are evoked by or associated with the figure of Morgan, are flattened and distanced by the writer's game. Like the masks used in Greek theater to represent unrepresentable or unspeakable crime (incest, infanticide, and parricide), like the Brechtian *Verfremdungseffekt*, Robbe-Grillet's play with such sado-erotic elements seeks—perhaps in vain—to establish a new form of catharsis.

Robbe-Grillet's self-conscious generative mechanisms produce a seam, an alarm, a discomfort, a distance; what he has called "a grinding sound." The conscious staging of secret rooms or obscurely sensed monsters, in the self as in the world, may be, as he claims, the only space of possible liberation from them. Yet behind the flat scenery, behind the conventional masks of detective and assassin, move, anew, incoherent hidden monsters. Once again, in Robbe-Grillet's work, a particular sadomasochistic story recommences as the machinery of the criminal organization moves into gear. Against the abstract background of the generative cell's bare white walls, what Robbe-Grillet has called "the immobile ceremonial of violence and abstraction" (*Topologie* 43) unfolds once more. Within the cell and without, ambiguously, are zones of shadow. Lurking behind the detective is the brutal male assassin with his instruments of torture and of terror, he who is provoked to violence by the frail rose or its avatars—a tiny tender butterfly, a starfish stranded on the shore, or a fearful captured virgin—in Robbe-Grillet's various works. Within the body, there is the dull sound of axes "striking deep within my breast," axe-blows from deep in the forest of heartbeat, passion, the fear of and fascination with the oceanic feeling of a feminine takeover, of capture by time and death. Outside the body, there is ensnaring language, "the vast lost forest . . . like a sly sea alive with adjectives and metaphors ready to swallow you up." In all of Robbe-Grillet's recent films and novels, jackbooted soldiers tramp narrowing corridors down which the unmasked Doctor, "chased outside himself," is forced to seek his way (*Topologie* 198, 175). Firing squads irrupt into his cell.

The premise of an essential "criminality" or "original sin," and their corollary "guilt," has no relevance in a postmodernist frame that denies the existence of originality and metaphysics. (In the beginning was the sign system.) Using the quantum model of "complementarity" as an analogy, I would argue that Dr. Morgan is, however, more than a ludic or linguistic function(ing) of a sign system. He stages the monstrous texts of self and history that postmodernist French culture and post-Freudian French psychoanalysis have repressed, in their emphasizing the decentered self of language (Jacques Lacan) at the expense of its hidden monsters (Melanie Klein).

Robbe-Grillet's work is not only a detective fiction of a monstrous Id, a Minotaur hidden among stage properties and conventional masks. It investigates both a historical discourse whose inversions of signs concealed the Holocaust, and the personal seduction exerted by that discourse. The ludic and fantastical figure of the criminal scientist, Dr. Morgan, conducts experiments, including insemination, on young girls' bodies with a scientific precision that recalls the secret Organization in *Souvenirs* and its minute distribution of murderous tasks to be performed with exactness and efficiency (22). But the reference is not wholly intertextual or phantasmic. This figure indirectly reflects Robbe-Grillet's own experiences during World War II, in particular the historical revelation of the monsters of Nazism and his personal discovery of the drive for power concealed behind the face of order, science, and progress presented by an initially admired Third Reich. The Nazi censorship of representations of sexuality and blood—masked in metaphors of purity and morality, even as unspeakable mass killings took place—are figured in Dr. Morgan/Inspector Francis. So, too, is the personal discovery of hidden violence behind the mask of apparent order in the institution, the world, and the self. Guilt is incompletely exorcised by the play of language.

Morgan's persona(e) explore the imprisonments within language and the struggle for power secreted by discourses. He is both a historically situated collective "we" (history) and an individuated "I" (Robbe-Grillet's own experience), an ironic and experimental yet historically situated self. The detached doctor and his methodical experiments, his pleasure in dominating and controlling the innocent sex/text, become uncertain and fatigued. Morgan also suggests the anxiety behind the deconstructionist enterprise: that the analytical staging (deconstruction) of metaphysical concepts of rational self and will may be, in its turn, "sequestered between mirror and window" like the adolescent girls of David Hamilton's photography in *Topologie*, reflected by the smooth surfaces in infinite replication and absence from self. The fear that the reconfigured self/space of the skeptical posthumanist enterprise may be only a cool simulacrum or intertext, without ethics and denying political agency, characterizes much of the present rethinking of postmodernism.

The writers of the French *nouveau roman* have consistently maintained a critical distance from Derrida's (de)constructions. For Nathalie Sarraute, Marguerite Duras, Michel Butor, Claude Simon, Robbe-Grillet, and even Barthes, there is an unknown multiple "real" outlined in the gaps of our conventional realist representations and constructions. The ordering and play of polished surface, number, plane, and meticulously observed object constitutes a "voice" that is distinctly Robbe-Grilletian within the diverse modes of the *nouveau roman*. However, these apparently objective surfaces are flawed; something moves within or behind the smooth, ludic words. What these writers investigate, in addition to the masking of Dr. Morgan's monsters by our ready-made languages, is the knowability (the origin) of these monsters. If words "don't develop scar tissue," as the poet Jack Spicer puts it (218), then the gap between text and life increases, and with it the writer's secret fear of impotence. Yet the deconstruction of conventional psychosocial masks, and the stripping of the masks of writer-scientist or writer-monster, is not always-already infinite regress. The narrator/character Ben Said, indeterminately both hero and villain as he pulls off layers of rubber masks in *Projet*, has, without noticing, pulled away "strips of his own skin" in the process. There is a "real" (skin), and all is not simulacrum.

Science, too, like the literary text, is a product of discourse and the structures of the human mind, rather than a privileged medium for acquiring knowledge of an external world. The new scientist knows that his measure is not determined by an objective external body but by the relationship between the theoretical (and affective) constructions of his mind and the world. The investigator Morgan is caught up in fantasies—of marching masculine boots, beautiful captives, and violent death—that make him both a prisoner (or victim) and a potential criminal (or agent of victimization). He attempts to control his situation by meticulously measuring the parameters of his cell, but his instruments are ready-made and his detecting is further contaminated by the very subjectivities he attempts to repress. The masculine detective enterprise is unable to suppress what threatens it: the feminine fissures between the language and the thing, the fluid tidal swell and seduction of the monsters of un-knowledge, the dissolution of the boundaries of self, and the new "self" constituted by relation to the Other. The beautiful captive, sequestered in the cell and interrogated by Morgan for his pleasure, is finally not only the dangerous, seductive Other to be controlled or suppressed (as in pornography), but another side of Morgan himself. Yet their disjunction is not a source of polarity and ultimate mediation and unification, as in traditional dialectic. It becomes a redistribution of same and different in the "complementarity"—the dynamic contradictions without exclusion—of the scientist/monster imprisoned with his captive in the secret room. Detective metaphor, like artistic metaphor, need not be only the production of a polarizing "language of the tribe." Monstrous Morgan and his female objects of interrogation share common features. The apparent binary opposites—vamp and vampire, siren and sadist—exchange signs of complicity between their respective cells. In Robbe-Grillet's ludic *and* confessional "new autobiographies," *Le Miroir* and *Angélique*, the analytical "deconstruction" of the feminine as Other in Western culture has an individuated and local origin in his own sado-erotic sexual orientation and experience.

The "complementary" figure of the cell—both laboratory and prison —points to the new character of these texts. The cell emphasizes imprisonment both in the commonality of language and in the individual psychosexual impulse toward what Duras calls "ravishing" (that is, an impulse to both dominate and submit to the Other, textual or sexual, to both master language and to lose oneself in the otherness that language reflects). It is thus a place from which the investigation and reordering of textual/sexual imprisonments can proceed. Detecting the crimes in and behind our collective representations, Robbe-Grillet's texts do not themselves escape guilt, criminal subjectivity, and individuated obsessions. In the austerity of the metafictional cell, there is a self-conscious detective investigating Morgan. Yet also in the cell, beyond language and the metafictional violation or generation of language, there is a hidden monster to be sought behind the postmodernist investigator's ludic mask.

Notes

1. All translations are my own.
2. Robbe-Grillet often uses the term *homage* (homage) in relation to its alphabetical predecessor, *gommage* (erasure). *Homage* thus both designates an influence and constitutes a sign of his own imminent work of deconstruction. Freud's theories become the "material" of a "bricolage": that is, a new kind of construction in which their meanings, like those of detective fictions, are placed, to use Derrida's expression, "under erasure" ("sous râture"). As Barthes says in his study of mythology, these meanings do not disappear but remain displayed or "in reserve."
3. "Lorsque les sèmes identiques traversent à plusieurs reprises le même Nom propre et semblent s'y fixer, il naît un personnage" (Barthes, *S/Z* 74).

Works Cited

Barthes, Roland. "Le Mythe aujourd'hui." *Mythologies.* Paris: Seuil, 1957. 215–68.
———. *Roland Barthes par Roland Barthes.* Paris: Seuil, 1975.
———. *S/Z.* Paris: Seuil, 1970.
Boyer, Alain-Michel. "Du Double à la doublure: L'image du détective dans les premiers romans de Robbe-Grillet." *L'Esprit Créateur* 26, 2 (1986): 60–70.
———. "L'Enigme, l'enquête et la quête du récit: La fiction policière dans *Les Gommes* et *Le Voyeur* d'Alain Robbe-Grillet." *French Forum* 6, 1 (1981): 74–83.
Brock, Robert. "Robbe-Grillet's *Les Gommes* and Graham Greene's *This Gun for Hire*: Imitation or Initiation?" *Modern Fiction Studies* 29, 4 (1983): 688–94.

Deneau, Daniel. "Little Mysteries in Robbe-Grillet's *The Erasers.*" *Notes on Contemporary Literature* 11, 1 (1981): 2–4.

Derrida, Jacques. *Glas.* Paris: Galilée, 1974.

Morrissette, Bruce. "Postmodern Generative Fiction." *Novel and Film: Essays in Two Genres.* Chicago: University of Chicago Press, 1985. 1–11.

Ricardou, Jean. *Problèmes du nouveau roman.* Paris: Seuil, 1967.

Robbe-Grillet, Alain. *Angélique ou l'enchantement.* Paris: Minuit, 1987.

———. *Dans le labyrinthe.* [*In the Labyrinth*]. Paris: Minuit, 1959.

———. *Djinn: Un trou rouge entre les pavés disjoints.* [Trans. Yvone Lenard as *Le Rendez-vous*, trans. Yvone Lenard and Walter Wells as *Djinn*]. Paris: Minuit, 1981.

———. *Glissements progressifs du plaisir.* [*Slow Slidings into Pleasure*]. Ciné-novel. Paris: Minuit, 1974.

———. *Glissements progressifs du plaisir.* Film. 1974.

———. *La Belle captive.* Film. 1982.

———. "La Chambre secrète." ["The Secret Room"]. *Instantanés.* [*Snapshots*]. Paris: Minuit, 1962.

———. *La Jalousie.* [*Jealousy*]. Paris: Minuit, 1957.

———. *L'Eden et après.* Film. 1971.

———. *Le Miroir qui revient.* [*Ghosts in the Mirror*]. Paris: Minuit, 1984.

———. *Les Gommes.* [*The Erasers*]. Paris: Minuit, 1953.

———. *Le Voyeur.* [*The Voyeur*]. Paris: Minuit, 1955.

———. *Pour un nouveau roman.* [*Towards a New Novel*]. Paris: Minuit, 1963.

———. *Projet pour une révolution à New York.* [*Project for a Revolution in New York*]. Paris: Minuit, 1970.

———. *Souvenirs du triangle d'or.* [*Memories of the Golden Triangle*]. Paris: Minuit, 1978.

———. *Topologie d'une cité fantôme.* [*Topology of a Phantom City*]. Paris: Minuit, 1976.

———. *Trans-Europ-Express.* Film. 1966.

Sarraute, Nathalie. *L'Ere du soupçon.* Paris: Gallimard, 1956.

Spicer, Jack. "Sporting Life." *The Collected Books of Jack Spicer*, ed. Robin Blaser. Los Angeles: Black Sparrow Press, 1975. 218.

Forging Identities

Chapter 10
Detecting Identity in Time and Space
Modiano's *Rue des Boutiques Obscures* and
Tabucchi's *Il Filo dell'orizzonte*

Anna Botta

> The present epoch will perhaps be above all the epoch of space. We are in the epoch of simultaneity; we are in the epoch of juxtaposition, the epoch of the near and far, of the side-by-side, of the dispersed. We are at a moment, I believe, when our experience of the world is less that of a long life developing through time than that of a network that connects points and intersects with its own skein.
>
> —Michel Foucault, "Of Other Spaces" (22)

Among contemporary novelists concerned with a problematics of time, the names of Patrick Modiano and Antonio Tabucchi figure prominently. They have made their reputation on the French and Italian literary scenes as authors of a distinctive and consistent body of work, characterized by unfathomable pasts and irretrievable identities. As a consequence, their protagonists are often detective-philosophers hot on the trail of existential and metaphysical conundrums, new Sherlock Holmeses who have turned the magnifying lens on themselves.

The occupation of France during World War II marks Modiano's narrators, depriving them of an origin and consequently a stable identity. In Tabucchi's works, the protagonists' quest for the traces of a dead (or disappeared) person serves as pretext for their search for self through the other. Both Modiano's and Tabucchi's narrative universes are saturated with nostalgias, memory gaps, blurred images, transitional stages. Yet this sense of temporal uncertainty (similar to an effect of cinematic *flou*) is countered by an equally strong obsession with spatial precision, an insistence on geometrical and architectural configurations. As Gerald

Prince remarks of Modiano: "Time is dilated, bloated, difficult, imprecise (that year, that winter, that day . . .). Space is obsessively evoked and
traversed: its mazes are those of accident and wandering, and a famil-
iarity with them proves necessary to those who must escape or hide"
("Re-Membering" 40).[1] It is as if a momentarily stable spatial orientation
serves to overcome the anxiety of an enigmatic temporal detection.

Two of their novels—Modiano's *Rue des Boutiques Obscures* (1978) and
Tabucchi's *Il Filo dell'orizzonte* (1986), henceforth *Rue* and *Filo*—confirm
Foucault's speculation that "the anxiety of our era has to do fundamentally with space, no doubt a great deal more than with time. Time probably appears to us only as one of the various distributive operations that
are possible for the elements that are spread out in space" (23). Both
texts are permeated by the tension between a traditional hermeneutics
of time and a more modern hermeneutics of spatial detection. The epistemological strategy originally adopted by the two protagonists—the
investigation of identity through temporality—is superseded by a hermeneutics of space which is affirmed, at least at the level of writing, as a
textual response to the failure of the first methodology.

My decision to focus on Modiano's *Rue* and Tabucchi's *Filo* is partly
motivated by their shared affinity with the detective story, a genre that
narrativizes hermeneutic structuration. The two novels adopt certain
conventions of the detective genre, but subvert them as well, by playing
them off against a narrative structure that defies any attempt at closure
and leaves the story's initial enigma unresolved. Describing this adoption and manipulation of detective-story codes will facilitate a more specific study of narrative strategies in the two novels.

I

In *Rue*, in place of a crime, there is an identity to be investigated; the
first-person narrator (introduced under his newly borrowed name, "Guy
Roland") has been the victim of total amnesia. As the book opens, "Guy"
is a private detective on the trail of his own identity; searching for information, he traces missing witnesses, hunts for clues, and follows false
leads. In fact, the amnesiac Guy brings together two functions of the
detective story: the detective and the corpse. He is simultaneously the
one who advances and the one who blocks the story. The corpse and
the amnesiac share the status of privileged narrators of their hidden experiences, despite their obvious inability to tell tales. As Uri Eisenzweig
writes: "The amnesiac, a favorite actantial figure in detective fiction, is
equivalent to a walking, potentially revivable corpse" (13; my trans.).
Little by little, this narrator reconstructs fragments of his past—recover-
ing names he has perhaps been known by ("Pedro McEvoy," "Jimmy

Pedro Stern")—but even these fragments fail to bridge the many lacunae that remain. The end result of such lacunae is to put in doubt the meaning of the few clues he manages to obtain. The last chapter stages the narrator's refusal to give up his quest; he departs on a new trail,[2] although bitterly commenting: "Do not our lives dissolve into the evening as quickly as [the] grief of childhood?" (159).[3]

Antonio Tabucchi's *Filo* exhibits a similarly deceptive use of *racconto giallo* conventions.[4] The novel begins when the corpse of an unidentified young man is brought to the morgue. His death "in a vacuum" (37) triggers in Spino, a worker at the morgue, an inexplicable urge to investigate. A sympathetic association between the protagonist and the dead man is made clear when Spino decides to call the anonymous corpse "The Kid," a name derived from his recollection of an old movie scene. In Spino's mind, it is as if the gunshot in the film, which murdered a criminal named "The Kid," also hit the young Spino sitting in the audience. In the course of the novel, Spino is asked several times to explain his curiosity about this dead stranger. His responses clearly show that the investigation serves as a pretext for his own interior quest. The first time, Spino replies: "Because he is dead and I am alive" (32). Later, he gives a better formulated answer to the same question:

"But who's he to you?" [Beppe Harpo] asked softly. "You don't know him, he doesn't mean anything to you." . . . "And you?" Spino said. "Who are you to yourself? Do you realize that if you wanted to find that out one day you'd have to look for yourself all over the place, reconstruct yourself, rummage in old drawers, get hold of evidence from other people, clues scattered here and there and lost? You'd be completely in the dark, you'd have to feel your way." (61–62)

After following a series of increasingly mysterious clues, Spino seems close to solving this twofold enigma—the "meaning" of the stranger's assassination and the answer to his own existential questioning. The last chapter defies such a resolution, however, by disappointing Spino's expectations and deferring closure. Just as the protagonist of *Rue* exits into the symbolic obscurity of the titular street, so the protagonist of *Filo* exits into a solitary darkness, still determined to continue his inquiry: "Only then did he suddenly feel absolutely certain that no one was there. Despite himself he began to laugh, first softly, then more loudly. He turned round and looked at the water a few meters away. Then stepped forward in the dark" (83). In a sense, Spino also disappears into the title of his story, since the darkness of this ending might lead to "the edge of the horizon." Tabucchi himself suggests as much in his note at the end of the novel: "The horizon, in fact, is a geometrical location, since it moves as we move. I would very much like to think that by some sorcery my character did manage to reach it, since he too had it in his eyes" (84).

As should be clear even from these synopses, a great number of the stock elements of *roman noir* can be found in the two novels, elements which successfully evoke the genre's distinctive tone.[5] But the typical narrative structure of the genre has been profoundly altered in the cases at hand, given that their initial enigmas are never resolved. The basic structure of detective fiction involves the interplay between an absent, "real" story (the story of the crime) and a present, derivative story (the story of the investigation) which mediates between the reader and the crime (Todorov 11). The implication of this dual system — "one story in search of another" (Eisenzweig 9; my trans.) — is that the detective novel is founded on an absence, that is, on a difficulty in narrating. As Eisenzweig argues, "It is the absence of the crime story (that is to say, finally, the mystery) which both calls for and allows the development of the story of the investigation. . . . Such impossibility [of narrating] concerns of course only the crime story, and it is only relative insofar as the mystery itself is relative" (11; my trans.). In traditional detective stories, the power of this "mystery," and with it the "impossibility" of narrating, is limited — it disappears when the investigation comes to an end.

Such is clearly not the case in *Rue* and *Filo*, in which the story's initial enigma is not solved. Difficulty in narrating the mystery becomes a veritable impossibility. If traditional detective novels originate in a frustrated desire — their narration being an expression of that frustration (Eisenzweig 11) — then narrative closure fulfills that original desire. In *Rue*, on the contrary, the protagonist is haunted by the same "panic fear" at the beginning of his investigation — when he is nothing but a blank page that awaits inscription — as at the end, in the midst of the most extensive fragment of his past that he has managed to rewrite:

From the Rue Anatole-de-la-Forge, we emerged into the Avenue de la Grande-Armée and I was tempted to jump out. . . . Until we reached the Porte de Saint-Cloud, I had to struggle with the panic fear that gripped me. (12)

There was nothing more disheartening than those mountains which blocked out the horizon. Panic took over. (144)

I wanted to open the door and tell her to get out. The two of us would have gone off together. (147)

In *Filo*, the imagery of weariness permeates the entire description of the corpse's arrival at the morgue; fatigue irradiates the ambulance, the policemen, Spino, the hospital courtyard, the city, and finally even the stars. This imagery resurfaces in the penultimate chapter, just when Spino appears able at last to formulate satisfying hypotheses: "He got up slowly, overcome by a great tiredness. But it was a calm, peaceful tiredness that led him by the hand towards his bed as if he were a boy again" (79). It might seem that a sense of relief has infiltrated the cosmic fatigue, now described as "calm, peaceful tiredness." Nonetheless, in the final chapter disillusionment undermines this false calm, eliciting from the protagonist an absurd and enigmatic laugh (83).

What both novels lack is a dénouement, a final reconstruction of events narrated into a stable pattern of significance. Such resolution (or solution) is typical of the traditional detective story, as Robbe-Grillet explains: "Traditionally, this is what a good detective novel looks like: there are disorderly pieces with a few gaps; somebody, a policeman, must order them and fill in the gaps; once the novel ends, there is no obscurity left. In other words, the detective novel is a novel highly charged with the ideology of realism; everything has a meaning, *one* meaning" (16; my trans.). According to generic codes, not only must the meaning (*sens*) be a single meaning, as pointed out by Robbe-Grillet, but *sens* should also be understood in terms of its etymological root of "direction." The detective must be able to assemble the given elements into causal relationships arranged on a continuous and vectored temporal line. The genre not only offers an application of what Roland Barthes calls "the *post hoc, ergo propter hoc* fallacy" (22), but this fallacy in fact constitutes the genre's raison d'être. Although many crime stories disregard this fallacy, they must still come to terms with it. At the end of the narration, clues will find their place in the diegetic series, while false leads will be discarded as digressions or instances of what Gerald Prince calls "the disnarrated."[6] The story of the crime is thus ultimately reconstituted by the story of the investigation, which works backward from murder to its motive, from effects to causes.

Both Guy Roland and Spino desire to construe their stories in a linear temporal sequence, attempting to make sense of disturbing events and thus rid themselves of fear (*Rue* 12, 109, 144), feelings of suffocation (*Rue* 111, 144, 146), or fatigue (*Filo* 11–13, 79). Of course, for Guy, amnesia prevents such ordering of the past. The "Ariadne's thread" of memory, instead of lending meaning to be reconstituted backward, continually dissolves itself into the lacunae of mystery (*Rue* 133). Describing another character affected by amnesia, Guy comments: "If he felt drawn to me, it was because he too—I learnt later—had lost track of himself and a whole section of his life had been engulfed without leaving the slightest trace, the slightest connection that could still link him with the past" (10). Instead of forming a signifying chain, traces of the past refuse to become visible ("But nothing caught my eye" [80]) or evaporate like fog on window panes (48, 139) or a child's tears (159). As Jeanne C. Ewert remarks, Guy Roland "is, as he says constantly, 'sur la piste,' but it is a trail that appears from nowhere and leads nowhere" (168).

Spino's attempts to reconstruct the meaning of his past (and that of

"The Kid") along a linear itinerary are equally frustrated. As in the children's game *il gioco dell'oca*—a popular board game, known in English as "snakes and ladders" or "chutes and ladders," in which players move pawns along an itinerary of consecutive squares—his movements are continually mocked by empty squares and traps, yet he still hopes for a moment of transcendence when, as in roulette, "sooner or later the dice will take him to a square that will give the whole thing meaning" (54). Opposing himself to imaginary others who are "wiping out" The Kid's past (61), Spino determines to recreate the unique sequence of events that will simultaneously make sense of his own past, and of The Kid's destiny:[7] " 'But you can't let people die in a vacuum,' Spino said. 'It's as if they'd died twice over' " (37). Here the collapse of logic and linear temporal order is evident: left without explanation, death amounts to a double break in the causal/chronological chain. Moreover, for Spino (as for any detective-story writer), an absurd death represents the reiteration, at the level of the investigation, of the impossibility of narrating that is uncovered at the level of the crime. Despite Spino's efforts, the past refuses narrativization; in its final pages, the story dissolves into darkness, and *sens* halts before the incomprehensibility of nothingness (83).

II

Through constant references to, and violation of, the generic codes of detective fiction, *Rue* and *Filo* manage to uncover the essential impasse of a hermeneutical project founded on a traditional concept of time. In place of the "suspense" convention of detective fiction, they substitute a hermeneutical "suspension" of closure. Hence the two protagonists are more than mere detectives, they are philosophers engaged in investigative reflection (in fact, as Tabucchi's note tells us, "Spino" is in part an affectionate reference to Spinoza [85]). The mystery they confront is the concept of identity: the relation of the subject to itself and to the phenomenological world. Identity for these subjects, however, is resistant to objectification; it cannot be manipulated a posteriori into narrative form. Since no final solution to the enigma is given, the subject cannot grasp itself as a being whose nature is clarified through "history/story." Modiano's and Tabucchi's protagonists seem to endorse what Paul Ricoeur calls a hermeneutics of suspicion, the fallacy of crediting self-identity with certainty and stability.

    The opening lines of *Rue* set the tone of a philosophical quest: "I am nothing. Nothing but a pale shape, silhouetted that evening against the cafe terrace" (7).[8] The first chapter of *Filo* similarly depicts Spino's occupation at the morgue as that of "a posthumous guardian, impassive and objective" (2), and his rigorous taxonomy of death assumes evident philosophical overtones: "And in a way this is life's storehouse. Before their final disappearance, the discarded products of the scene find a last home here while waiting for suitable classification, since the causes of their deaths cannot be left in doubt. That's why they are lying here, and he looks after them and watches over them" (1).

One of the first steps in both characters' search for identity is to find a name, a legible and durable trace left in official documents (telephone directories, passports, birth and marriage certificates in *Rue*) or objects (a doorbell, an engraved ring, a label sewn inside a coat in *Filo*). But names prove to be unreliable, given that the relationship between sign and referent is anything but certain. The names "Pedro McEvoy" and "Jimmy Pedro Stern" turn out to be just as borrowed as the name "Guy Roland"; "Carlo Nobodi," the most credible name with which Spino can label The Kid's corpse, is clearly symbolic (*Filo* 26).[9] In her analysis of *Rue*, Marja Warehime points out that such names, "as fragments of a chronology, suggest a linear narrative by locating an individual in a place at a certain period in time" (339). Guy and Spino make precisely this methodological error when they attempt to use names as reference points in reconstructing a biographical history.

Objects and photographs prove to be unreliable for similar reasons; they either mislead the investigation or leave it at a dead end. In spite of Guy's prompting, other characters do not recognize him in the old photograph he shows them. The picture found by Spino in the dead man's pocket does not help to identify him; neither does the school picture found at his old boarding house (*Filo* 39–41, 52–53). In *Rue*, old objects and pictures circulate excessively, becoming nearly free-floating signifiers. When given a box of memorabilia for the third time, the protagonist ironically comments: "It certainly seemed everything ended with old chocolate or biscuit or cigar boxes" (64). It is as if the other characters had waited all these years for someone to narrate their pasts, someone able to turn those old boxes into texts. For them, identity is as uncertain and as untellable as it is for the protagonist. In *Filo*, the past is stored in drawers whose contents prove to be of no real use but cause an "indefinable sadness" (80). Moreover, such objects also tell unreliable stories. After failing to remember the story of his old coat, one of the characters in *Filo* comments: "you know, belongings, they're always so slippery, these belongings of ours, they move about, they even get the better of your memory" (50).

What the protagonists of *Rue* and *Filo* lack is a hermeneutics that would forge links between isolated fragments (such as names, persons, objects, photographs) and establish them as events in a stabilized, consecutive, causal chain. Guy and Spino both mistakenly rely on inter-

pretations founded on a traditional concept of time. From their perspective, consciousness is a cognitive process that constitutes entities as
objects susceptible of narration, possessing beginnings and ends. Insofar as temporality in these two novels is not organized in terms of plot
or chronology, such a hermeneutics of linear time must be abandoned.

In response to this failed strategy, the two novels develop a hermeneutics of spatial detection evidently influenced by Heideggerian philosophy. For Heidegger, "placement" is a key concept in understanding
the condition of *Dasein*. As Ricoeur notes, *Dasein* is "not a subject for
which there is an object, but rather a being within Being" (56). Herman
Rapaport explains that "*Dasein*, in other words, is proximate, attitudinal,
attentive to wordly clues through which is achieved both a sense of clari-
fication and occultation . . . [what] Heidegger calls 'tuned correspondence' " (48). "Tuned correspondence" is also the attitude suggested by
both *Rue* and *Filo*, in response to the protagonists' assumption that there
is a subject who can truly know. The initial idea of "identity" as an accessible object (accessible to both cognition and narration) is gradually
replaced in these texts by a concept of identity as a multitude of momentary, changeable, phenomenological horizons.

The horizon of the title in Tabucchi's novel thus acquires Heideggerian connotations. The port city of Genoa—never directly named, yet as
determining in the text as the protagonist's lack of destination—offers
to Spino, at each moment, an unobstructed view of the horizon. Its presence, as familiar as it is unreachable, seems to ridicule his interpretive
pretensions. In the passage cited earlier, in which Spino fantasizes about
a chance solution, the sea appears to refute his idle dreaming just by
being there:

> And so here he is again wandering about in search of nothing. The walls of these
> narrow streets seem to promise a reward he never manages to arrive at, as if they
> formed the board of a game of snakes and ladders [*gioco dell'oca*], full of dead
> ends and trap doors, on which he goes up and down, round and round, hoping
> that sooner or later the dice will take him to a square that will give the whole
> thing meaning. And meanwhile over there is the sea. He looks at it. Across its
> surface pass the shapes of ships, a few seagulls, clouds. (54)

Tabucchi further explicates the philosophical meaning of the horizon
in his Author's Note, where he comments that "the edge of the horizon
is a geometrical location" (85), an inner landscape that conditions our
way of being in the world.

Both protagonists' recurring need to determine their spatial coordinates also manifests the Heideggerian imperative of "placement." As
Warehime says of Guy's obstinate search for his identity in *Rue*, "His
sense of self is less an identity than an itinerary where names and streets

and places figure prominently" (340). It is almost as if Guy seeks identity through his metonymic relationship with the toponymy of Paris: "I often mention bars or restaurants, but if it were not for a street or café sign from time to time, how would I ever find my way?" (108). Moreover, Guy's itineraries are often labyrinths whose walls form menacing, insuperable obstacles, mazes of stairways and escalators (32), streets and avenues (97), or garden hedges (60). Lost memories are compared to walled passageways: "Why try to renew ties that had been broken and look for passageways that had been walled off long ago?" (42; my trans.). The past seems as sealed off ("under seal" [63]) as the upper floors of one character's country mansion, and people's identities resemble noncommunicating rooms: "People certainly lead compartmentalized lives and their friends do not know each other. It's unfortunate" (76).

The neighborhoods of Genoa where Spino searches for traces of The Kid are equally oppressive, although exhibiting less toponymic precision. Houses, streets, squares, walls loom as concrete presences hanging down over the passing protagonist. The feeling of confinement culminates in the cemetery scene, in which the imposing presence of monumental tombs contrasts mockingly with the absence of the person Spino is supposed to meet there. But Spino follows a precise itinerary even in open spaces, skirting walls, detouring around obstacles, and following railways as if he were constantly afraid of losing touch with his spatial coordinates. The itinerary that he follows to the last appointment is laid out as neatly as a labyrinth that penetrates into a temple's *sancta sanctorum.*

The insistence in both novels on architectural and geometrical imagery gives rise to an excessive determination of exterior space. For Foucault, the opening of a "site," the space of living, results from such description:

The space in which we live, which draws us to ourselves, in which the erosion of our lives, our time and history occurs, the space that claws and gnaws at us, is also, in itself, a heterogeneous space. In other words, we do not live in a kind of void, inside of which we could place individuals and things. We do not live inside a void that could be colored with diverse shades of light, we live inside a set of relations that delineates sites which are irreducible to one another and absolutely not superimposable on one another. (23)

Like that in Foucault's description, the heterogeneous space inhabited by Modiano's and Tabucchi's characters is traversed by multiple sets of lines delineating "irreducible," concretely partitioned sites. Moreover, an identical topography characterizes their interior space: if placement is a constitutive condition of *Dasein,* then exterior and interior space are indistinguishable.[10] For these characters, dispersed fragments of identity can thus be interpreted as positional sites, horizons of being, placed in a network that connects points in transient relations. It is important to restate, however, that neither Heidegger nor Foucault call for a denial of time. They simply no longer view time and history only in terms of linear connection on a temporal axis. A Heideggerian hermeneutics based on "tuned correspondence" considers time as a manifold of temporal moments that refuse chronological closure; Foucault views time as an ensemble of relations, in which events may appear juxtaposed or disseminated in a spatial constellation. For both philosophers, however, insofar as spatial detection becomes the only possible interpretive strategy, time loses its privileged position and becomes merely "one of the various distributive operations that are possible for the elements that are spread out in space" (Foucault 21).

Modiano's and Tabucchi's texts affirm a hermeneutics of spatial detection in spite of their characters' efforts to investigate identity within traditional temporal parameters. Guy and Spino find themselves positioned at the intersections of a web of continually changing relations. Identity, for them, is thus a heterogeneous space traversed by a grid, in which the only possible hermeneutic activity is to establish precarious relations of proximity rather than continuity. Memory gaps and lacunae of meaning cannot be bridged, but can be repositioned in different spatial configurations. Modiano's image of errant voices on abandoned telephone lines could be read as a metaphor for such spatial hermeneutics. Reconfirming the isolation and fragmentation of identity, this metaphor still leaves open the possibility of contact (if not communication): "Skeletal conversations, voices seeking each other out, in spite of the ringing which obliterated them at regular intervals. And all these faceless beings trying to exchange telephone numbers, passwords, in the hope of some rendez-vous" (96). Intersecting networks and chance encounters also determine the relationship of past and present for Guy: "Denise Coudreuse and I had met one day in this maze of roads and boulevards. Paths that cross, among those of thousands and thousands of people all over Paris, like countless little balls on a gigantic, electric billiard table, which occasionally bump into each other. And nothing remained of this, not even the luminous trail a firefly leaves behind it" (97). Guy's frustration comes from his inability to reconstruct that enormous pinball machine's "thousands and thousands of paths" into one distinct line, to extract from his positional being an identity that can be known as an object, separate from the investigating subject and susceptible to a linear narration (or at least "the luminous trail of a firefly"). In a rare moment, however, the novel briefly adopts a more productive hermeneutics when Guy surrenders to an attitude of "tuned correspondence," positioning himself at a nodal point in a fabric of relations: "Perhaps, after all, I never was this Pedro McEvoy, I was nothing, but waves passed through me, sometimes faint, sometimes stronger, and all these scattered echoes afloat in the air crystallized and there I was" (82). In *Filo*, Spino feels from the beginning that he has to rearrange the "architecture of things" in order to accommodate that "insignificant corpse with no name and no history." He believes that The Kid, instead of being an absurd remainder ("a waste fragment"), represents a silence in which he feels caught, a silence traversed by a network of invisible relations: "In this silence [Spino] had the sensation of moving like a fish caught in a net" (23–24). That network becomes textually visible in the penultimate chapter. There, in a sort of epiphany, Spino's memory of a deathbed, the objects in his room, and the trajectory of the bullets that killed The Kid all come together in a single weblike nexus of significance in his mind. This nexus of relations, however, can only be inferred intuitively by Spino, since the existential condition of "placement" does not allow for a privileged point of observation, from which alone a comprehensive description of the general pattern could be given:

an implacable logic, as of some unknown geometry, something one might intuit but could never pin down in a rational order or in an explanation. And he thought that things do follow an order and that nothing happens by chance, but chance in fact is just this: our incapacity to grasp the true connections between things. And he sensed the vulgarity and the arrogance with which we bring together the objects that surround us. (78)

Such sentiments notwithstanding, Spino's whole investigation has been motivated by that "vulgarity and arrogance" by means of which we make connections among the things surrounding us and believe that we have uncovered, and not merely invented, the architecture of Being. As Spino remarks here, there may be an implacable geometry, but it is still as unknowable as it is necessary. In actuality, the connections we draw are merely ad hoc distributive operations, unable to claim the stable status of knowledge. Initially, Spino thinks that he can reconstruct The Kid's (and his own) identity according to a rational and chronological order. His investigation leads him, instead, to a series of dispersed fragments that cannot cohere into an organized narrative, but can only be interpreted as transient spatial constellations projected onto a narrative horizon.

In the penultimate chapter, Spino literally enacts this hermeneutical strategy when he tries to establish connections between his last clue and the pattern of things. He takes the sheet of paper on which he has jotted down that last clue, goes out on his terrace, and pegs it out on the clothesline against the horizon: "then came back in, sat in the same position as before, and looked at it. . . . He just watched it for a long time, establishing again a connection between that piece of paper flapping in the dusk and the edge of the horizon that was ever so slowly dissolving away into darkness" (79). This image offers a *mise en abyme* of the author's relation to his fiction. Since the sheet of paper carries a verse from a Greek tragedy, it also functions as a *mise en abyme* of the hermeneutical value of literature itself. Tabucchi, however, like his characters, has been unable to construe identity as a knowable object accessible to narration. In his novels, exploring the past does not resolve the initial enigma posed by identity; instead, it releases only isolated narrative fragments. Nonetheless, Tabucchi continues to write about the quest for identity and the structure of memory. His work, as improbable and nonexistent as the edge of the horizon, presents the same instability and fragility as the configurations of meaning realized by Spino. Tabucchi's writing constantly weaves and unweaves a fine web of lines that does not pretend to grasp the edge of the horizon, but nevertheless is able to help construct an intuition of proximity.

In *Rue*, the impossibility of Guy's narrating his past parallels Modiano's inability to integrate the story's different elements into a single narrative line. As Francine de Martinoir explains, "Patrick Modiano's world is made up of pieces [or, more literally, "is the world of the fissure"]. For his heroes, narration is no longer possible. One can understand how, for this writer more than any other, it could be said that after Auschwitz it was difficult, if not impossible, to write as if nothing had happened. The narrative is shattered, and writing sketches a discontinuous world" (106–7; my trans.). In spite of his characters' restless efforts to determine their identity by anchoring it to a chronological axis, identity resists organization and representation on the page. Nonetheless, like Tabucchi, Modiano continues in his necessarily incomplete project of writing. The original "crack" in the world (both a historical and a biographical break) makes it impossible to retrieve anything but dispersed fragments of the past which, like beauty queens and butterflies, "spring out of nothing one fine day and return there, having sparkled a little." Like hermeneutical horizons, such sparks are accessible only as relations which change through time. Modiano's writing constantly both delineates and erases this network of relations. Like his character, Hutte, he knows that "in the end we were all 'beach men' and that 'the sand' . . . keeps the traces of our footsteps only a few moments" (49). Such instability, however, is the necessary precondition to a hermeneutics of spatial detection.

This tension between a traditional hermeneutics of time and a more modern hermeneutics of space places Modiano and Tabucchi at the center of the ideological debate that, according to Foucault, characterizes our epoch: "One could perhaps say that certain ideological conflicts animating present-day polemics oppose the pious descendants of time and the determined inhabitants of space" (22). By privileging space over time, Modiano and Tabucchi clearly join the party of "the determined inhabitants of space." However, it is necessary to recognize the ways in which space itself has changed. For these authors, space is constituted through a flexible fabric of relations that refuses stable determinations and requires constant repositioning. By developing their project of spatial detection, Modiano and Tabucchi do not renounce the representational precision of geometry. They claim instead a more precarious role—that of geometers of the horizon.

Notes

1. I would like to take this opportunity to thank Gerald Prince, in whose seminar course (many years ago) I read Modiano's novels for the first time.

2. Modiano gives an ironic twist to his novel by choosing the name "Rue des Boutiques Obscures" for both the protagonist's final destination and the novel's title. Such a name offers a *mise en abyme* of the same hermeneutic movement presented and deferred by the last chapter. On the literal level, it provides the quest with a definite point of arrival (a real "Via delle Botteghe Oscure" exists in Rome), while figuratively it brings the protagonist to a new dead end.

3. All quotations from *Rue* and *Filo* are from their English translations unless otherwise indicated.

4. *Racconto giallo*—literally, "yellow short story"—is the generic Italian term for detective fiction. The phrase comes from the colored book covers of a very popular detective fiction series.

5. Of course, style also contributes to the standard *roman noir* effect: both novels are written in the simple, unobtrusive prose characteristic of this genre (cf. Todorov 13).

6. Gerald Prince defines the disnarrated as the narrative category that "covers all the events that do not happen but, nonetheless, are referred to (in a negative or hypothetical mode) by the narrative text"; it generates suspense and "articulate[s] the narrative in hermeneutic terms (in detective novels, for instance, the possible solutions it introduces are contrasted with the real ones)" ("Disnarrated" 2, 5).

7. Barthes writes: "the formula *post hoc, ergo propter hoc* . . . could be seen as the motto of Destiny, while the story is reduced to Destiny's 'language' " (22; my trans.).

8. This beginning closely resembles that of Raymond Queneau's *Le Chiendent*, a novel which itself rewrites Descartes's *Discours de la méthode* into contemporary vernacular French.

9. I am grateful for Susan Elizabeth Sweeney's suggestion that "Carlo Nobodi" may refer to Carlo Collodi, author of *The Adventures of Pinocchio* (a tale about the search for selfhood), and a writer from Tuscany, like Tabucchi. I would also like to thank her for her careful reading of my essay and her many appropriate stylistic suggestions.

10. Foucault does maintain this distinction, declaring his intention to treat exclusively external space, in contrast to Bachelard, whose work dealt with internal space (Foucault 23). In my opinion, however, Foucault's essay collapses the two realms, especially in his treatment of the garden, the carpet, and the ship as both actual heterotopias and topoi of the imaginary.

Works Cited

Bachelard, Gaston. *The Poetics of Space.* Trans. Maria Jolas. New York: Orion, 1964.
Barthes, Roland. "Introduction à l'analyse du récit." *Poétique du récit,* by Barthes et al. Paris: Seuil, 1977. 7–57.
Collodi, Carlo. *The Adventures of Pinocchio.* [*Le Avventure di Pinocchio.*] Trans. Nicolas J. Perella. Berkeley: University of California Press, 1986.
De Martinoir, Francine. "Patrick Modiano: *Rue des Boutiques Obscures.*" *La Nouvelle Revue Française* 310 (1978): 105–8.
Descartes, René. *A Discourse on Method and Meditations on the First Philosophy.* [*Discours de la méthode*]. Trans. Donald A. Cress. Indianapolis, Ind.: Hackett, 1993.
Eisenzweig, Uri. "Présentation du genre." *Littérature* 49 (1983): 3–15.
Ewert, Jeanne C. "Lost in the Hermeneutic Funhouse: Patrick Modiano's Postmodern Detective." In *The Cunning Craft: Original Essays on Detective Fiction and Contemporary Literary Theory,* ed. Ronald G. Walker and June M. Frazer. Macomb: Western Illinois University Press, 1990. 166–73.
Foucault, Michel. "Of Other Spaces." *Diacritics* 16, 1 (1986): 22–27.
Heidegger, Martin. *Being and Time.* Trans. John Macquarrie and Edward Robinson. New York: Harper, 1962.
Modiano, Patrick. *Rue des Boutiques Obscures.* [*Missing Person,* trans. Daniel Weissbort, London: Jonathan Cape, 1980]. Paris: Gallimard, 1978.
Prince, Gerald. "The Disnarrated." *Style* 22, 1 (1988): 1–8.
———. "Re-Membering Modiano; or, Something Happened." *SubStance* 15, 49 (1986): 35–43.
Queneau, Raymond. *Le Chiendent.* Paris: Gallimard, 1956.
Rapaport, Herman. "Literature and the Hermeneutics of Detection." *L'Esprit Créateur* 26, 2 (1986): 48–59.
Ricoeur, Paul. "The Task of Hermeneutics." In *Hermeneutics and the Human Sciences,* ed. J. B. Thompson. London: Cambridge University Press, 1981. 52–68.
Robbe-Grillet, Alain. "Entretien." Interview with Uri Eisenzweig. *Littérature* 49 (1983): 16–22.
Tabucchi, Antonio. *Il Filo dell'orizzonte.* [*The Edge of the Horizon,* trans. Tim Parks, New York: New Directions, 1990]. Milano: Feltrinelli, 1986.
Todorov, Tzvetan. "Typologie du roman policier." *Poétique de la prose.* [*The Poetics of Prose*]. Paris: Seuil, 1971. 9–19.
Warehime, Marja. "Originality and Narrative Nostalgia: Shadows in Modiano's *Rue des Boutiques Obscures.*" *French Forum* 12 (1987): 335–45.

Chapter 11
"Premeditated Crimes"
The Dis-Solution of Detective Fiction in Gombrowicz's Works

Hanjo Berressem

> A paranoic delusion is a caricature of a philosophical system.
> —Sigmund Freud, *Werke* (9: 363)

In the following essay, I will trace elements of the metaphysical detective story in the works of Witold Gombrowicz and align them within a psychoanalytic (in particular, Lacanian) framework. For this project, I will draw on the elective affinity between detective fiction and psychoanalysis, which is based—at least partly—on the fact that, like the criminal case, the psychoanalytic case is a knotty problem with death at its center. Jacques Lacan, in fact, defines human reality in general as "The Case of the Borromean Knot," the structure he draws upon to describe the interrelated realms of the symbolic, the imaginary, and the real, which compose the complex topography of human reality:[1]

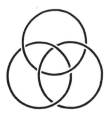

This imbroglio (*Encore* 112) might serve as an epigraph for a study of Gombrowicz, who, beginning with his first collection of short stories, *Memoirs from the Epoch of Maturation* (1938), uses the genre of metaphysical detective fiction to show the intervention of the imaginary in the symbolic, and the belated effect of the real in the imaginary and the symbolic.

Although the metaphysical detective story is the genre that describes this complex topography, and shows the interrelatedness of these various levels, classic detective fiction is also a fascinating genre for psychoanalysis, because its structure carefully separates these generally interwoven realms. While the symbolic (the realm of language, reason, and logic) is related to the detective, the imaginary (the realm of visual identification, desire, and the logic of desire) is related to the criminal. The real, finally (that which is neither symbolic nor imaginary), is related to the evidence.

From the standpoint of detection, the real and the symbolic are relatively unproblematic because they are unambiguous. While the former is not structured at all, the latter is completely structured. In detective fiction, the former is related to observation and the search for clues, and the latter to logical reasoning. Although either of these realms can be problematic, usually it is the imaginary that poses difficulties.

The criminal can intervene in each of these three realms in order to cover up his crime: in the imaginary, for instance, by concealing his motive; in the symbolic, by engineering a fake alibi, which would imply the logical impossibility of having been in a position to commit the crime; or in the real, by getting rid of the evidence. It is ultimately this evidence—in ninety-nine cases out of a hundred, a corpse—which has to be accounted for as the alien parameter in the symbolic universe, and over which the criminal stumbles. In Alfred Hitchcock's film *The Trouble with Harry* (1955), for instance, Harry's corpse is quite literally such a stumbling block, a part of the real that, although everyone tries to get rid of it, resurfaces with the relentless persistence of the return of the repressed. Only after it has been integrated into the symbolic—when it becomes clear that Harry has not been murdered at all—can the corpse finally come to rest.

Hitchcock underscores the corpse's detour through the symbolic with the circular structure of the film, whose first and last scenes are identical: Harry's corpse lying in the woods. The temporal loop which this circular structure implies is made possible by little Arnie's private temporal reckoning, according to which "today is tomorrow" and "tomorrow yesterday."[2] Yet apart from a temporal loop, *The Trouble with Harry* is also defined by a logical loop, because the corpses of the first and last scenes are not identical. Although the material, real corpse is at the same place, and the time between the two scenes has been erased, the symbolic universe around it is completely different.

In *The Trouble with Harry*, Calvin Biggs, the sheriff, feels intuitively that something is wrong, although he (unlike the spectator) will never be able to integrate the real events fully into the symbolic. A natural correspondence between the symbolic and the real, which can be sensed intuitively—the one that is withheld from Biggs in *The Trouble with Harry*—has always been the logocentric idea(l) on which classic detective fiction rests. While, as a rule, the detective unveils this hidden correspondence and thus shows the triumph of the spirit over the literal, Hitchcock's example suggests that detective fiction can also be the perfect genre in which to problematize and deconstruct this correspondence.

I

Before I discuss Gombrowicz's work—in which, as I will argue, this correspondence is relentlessly deconstructed—I will show what happens to the concept of intuition in the passage from Poe's to Lacan's texts.

Poe deals with intuition in his theory of ratiocination, which stresses that Auguste Dupin's success is not based on intuition (the spirit) but on a specific method (the letter). The results of this method, however, although "brought about by the very soul and essence of method, have, in truth, the whole air of intuition" ("Murders" 141). This seems at first to be itself a deconstruction of the logocentric idea(l) of intuition, yet a closer look reveals that it is only a clever ruse to cover up, and get away with, a more initial and fundamental logocentrism.

It is Poe's theory of visual identification that reintroduces intuition into the analytic process. In his example—the game of "even and odd" ("Purloined" 215)—this imaginary identification takes place on a level outside the symbolic, axiomatic, and thus logical rules of the game, on the level of "things external" to it and, by analogy, seemingly "irrelevant" to the case ("Murders" 142; "Mystery" 191). Poe's Dupin provides an exact method for this identification, based on the analyst's imitation of his opponent's visual expression. This imaginary, specular identification, in which the analyst's face becomes the mirror image of the opponent's, invariably—and necessarily—results in a correct symbolic admeasurement of the opponent's intellect.

The right balance between, and yet the precise separation of, "[imaginary] observation and [symbolic] admeasurement" defines Dupin's method, as well as his separation of the two parts of his personality, the "resolvent and the creative," whose combination distinguishes the true detective ("Purloined" 215; "Murders" 141). In fact, one only fails to come to the right conclusions if one allows one's own imaginary to interfere within the symbolic, as the police do in their search for the purloined letter, in which they "consider only their *own* ideas of ingenuity and . . . advert only to the modes in which *they* would have hidden it" ("Purloined" 216; my emphasis). It is thus ultimately the visual identification with the criminal's imaginary that decides between success and failure. Dupin's invariably exact identifications do make intuition superfluous, but only because they are themselves intuitive.[3] The spirit wins out over the letter.

It is here that Lacan differs from Dupin. Although, like Dupin, he sees the symbolic—which for him denotes the mechanics of the network of signifiers, "the possible combinatory of the machine" (*Ego* 181)—as itself strictly logical, Lacan counters the ideal imaginary mapping with his contention that all knowledge is always already paranoic. Due to the specifically human "*prematurity of birth*" (*Écrits* 4), the formation of the imaginary instance of the ego results in the double movement of an always "alienating identification" (128) which defines it as an essentially "fragmented" (4), hallucinated entity connected to a "function of *méconnaissance* [misrecognition] that characterizes . . . [it] in all its structures" (6). Because human reality results from a projection of narcissistically and therefore libidinously charged images onto actual objects and people, it is inevitably fictional and paranoic. Reality, "inasmuch as it is supported by desire, is initially hallucinated" (*Psychoses* 84).

Because "The Purloined Letter" (1844) thematizes the relation between the symbolic and the imaginary, it is a perfect pretext for Lacan to develop the subversion and "decisive orientation which the subject receives from the itinerary of the signifier" ("Seminar" 29), and to illustrate his belief in the predominance of the letter over the spirit. For my purposes, it is crucial that, beginning with Poe, the relation of the detective to the crime has been a professional, impersonal, and impartial one. This position outside the sphere of the crime ensures that the detective can be fully within the symbolic. Lacan comments on the shift from this outside position to the inside when he detects a "certain dissonance" between "the admittedly penetrating . . . remarks" with which Dupin "introduces us to his method," and "the manner in which he in fact intervenes" (33). Dupin's symbolic detachment is ensured by "The profit" he "so nimbly extracts from his exploit." Yet, Lacan comments, this profit, "if its purpose is to allow him to withdraw his stakes from the game, makes all the more paradoxical, even shocking, the partisan attack . . . he suddenly permits himself to launch against the Minister" (49). Through this partial action, which Lacan relates to the simple fact that Dupin "*has* the letter," he becomes "fully participant in the intersubjective triad, and, as such, in the median position previously occupied by the Queen and the Minister" (50). In this shift, Dupin loses his perspective from outside the "symbolic circuit" (49), and enters the imaginary realm of the crime.

Ultimately, Poe's story allows Lacan to show the link between the repetition compulsion—itself a highly criminal term—and the agency of the letter. The entry into the symbolic entails the separation from the real. From that moment onwards, each object is defined within the conjunction of the symbolic and the imaginary (what Lacan calls an "object *o*"). This human(ized) object can never completely substitute for the lost, absolute object—the real, which "resists symbolization completely" (*Freud's* 66). Human reality is forever pervaded by the fundamental "*Manque-à-être*"—that is, the "lack-of-being" or the "want-to-be"—entailed by this loss (*Ecrits* 323; original emphasis), which is why Lacan writes the subject as "$." Although the repetition compulsion has its roots in the desire to recreate the real, this recreation is impossible because one cannot escape the symbolic. This impossibility is the reason why the repetition compulsion "finds its basis in what we have called the insistence of the signifying chain," and why "the signifier materializes the agency of death" ("Seminar" 28, 38). In order to bring about an approximation of the symbolic and the real, the subject must forever "pass through the channels of the symbolic" (43).

Although the intervention of the signifier in the subject's reality is easily repressed by the subject, the letter "does not forget" the subject. In fact, the letter brings about the relentless "return of the repressed" (47). In Freudian terminology, this repressed real is "an instinct or a part of an instinct which has not followed the normal development [and] . . . has remained in a more infantile stadium" (*Werke* 7: 190).[4] In this context, Freud notes especially the "narcissistic" fixation (185)—the cathexis of the ego with libido—with its imaginary illusion of fullness, and the repression of the lack-of-being and death it entails. The return of the repressed in the symbolic is triggered by the intervention of present events which stir up the repressed material. Lacan stresses that because of the letter's insistence in the unconscious, the repressed is always already "something which will be realized in the symbolic," and something that "*will have been*" (*Freud's* 158; original emphasis). Its representation within the symbolic is therefore always belated and distorted. This belatedness defines the temporal loop in which real "psychic traces" cause a "belated effect" within the symbolic (Freud, *Werke* 5: 31).

This belatedness defines both *The Trouble with Harry* and "The Purloined Letter," which also ends with a temporal loop. A seemingly identical letter, like Harry's corpse, is back in its place and, like Harry's corpse, defines a different symbolic framework around it. Unlike *The Trouble with Harry*, however, at the end of Poe's story the real letter is still not at rest, because its ultimate destination is the King. That it does not get there is (at least partly) the result of Dupin's slip into the imaginary. Yet while in Poe's tale this shift into the imaginary is merely an *aperçu*, in Gombrowicz's story "A Premeditated Crime" (1936) it marks the very beginning of the narrative.

II

"A Premeditated Crime" relates how H., an investigating magistrate, travels to Ignatius K.'s home in the country in order to clear up some monetary questions. It takes some time before the strange behavior of K.'s family is explained by the fact that K. died during the night before H.'s arrival. Although K. is obviously the victim of a heart attack, and there are no strangulation marks on his neck, H. maintains that K. has been strangled. After a "thorough" investigation, he accuses K.'s son Anton of murder. In the end, Anton admits to the crime, although it is still obvious that, in actual fact, K. died a natural death. Anton even strangles the corpse, so that he himself, belatedly, produces the missing real evidence.

In this tale of a belated crime after the event, Gombrowicz completely reverses the structure of the detective story. If, generally, the facts—the real—are the immutable evidence that must be incorporated into a symbolic system, then the question in "A Premeditated Crime" is how to change the real belatedly from within the immutable logic of an imaginary obsession: the method of madness. Because "the real . . . is always in its place," and "it can *literally* be said that something is missing from its place only of what can change it: the symbolic" (Lacan, "Seminar" 40), this change is only possible via a detour through the symbolic.

From the beginning of the story, H. is described as a highly ambivalent character. On the one hand, he loves "cleanliness and order," which are related to the symbolic ("Premeditated" 46).[5] On the other, he considers himself "sensitive and above all irritable," and at one point even talks about his "wretched character," all traits which point toward the imaginary (44, 46). Although he generally represses the aggressive part of his character, especially in his official function as magistrate, his trip is marked by eruptions of this aggressivity. As soon as he arrives at the train station, he is annoyed that no one is there to pick him up. These irritations continue: after a strenuous ride, he arrives at the house, where he is attacked by the dogs; and when Anton finally opens the door, he tells H. that they have simply "forgotten" the telegram he had sent about his arrival. Nothing, then, is "in order." Even the presence of Cäcilie, K.'s daughter, cannot please H., although "femininity can never hurt. But the hand which she held out to me is sweaty—and the femininity . . . is somehow . . . sweaty and indifferent . . . mashed and uncombed" (38). Furthermore, H. is "angry" that the family is "busy only with itself," and they seem to him as if "insulted by me, or as if they were afraid of me, or as if they were pitying me, or also as if they were ashamed of me" (39). When, during dinner, the mother informs H. of K.'s death, the atmosphere is already so poisoned that the only thing he is really—and excessively—angry about is being unable to finish his cutlet, because he has to go up to see the corpse: "is it my fault that she terrorized me in this way, that my cutlets as well as myself seemed to me to be trivial and not worth mentioning?" (43).

The carefully developed sequence of H.'s growing annoyance charts his gradual regression from symbolic to imaginary registers—which entails a regression from the reality principle to the pleasure principle, and to narcissistic, aggressive structures and images which result, according to Lacan, in a "more and more paralyzing, vast concentric hallucination" (*Ego* 169). In this context, his feelings of being slighted and neglected should be read as projections of the repressed feelings of shame and inadequacy that are the reverse side of a heightened narcissism.[6]

As in "The Purloined Letter," this shift results in a loss of perspective, which culminates in H.'s irrational statement that K. has been murdered. Afterward, H. himself muses that if he had asserted himself and told them that he would first finish his cutlets, "perhaps many tragic events might have been averted." Because he missed this chance, however, he now has to avenge himself via a complicated detour: "The deceased lay on the bed. . . . The blue, swollen face looked as if strangled, which is normal with a heart attack. 'Strangled,' I whispered, although I saw very well that it had been a heart attack" (43). This statement, uttered completely against his better judgment, is not so much the result of a real observation as of an hallucination, a projection of feelings of shame, aggressiveness, and revenge onto the real, in which what is repressed in the symbolic reappears. The intimate relation of the "murder" to H.'s mental state is further underscored by a scene that shows him reenacting the murder in a condensed and displaced manner. Symptomatically, he relates this reenactment, in which he is already in the position of passive spectator, to the fact that "they have ridiculed me. . . . When I was finally alone in my small chamber I took off the collar, and instead of putting it on the table, I threw it on the floor and then I even stamped on it with my foot. My face became distorted and turned blood-red, and the fingers pressed together convulsively, in a very unexpected manner" (46).

The basic, real fact that H. has to incorporate into the logic of his paranoic system is that because K. died of a heart attack, there are no strangulation marks on his neck. His attempt to change the real is therefore ultimately a fight against the corpse, which represents the real, death, and the materiality of physical objects, while H.'s paranoic system, which represents the symbolic and the imaginary, stands for life and the realm of the psyche. H. himself identifies these two sides very clearly: "Can this dead object with human traits . . . can this stiffened face offer a true resistance to my flexible, changeable physiognomy, which can find the fitting expression for every situation?" (52). Throughout the story, the neck of the corpse is the part of the real against which H.'s paranoic construction of reality stumbles: "It was as if I fought against a stool. However much I strained the imagination, intuition, logic—the neck remained a neck, and the white, white, with the resistance so characteristic of a dead object" (64). Even at the end, H. wonders "what can thought do against the thoughtlessness of a corpse?" (72).

Because this real can be neither eliminated nor incorporated into a logical system, one has to evade it, because, as H. states, "what cannot be gotten rid of, one has to jump over" (52). All of H.'s ideas, in fact, are attempts to "fool" the real by cleverly replacing the realm of logic with the logic of desire: "When the appearance speaks against a crime— I said cleverly—let's be smart and let's not be fooled by the appearance. If on the contrary, however, logic, common sense, and finally obviousness make themselves the counsel for the criminal, and the appearance speaks against him, let's trust the appearance" (52). The complicated and ultimately impossible fight against the real is extremely tiring, however, because it involves continual repression.[7] Although the structure of the "vast concentric hallucination" (Lacan, *Ego* 169) of H.'s delusional system is taken up by images of the noose around the murderer's neck, and of his strangulation, this noose is always only an "imaginary" one: "The net pulled itself together more and more, the noose, which contracted around the murderer's neck, became more and more visible— But why, instead of showing triumph, did I merely smile rather stupidly? Because—unfortunately, one has to admit—something just as important as the noose around the murderer's neck was missing, namely, the noose around the neck of the victim" (58–59).

What H. represses is the reality of death. It is, however, not any corpse, and thus not death in general, but a specific form of death that disturbs him: "an ugly . . . corpse of a murder victim is one thing; and someone who has died a respectable, natural death is something else completely . . . a certain formlessness is one thing; and a . . . [natural] death in all of its majesty is something else completely" (41). A natural death is more terrible than a murder because it is a triumph of both nature and the real, while a murder is precisely a triumph of the symbolic over the real. The attempt to change the natural "death in all of its majesty" into a "formless" murder, then, results from a repression and foreclosure of the reality of death and the real.

As a first step in the transposition of the real into the symbolic, H.'s paranoic system transfers the natural situation into a theatrical and thus symbolic one. This is why H. has the "annoying, strangely persistent idea that this was a prearranged theatrical scene. Everything looked as if it were staged" (45). The second step is the transposition of the reality of the death into a metaphorical and thus verbally symbolic realm, to transpose the fact from the outside to the inside and from the physical to the psychic: "This obstacle bothered me so much that during dinner . . . I began to prove that the crime was, according to its nature, not physical, but, par excellence—psychic" (60). H. turns the death into an "inner crime" (55) by metaphorizing the heart of the matter, and thus staking the real heart against the symbolic one. This is easy, because "the heart is a very elastic, even symbolic term . . . We know how intricate, how ambiguous a heart can be." H.'s conclusion is that "the deceased has been strangled, and this strangulation has a heart-character" (53). He connects this character to the house's interior and ambience: "Everything was combined to an atmosphere of special care, great *heartiness*— at every step, the heart found nourishment for itself. . . . And one had to admit that the house was also exceptionally 'internal' " (54; my emphasis).

The middle of the story is marked by a moment which once again highlights the ambivalence of H.'s psychic state and shows the last time he feels any control over his paranoic system. This instance of control is, symptomatically, the highest one—God. Evoking the Last Judgment, H. imagines being accused of having only imagined the murder, of having "in my base way of thinking . . . mixed up crime and mourning" (59). This is again symptomatic, because mourning entails the acceptance of the "lack-of-being" and of death, exactly that which H. represses. Immediately after this scene, however, he plays down the importance of the real with renewed vigor in a moment that describes his final shift into psychosis. In a conversation, he gives three completely absurd and "mad" examples of murder, all of which serve to prove that "the actual crime always happens in the soul" (60), and that the subsequent, belated, real murder is only a minor matter, a mere formality: "such a big psychic crime, and such a small, unrecognizable physical trace . . . physically speaking, the crime is a trifle, only psychically is it difficult. As a result of the exceptional frailty of the organism, one can kill by accident . . . by absentmindedness—without knowing how, suddenly, bang, there lies a corpse" (60–61).

Gradually, H.'s paranoic system contracts around Anton, who is an easy target: like H., he has an especially "nervous nature. Nervous nature, bashfulness, excessive sensitivity, excessive heartiness"; and, as his mother states, he has completely repressed his feelings for his father: "he even forbids the trembling of one's hands. . . . He has not cried. . . . Oh, if at least he would cry once" (57, 43). Because of this repression, he is especially susceptible to the ambivalence of the psychic rift that aligns love and hate, to the fact that "love and hate are two faces of one and the same thing" (71). It is through this analogy (that excessive mourning can be interpreted as excessive hate) that H. convinces Anton—who is in many ways his alter ego—that he has indeed (perhaps "unconsciously") killed his father. In a scene that is itself highly "psychoanalytic," he "suggests" to him his own repressed Oedipal fantasy—"the murder of the father" (56)—and his own repression of death, which Anton finally admits when he states that he has locked his father's room because "we wanted . . . father . . . [to deal] with it alone" (70).

At the very beginning of the story, Gombrowicz stresses the fact that H.'s arrival has a special relevance to Anton. When Anton opens the door, he looks upon H. as if he were indeed his own repressed returning to him from the outside, a "truth" that he does not want to face: " 'Go with God,' he suddenly sa[ys] softly, as if he ha[s] seen a special sign; his eyes fle[e] to the side. . . . 'With God, with God, Sir! God be with you!' " and he wants to retreat back into the house (37). Yet H. succeeds in bringing out this repressed: "Did he see something there in his depths? Maybe he saw himself get off the bed. . . . It is possible that at this one second, hate seemed to be a fulfillment of love" (70–71).

But even at the moment when Anton admits the murder—" 'Strangled,' he exclaim[s] with a kind of strange satisfaction" (66)—and H.'s paranoic system has found its own logical stability, H. has to test it against the real. Because this is still impossible, he again grows "weak and tired" (72) and, in turn, confesses to Anton: "Look . . . here is a certain obstacle, a cliff—a purely formal one, by the way—nothing important. It has to do with the fact that . . . the body does not show any signs of strangulation. Physically speaking—he has not been strangled at all, but has simply died of a heart attack. The neck, you know, the neck! . . . The neck is untouched!" (72). Yet by means of his detour through the symbolic, H. does finally cause a belated change of the real, by bringing about a situation which "gives birth to . . . something not fictive anymore, but something substantial" (65). When Anton actually changes the real and thus solves H.'s problem, this is the final proof that the delusional system is stronger than the real and can overrule it. While H. hides in a closet in K.'s bedroom, Anton enters, and "then I heard a terrible sound, the bed creaked like crazy—in complete silence, ex post facto, all formalities were taken care of!" (73). Although the change of the real is only a formality after the change of the symbolic, order (which is, of course, by now a completely paranoic one) must be re-established.

With this formality, the fight against the real has been won, and the subsequent trial and conviction are again merely a purely symbolic chain of cause and effect. Thus, just like *The Trouble with Harry* and "The Purloined Letter," "A Premeditated Crime" describes a temporal loop. This loop shows how the symbolic and the imaginary can be "earlier" than the real. At the end of the story, the real "*will have been*" (Lacan, *Freud's* 158; original emphasis); K. will have been strangled.

III

Although the criminal aspect is missing in Gombrowicz's first book, *Ferdydurke* (1937), it is present in varying degrees in all his other novels. In *Trans-Atlantyk* (1952), Ignacy's patricide, which Gonzalo tries to bring about, stands metaphorically for the "killing" of the "reality principle" and the "Law-of-the-Father," in order to inaugurate the libidinous, imaginary "Law-of-the-Son": "Let Son murder Father" (156). Yet, as in *Cosmos* (1965), the murder does not come about, and the book drowns in a Rabelaisian riot of laughter: "Whilst he so at his Father Swoops, Swoops, Swoops, and yet Swoops, is Swooping, nigh, nigh Swooping down, upon him Laughter, oh, on him Laughter" (157). In *Pornografia* (1960), the murder motif is linked to the attempt to bring about the union of a young couple (Henia and Karol) with an old one (Witold and Frederick). This union is described as an artificially created chemical re-action, in which murder and sin function as catalysts. The final scene, in which Karol kills an adult while Frederick kills a young boy, brings about a momentary union of the four people: "And for a split second, we all four of us smiled" (160). Yet in both *Trans-Atlantyk* and *Pornografia*, the murders are treated less as criminal cases and problems than as "per-verted" sexual acts.

In *Cosmos*, however, the intervention of the realm of desire and sexu-ality into that of reason and logic is related, again, to the problem of criminalistic deduction (see also Merivale) and to the temporality of be-latedness. Actually, Gombrowicz himself described the book as "some-thing of a thriller" (*Kind* 137). Like "A Premeditated Crime," *Cosmos* brings the desire for logic and the logic of desire into a collision course. In fact, this novel takes up many of the concerns of "A Premeditated Crime." It is in a discussion of *Cosmos*, for instance, that Gombrowicz poses the question as to whether reality is "obsessive by its very essence" (*Diary* 3: 162).

Cosmos begins with the enigmatic image of a hanged sparrow and ends, after this image has been amplified by various other hangings, with the equally enigmatic image of a hanged man—an identical, yet different version of the hanged sparrow. Like "A Premeditated Crime," then, *Cosmos* has the structure of a temporal and logical loop. There are, in fact, so many correspondences between them that the earlier story might be considered a primal scene for *Cosmos*. The hanged sparrow, for instance, takes up the motif of the suffocating and contracting charac-ter of the paranoic system described in "A Premeditated Crime." Simi-larly, Witold's problems with his family, and the mysterious aversion that Fuchs's boss harbors for him, resemble H.'s repressed aggressivity.

Structurally, such elements of the novel as the hanged sparrow, the "innocent" mouth of Lena, and the mutilated, "perverse" mouth of Katasia function, like K.'s corpse, as events in the present that trigger a return of the repressed. Yet while "A Premeditated Crime" centers on death, and *Pornografia* on sexuality, in *Cosmos* the return of the repressed combines these two fundamentally enigmatic realms which relate the real and reality—because "both death and sex" are situated at the threshold between them, "at this locus of the irreconcilable, between the lack and the word" (Leclaire 23).

Like the ambivalent rift between love and hate in "A Premeditated Crime," the connotations of orality in *Cosmos* are divided into those related to Katasia's mouth (aggression, revulsion, fascination, perversion, defilement, debasement, and sin), and those related to Lena's mouth (mildness, attraction, longing, normality, purity, elevation, and virtue). These conflicting elements of sexuality are linked in an ambivalent whole. Death, which is related to the hangings, functions—as in *Pornografia*—as a catalyst in the linking process.

In the middle of the book, Witold tries to find out the naked truth about Lena's sexuality by climbing a tree to watch her undress. His voyeuristic desire and curiosity is at least partially gratified: "She removed the towel from her shoulders, and I received the shock of her nudity, her breasts and shoulders" (*Cosmos* 67). But the ultimate truth, here quite directly equated with the female sex, remains veiled: "I stayed there, thinking that now I was going to find out what she was like when she was with him in the nude, whether she was vile, sensual, elusive, saintlike, sensitive, pure, faithful, fresh, alluring, or perhaps coquettish. . . . Her thighs appeared, first one and then the other . . . at last something definite was going to be revealed to me" (67).

Before the secret of her nudity—the truth about sexuality—is unveiled completely, the real, in the guise of a teapot, quite literally blocks Witold's revelation by blocking his gaze. Already, before, Lena's husband Louis had shown her this teapot: "I had been ready for everything, but not for a teapot. Enough is enough. There is a sort of excess of reality, and after a certain point it can become intolerable" (66). Now Louis takes the teapot, puts it on a shelf, walks to the door, and turns out the light. The impossibility of seeing forces Witold to imagine—a shift similar to the one from naturality to theatricality, and from the real to the imaginary, in "A Premeditated Crime": "I went on looking though I could not see, I went on gazing blindly into the pitch-black darkness. What were they doing? . . . There was nothing on their part that was inconceivable, the darkness was impenetrable. . . . I should never know" (67). As in "A Premeditated Crime," this intervention of the real causes a temporary collapse of the paranoiac system: "After so many things that I could no longer enumerate . . . here was this teapot popping up like a jack-in-the-box without rhyme or reason, extra, gratis, and for nothing . . . an ornament of chaos. I had had enough. My throat contracted. This teapot was too much, and I could not swallow it. I had had enough. There was nothing for it but to pack up and go home" (66–67).

Because the teapot has blocked the direct route to Lena, Witold— or, better yet, his paranoic system—now attempts to get to her via a detour and through another catalyst: her cat. In this displacement, Witold comes to participate in the series of hangings himself: "I grabbed [the cat] by the throat and started throttling it, wondering why, but it was too late, it happened to me in a flash and I could not help it, I put all my strength into throttling it" (68). With this action, Witold himself becomes a criminal: "As if the cat had put me on the obverse side of the medal and I was now in a realm of hieroglyphics, where occult and mysterious things took place" (72). Yet like H., who is overcome "in a very unexpected manner" by his reenactment of the "murder" ("Premeditated" 46), Witold is surprised that "It was I who had done it. This shattered me" (*Cosmos* 70).

It is only when Witold detects a trace of shame in Lena, his ultimate object of desire, that he can relate to her again: "She was useless for anything but love . . . and that was why she felt ashamed of the cat, for she knew that everything connected with her must have an amorous meaning" (72). As in "A Premeditated Crime," it is through such shame that Witold can for the first time—although only provisionally—connect the hangings with the mouths. The series of deadly hangings become amorous, while the amorous mouths become deadly: "Thanks to her shame the cat linked up with Katasia's lip like a cogwheel engaging with another" (73). The expansion of Witold's paranoic system can be measured directly by such logical syllogisms as his remark that "If I strangled and hanged the cat I ought to strangle and hang her too" (116), which show the gradual replacement of rational logic by the logic of paranoia.

The obsessive, sexually connoted mouth-series is finally mapped onto the deadly hanging-series when Witold finds Louis, Lena's husband, hanging from a tree—the amplified mirror image of the introductory tableau with the hanged sparrow. Enumerating the countless possibilities that might have led to Louis's death, Witold is soon overwhelmed: "I smiled in the moonlight at the impotence of reason in the face of the overflowing, destroying, enveloping reality. Everything was possible and nothing was impossible" (156). Yet all such apparent connections are, like the constellations of the night sky, merely projections; and, like the paranoiac rationalizations in "A Premeditated Crime," they are illuminated only by a "second-hand" glow, "unreal, artificial, imposed; they were the obsessions of the luminous sky" (157).

Witold's system finds its largest expansion when the whole world—

the cosmos itself—is obsessed. Yet this obsession attributed to the real is only a projection of his own paranoic system, which is why Witold feels that the consistency and logic is "a clumsy sort of logic, a rather too personal and private logic of my own" (155). This realization coincides with the final connection between hangings and mouths. Just as H. touched K.'s corpse—"Nevertheless I suddenly approached the bed and touched the neck with the finger" ("Premeditated" 50)—so Witold finally brings about a real connection between the two series by putting his finger first into Louis's and later into the priest's mouth: "I felt a deep satisfaction that at last a link had been established between 'mouth' and 'hanging.' It was I who had done it. . . . And now I must go and hang Lena. . . . Hanging and I were one" (*Cosmos* 160). Witold's complete identity with his obsession denotes the final closure of the "more and more paralyzing, vast concentric hallucination" (Lacan, *Ego* 169) of his paranoic system.

At this point, Witold's obsessive logic has finally brought about the paranoic unity of love and death: "for we were in love, she was just as much in love with me as I was with her, there could be no doubt about that, because if I wanted to kill her it followed that she must be in love with me" (161).[8] Yet the final act of a loving murder, or a murderous love, fails to come about. At the very moment that the obsessive system finds a stable consistency, the real intervenes within Witold's obsessive logic for a final time. It begins to rain, a rain that literally sweeps the story to its ending. This final cataclysm results in the return to Witold's home, which unveils the adventure in the country as a fictional—perhaps even hallucinatory—escape from the domestic problems that frame it: "I went back to Warsaw and my parents—warfare with my father was resumed—and to other things, problems, difficulties and complications. Today we had chicken and rice for lunch" (166).

On the level of language, the paranoic structure of reality and the impossibility of reaching a stable truth is mirrored in the inability to create a "real" story: "Such a continual accumulation and disintegration of things can hardly be called a story" (153). Because storytelling is an obsessive activity that inevitably involves selection and ordering, it mirrors the obsessive quality of perception. Yet within each signification, the loss of the real "insists." It is this lack that sets the paranoic machine in motion in the first place. This insistence is the result of the unbridgeable breach between the symbolic and the real: "we say 'forest,' but the word implies the unknown, the inconceivable, the unknowable. Earth and stones" (131). All of Gombrowicz's deconstructions revolve around this impossible insistence. If classic detective fiction separates the realms of the imaginary, the symbolic, and the real, then the metaphysical detective story—as represented by Gombrowicz's "A Premeditated Crime" and *Cosmos*—knots them together again in new and unexpected ways.

The paranoiac, obsessive systems that Gombrowicz portrays, and with which he replaces the symbolic system that underlies the detective story, create their own symbolic as well as their own real: the former through the logic of desire, the latter through hallucination. Ultimately, both of these simulations serve to cover up the reality of death. As the fictional text is also such a "cover up," Gombrowicz's texts might themselves be considered the ultimate crime.[9]

Notes

1. Throughout this essay, I use quotation marks to indicate whenever these words—symbolic, imaginary, and real—are not used in the Lacanian sense.

2. This temporal structure is itself a perfect model of the backward and forward movement of Lacan's structuration of psychic time, which is in turn based on the structure of a knot (*Encore* 111):

3. This becomes especially obvious in Peirce's theory of abduction, which conflates abduction and perceptual judgment, "the first premise of all critical and controlled thinking" (5: 112). In a logical loop, the final abduction "shades into perceptual judgment without any sharp line of demarcation between them," so that abduction is ultimately the exteriorized version of the internal, ideal(ized) perceptual process. The beginning and end of his argument are thus not only related, but in fact identical. Perceptual judgment is the "reverse side" of abduction, of which it is only an "extreme case." Like Poe's visual identification, perceptual judgment is outside of theoretical reach, the "result of a process . . . not controllable and therefore not fully conscious" (5: 113). Actually, its existence can only be abducted: as in any good detective novel, an abduction ends with a conviction.

4. All translations of Freud are my own.

5. All translations of "A Premeditated Crime" are my own.

6. "An inner perception is repressed, and as a substitute, its content, after it has been distorted, enters consciousness as a perception from the outside" (Freud, *Werke* 7: 189).

7. H.'s remarks indicate how wearying this process is: "And I began, with all perspicacity, to combine the chain of facts, to create syllogisms, spin threads and look for clues. But soon, tired by the abortiveness of this undertaking, I fell asleep, yes, yes. . ." (47).

8. Freud sees a similar reversal in the obsessive neurosis, which implies "the regression of the libido to the earlier sadistic-anal organization. . . . The obsessive perception 'I want to kill you' means . . . nothing other than 'I want to enjoy you in love' " (*Werke* 1: 337).

9. I expand on this argument in my book, *Lines of Desire: Reading Gombrowicz's Fiction with Lacan*, forthcoming from Northwestern University Press.

Works Cited

Freud, Sigmund. *Werke. Studienausgabe.* Frankfurt am Main: Fischer, 1969.
Gombrowicz, Witold. *Cosmos.* [*Kosmos*, 1965]. Trans. Eric Mosbacher. New York: Grove, 1970.
———. *Diary.* 4 vols. Vol. 3 (1961–1966). Evanston, Ill.: Northwestern University Press, 1993.
———. *Ferdydurke.* [1937]. Trans. Eric Mosbacher. New York: Harcourt, 1961.
———. *A Kind of Testament.* [1968]. Ed. Dominique de Roux, trans. Alastair Hamilton, intro. Maurice Nadeau. London: Calder and Boyars, 1973.
———. *Memoirs from the Epoch of Maturation.* [1938]. *Bacacay.* [1957]. München: Hanser, 1984.
———. *Pornografia.* [1960]. Trans. Alastair Hamilton. New York: Grove, 1966.
———. "A Premeditated Crime." [1936]. *Memoirs* 37–73.
———. *Trans-Atlantyk.* [1952]. New Haven, Conn.: Yale University Press, 1994.
Lacan, Jacques. *Ecrits.* [1966]. Trans. Alan Sheridan. New York: Norton, 1977.
———. *The Ego in Freud's Theory and in the Technique of Psycho-Analysis, 1954–55.* [Seminar book 2]. Trans. Sylvana Tomaselli. Cambridge: Cambridge University Press, 1988.
———. *Encore, 1972–73.* [Seminar book 20]. Paris: Seuil, 1975.
———. *Freud's Papers on Technique, 1953–54.* [*Les Ecrits techniques de Freud,* 1975. Seminar book 1]. Trans. John Forrester. Cambridge: Cambridge University Press, 1988.
———. *The Psychoses, 1955–56.* [Seminar book 3]. New York: Norton, 1993.
———. "Seminar on 'The Purloined Letter.'" Trans. Jeffrey Mehlman. *The Purloined Poe: Lacan, Derrida, and Psychoanalytic Reading,* ed. John P. Muller and William J. Richardson. Baltimore: Johns Hopkins University Press, 1988.
Leclaire, Serge. *Démasquer le réel: Un essai sur l'objet en psychanalyse.* Paris: Seuil, 1971.
Merivale, Patricia. "The Esthetics of Perversion: Gothic Artifice in Henry James and Witold Gombrowicz." *PMLA* 93, 5 (1978): 992–1002.
Peirce, Charles Sanders. *Collected Papers of Charles Sanders Peirce.* 8 vols. Cambridge: Belknap Press, 1965.
Poe, Edgar Allan. *The Complete Tales and Poems of Edgar Allan Poe.* New York: Modern Library, 1983.
———. "The Murders in the Rue Morgue." *Complete* 141–68.
———. "The Mystery of Marie Roget." *Complete* 169–207.
———. "The Purloined Letter." *Complete* 208–22.
The Trouble with Harry. Dir. Alfred Hitchcock. Perf. Edmund Gwenne, John Forsythe, and Shirley MacLaine. Universal Studios, 1955.

Chapter 12
"Subject-Cases" and "Book-Cases"
Impostures and Forgeries from Poe to Auster

Susan Elizabeth Sweeney

Supposing

> . . . we suppose a case, and put ourselves into it, and hence are in
> two cases at the same time, and it is doubly difficult to get out.
> —Henry David Thoreau, *Walden* (443)

> To suppose, we suppose that there arose here and there that here
> and there there arose an instance of knowing . . .
> —Gertrude Stein, "An Elucidation" (430)

What does it mean, in Thoreau's terms, to "suppose a case"? "To suppose," as Stein suggests, is to substitute some faraway, remotely possible
"instance" for one's real position. ("Suppose" derives, in fact, from the
roots of *substitute* and *position*.) A "case" is a set of circumstances or conditions. Supposing a case, then, must mean thinking in the subjunctive
mood: imagining scenarios, developing hypotheses, speculating that "if
this were the case," or "in that case," or even "in any case. . . ." But "case"
also has another meaning: a crime that requires investigation.[1] Indeed,
the best way to solve such a case, according to theorists of mental analysis from C. Auguste Dupin to C. S. Peirce, is to imagine possible cases.

In Paul Auster's metaphysical detective story *Ghosts* (1986), a private
eye named Blue engages in just such speculation about his current as-
signment, which he always calls "the case": "It seems perfectly plausible
to him that he is also being watched. . . . If that is the case, then he
has never been free. From the very start he has been the man in the
middle, thwarted in front and hemmed in from the rear" (200). Yet
Blue's thought is not narrated in the present subjunctive mood ("if that
be the case"), but in the indicative—as if it were, in fact, the case. Blue
may be unaware, then, of this subtle but crucial grammatical distinction

between imagination and reality. Like other metaphysical detectives, he may forget that when he supposes a case he is only supposing. By thus confusing subjunctive and indicative modes of thought, Thoreau suggests, one loses track of one's own case. Indeed, Blue's position seems even more tenuous when he tries to express it by quoting this very passage from Thoreau's 1847 masterpiece: "Oddly enough, this thought reminds him of some sentences from Walden, and he searches through his notebook for the exact phrasing, fairly certain that he has written them down. We are not where we are, he finds, but in a false position. Through an infirmity of our natures, we suppose a case, and put ourselves into it, and hence are in two cases at the same time, and it is doubly difficult to get out" (200). Even as Blue describes the dangers of supposing a case, then, he substitutes Thoreau's words for his own.[2] And as he tries to imagine another man's life in the course of his investigation, he becomes "a prisoner of the case itself" and risks losing his own identity altogether (201).

Supposing a case and then finding oneself in two cases at once is a common occupational hazard for literary detectives, of course. The detective's penchant for doubling and disguise, his empathy for others, his uncanny ability to intuit a criminal's motives and methods—these are defining traits of such famous sleuths as Edgar Allan Poe's Dupin and Arthur Conan Doyle's Sherlock Holmes. But no matter how much Dupin and Holmes speculate about their opponents, neither ever seems to endanger his own singular identity. The protagonist of a metaphysical detective story, however, may find that he cannot distinguish between supposing and knowing.[3] A "doomed detective" (in Stefano Tani's phrase), he may even learn that he himself is the victim he avenges, the criminal he seeks, or both at once. In such tales, the answer to the detective story's perennial question—"Whodunit?"—is "I." And "Who is 'I'?" is another question entirely.

The metaphysical detective thus discovers, as Blue does, that "however he might present the case to himself, he is a part of it, too" (217). Detective fiction has always acknowledged the *possibility* that a search for truth might lead to the mystery of one's own identity. Such a dénouement occurs, in fact, in *Oedipus Rex*, which some critics call the first detective story (Holquist 154; van Meter). Oedipus, ostensibly a disinterested investigator, is so horrified to find that he is the victim's son and murderer that he puts out his own eyes, as if to obliterate the very source of such painful self-recognition. Sophocles's tragedy epitomizes the horror of being unable to extricate oneself from what one has supposed—an epistemological nightmare also explored in metaphysical detective stories, which often allude to *Oedipus*.[4]

The metaphysical sleuth's self-discovery, however, reveals a more modern anxiety about identity: a fear of being trapped within one's self, on the one hand, and of being without a self, on the other. The crime that is plotted and detected in metaphysical detective stories, therefore, is usually suicide rather than patricide. The self-murder that is merely implied by Oedipus's blinding, or by Dupin's and Holmes's punishment of their criminal doubles, becomes explicit and endemic in these later works. In metaphysical detective stories by Felipe Alfau, Vladimir Nabokov, Jorge Luis Borges, and Auster, in particular, detectives as well as criminals stage their own deaths in order to usurp others' lives.

Such substitution, moreover, usually occurs on two levels: first, the text's diegetic plot (that is, the protagonist's apparent death constitutes the crime); second, its extradiegetic narration (that is, the protagonist seeks metafictional immortality within the text).[5] The tales of Alfau, Nabokov, Borges, and Auster, in other words, involve both "subject-cases" (Stein's phrase, which I define as crimes of stolen subjectivity) and "book-cases" (my own term for crimes of forged authorial identity). Indeed, the tales' would-be criminal and detective masterminds confuse these two levels; that is, they fail precisely because they cannot distinguish the subjunctive from the indicative, the figurative from the literal, the hypothetical from the real, or the story of a crime from the crime itself. Each protagonist tries to get out of his own case by supposing another. By doing this in actuality rather than in imagination, however, he places himself in two cases at once—and, as Thoreau says, he then finds it "doubly difficult to get out."

Doubly Difficult: Poe

> In sane moments we regard only the facts, the case that is.
> —Henry David Thoreau, *Walden* (433)

Before I turn to staged deaths in metaphysical detective stories, I want to trace their origin in the doubled identities of classic detective fiction. Poe refined this theme in his Dupin series—"The Murders in the Rue Morgue" (1841), "The Mystery of Marie Rogêt" (1842–43), and "The Purloined Letter" (1844)—which culminates, in the final story, with a proliferation of "brotherly couple[s]" (Richard 8) and the possibility that Dupin and D——, the criminal, are not only similar but the same (Babener). But Poe first experimented with a doubled detective in "William Wilson" (1839). The eponymous (and pseudonymous) narrator of this tale recounts his vain attempts to flee a pursuer who resembles him in every way, including his name. This nemesis somehow deduces, foils, and avenges all the narrator's crimes; meanwhile, the narrator conducts his own investigation—from a stealthy visit to his rival's bedroom to a "minute scrutiny" of his methods and mannerisms—so as to discover the other's identity (445). Their relationship—like that between the narrator of Poe's next tale, "The Man of the Crowd" (1840), and the old man whom *he* pursues—thus anticipates the doubling of detective and criminal in the Dupin stories.

William Wilson finally confronts his pursuer at a masked ball, and drags him into an antechamber that completes the series of closets and vestibules where they have met throughout the tale. Here, after a "brief" but "furious" struggle, he stabs his rival through the heart. But someone else tries to open the door, and the narrator, "hasten[ing] to prevent an intrusion," apparently locks it (447). When he returns to his victim, he is horrified at what he sees:

The brief moment in which I averted my eyes had been sufficient to produce, apparently, a material change. . . . A large mirror—so at first it seemed to me in my confusion—now stood where none had been perceptible before. . . . Thus it appeared, I say, but was not. It was my antagonist—it was Wilson, who then stood before me in the agonies of his dissolution. His mask and cloak lay, where he had thrown them, upon the floor. Not a thread in all his raiment—not a line in all the marked and singular lineaments of his face which was not, even in the most absolute identity, *mine own!* . . . I could have fancied that I myself was speaking while he said: "*You have conquered, and I yield. Yet, henceforward art thou also dead—dead to the World, to Heaven, and to Hope! In me didst thou exist—and, in my death, see by this image, which is thine own, how utterly thou hast murdered thyself.*" (447–48; Poe's emphasis)

This disturbing dénouement—in which the narrator realizes that he is at once victim, criminal, and investigator of the crime—prefigures similar endings in metaphysical detective stories. It also anticipates the way that detective fiction narrates such a revelation. Poe's references to visual perception, recognition, and reflection echo the association of seeing with solving a mystery in *Oedipus*, and look toward the scopic nature of investigation in later works.[6] Poe complicates this dénouement, moreover, by stressing the narrator's unreliable senses (a mirror, "*apparently*, . . . it *seemed* . . . stood where none had been *perceptible*") and untrustworthy sensibility ("in my *confusion* . . . I could have *fancied*" [447–48; my emphasis]), and by using images of disclosure such as the discarded mask and cloak and the speaking mirror. The mirror, in particular—which suggests that all of Wilson's encounters with his double may have been with his reflection—makes the narrator's self-discovery even more ambiguous. He sees in it first his "own image, but . . . all pale and dabbled in blood," then that of an "antagonist" whose every feature is, "even in the most absolute identity, [*his*] *own*"; this antagonist then proclaims, in turn, that *his* image represents *the narrator's* self-murder. The pronouns in the story's last lines—"I," "he," "you," "thou," "own," "self"—become almost interchangeable as Poe dissolves the connections among Wilson's identity and his name, image, and voice (448). Wilson's "arch-enemy and evil genius" (445), whom he pursues and by whom he is pursued, turns out to be . . . himself.

This self-recognition takes place at the end of the tale—or rather, takes the place of its ending. Wilson explains at the outset that his tale is not a "record of [his] later years of . . . unpardonable crime," but an investigation of the "one event" that caused them (426). But because his confession ends with the assertion that he has murdered himself, that self-murder seems to lead, in turn, to the composition of this very confession—which is motivated, he tells us, by the approach of "Death . . . and the shadow which foreruns him" (427). Such narrative circularity resembles the structure of detective fiction, which begins with results, ends with causes, and produces stories to explain crimes that have already occurred. By exploiting that structure, in fact, "William Wilson" anticipates the recursive endings of much later works like Nabokov's *The Real Life of Sebastian Knight* (1941) or Alain Robbe-Grillet's *The Erasers* (1953).

It is the narrator's uncanny "self-murder," in particular, that facilitates the tale's conundrums at both diegetic and extradiegetic levels. At the diegetic level, this act culminates the progressive series of his crimes (mischief, drinking, gambling, adultery), even as it completes his pursuit of his rival. Such an ending, in which one double defeats the other, is typical of *Doppelgänger* tales. But in this case, it is unclear whether to read the narrator's act literally (as a suicide or a botched murder attempt), figuratively (as the death of his conscience), or both at once. At the extradiegetic level, too, his self-murder makes matters more complicated. By killing his double he becomes the narrator of his story, even attaining a new identity (or at least a new name) in the process: "Let me call myself, for the present, William Wilson" (426). The tale's circularity thus implies that he has the last word, because he lives to tell the tale; yet that tale ends with his double's last words, which are his own death sentence. And all these riddles reflect the deeper mystery of Wilson's self-deceiving self.

"William Wilson" is not usually considered a detective story, but I wish to cite it as Poe's first major contribution to the genre. It influenced his initial tale about Dupin, "The Murders in the Rue Morgue,"[7] as well as later writers and later texts. Wilson's cryptic self-murder, in particular, is as important as the armchair detective, the locked room, and all of Poe's other inventions. Indeed, this tale eventually led to metaphysical detective stories by Alfau, Nabokov, Borges, and Auster—whose protagonists also stage their own deaths, in order to attain new identities and gain control of the very texts in which they appear.

One Way Out: Doyle

> There was the case, and of course there was but one way out of it.
> —Arthur Conan Doyle, "The Man with the Twisted Lip" (230)

Doyle, however, was the first to borrow this device. In the Holmes tales, he reworks Poe's detective—and sometimes Poe's detective stories—by adding details of character, plot, and setting that heighten the genre's suspense but diminish its metaphysical import (Sweeney, "Purloined" 216–22). Doyle revises the motif of self-murder, in this fashion, in "The Man with the Twisted Lip" (1891).[8] The story begins when Watson visits an opium den in search of a friend's errant husband, and there finds Holmes investigating a locked-room mystery. Mrs. Neville St. Clair, wife of a well-to-do businessman, was walking through a seedy part of London when she saw her husband waving "frantically" from the opium den's second-story window. Frightened, she tried in vain to enter the building, then summoned the police, who forced their way upstairs—but St. Clair was nowhere to be found. The only person there was one Hugh Boone—a beggar, "a crippled wretch of hideous aspect"—and the only other exit a window opening onto the Thames (234). The police arrest Boone for St. Clair's murder. But Holmes deduces that they are one and the same: St. Clair earned his fortune by begging, and when his wife spied him in the rented room where he disguised himself as Boone, he saw no way out but staging his own death.

Although Mrs. St. Clair spots her husband at the window, she cannot recognize him when he is dressed, painted, and wigged as a beggar, because "even a wife's eyes could not pierce so complete a disguise" (243). But Holmes's eyes can, especially when he notices that both men bear a self-inflicted wound on the right hand (236, 239, 243). The story thus shows Holmes's ability to recognize that St. Clair has altered his appearance and deduce that he is ensnared by the alternate life he imagined for himself. Holmes unmasks him, moreover, in yet another locked room—a prison cell—before the astonished eyes of Watson, a police inspector, and the reader. "Never in my life have I seen such a sight," Watson says. "Gone was the coarse brown tint! Gone, too, was the horrid scar which had seamed it across, and the twisted lip. . . . A twitch brought away the tangled red hair, and there . . . was a pale, sad-faced, refined-looking man" (242).

Despite Watson's amazement, however, he has "seen such a sight" before. At the beginning of this very story, he encountered an elderly opium addict, "very thin, very wrinkled, bent with age," whom he did not know. Before Watson's eyes, this person also became someone else: "His form had filled out, his wrinkles were gone . . . and there, sitting by the fire, and grinning at my surprise, was none other than Sherlock Holmes" (231–32). Together, these two scenes emphasize the sleuth's similarity to the man he unmasks. Like Holmes himself, St. Clair is a brilliant fellow with a knack for disguise, a talent for detection (he was an investigative journalist), and the ability to earn a living by his wits alone.[9] It is because he understands St. Clair so well, in fact, that Holmes can deduce his true identity.

The solution to this crime, then, is that there is no crime. St. Clair can't be charged with his own murder, the police inspector admits, "unless they make [it] a case of attempted suicide" (242). What remains unsolved, however, is the mystery of a comfortably married man's longing for a double life—a theme on which Nathaniel Hawthorne, Dashiell Hammett, and Paul Auster, among others, have played intriguing variations.[10] In this case, too, an individual tries to leave his original identity behind, only to learn—as Hawthorne puts it in "Wakefield"—that "by stepping aside for a moment a man exposes himself to a fearful risk of losing his place forever" (298). Doyle's classic tale thus expresses a profoundly modern sense of alienation. And yet "The Man with the Twisted Lip" is not a metaphysical detective story, because the existential questions raised by St. Clair's situation do not extend to either the detective's investigation of the crime or the reader's investigation of the text.[11]

"The Man with the Twisted Lip" does indicate how Poe's immediate followers transformed the theme of self-recognition—and self-murder—in "William Wilson." The classic sleuth learns much about others yet little about himself; later tales acknowledge the possibility of his self-discovery,[12] but only in metaphysical detective fiction does it truly occur. Indeed, in a "real metaphysical detective story," Patricia Merivale says, "the detective hero himself becomes . . . the murderer he has been seeking" (210). Alfau, Nabokov, Borges, and Auster, in particular, elaborate on Poe's use of self-murder—a device also employed by G. K. Chesterton in "The Secret Garden" (1910) and "The Wrong Shape" (1911), and by Agatha Christie in *Ten Little Indians* (1939)—as the most elegant way to investigate the nature of subjectivity in detective-story terms. In their tales, the roles of victim, murderer, and sleuth may be played by a single consciousness trying to free itself from itself. More precisely, each protagonist stages his own death in order to usurp another's identity. And like the murderer in Chesterton's "The Wrong Shape"—who makes believe that his victim's last message was a suicide note—each protagonist compounds his initial crime by attempting to alter the way it is represented in the text.

A Case in Point: Alfau

> All cases are unique, and very similar to others.
> —T. S. Eliot, *The Cocktail Party* (2)

A tale from Felipe Alfau's first novel, *Locos* (1936), illustrates both the existential and the metafictional implications of self-murder. *Locos* is not so much a novel as a series of interlocking metaphysical detective stories that feature assorted crimes, criminals, policemen, Holmesian allusions, and parodies of "official" solutions to the riddle of being. Alfau thus uses the detective genre to investigate the mystery of identity (Sweeney, "Aliens").

The first story in *Locos* is actually entitled "Identity," and it describes a case of staged suicide. Fulano, the protagonist, is "the least important of men" (3), according to the narrator. He longs for fame, popularity, or even the merest acknowledgment of his existence: "Poor Fulano's unimportance had arrived at the degree of making him almost invisible and inaudible. His name was unimportant, his face and figure were unimportant, his attire was unimportant and his whole life was unimportant. In fact, I don't know how I, myself, ever noticed him" (4). Just as this passage emphasizes Fulano's insignificance by repeating the adjective "unimportant" four times, so the story reiterates the same point by recounting his increasingly desperate attempts to find anyone who will acknowledge his existence. He shouts "Fire!" in a crowded square, for example, but no one hears him and a trolley nearly runs him down. He breaks a shop window, but the owner does not see him and wonders aloud how it happened. This series of ludicrous anecdotes culminates when Fulano begs for help from the narrator—after first rapping on a table, grabbing his collar, and shouting to get his attention. Would the narrator help him become famous and important, he asks, by making him into a literary character—one who is actually noteworthy for his "very lack of importance" (6)?

Like most characters in *Locos*, then, Fulano aspires to a richer, more independent existence. But whereas the others are often fictional beings with "a strong desire to become real" (Prologue xii), Fulano already is real. Instead, convinced that he does not exist unless others hear or see him, he wants to become a character so that he can be assured of an audience. Like a reverse Pinocchio, he wants to become a puppet and *not* a human being.

How can Fulano stop being who he already is? Dr. José de los Rios, overhearing his conversation with the narrator, tells him that he can become a character only by committing "an official suicide." Dr. de los Rios explains, "This evening as soon as it gets dark, you walk over the bridge of Alcantara and leave your coat on the ground with all your personal identification, all your credentials, your money, bankbook, etc., and a note saying that you have thrown yourself into the Tajo. Then you go back to Madrid, having lost your official identity, and there we will try to make a character out of you" (6). This staged suicide is a would-be solution to the problem of "being," to begin with; that is, it would solve the problem of being Fulano. As Ann Smock says in *Double Dealing*, "Being, being you—identity—is a crime foisted off upon you as though it were yours. To assume one's identity is blindly to fall for this deception, taking it for self-recognition. Life is a crime pinned on its victim, who obligingly mistakes himself for the guilty party" (49). Fulano attempts, instead, to assume a *new* identity, and to pin that crime on life itself—by penning a fictitious suicide note and "pinning" it to his empty coat (11).

But this plot backfires when someone else assumes *his* identity. Instead of Fulano becoming someone, someone else becomes him—by finding his suicide note, taking his credentials, and substituting his own. This someone else has been identified only as "a man of evil appearance," "So-and-so who had escaped from prison," but he now possesses Fulano's name and thus his identity (11, 12). Fulano, meanwhile, becomes literally as well as figuratively anonymous; as he says, "every identity has its owner and I am nothing, nothing. I do not exist" (13). Once again, Dr. de los Rios proposes a solution. He tells Fulano that he must now commit, in earnest, the suicide that he had only staged before: "There is only one superfluous identity as superfluous as yourself, and that identity is under the river Tajo. Yes, Señor Fulano, officially that identity is under that river and lately you must have realized the importance of official things. That soul upon the bed of the Tajo is craving for a body as much as you crave a soul. Go join it and end your mutual absurdity. After that I am sure that my friend will try to revive you in a story" (15). The "mutual absurdity" that Fulano shares with the nonexistent corpse is reflected here in the parallel constructions, repeated phrases, and reiterated words of the doctor's speech. According to such tautological discourse, the only name available to Fulano is that of the "official" suicide, "So-and-so" (12); and the only way to earn this obscure, unnamed name is to jump off the bridge to his death. And so he does. Fulano's story is a case study, then, of that paradox whereby individuals try to escape the "net of fingerprints" that constitutes their identity, only to find that without it they do not exist (Alfau, "Fingerprints" 73).

This tale expresses Fulano's unimportance, anonymity, and desire to become someone, moreover, in textual terms. Like other stories in *Locos*, "Identity" describes a world where individuals exist only on paper—that is, only if their existence is verified by written documents. Consider, for example, the document that Fulano writes earlier in this story, "a note saying: *I have committed suicide by jumping into the Tajo*" (9). His suicide note—supposedly the most personal, most candid text one would ever write—does not really belong to him at all. First, it is more or less dictated to him by Dr. de los Rios. Second, he neglects to sign it. That missing signature, in fact, allows someone else to appropriate his identity, by leaving the unsigned note there and substituting other "documents and credentials" for Fulano's own (10).

Given this emphasis on textual constructions of identity, it is fitting that Fulano learns that his "official suicide" has failed only by reading about it in the paper: first, in reports on an escaped prisoner's drowning in the Tajo; later, in headlines about someone else with Fulano's name. Indeed, his staged suicide may itself be based on a prior text, Luigi Pirandello's 1904 novel *Il Fu Mattia Pascal* (Zangrilli 217–19). More important, after Fulano dies in earnest he finally achieves the fame that he sought as a literary character. He is truly nonexistent at the story's end, whereas he only seemed so before; yet he also exists for the first time, because the narrator keeps his promise and immortalizes him in the text of "Identity," the very story we are reading. Alfau's story shows, then, how a crisis of subjectivity (in other words, a "subject-case") turns into a matter of textuality (that is, a "book-case"). And in this case, that outcome even produces a happy ending—which is quite rare in metaphysical detective fiction.

Strange Cases: Nabokov

> Resemblances are the shadows of differences.
> —Vladimir Nabokov, *Pale Fire* (265)

> they found my corpse . . . in a certain vacant plot I was known to frequent.
> —Jean Lahougue, "La Ressemblance" (241; trans. Jeff Edmunds)

Nabokov's protagonists also seek literary immortality, but they pursue it by becoming narrators instead of characters. His novels express this metafictional search for identity, moreover, in detective-story terms. Nabokov included Poe, Doyle, and Chesterton among his favorite writers as a child (*Strong* 42–43), and when asked why he parodied the detective genre, answered: "My boyhood passion for the Sherlock Holmes and Father Brown stories may yield some twisted clue" (174). Twisted, indeed. Some of his best novels, such as *The Real Life of Sebastian Knight* (1941), *Lolita* (1955), and *Pale Fire* (1963), invert the genre's narrative form.[13] And two early works, in particular—*The Eye* (1930) and *Despair* (1934)—depict protagonists who try to stage their own deaths at both diegetic and extradiegetic levels. In *The Eye*, a would-be suicide narrates his suicide attempt as if he had succeeded, even describing his surviving self in the third person. In *Despair*, a man murders someone else in order to fake his own death; but it turns out that his double looks nothing like him, and he realizes, on rereading his narrative, that he has left behind traces of the other's true identity. One protagonist tries to divide himself in two; the other, to make himself and another man into one. But in each case, he fails to enact his own death convincingly—either in actuality, or in the tale that he tells about it.

The Eye, the English title of Nabokov's novella, neatly expresses the split in his narrator's psyche between "I" (his self) and "eye" (his acute self-consciousness). Nabokov also uses mirrors and masks to describe such doubling, as Poe did in "William Wilson."[14] The narrator longs to "stop being aware of myself"; that is, rather than have a self that can be observed, he wants only "to spy, to watch, to scrutinize oneself and others, to be nothing but a big, slightly vitreous, somewhat bloodshot, unblinking eye" (17, 113). Eventually, unable to bear his self-consciousness, his feelings of failure and impotence, and the same sense of alienation that afflicted Doyle's St. Clair and Alfau's Fulano, he decides to kill himself. This decision makes Nabokov's narrator feel "unbelievably free" (29); and after he dies, he feels even freer when he discovers that, as a ghost, he can observe others and speculate about them with impunity.

He studies one character in particular: Smurov, a dashing figure, "a daredevil who liked to flirt with death" (45), a man who is everything the narrator is not. He even begins to gather "evidence," in the form of others' perceptions, in order to solve "the mystery of Smurov's personality" (83). The narrator describes this endeavor, in detective-story terms, as the effort to "penetrat[e]" the other's "secret," as "the hunt, the watch, the insane attempt to corner Smurov" (93), as "this house-to-house search, this quest of mine for the real Smurov" (99). And Smurov's identity is revealed, in keeping with generic tradition, at the story's end —when the narrator himself is addressed by that name. As Smurov, the narrator is not at all the romantic figure that he has made himself out to be. He apparently bungled the suicide that he thought would allow him to escape his identity; more pathetically, he also fails in his ludicrous effort to obviate that failure—and to try, once more, to escape from himself—in the way that he narrates his tale.[15] At his story's end, he still feels vulnerable to others' condemning eyes: "I do not exist: there exist but the thousands of mirrors that reflect me. . . . And then will come the day when the last person who remembers me will die. A fetus in reverse, my image, too, will dwindle and die within that last witness of the crime I committed by the mere fact of living" (113). In the novella's last lines, he even includes us among these accusers: "I am happy—yes, happy! What more can I do to prove it, how to proclaim that I am happy? Oh, to shout it so that all of you believe me at last, you cruel, smug people" (114). *Despair* is yet another *Doppelgänger* story. It begins, in fact, when the first-person narrator, Hermann—a successful, happily married business-man, like Doyle's St. Clair—finds a sleeping tramp who he thinks looks just like him. He immediately begins to plan the perfect crime: turning poor Felix into his own "dead double" (177). When the body is discovered, Hermann reasons, the police will think that *he* has been murdered, and he can then do whatever he wants—especially once his wife cashes in his life insurance policy.[16] The ensuing plot employs such conventions of *Doppelgänger* fiction as mirror images, twin brothers, and Hermann's sense, after shooting Felix, that "really I could not say who had been killed, I or he" (172). Hermann smugly compares his crime's verisimili-tude to a work of art, even thinking himself superior to the only artist he knows, his wife's cousin (who he does not realize is cuckolding him). After he carries out this mad scheme, however, Hermann discovers that the police never believed him to be the victim, but knew all along that he was the murderer. No one else, apparently, saw any resemblance be-tween Felix and himself.

In *Despair*, as in *The Eye*, the failed staging of the protagonist's death is duplicated by the flaws in his first-person narration. Hermann him-self emphasizes this connection by comparing his crime to a literary composition (171, 191) and to a detective novel read by his wife (24). And just as he fancies that he has committed the perfect murder, so he has great hopes for the book he has written about it. His manuscript, in fact, is another version of his masquerade. Hermann explains at the beginning that "inspired lying" is one of his "essential traits" (4), and he later concocts a make-believe ending to his tale (178–80). He even disguises his actual identity in the narration, as Smurov did: after the murder, he opens the next chapter in Felix's first-person voice instead of his own (175–76). As an imposture, however, Hermann's narrative is no more successful than his crime. At the end of the novel, hiding in a hotel under an assumed name, he happily settles down to reread his account of the perfect murder—and discovers there, to his horror, that he left a telltale item at the crime scene with Felix's name on it. Real-izing that his crime and his manuscript are both irreparably flawed, Hermann promptly titles the book *Despair* (204). In addition to this tell-ing title, Nabokov adds a final metafictional twist that emphasizes his narrator's lack of authority (in all senses). Hermann has decided to send his "masterpiece" to a certain "*émigré* novelist"—apparently Nabo-kov himself—so that it might be published under the other's name (195, 158). The book we are reading, then, is the textual equivalent of

Hermann's own crime of identity. *Despair* thus shows how a subject-case can become a book-case, and one that involves the reader in the very transgressions that it describes. Indeed, one of Nabokov's readers, Jean Lahougue, has dramatized this complicity in his own tale about a book-case—"La Ressemblance" (1989)—which, as Michel Sirvent has shown, is an overt, overdetermined parody of *Despair* and of Nabokov's status as its author. Nabokov continues this theme, moreover, in his own novels *The Real Life of Sebastian Knight* and *Pale Fire*—whose embedded authors seem to stage their own deaths so as to die, as it were, *into* the text.[17]

Case Histories: Borges

> I do in this case. Possibly for you in this case. I do in this case. Possibly not only possibly, but they will, possibly, be you.
> —Gertrude Stein, *Blood on the Dining-Room Floor* (35)

Jorge Luis Borges was also influenced by Poe's and Chesterton's sleuths, and was familiar with "William Wilson" in particular ("Commentaries" 266, 273). In his case, too, those precursors inspired several metaphysical tales—of which the most famous is "Death and the Compass" (1941), whose doomed detective, Borges says, represents "a man committing suicide" ("Commentaries" 269). Because Borges is fascinated by the notion that all individuals and texts are versions of one another, or of an unknowable original, many of his detective stories assert the impossibility of establishing a singular identity. "Death and the Compass" uses a staged death, although a peripheral one (Scharlach's imposture as the murdered Gryphius), to make that point. Three subsequent tales use this same plot device to express the complementarity of criminal and victim—or, as one title puts it, the "theme of the traitor and hero." The enigma, in each case, is an uncanny connection between the opposed individuals. Each detective solves this mystery by discovering that the crime is a form of self-murder. But each detective also realizes that he himself is part of the historical pattern he investigates—and that that pattern prevents him from divulging the criminal's and victim's true identities. Borges first stated this theme in "The Form of the Sword" (1942), and then elaborated on it in "Theme of the Traitor and Hero" (1944) and, to a lesser extent, "Three Versions of Judas" (1944).

"The Form of the Sword" begins when the narrator, briefly stranded at a stranger's house, wonders about his host's mysterious scar and asks its origin. His host agrees to tell him on one condition: that he not hide any contempt the tale makes him feel. The host then recounts his involvement, twenty years earlier, with a group of Irish rebels. One of them was John Vincent Moon, a cowardly, arrogant young man whose life he saved—and who repaid that kindness by betraying him to the British. "At this point," the host says, "my story becomes confused, its thread is lost. I know I pursued the informer down the dark corridors of nightmare." At last he cornered him, seized a curved scimitar, and marked his face "with a half-moon of blood." The narrator, listening to this embedded tale, misses the significance of such clues as the "half-moon" scar, so that his host must finally confess outright: "I told you the story the way I did so that you would hear it to the end. . . . I am Vincent Moon" (122).

"The Form of the Sword," then, is another story about a staged death. Like Poe's "William Wilson," this tale features an uncanny climactic duel between paired doubles, set among the "vain antechambers" of an ancient mansion (120); in this case, Borges makes the doubles' encounter even more ambiguous, because it is unclear whether Moon was wounded by himself or by the other man.[18] Like "William Wilson," too, the tale extends such ambiguity to its narration. In telling his story, Moon pretends (as Nabokov's Hermann did) to be the man whom he betrayed—an impersonation that may indicate either his inconsolable remorse or his incurable deceit. Moon's storytelling, indeed, is another instance of his "informing" on the other man. Borges further complicates this *mise en abyme* by adding yet another level: the narrator, in turn, supposedly repeats the tale to us as it was told to him, without "belittl[ing] a single infamous circumstance" (118). And even as the host divulges that he himself is Moon, he reveals the narrator's identity, too, by addressing *him* as "Borges" (122). This series of embedded narrative frames—which connects us to "Borges," Moon, and the man he betrayed—reiterates in metafictional terms an idea of Moon's: "What one man does is something done, in some measure, by all men. . . . Perhaps Schopenhauer is right: I am all others, any man is all men, Shakespeare is in some way the wretched John Vincent Moon" (120–21). Moon's subject-case, in other words, has become a book-case that implicates us as well.

"Theme of the Traitor and Hero" extends such self-reflexivity even further. Like many of Borges's tales, it is a précis of a text that the narrator (again, perhaps, "Borges" himself) has just read or has not yet written. Under the influence of Leibniz and "the flagrant Chesterton," the narrator says, he has imagined the following detective story, which is narrated, in turn, by Ryan, great-grandson of an Irish rebel named Kilpatrick who had been mysteriously assassinated. Ryan, "compiling a biography" of his famous great-grandfather, discovers that "the circumstances of the crime are enigmatic" and that "the enigma goes beyond the merely criminal" (124). He finds, in fact, that details of the assassination (an unread message, a fallen tower, a conversation) echo incidents, images, and words from Shakespeare's *Julius Caesar* and *Macbeth*. After pondering this metafictional impossibility at length, Ryan finally "succeeds in solving the enigma" (125). He learns that the rebels' attempts to incite revolt always failed because of a traitor in their midst. Kilpatrick, the leader, ordered his friend Nolan to ferret out the traitor, and after investigating the matter, Nolan announced that the traitor was Kilpatrick himself, demonstrating "the truth of his accusation with irrefutable proofs" (126). The rebels condemned Kilpatrick; he signed his own death sentence, but begged that his death not harm the cause. Accordingly, Nolan proposed that he die "at the hands of an unknown assassin, in circumstances deliberately dramatic, which would engrave themselves upon the popular imagination and . . . speed the revolt" (126). Kilpatrick conspired, then, in his own martyrdom, in a death specifically designed to make him a hero instead of a traitor. But, like Alfau's Fulano, he had to die in earnest in order to stage his death successfully.

That staging, moreover, takes textual form. The assassination was devised, and even scripted, by Nolan (a playwright and translator as well as a sleuth); it was "plagiarize[d]," to some extent, from Shakespeare's tragedies; and it subsequently persists in "the books of history" (126). Ryan's detection is equally literary. Indeed, he thinks that Nolan may have stolen from Shakespeare "so that one person, in the future, might realize the truth," and that he himself, therefore, "forms part of Nolan's plan." His response to this insight is disturbing: "At the end of some tenacious caviling, he resolves to keep silent. . . . He publishes a book dedicated to the glory of the hero; this, too, no doubt was foreseen" (127). Borges's detective thus knowingly perpetuates the very case of mistaken identity that he has apparently solved.

Borges expands on the theme's historical implications in "Three Versions of Judas," which he calls a "Christological fantasy" (Prologue 106). In this story, a scholar, trying "to decipher a central mystery of theology" (151–52), proposes that Christ's martyrdom took the form of the most "infamous destiny" imaginable: being Judas. When his book goes unread and unheeded, however, the scholar concludes that "God did not wish His terrible secret propagated in the world" (156). This tale of self-murder also refers to texts, then, but it lacks the metafictional aspects of "The Form of the Sword" and "Theme of the Traitor and Hero."

Borges's literary case histories led, in turn, to later metaphysical research novels such as Peter Ackroyd's *Chatterton* (1987), which is a Borgesian meditation on counterfeiting, intertextuality, and identity,[19] as well as a tale of staged suicide. Ackroyd's sleuth discovers clues—a portrait, an autobiography, manuscripts—which hint that Thomas Chatterton, the famous literary forger, "forge[d his] own death" to win lasting fame (92). The same evidence indicates that he forged poems ascribed to Blake, Cowper, and others. Like Borges's tales, then, *Chatterton* offers a vertiginous rewriting of actual history. *Chatterton* also qualifies as a metaphysical detective story, because the sleuth dies before solving the mystery—that is, before discovering that the evidence of the forger's faked death had itself been forged. Indeed, the novel proposes another explanation of Chatterton's death not deduced by any of the characters: that he died not in a suicide attempt, but in a misguided effort to cure himself of venereal disease. Like another of Borges's fictitious metaphysical detective stories, then, *Chatterton* is designed so that its readers may be "more discerning than the detective" ("Examination" 74).

In Any Case: Auster

> He was alive, and the stubbornness of this fact had begun to fascinate him—as if he had managed to outlive himself, as if he were somehow living a posthumous life.
> —Paul Auster, *City of Glass* (6)

Auster's *New York Trilogy* demonstrates the extreme manifestation of all these cases of supposition in which characters assume other identities and lose their own. Each of his protagonists—Quinn, the detective novelist turned sleuth in *City of Glass* (1985); Blue, the private eye in *Ghosts* (1986); and the anonymous man of letters in *The Locked Room* (1986)— seems to abandon his self altogether, becoming instead a simulacrum of the man he pursues. For these men, the very process of detection involves a kind of self-murder, in which one becomes dead to the world, lost to friends and family, and known by other names if known at all. *The Locked Room*, moreover, features an actual case of fabricated death. Like Wakefield, St. Clair, Hermann, and many others, Fanshawe has left his wife in order to leave behind the man she knows. He doesn't pretend to commit suicide; but he does stage his own death, live "like a dead man" (366), and eventually threaten to kill himself for good. It is, the book concludes, "as though in the end the only thing he had really wanted was to fail—even to the point of failing himself" (370).

But escaping one's identity may require tricking another into taking one's place—just as "So-and-so" did to Fulano in "Identity," Hermann did to Felix in *Despair*, and Black did to Blue in *Ghosts*. Accordingly, Fanshawe chooses the narrator, a childhood friend, to be his stand-in. And the narrator becomes just that: he marries Fanshawe's wife, adopts his child, publishes his books (as his literary executor), and even feels flattered by rumors that he himself wrote the novels, poems, and plays printed under Fanshawe's name. At first all goes well. But when the narrator of *The Locked Room* learns that Fanshawe is still alive, he begins to pursue him—according to the tradition of the metaphysical research novel—through the textual traces he has left behind. Although he cannot find Fanshawe, he becomes more and more like him in the course of his pursuit. Eventually, Fanshawe summons him to a locked room in an elegant, "dilapidated," "nineteenth-century" house (358), and there they have a conversation, through "closed double doors" (359), in which Fanshawe refuses to answer to that name and disavows everything published under it. This encounter, with its doubles, doors, and disembodied voices, recalls Poe's "William Wilson," and the title *The Locked Room* may have been inspired by that tale.[20] Indeed, "William Wilson," the pseudonym of Poe's narrator, is the name under which Auster's protagonist writes detective novels in *City of Glass* (3).

Such noms de plume are important because *The Locked Room*, like the other metaphysical detective stories under investigation here, features a subject-case (the crime of identity in which both Fanshawe and the narrator are complicit) that becomes a book-case. Outside the locked room, Fanshawe has left a red notebook, written expressly for the narrator, that he says explains everything. Auster skillfully witholds its contents from us, even as he implicitly identifies it, in the novella's last pages, with the recursive circularity of *The Locked Room* itself: "Each sentence erased the sentence before it . . . and therefore everything remained open, unfinished, to be started again" (370). The narrator reveals, in fact, that Fanshawe's last words, like those of William Wilson's double in Poe's story, lead to his own narration of the text: "without that end inside me now, I could not have started this book." He adds, more disturbingly: "The same holds for the two books that come before it, *City of Glass* and *Ghosts*. These three stories are finally the same story" (346). Fanshawe's double thus becomes the narrator, and the author, of this novella—and of the earlier ones as well.

In *The New York Trilogy*, then, subject-cases lead not only to book-cases, but to an irresolvable confusion of textual, narratorial, and authorial identities among all three novellas. The separate cases—Quinn's pursuit of Peter Stillman Sr. in *City of Glass*, Blue's pursuit of Black in *Ghosts*, the critic's pursuit of Fanshawe in *The Locked Room*—repeat and contradict each other, as oddly duplicitous as those red notebooks in which, it turns out, each case has been recorded. Blue's sense of entrapment, in the passage quoted at the very beginning of my essay, thus becomes an eerie metafictional joke: as the protagonist of the second novella, he is indeed "the man in the middle, thwarted in front and hemmed in from the rear" (200). But Auster's detectives, narrators, and readers must all feel this way: his trilogy forms a series of recursive *mises en abyme* from which it is not doubly but triply difficult to get out.

Case Closed?

> But the world is neither meaningful nor absurd. It quite simply *is*.
> And that, in any case, is what is most remarkable about it.
> —Alain Robbe-Grillet, "A Path for the Future Novel" (56)

> There is the world. . . . It means only what it is. Nothing more,
> nothing less.
> —Paul Auster, *The Invention of Solitude* (148–49)

> The world is all that the case is.
> —Thomas Pynchon, *V.* (259)

In closing, I want to cite the opening words of Gertrude Stein's "Subject-Cases: The Background of a Detective Story" (1923). Stein's cryptic essay begins with a poem that eventually generates the hyphenated phrase in its title (thus providing the background, in a sense, for the title of my own essay).[21] And in that poem, Stein shows how speculating "in case of this"—that is, supposing a case—involves making a series of logical, linguistic, and grammatical substitutions "in place of this and in place of this." Such substitutions, Stein suggests, are the source of narrative. For a detective, in particular, they produce a "story" that takes the "place of this," that is, of whatever may have actually taken place:

In case of this.
A story.
Subjects and places.
In place of this.
A story.
Subjects and traces.
In face of this.
A story.
Subjects and places.
In place of this and in place of this.
A story.
Subject places.
In place of this.
A story. (200)

Now, any narrative substitutes words for the things they represent, as the poem's refrain ("A story") suggests. But Stein is concerned with narratives in and of detective stories, in particular. Consider the generic tropes evoked by her word choice: crimes ("cases"), suspects ("subjects"), crime scenes ("places"), and clues ("traces"). In addition to suggesting these plural nouns, however, Stein's words also serve as third-person, singular, present-tense verbs that denote the detective's

process as he "cases" a crime scene, "subjects" witnesses to interrogation, "places" suspects at the scene or under arrest, and "traces" the
circumstances that led to a crime. Such grammatical ambiguity underscores the unreliability of any narrative substitution "in place of this."
At the same time, the confusion about these words' syntactic function
makes the poem itself a hermeneutic puzzle. Its phrases can combine
into various sentences, with the refrain "A story" designating both agent
(that is, "A story subjects and traces") and object ("in face of this, a
story"). Stein emphasizes her own artful undermining of grammatical
structure, moreover, by choosing words that refer, themselves, to either
nouns ("subjects") or verbs ("cases").

Stein's poem examines, then, with a similar degree of self-reflexivity,
the same crisis of identity and textuality as the detective stories discussed in this essay. In each of those tales, too, the subject places a
"story" in "place of this." That is, the would-be detective or criminal confuses the subjunctive and the indicative, the figurative and the literal,
the hypothetical and the real. In confusing those two levels, moreover,
he always seems to forget about "this," to ignore some sign of his original, actual, corporeal identity that ultimately gives him away—whether
it be his body (in "Identity" and *The Locked Room*), his physical appearance (*Despair*), or a specific wound or scar ("William Wilson," "The Man
with the Twisted Lip," *The Eye*, "The Form of the Sword"). That telltale
sign, unsuccessfully repressed or hidden by the embedded narrative (in
Despair and "The Form of the Sword," for example), gives rise to the
text that readers read. And yet, at the same time, the sheer persistence
of this physical evidence—despite all the protagonist's suppositions and
substitutions—reminds us that, as Robbe-Grillet says, the world is still
there no matter how many stories we invent in order to explain it. Similarly, in Stein's "Subject-Cases," "this" always seems to remain, no matter
how many other words are put in its place—even if exactly what that
pronoun refers to remains teasingly and poignantly obscure.

The metaphysical detective story suggests, in fact, that all our investigations are doomed to remain only cases of supposition, mere stories "in
place of this," narratives that try, in vain, to substitute for the mysterious,
irreducible, stubbornly unknowable world outside us. And this is why
our investigation of *that* case in particular—the only case there is, according to Wittgenstein, and later Pynchon—cannot possibly be closed.

Notes

1. A "case" is also a "box," of course—as Thoreau's imagery of being "put . . .
into" and unable "to get out" of one suggests.
2. Note that this passage obscures authorial identity—a recurrent theme in

Auster's trilogy—by not italicizing *Walden,* and by eliminating quotation marks around the quote and inserting the phrase "he finds" into it.

3. See Merivale, Holquist, and Tani for definitions of metaphysical detective fiction.

4. Consider, for example, the "Oedipe" eraser and other allusions in Robbe-Grillet's *The Erasers* (1953); "Oedipa Maas," the detecting housewife in Pynchon's *The Crying of Lot 49* (1966); and the tale of "Oidipus" in Perec's *A Void* (1969).

5. On the distinction between diegetic and extradiegetic levels, see Genette.

6. On other connections between "William Wilson" and *Oedipus,* see Irwin 214–16. Wilson's scrutiny of the "thread[s]," "line[s]," and "lineaments" of his rival's appearance (448) prefigures the link between "clue" and "clew" in Poe's "The Murders in the Rue Morgue" (Irwin 196), as well as the classic detective story's magnifying glass and the hard-boiled novel's "private eye."

7. "The Murders in the Rue Morgue" transforms William Wilson into "a double Dupin—the creative and the resolvent" (533), and into dual relationships among detectives (Dupin and the narrator), victims (Mme. L'Espanaye and her daughter), and criminals (the sailor and his Ourang-Outang); that story, too, relates the doubles' confrontation to locked rooms, mirrors, pursuit, and assault.

8. In Doyle's "A Case of Identity," a man disguises himself as his stepdaughter's suitor and stages a disappearance in order to discourage her from marriage and keep control of her money; this tale, however, lacks the existential implications of "The Man with a Twisted Lip."

9. See Jaffe on the purely intellectual nature of Holmes's labor.

10. Consider Hawthorne's "Wakefield" (1835); Hammett's *The Maltese Falcon* (1930), which contains Flitcraft's story; and Auster's *Ghosts,* in which the sleuth abandons "the future Mrs. Blue" (9) to pursue his case and discovers that he has become another Wakefield. See Swope on the Wakefield theme in metaphysical detective stories.

11. Holmes never acknowledges his likeness to St. Clair, for example, although the tale's parallels to "William Wilson" and Stevenson's *Strange Case of Dr Jekyll and Mr Hyde* (1886) hint that he may do so. Doyle's tale recalls Poe's in its ironic self-enclosure (here victim and criminal are one), its locked-room mystery, and its emphasis on St. Clair's telltale wound. It also evokes Stevenson's detective tale of suicidal doubles by describing St. Clair's alter ego as "a hideous wretch" and identifying his transformation with a secret room (234).

12. Christie deceptively depicts the identities of "the Watson" in *The Murder of Roger Ackroyd* (1926) and the detective in *The Mousetrap* (1950); Sayers explores a mystery's relevance to her detectives' lives in *Gaudy Night* (1935); and Hammett and Chandler create private eyes who realize their complicity in a corrupt world, even acknowledging—as Marlowe says in *The Big Sleep* (1939)—that they themselves are "part of the nastiness now" (216).

13. On Nabokov's metaphysical detective stories, see Merivale; on his generic parody in *Real Life,* see my essay "Purloined Letters"; on *Despair,* see Smock.

14. The narrator, "always hidden behind a mask" (103), spies his reflection—described in the third person—just before attempting suicide (27). Later he says that he and a reflection have "merged into one" (107), even as his identity and Smurov's merge in the narration.

15. His deceptive narration is echoed in a lie that he tells the other characters, about the daring escapade in which he received a slight bullet wound—a wound that actually resulted from his suicide attempt (56–59).

16. On the existential and psychoanalytical implications of Hermann's crime, see Smock.

17. *Real Life* includes evidence that its text—supposedly an investigation of a novelist's death—may be his latest novel; *Pale Fire* encodes clues that the commentary on the late John Shade's poem, ostensibly penned by a madman, could conceivably have been written by Shade himself.

18. Another subtext, no doubt, is Chesterton's "The Sign of the Broken Sword," which features a similar telltale sword and a somewhat similar confusion about identity that also results from national antipathies—in this case, appropriately enough, between the British and the Argentine.

19. A librarian, for example, who imagines that forgotten volumes have "been speaking to each other" (71), finds a book that another character has plagiarized; that book not only concerns another case of posthumous plagiarism and thus parallels the plot of this very novel, but its title, *The Last Testament*, alludes to one of Ackroyd's own works.

20. See also Bernstein on doubling (89–90) and locked rooms (95–96) in Auster's novella.

21. The title comes from a remark on the difficulty of writing that occurs as the poem shifts into prose: "how hardly to place in face of this, subject cases, to place in case of this, to place this subject in case of this in place of this. Subject cases in place of this" (200).

Works Cited

Ackroyd, Peter. *Chatterton*. New York: Grove, 1987.
———. *The Last Testament of Oscar Wilde*. London: Hamish Hamilton, 1983.
Alfau, Felipe. "Fingerprints." *Locos* 57–74.
———. "Identity." *Locos* 3–15.
———. *Locos: A Comedy of Gestures*. [1936]. New York: Vintage, 1988.
———. Prologue. *Locos* ix–xii.
Auster, Paul. *City of Glass*. [1985]. *New* 1–158.
———. *Ghosts*. [1986]. *New* 159–232.
———. *The Invention of Solitude*. New York: Sun, 1982.
———. *The Locked Room*. [1986]. *New* 235–71.
———. *The New York Trilogy*. New York: Penguin, 1990.
Babener, Lianha Klenman. "The Shadow's Shadow: The Motif of the Double in Edgar Allan Poe's 'The Purloined Letter.'" *Mystery and Detective Annual* (1972): 21–32.
Bernstein, Stephen. "Auster's Sublime Enclosure: *The Locked Room*." In *Beyond the Red Notebook: Essays on Paul Auster*, ed. Dennis Barone. Philadelphia: University of Pennsylvania Press, 1995. 88–106.
Borges, Jorge Luis. "Commentaries." *The Aleph and Other Stories, 1933–1969*. Trans. and ed. Norman Thomas di Giovanni with the author. New York: Dutton, 1970. 263–83.
———. "Death and the Compass." ["La Muerte y la brújula," 1942]. Trans. Anthony Kerrigan. *Ficciones* 129–41.
———. "An Examination of the Work of Herbert Quain." ["Examen de la obra de Herbert Quain," 1941]. Trans. Anthony Kerrigan. *Ficciones* 73–78.
———. *Ficciones*. [1956]. Ed. and intro. Anthony Kerrigan. New York: Grove, 1963.

———. "The Form of the Sword." ["La Forma de la espada," 1942]. Trans. Anthony Kerrigan. *Ficciones* 117–22.

———. Prologue to "Artifices." Trans. Anthony Kerrigan. *Ficciones* 105–6.

———. "Theme of the Traitor and Hero." ["Tema del traidor y del héroe," 1944]. Trans. Anthony Kerrigan. *Ficciones* 123–27.

———. "Three Versions of Judas." ["Tres versiones de Judas," 1944]. Trans. Anthony Kerrigan. *Ficciones* 151–57.

Chandler, Raymond. *The Big Sleep.* [1939]. New York: Random House, 1976.

Chesterton, G. K. *The Annotated Innocence of Father Brown,* ed. Martin Gardner. New York: Oxford University Press, 1988.

———. "The Secret Garden." [1910]. *Annotated* 41–63.

———. "The Sign of the Broken Sword." [1913]. *Annotated* 217–37.

———. "The Wrong Shape." [1911]. *Annotated* 138–59.

Christie, Agatha. *The Mousetrap.* [1950]. London: French, 1954.

———. *The Murder of Roger Ackroyd.* New York: Grosset and Dunlap, 1926.

———. *Ten Little Indians.* [*And Then There Were None*]. New York: Pocket, 1939.

Doyle, Arthur Conan. "A Case of Identity." [1891]. *Complete* 1: 190–201.

———. *The Complete Sherlock Holmes.* 2 vols. New York: Doubleday, 1930.

———. "The Man with the Twisted Lip." [1891]. *Complete* 1 : 229–44.

Eliot, T. S. *The Cocktail Party.* [1949]. New York: Harcourt, 1950.

Genette, Gerard. *Narrative Discourse: An Essay in Method.* [*Figures III*, 1972]. Trans. Jane E. Lewin and intro. Jonathan Culler. Ithaca, N. Y.: Cornell University Press, 1980.

Hammett, Dashiell. *The Maltese Falcon.* New York: Grosset and Dunlap, 1930.

Hawthorne, Nathaniel. "Wakefield." [1835]. *Tales and Sketches,* ed. Roy Harvey Pearce. New York: Library of America, 1982. 290–98.

Holquist, Michael. "Whodunit and Other Questions: Metaphysical Detective Stories in Postwar Fiction." *New Literary History* 3 (1971–72): 135–56. Reprinted in *The Poetics of Murder: Detective Fiction and Literary Theory,* ed. Glenn W. Most and William W. Stowe. San Diego: Harcourt, 1983. 149–74.

Irwin, John T. *The Mystery to a Solution: Poe, Borges, and the Analytic Detective Story.* Baltimore: Johns Hopkins University Press, 1994.

Jaffe, Audrey. "Detecting the Beggar: Arthur Conan Doyle, Henry Mayhew, and 'The Man with the Twisted Lip.' " *Representations* 31 (1990): 96–117.

Lahougue, Jean. "La Ressemblance." ["The Resemblance," trans. Jeff Edmunds, *Nabokov Studies* 2 (1995): 235–50]. *La Ressemblance et autres abus de langage.* Paris: Impressions Nouvelles, 1989.

Merivale, Patricia. "The Flaunting of Artifice in Vladimir Nabokov and Jorge Luis Borges." In *Nabokov: The Man and His Work,* ed. L. S. Dembo. Madison: University of Wisconsin Press, 1967. 290–324. Reprinted in *Critical Essays on Jorge Luis Borges,* ed. Jaime Alazraki. Boston: G. K. Hall, 1987. 141–53.

Nabokov, Vladimir. *Despair.* [*Otchaianie,* 1934, 1936; rev. and trans. by the author, 1965]. New York: Vintage, 1990.

———. *The Eye.* [*Sogliadatai,* 1930]. Trans. Dmitri Nabokov with the author. New York: Phaedra, 1965.

———. *Lolita.* [1955]. New York: Vintage, 1990.

———. *Pale Fire.* [1963]. New York: Vintage, 1990.

———. *The Real Life of Sebastian Knight.* [1941]. New York: New Directions, 1959.

———. *Strong Opinions.* New York: Vintage, 1989.

Perec, Georges. *A Void.* [*La Disparition,* 1969]. Trans. Gilbert Adair. New York: HarperCollins, 1994.

Poe, Edgar Allan. *Collected Works of Edgar Allan Poe*, ed. Thomas Ollive Mabbott. 3 vols. Cambridge, Mass.: Harvard University Press, 1978.

———. "The Murders in the Rue Morgue." [1841]. *Collected* 2: 521–74.

———. "The Purloined Letter." [1844]. *Collected* 3: 972–97.

———. "William Wilson." [1839]. *Collected* 2: 422–51.

Pynchon, Thomas. *The Crying of Lot 49*. Philadelphia: Lippincott, 1966.

Richard, Claude. "Destin, Design, Dasein: Lacan, Derrida, and 'The Purloined Letter.'" *Iowa Review* 12 (1981): 1–11.

Robbe-Grillet, Alain. *The Erasers*. [*Les Gommes*, 1953]. Trans. Richard Howard. New York: Grove, 1964.

———. "A Path for the Future Novel." ["Une Voie pour le roman futur," 1956]. *Snapshots* and *Towards a New Novel*, trans. Barbara Wright. London: Calder and Boyars, 1965. 50–57.

Sayers, Dorothy. *Gaudy Night*. London: Gollancz, 1935.

Sirvent, Michel. "(Re)Writing Considered as an Act of Murder: How to Rewrite Nabokov's *Despair* in a Post-Nouveau Roman Context." *Nabokov Studies* 2 (1995): 251–76.

Smock, Ann. *Double Dealing*. Lincoln: University of Nebraska Press, 1986.

Stein, Gertrude. *Blood on the Dining-Room Floor*. [1935]. Ed. John Herbert Gill. Berkeley, Calif.: Creative Arts, 1982.

———. "An Elucidation." [1923]. *A Stein Reader*, ed. and intro. Ulla E. Dydo. Evanston, Ill.: Northwestern University Press, 1993. 429–42.

———. "Subject-Cases: The Background of a Detective Story." [1923]. *The Yale Gertrude Stein*, ed. Richard Kostelanetz. New Haven, Conn.: Yale University Press, 1980. 200–29.

Stevenson, Robert Louis. *Strange Case of Dr Jekyll and Mr Hyde*. [1886]. *The Strange Case of Dr Jekyll and Mr Hyde* and *Weir of Hermiston*, ed. Emma Letley. New York: Oxford University Press, 1987.

Sweeney, Susan Elizabeth. "Aliens, Aliases, and Alibis: Felipe Alfau's *Locos* as a Metaphysical Detective Story." *Review of Contemporary Fiction* 13, 1 (1993): 207–14.

———. "Purloined Letters: Poe, Doyle, Nabokov." *Russian Literature Triquarterly* 24 (1991): 213–37.

Swope, Richard. "Approaching the Threshold(s) in Postmodern Detective Fiction: Hawthorne's 'Wakefield' and Other Missing Persons." *Critique* 39, 3 (1998): 207–227.

Tani, Stefano. *The Doomed Detective: The Contribution of the Detective Novel to Postmodern American and Italian Fiction*. Carbondale: Southern Illinois University Press, 1984.

Thoreau, Henry David. *Walden*. [1847]. *The Annotated Walden*, ed. Philip Van Doren Stern. New York: Clarkson Potter, 1970.

Van Meter, Jan. "Sophocles and the Rest of the Boys in the Pulps: Myth and the Detective Novel." In *Dimensions of Detective Fiction*, ed. Larry N. Landrum, Pat Browne, and Ray B. Browne. Bowling Green, Oh.: Bowling Green University Popular Press, 1976. 12–21.

Zangrilli, Franco. "Pirandello and Alfau." *Review of Contemporary Fiction* 13, 1 (1993): 215–20.

In Place of an Ending

Suggestions for Further Reading
Patricia Merivale and
Susan Elizabeth Sweeney

Theorizing Detective Fiction

We list here selected studies of the "classic" detective story, ranging from early genre histories and debates to more recent, often complex theoretical accounts.

Black, Joel. *The Aesthetics of Murder: A Study in Romantic Literature and Contemporary Culture*. Baltimore: Johns Hopkins University Press, 1991. On murder as literary theme and cultural spectacle.

Bloch, Ernst. "A Philosophical View of the Detective Novel." Trans. R. Mueller and S. Thaman. *Discourse* 2 (1980): 32–51. Elegant analysis of the genre's narrative form and its implications.

Caillois, Roger. "Order and License: The Ambiguity of the Detective Story." Trans. William Jay Smith. *Chimera* 5, 4 (1947): 67–79. Discusses the genre's paradoxical combination of sensational content and rigorous form.

Cawelti, John G. *Adventure, Mystery, and Romance: Formula Stories as Art and Popular Culture*. Chicago: University of Chicago Press, 1976. Cites detective fiction as an example of formulaic narrative's cultural significance.

Champigny, Robert. *What Will Have Happened: A Philosophical and Technical Essay on Mystery Stories*. Bloomington: Indiana University Press, 1977. Interesting philosophical meditations on the narration of detective stories.

Charney, Hanna. *The Detective Novel of Manners: Hedonism, Morality, and the Life of Reason*. East Brunswick, N.J.: Associated University Press, 1981. Discusses the genre's ironic and self-reflexive aspects.

Dove, George. *The Reader and the Detective Story*. Bowling Green, Ky.: Bowling Green University Popular Press, 1997. Thorough account of the genre in terms of reader-response and reception theory.

Eco, Umberto and Thomas A. Sebeok, eds. *The Sign of Three: Dupin, Holmes, Peirce*. Bloomington: Indiana University Press, 1983. Compares literary and philosophical theories of the detective process.

Gilbert, Elliot L. "The Detective as Metaphor in the Nineteenth Century." *Journal of Popular Culture* 1 (1967): 256–620. Reprinted in *The Mystery Writer's Art*, ed. Francis M. Nevins, Jr. Bowling Green, Oh.: Bowling Green University

Popular Press, 1976. 286–94. Discusses the idea of order implied by positivistic detection.

Grossvogel, David I. *Mystery and Its Fictions: From Oedipus to Agatha Christie.* Baltimore: Johns Hopkins University Press, 1979. Compares the ways that mystery is defined as either easily solved or irremediable in works by Pirandello, Borges, Kafka, and Robbe-Grillet, among others.

Haycraft, Howard. *The Art of the Mystery Story.* New York: Grosset and Dunlap, 1946. A lively collection of early responses to detective fiction.

———. *Murder for Pleasure: The Life and Times of the Detective Story.* [1941]. New York: Carroll and Graf, 1984. A standard history of the genre.

Hühn, Peter. "The Detective as Reader: Narrativity and Reading Concepts in Detective Fiction." *Modern Fiction Studies* 33, 3 (1987): 451–66. Analyzes the way the genre thematizes hermeneutics.

Klein, Kathleen Gregory. *The Woman Detective: Gender and Genre.* Chicago: University of Illinois Press, 1995. A general but thorough survey.

Knight, Stephen. *Form and Ideology in Crime Fiction.* Bloomington: Indiana University Press, 1980. Marxist analysis of the genre.

Lehman, David. *The Perfect Murder: A Study in Detection.* New York: Free Press, 1989. A witty and succinct survey.

Most, Glenn W. and William W. Stowe, eds. *The Poetics of Murder: Detective Fiction and Literary Theory.* New York: Harcourt, 1983. Includes a range of sociological, psychoanalytical, and narratological approaches.

Muller, John P. and William J. Richardson, eds. *The Purloined Poe: Lacan, Derrida, and Psychoanalytic Reading.* Baltimore: Johns Hopkins University Press, 1988. A useful casebook of psychoanalytic and deconstructive readings of "The Purloined Letter."

Porter, Dennis. *The Pursuit of Crime: Art and Ideology in Detective Fiction.* New Haven, Conn.: Yale University Press, 1981. Combines cultural analysis with attention to narratology and hermeneutics.

Priestman, Martin. *Detective Fiction and Literature: The Figure on the Carpet.* New York: St. Martin's Press, 1991. A thorough history of the genre's relationship to broader literary genres and concerns.

Pyrhönen, Heta. *Murder from an Academic Angle: An Introduction to the Study of the Detective Narrative.* Columbia, S.C.: Camden House, 1994. Surveys the theory and criticism of detective fiction.

Rapaport, Herman. "Literature and the Hermeneutics of Detection." *L'Esprit Créateur* 26, 2 (1986): 48–59.

Steele, Timothy. "The Structure of the Detective Story: Classical or Modern?" *Modern Fiction Studies* 27, 4 (1981–82): 555–70.

Symons, Julian. *Bloody Murder: From the Detective Story to the Crime Novel: A History.* 2nd rev. ed. New York: Penguin, 1985. A standard history of the genre.

Todorov, Tzvetan. "The Typology of the Detective Story." *The Poetics of Prose.* [*Poétique de la prose*, 1971]. Trans. Richard Howard. Ithaca, N.Y.: Cornell University Press, 1977. 42–52. Succinct, insightful, influential discussion of the genre's narrative form.

Walker, Ronald G. and June M. Frazer, eds. *The Cunning Craft: Original Essays on Detective Fiction and Contemporary Literary Theory.* Macomb: Western Illinois University Press, 1990. Investigates the genre's relevance to literary theory.

Winks, Robin W., ed. *Detective Fiction: A Collection of Critical Essays.* Englewood Cliffs, N.J.: Prentice-Hall, 1980. Classic essays on the genre's history and interpretation.

Defining Metaphysical Detective Fiction

These sources all contribute to a theory of the metaphysical detective story, although they assign the genre various names and distinguishing characteristics.

Borges, Jorge Luis. *Borges: A Reader*, ed. Emir Rodríguez Monegal and Alastair Reid. New York: Dutton, 1981. See especially "Narrative Art and Magic," trans. Norman Thomas di Giovanni (34–38), "Chesterton and the Labyrinths of the Detective Story," trans. Mark Larsen (71–73), and "Modes of G. K. Chesterton," trans. Mark Larsen (87–91). In these essays, Borges applauds Chesterton for his shapely narratives and for his provocative distinction between the detective plot and the metaphysical mysteries that it implies but does not resolve.

Christ, Ronald. "Forking Narratives." *Latin-American Literary Review* 14 (1979): 52–61. Describes texts, like Borges' "The Garden of Forking Paths," that enact bifurcated temporal structures.

Eco, Umberto. *Postscript to* The Name of the Rose. Trans. William Weaver. New York: Harcourt, 1983. Analyzes the self-reflexive hermeneutics of metaphysical detective stories, using Eco's own novel as an example.

Gomel, Elana. "Mystery, Apocalypse, and Utopia: The Case of the Ontological Detective Story." *Science Fiction Studies* 22, 3 (1995): 343–56. Proposes a connection between mystery and apocalypse, and analyzes science fiction in which protagonists investigate the world itself.

Holquist, Michael. "Whodunit and Other Questions: Metaphysical Detective Stories in Post-War Fiction." *New Literary History* 3 (1971–72): 135–56. Reprinted in Most and Stowe (149–74). An early and prescient account of detective fiction as a pervasive subtext in postmodernist literature.

Hutcheon, Linda. *Narcissistic Narrative: The Metafictional Paradox*. New York: Methuen, 1980. Cites the metaphysical detective story as a paradigm of self-reflexive narrative.

———. *A Theory of Parody: The Teachings of Twentieth-Century Art Forms*. New York: Methuen, 1985.

Irwin, John T. *The Mystery to a Solution: Poe, Borges, and the Analytic Detective Story*. Baltimore: Johns Hopkins University Press, 1994. Incorporates his previously published essays on the numerical, geometrical, narratological, and philosophical games that Poe and Borges play—including "Mysteries We Reread, Mysteries of Rereading," excerpted in the present volume.

McHale, Brian. *Constructing Postmodernism*. New York: Routledge, 1992. Clarifies the metaphysical detective story's position in postmodernism.

———. *Postmodernist Fiction*. New York: Methuen, 1987. Explains how metaphysical detective stories and other postmodernist texts are formally constructed so as to raise ontological questions.

Merivale, Patricia. "The Flaunting of Artifice in Vladimir Nabokov and Jorge Luis Borges." In *Nabokov: The Man and His Work*, ed. L.S. Dembo. Madison: University of Wisconsin Press, 1967. 290–324. Reprinted in *Critical Essays on Jorge Luis Borges*, ed. Jaime Alazraki. Boston: G. K. Hall, 1987. 141–53. A pioneering essay that, within the context of these authors' works, defined the metaphysical detective story for the first time.

Most, Glenn W. and William W. Stowe, eds. *The Poetics of Murder: Detective Fiction and Literary Theory.* New York: Harcourt, 1983. Reprints Holquist's influential essay cited above (149–74). See also Fredric Jameson's discussion of post-modernist murder mysteries in "On Raymond Chandler" (122–48), Geoffrey Hartman's reading of Pynchon and Robbe-Grillet in "Literature High and Low: The Case of the Mystery Story" (210–29), and Frank Kermode's account of the detective story's influence on the new novel in "Novel and Narrative" (175–89).

Spanos, William V. "The Detective and the Boundary: Some Notes on the Post-modern Literary Imagination." *Boundary 2* 1, 1 (1972): 147–68. Reprinted in *Repetitions: The Postmodern Occasion in Literature and Culture.* Baton Rouge: Louisiana State University Press, 1990. 322–42. This influential essay proposed the first definition of "anti-detective" fiction.

Swope, Richard. "Approaching the Threshold(s) in Postmodern Detective Fiction: Hawthorne's 'Wakefield' and Other Missing Persons." *Critique* 39, 3 (1998): 207–27. Provides a thorough taxonomy of the missing person as illustrated by Hawthorne's tale, McElroy's *Lookout Cartridge*, DeLillo's *The Names*, Pynchon's *The Crying of Lot 49*, Fowles's *The Maggot*, Ackroyd's *Hawksmoor*, and Auster's *New York Trilogy.*

Tani, Stefano. *The Doomed Detective: The Contribution of the Detective Novel to Postmodern Italian and American Fiction.* Carbondale: Southern Illinois University Press, 1984. The first book-length study of the metaphysical detective story. Discussing a number of Italian and American novels, Tani divides "anti-detective" fiction into three categories: the innovative, the deconstructive, and the meta-fictional.

Walker, Ronald G. and June M. Frazer, eds. *The Cunning Craft: Original Essays on Detective Fiction and Contemporary Literary Theory.* Macomb: Western Illinois University Press, 1990. See especially William J. Scheick's "Ethical Romance and the Detecting Reader: The Example of Chesterton's *The Club of Queer Trades*" (86–97) and Susan Elizabeth Sweeney's "Locked Rooms: Detective Fiction, Narrative Theory, and Self-Reflexivity" (1–14).

Wilson, Robert Rawdon. "Godgames and Labyrinths: The Logic of Entrapment." *Mosaic* 15, 4 (1982): 1–22. Explores the labyrinth as a model for the structure and hermeneutics of postmodernist narratives.

See also Lehman's and Porter's books, cited above under "Theorizing Detective Fiction." The former examines the "subversive tradition" of Borges and Eco in its final chapter; the latter concludes with a description of "anti-detective" novels.

Analyzing Metaphysical Detective Fiction

Here we list selected criticism of metaphysical detective stories written in varous genres and traditions by both canonical and little-known authors. (Because many of these writers are widely studied, we include only criticism that focuses specifically on detective-story elements in their work.) We conclude with some more broadly comparative studies.

Major Figures

Paul Auster

Barone, Dennis, ed. *Beyond the Red Notebook: Essays on Paul Auster.* Philadelphia: University of Pennsylvania Press, 1995. See especially Stephen Bernstein's "Auster's Sublime Enclosure: *The Locked Room*" (88–106) and Madeleine Sorapure's "The Detective and the Author: *City of Glass*" (71–87).
De Los Santos, Oscar. "Auster vs. Chandler: or, Cracking the Case of the Postmodern Mystery." *Connecticut Review* 18, 1 (1994): 75–80.
Handler, Nina and Dale Salwak. *Drawn into the Circle of Its Repetitions: Paul Auster's New York Trilogy.* San Bernardino, Calif.: Borgo Press, 1997.
Holzapfel, Anne M. *The New York Trilogy: Whodunit? Tracking the Structure of Paul Auster's Anti-Detective Novels.* Frankfurt am Main: Peter Lang, 1996. Master's thesis.
Lewis, Barry. "The Strange Case of Paul Auster." *Review of Contemporary Fiction* 14, 1 (1994): 53–61.
Malmgren, Carl D. "Detecting/Writing the Real: Paul Auster's *City of Glass.*" In *Narrative Turns and Minor Genres in Postmodernism,* ed. Theo D'haen and Hans Bertens. Amsterdam: Rodopi, 1995. 177–201.
Merivale, Patricia. "The Austerized Version." Review of *Beyond the Red Notebook,* ed. Dennis Barone; *Review of Contemporary Fiction* Paul Auster issue, ed. Dennis Barone; and *L'Oeuvre de Paul Auster,* ed. Annick Duperray. *Contemporary Literature* 38, 1 (1997): 185–97.
Rosello, Mireille. "The Screener's Maps: Michel de Certeau's 'Wandersmanner' and Paul Auster's Hypertextual Detective." In *Hyper/Text/Theory,* ed. George P. Landow. Baltimore: Johns Hopkins University Press, 1994. 121–58.
Rowen, Norma. "The Detective in Search of the Lost Tongue of Adam: Paul Auster's *City of Glass.*" *Critique* 32 (1991): 224–34.
Russell, Alison. "Deconstructing *The New York Trilogy:* Paul Auster's Anti-Detective Fiction." *Critique* 31, 2 (1990): 71–84.

Jorge Luis Borges

Bennett, Maurice J. "The Detective Fiction of Poe and Borges." *Comparative Literature* 35, 3 (1983): 266–75.
Boruchoff, David A. "In Pursuit of the Detective Genre: 'La muerte y la brujula' of J. L. Borges." *Inti* 21 (1985): 13–26.
Cortínez, Veronica. "De Poe a Borges: La creación del lector policial." *Revista Hispánica Moderna* 48, 1 (1995): 127–36.
Gillespie, Robert. "Detections: Borges and Father Brown." *Novel* 7 (1974): 220–30.
Hayes, Aden W. and Khachig Tölölyan. "The Cross and the Compass: Patterns of Order in Chesterton and Borges." *Humanities Review* 49, 4 (1981): 395–405.
Hernández Martín, Jorge. "Honorio Bustos Domecq, Six Problems and all That Skaz." *Symposium* 48, 2 (1994): 105–19. "Bustos Domecq" was the pseudonym under which Borges and Adolfo Bioy Cesares penned detective stories featuring Don Isidro Parodi.
Kushigian, Julia A. "The Detective Story Genre in Poe and Borges." *Latin-American Literary Review* 11, 22 (1983): 27–39.

Redekop, Ernest H. "Labyrinths in Time and Space." *Mosaic* 11, 3–4 (1980): 95–113. Analyzes labyrinthine structures in Borges with reference to Escher, Piranesi, and science fiction.

Schehr, Lawrence R. "Unreading Borges' Labyrinths." *Studies in Twentieth Century Literature* 10, 2 (1986): 177–89.

Solotorevsky, Myrna. "'La Muerte y la brujula': Parodia ironica de una convencion generica." *Neophilologus* 70, 4 (1986): 547–54.

Toro, Alfonso de. "El Eroductor 'rizomorfico' y el lector como 'detective literario': La aventura de los signos o la postmodernidad del discurso borgesiano (Intertextualidad-palimpsesto-deconstruccion-rizoma)." *Studi di Letteratura Ispano-Americana* 23 (1992): 63–102. Reprinted in *Jorge Luis Borges: Variaciones interpretativas sobre sus procedimentos literarios y bases epistemologicas*, ed. Karl Alfred Bluher and Alfonso de Toro. Frankfurt: Vervuert, 1992. 145–83.

See also Irwin's book and Merivale's essay "The Flaunting of Artifice," cited above under "Defining Metaphysical Detective Fiction," as well as a book by Hernández Martín and essays by Hudde, Moraldo, and Zlotchew, all listed below under "Comparisons."

Umberto Eco

Clerici, Carlotta. "Sulla tracce del giallo ne *Il Nome della rosa*." *Narrativa* 10 (1996): 101–18.

Inge, Thomas M., ed. *Naming the Rose: Essays on Eco's* The Name of the Rose. Jackson: University of Mississippi Press, 1988. See especially Michael Cohen's "The Hounding of Baskerville: Allusion and Apocalypse in Eco's *The Name of the Rose*" (65–76) and H. Aram Veeser's "Holmes Goes to Carnival: Embarrassing the Signifier in Eco's Anti-Detective Novel" (101–115).

Richter, David H. "Eco's Echoes: Semiotic Theory and Detective Practice in *The Name of the Rose*." *Studies in Twentieth-Century Literature* 10, 2 (1986): 213–36.

Schulz-Buschhaus, Ulrich. "Sam Spade im Reich des Okkulten: Umberto Ecos *Il Pendolo di Foucault* und der Kriminalroman." In *Poetik und Geschichte*, ed. Dieter Borchmeyer. Tubingen: Niemeyer, 1989. 486–504.

See also Hernández Martín's book and Wunderlich's essay listed below under "Comparisons."

Gabriel García Márquez

Alvarez Borland, Isabel. "From Mystery to Parody: (Re)Readings of García Márquez's *Cronica de una muerte anunciada*." *Symposium* 38, 4 (1984–85): 278–86.

Aronne-Amestoy, Lida. "La Mala hora de los generos: Gabriel García Márquez y la genesis de la nueva novela." *Inti* 16–17 (1982–83): 27–36.

Bandyopadhyay, Manabendra. "A Detective Story Turned Upside Down: Did They Not Warn Santiago Nasar?" In *García Márquez and Latin America*, ed. Alok Bhalla and introd. Ramesh Mohan. New York: Envoy, 1987. 89–100.

Hernández de Lopez, Ana Maria. "Sentido detectivesco en *Cronica de una muerte anunciada*." *Cuadernos de Aldeeu* 3, 2 (1987): 105–14.

March, Kathleen N. "*Cronica de una muerte anunciada*: García Márquez y el genero policiaco." *Inti* 16–17 (1982–83): 61–70.

Patrick Modiano

Ewert, Jeanne C. "Lost in the Hermeneutic Funbouse: Patrick Modiano's Postmodern Detective." In *The Cunning Craft: Original Essays on Detective Fiction and Contemporary Literary Theory*, ed. Ronald G. Walker and June M. Frazer. Macomb: Western Illinois University Press, 1990. 166–73.
Kaminskas, Jurate D. "Quête/enquête—à la recherche du genre: *Voyage de noces* de Patrick Modiano." *French Review* 66, 6 (1993): 932–40.

Vladimir Nabokov

Burch, Barbara. "Nabokov and the Detective." *Clues* 12, 1 (1991): 101–21.
Froidevaux, Genevieve. "Ou se cache la detective dans *Lolita* de Vladimir Nabokov?" *Etudes des Lettres* 1 (1983): 69–71.
Schroeter, J. "Detective Stories and Aesthetic Bliss in Nabokov." *Delta* 17 (1983): 23–32.
Sisson, Jonathan B. "Nabokov and Some Turn-of-the Century English Writers." In *The Garland Companion to Vladimir Nabokov*, ed. Vladimir Alexandrov. New York: Garland, 1995. 528–36.
Sweeney, Susan Elizabeth. "Purloined Letters: Poe, Doyle, Nabokov." *Russian Literature Triquarterly* 24 (1991): 213–37.

See also Merivale's essay on "The Flaunting of Artifice," cited above under "Defining the Metaphysical Detective Story," and Sirvent's essay on "(Re)Writing Considered as an Act of Murder," listed below under "Comparisons."

Manuel Puig

Boyer, Alain-Michel. "Le Recit lacunaire." *Textes et Langages* 12 (1986): 115–23.
Campos, René A. "Novela policial, film noir y *The Buenos Aires Affair*." *La Palabra y el Hombre* 69 (1989): 193–201.
Kerr, Lucille. "*The Buenos Aires Affair*: Un caso de repeticion criminal." *Texto Critico* 6, 16–17 (1980): 201–32.

Thomas Pynchon

Baylon, Daniel. "*The Crying of Lot 49*: Vrai Roman et faux policier?" *Caliban* 23 (1986): 111–25.
Das, Prasanta. "Pynchon's *The Crying of Lot 49* and the Classical Detective Story." *Panjab University Research Bulletin* 23, 2 (1992): 141–49.

See also Thompson's book chapter and Keesey's and Lord's essays, listed below under "Comparisons."

Ishmael Reed

Carter, Steven R. "Ishmael Reed's Neo-Hoodoo Detection." In *Dimensions of Detective Fiction*, ed. Larry N. Landrum, Pat Browne, and Ray B. Browne. Bowling Green, Oh.: Bowling Green University Popular Press, 1976. 265–74.
Paravisini, Lizabeth. "*Mumbo Jumbo* and the Uses of Parody." *Obsidian II* 1, 1–2 (1986): 113–27.

See also Soitos's book chapter and Weixlmann's essay listed below under "Comparisons."

Alain Robbe-Grillet

Boyer, Alain-Michel. "Du Double à la doublure: l'image du détective dans les premiers romans de Robbe-Grillet." *L'Esprit Créateur* 26, 2 (1986): 60–70.
———. "L'Enigme, l'enquête et la quête du récit: la fiction policière dans *Les Gommes* et *Le Voyeur*." *French Forum* 6 (1981): 74–83.
Brock, Robert. "Robbe-Grillet's *Les Gommes* and Graham Greene's *This Gun for Hire*: Imitation or Initiation?" *Modern Fiction Studies* 29, 4 (1983): 688–94.
Deneau, Daniel. "Little Mysteries in Robbe-Grillet's *The Erasers*." *Notes on Contemporary Literature* 11, 1 (1981): 2–4.
Morrissette, Bruce. *The Novels of Robbe-Grillet*. Ithaca, NY: Cornell University Press, 1975.
Ramsay, Raylene. *Robbe-Grillet and Modernity: Science, Sexuality, and Subversion*. Gainesville: University Press of Florida, 1992.

See also essays by Hudde, Law, and Mulder listed below under "Comparisons."

Leonardo Sciascia

Ambroise, Claude. "Sciascia: Lo storiografo e il giallo." *Narrativa* 2 (1992): 131–39.
Blaha, Franz. "The Detective Novel Unbound: The Novels of Leonardo Sciascia." *Clues* 4, 1 (1983): 3–18.
Cannon, JoAnn. "The Detective Fiction of Leonardo Sciascia." *Modern Fiction Studies* 29, 3 (1983): 523–34.
Lazzaro-Weis, Carol. "The Metaphysical Detective Novel and Sciascia's *Il contesto*: Parody or Tyranny of a Borrowed Form?" *Quaderni d'Italianistica* 8, 1 (1987): 42–52.
Moraldo, Sandro. "Leonardo Sciascia: Oder die Destruktion des Kriminalromans in *Il giorno della civetta*." *Neophilologus* 67, 2 (1983): 215–27.
Pietropaoli, Antonio. "Il Giallo 'contestuale' di Leonardo Sciascia." *Narrativa* 10 (1996): 5–39.
Schultz-Buschhaus, Ulrich. "Gli inquietanti romanzi polizieschi di Sciascia." *Problemi* 71 (1984): 289–301.
———. "Sciascia's Beunruhigende Kriminalromane." *Italienische Studien* 1 (1978): 43–53.

See also Hudde's and Moraldo's essays listed below under "Comparisons."

Other Texts and Authors

Abella, Encarna. "Satira y parodia de la novela policial en *El tunel* de Ernesto Sábato." *Romance Linguistic and Literary Review* 1 (1988): 66–75.

Alter, V. Jean. "L'Enquête policière dans le 'Nouveau Roman': *La Mise en scène* de Claude Ollier." In *Un Nouveau Roman? Recherches et tradition: La Critique étrangère*, ed. J. H. Matthews. Paris: Minard, 1964. [*La Revue des Lettres Modernes* 94–99]. 83–104.

Bjerring, Nancy E. "Reconstructing the 'Desert of Facts': Detection and Antidetection in *Coming Through Slaughter.*" *English Studies in Canada* 16, 3 (1990): 325–38. On Ondaatje's novel.

Bowen, Brian. "Identity Unknown: Exploring the Labyrinth of Abe Kobo's Inverted Detective Fiction." *Descant* (1985): 30–37.

Brown, Russell M. "*Blackout*: Hubert Aquin's Surreal Mystery." *Armchair Detective* 13 (1980): 58–60.

Butterfield, Bradley. "Enlightenment's Other in Patrick Susskind's *Das Parfum*: Adorno and the Ineffable Utopia of Modern Art." *Comparative Literature Studies* 32, 3 (1995): 401–48.

Cannon, JoAnn. "The Reader as Detective: Notes on Gadda's *Pasticciaccio.*" *Modern Language Studies* 10, 3 (1980): 41–50.

Clark, Beverly Lyon. "In Search of Barthelme's Weeping Father." *Philological Quarterly* 62, 4 (1983): 419–33. On "Views of My Father Weeping."

Colas, Santiago. "Un Posmodernismo resistente en America Latina: *El Diez por ciento de vida* y la historia." *Nuevo Texto Critico* 4 (1991) 7: 175–96. On Conteris's novel.

Dettmar, Kevin J. H. "From Interpretation to 'Intrepidation': Joyce's 'The Sisters' as a Precursor of the Postmodern Mystery." In *The Cunning Craft: Original Essays on Detective Fiction and Contemporary Literary Theory*, ed. Ronald G. Walker and June M. Frazer. Macomb: Western Illinois University Press, 1990. 149–65.

Dopp, Jamie. "Affirming Mystery in Eric McCormack's 'The Mysterium.'" *Canadian Literature* 154 (1997): 94–109.

Dusing, Wolfgang, ed. *Experimente mit dem Kriminalroman: Ein Erzahmodell in der deutschsprachigen Literatur des 20. Jahrhunderts*. Frankfurt: Peter Lang, 1993. See especially essays by Jochen Richter on Friedrich Dürrenmatt (141–53), Helga Schreckenberger on Gerhard Roth (171–83), Linda C. Merritt on Peter Handke (185–203), and Gottfried Willems on Patrick Susskind's *Das Parfum* (223–44).

Egan, James. "Antidetection: Gothic and Detective Conventions in the Fiction of Stephen King." *Clues* 5, 1 (1984): 131–46. Gothic mysteries problematize what seem to be detective stories.

Felman, Shoshana. "De Sophocle à Japrisot (via Freud)." *Littérature* 49 (1983): 23–42. On Japrisot's *Piège pour Cendrillon*.

Giffone, Tony. "*Twin Peaks* as Post-Modernist Parody: David Lynch's Subversion of the British Detective Narrative." *Mid-Atlantic Almanac* 1 (1992): 53–60.

Madden, David. "The Isaac Quintet: Jerome Charyn's Metaphysics of Law and Disorder." *Review of Contemporary Fiction* 12, 2 (1992): 164–72.

————. "Thomas Berger's Comic-Absurd Vision in *Who is Teddy Villanova?*" *Armchair Detective* 14, 1 (1981): 37–43.

McGovern, Lynn. "A 'Private I': The Birth of a Female Sleuth and the Role of Parody in Lourdes Ortiz's *Picadura mortal.*" *Journal of Interdisciplinary Literary Studies* 5, 2 (1993): 251–79.

Resina, Joan Ramon. "Detective Formula and Parodic Reflexivity: *Crim.*" In *The Garden Across the Border: Merce Rodoreda's Fiction,* ed. Kathleen McNerney and Nancy Vosburg. Selinsgrove, Penn.: Associated University Press, 1994. 119–34.

Rich, Lawrence. "Antonio Muñoz Molina's *Beatus ille* and *Beltenebros*: Conventions of Reading the Postmodern Anti-Detective Novel." *Romance Languages Annual* 8 (1994): 577–80.

Richter, David H. "Murder in Jest: Serial Killing in the Post-Modern Detective Story." *Journal of Narrative Technique* 19, 1 (1989): 106–15. On Ackroyd's *Hawksmoor.*

Sirvent, Michel. "Lettres volées (métareprésentation et lipogramme chez E. A. Poe et G. Perec)." *Littérature* 83 (1991): 12–30.

Sobejano-Moran, Antonio. "La novela metafictiva antipoliciaca de Luis Goytisolo: La parodoja del ave migratoria." *Bulletin Hispanique* 93, 2 (1991): 423–38.

Steiner, T. R. "Stanislaw Lem's Detective Stories: A Genre Extended." *Modern Fiction Studies* 29, 3 (1983): 451–62.

Sweeney, Susan Elizabeth. "Aliens, Aliases, and Alibis: Alfau's *Locos* as a Metaphysical Detective Story." *Review of Contemporary Fiction* 13, 1 (1993): 207–14.

————. "Formal Strategies in a Female Narrative Tradition: The Case of *Swann: A Mystery.*" In *Anxious Power: Reading, Writing, and Ambivalence in Narrative by Women,* ed. Carol J. Singley and Susan Elizabeth Sweeney. Albany: SUNY Press, 1993. 19–32. On Shields's novel.

————. "Gender-Blending, Genre-Bending, and the Rendering of Identity in Barbara Wilson's *Gaudí Afternoon.*" In *Multicultural Detective Fiction: Murder on the "Other" Side,* ed. Adrienne J. Gosselin. New York: Garland, 1998.

Comparisons

Bertens, Hans R. "The Detective." In *International Postmodernism: Theory and Literature,* ed. Hans R. Bertens, Douwe Fokkema, and Mario J. Valdes. Amsterdam: Benjamin, 1997. 195–202. Analyzes the recurrent figure of the detective in postmodernist literature.

Brantlinger, Patrick. "Missing Corpses: The Deconstructive Mysteries of James Purdy and Franz Kafka." *Novel* 20, 1 (1987): 24–40.

Carlson, Marvin. *Deathtraps: The Postmodernist Comedy Thriller.* Bloomington: Indiana University Press, 1993. A fascinating study of metaphysical detection on stage and film.

Charney, Hanna. "Pourquoi le 'Nouveau Roman' policier?" *French Review* 46, 1 (1972): 17–23.

Grimes, Larry E. "Stepsons of Sam: Re-Visions of the Hard-Boiled Detective Formula in Recent American Fiction." *Modern Fiction Studies* 29, 3 (1983): 535–44. On Jules Pfeiffer's *Ackroyd,* Richard Brautigan's *Dreaming of Babylon,* and Thomas Berger's *Who Is Teddy Villanova?*

Hernández Martín, Jorge. *Readers and Labyrinths: Detective Fiction in Borges, Bustos Domecq, and Eco.* New York: Garland, 1995.

Hudde, Hinrich. "Das Scheitern des Detektivs: Ein literarisches Thema bei

Borges sowie Robbe-Grillet, Dürrenmatt und Sciascia." *Romanistisches Jahrbuch* 29 (1978): 322–42.

Hurstfield, Julian G. "Mean Streets, Mystery Plays: The New Pathology of Recent American Crime Fiction." In *The New American Writing: Essays on American Literature Since 1970*, ed. Graham Clarke. New York: St Martin's, 1990. 165–81.

Keesey, Douglas. "The Ideology of Detection in Pynchon and DeLillo." *Pynchon Notes* 32–33 (1993): 44–59.

Law, Graham. " 'Il s'agissait peut-être d'un roman policier': Leblanc, Macdonald, and Robbe-Grillet." *Comparative Literature* 40, 4 (1998): 335–57.

Lord, Geoffrey. "Mystery and History, Discovery and Recovery in Thomas Pynchon's *The Crying of Lot 49* and Graham Swift's *Waterland*." *Neophilogus* 81, 1 (1997): 145–63.

Moraldo, Sandro. "Leonardo Sciascia's *Il contesto* und Jorges Luis Borges' 'La muerte y la brújula.' " *Neophilologus* 68, 3 (1984): 389–99.

Mulder, Hanneke. "De anti-detective als postmodernistische verschijnsel: Over *Les Gommes* van Alain Robbe-Grillet, *Cherokee* van Jean Echenoz en *Maurits en de Peiten* van Gerrit Krol." *Forum der Letteren* 30, 4 (1989): 241–54.

Occiogrosso, Frank. "Threats to Rationalism: John Fowles, Stanislaw Lem, and the Detective Story." *Armchair Detective* 13 (1980): 4–7.

Pavan, Lidia. "Ai Confini del giallo: Il giallo infinito: Gadda e Pontiggia." *Narrativa* 7 (1995): 147–52.

Pietropaoli, Antonio. "Evoluzione e rivoluzione del romanzo poliziesco: Giallo, giallo ocra e giallo infinito." *Narrativa* 2 (1992): 7–52.

Saltzman, Arthur. *Designs of Darkness in Contemporary American Fiction*. Philadelphia: University of Pennsylvania Press, 1990.

Schulz-Buschhaus, Ulrich. "Kriminalroman und Post-Avantgarde." *Merkur-Deutsche Zeitschrift fur Europaisches Denken* 41, 4 (1987): 287–96.

Sirvent, Michel. "(Re)Writing Considered as an Act of Murder: How to Rewrite Nabokov's *Despair* in a Post-Nouveau Roman Context." *Nabokov Studies* 2 (1995): 251–76. Comparison with Jean Lahougue's "La Ressemblance."

Sklodowska, Elzbieta. "Transgresion parodica de la formula policial en la novela hispanoamericana." *Hispanica Posnaniensia* 1 (1990): 71–83.

Soitos, Stephen. "The Black Anti-Detective Novel." *The Blues Detective: A Study of African-American Detective Fiction*. Amherst: University of Massachusetts Press, 1996. 179–219. On Ishmael Reed and Clarence Major.

Thompson, Jon. "Postmodern Fictions of Crime." *Fiction, Crime, and Empire: Clues to Modernity and Postmodernism*. Chicago: University of Illinois Press, 1993. 168–81. Discusses Pynchon's *The Crying of Lot 49* in particular and other texts in passing.

Weide, Jack van der. "Ontstaan en ontwikkeling van de anti-detective." *Forum der Letteren* 31, 2 (1990): 291–301. Examines the relationship between postmodernism and the anti-detective genre. Weide continues this argument in "Detective en anti-detective." *Forum der Letteren* 31, 4 (1990): 137–38.

Weixlmann, Joe. "Culture Clash, Survival, and Trans-Formation: A Study of Some Innovative Afro-American Novels of Detection." *Mississippi Quarterly* 38, 1 (1984–85): 21–32.

Wunderlich, Werner. "Monastic Thrillers: Detecting Postmodernity in the Middle Ages." *Comparative Literature Studies* 32, 3 (1995): 382–400.

Zlotchew, Clark M. "The Collaboration of the Reader in Borges and Robbe-Grillet." *Michigan Academician* 14, 2 (1981): 167–73.

Contributors

Stephen Bernstein is associate professor of English at the University of Michigan, Flint, where he teaches British literature. His research, ranging over the nineteenth and twentieth centuries, frequently focuses on gothicism, intertextuality, ideology, and the sublime. He is also the author of "Auster's Sublime Closure: *The Locked Room*," which appeared in *Beyond the Red Notebook: Essays on Paul Auster* (University of Pennsylvania Press, 1995), as well as essays and book chapters on Don DeLillo, Samuel Beckett, Virginia Woolf, Joseph Conrad, Charles Dickens, and Wilkie Collins, among others. His most recent project is an introduction to the novels of the Scottish writer Alasdair Gray.

Hanjo Berressem is professor of American literature at the University of Bielefeld, Germany. He is the author of *Pynchon's Poetics: Interfacing Theory and Text* (1992). Another book, *Lines of Desire: Reading Gombrowicz' Fiction with Lacan*, is forthcoming, and he is currently finishing a book-length study of spatial and temporal loops in postmodernist American literature, art, and architecture. He has also published many articles on British and American fiction, painting, and poststructuralist theory.

Joel Black studied at Columbia and Stanford, and has taught comparative literature at the University of North Carolina at Chapel Hill, Emory University, Hamilton College, and the University of Antwerp. He is presently associate professor of comparative literature at the University of Georgia. Besides writing extensively on romanticism, postmodernism, literature and science, and cultural studies, he has published several essays on Thomas Pynchon and is the author of *The Aesthetics of Murder: A Study in Romantic Literature and Contemporary Culture* (1991). He is now at work on two books, one on Freud and one on Oscar Wilde.

Anna Botta, who holds an advanced degree in modern languages from the University of Turin and a Ph.D. in comparative literature and literary theory from the University of Pennsylvania, is an associate professor of Italian at Smith College. Her publications include critical articles on Antonio Tabucchi (*Spunti e Ricerche*), Italo Calvino (*Modern Language Notes, Cultura italiana, Anthropos*), Cristina Campo (*L'opera di Cristina Campo*), and Georges Perec (*ISSEI*). Botta also conducted and published the very first interview with Tabucchi to appear in English (*Contemporary Literature*). She is currently studying representations of perception in postmodernist narratives.

Robert L. Chibka, associate professor of English at Boston College, is primarily concerned with narrative strategies and the ways in which they display and complicate the often vexed relations of authors, narrators, characters, and readers. His first novel, *A Slight Lapse,* was published by W. W. Norton in 1990. He has published critical articles on Sterne's *Tristram Shandy* (*Eighteenth-Century Fiction*), Fielding's *Tom Jones* (*The Eighteenth Century: Theory and Interpretation*), Behn's *Oroonoko* (*Texas Studies in Literature and Language*), Young's *Conjectures on Original Composition* (*ELH*), and Hawthorne's "Wakefield" (*ESQ*). He is at work on a second novel.

Jeanne C. Ewert is assistant professor of literature, communication, and culture at the Georgia Institute of Technology. She earned her Ph.D. in comparative literature and literary theory with a dissertation entitled "A Thousand Mysteries: Detection's Changing Formula" (University of Pennsylvania, 1995). Her publications include "Lost in the Hermeneutic Funhouse: Modiano's Postmodern Detective" in *The Cunning Craft: Original Essays on Detective Fiction and Contemporary Literary Theory* (1990), and she is now working on a book-length study of the detective in modernist and postmodernist fiction.

John T. Irwin is Decker Professor of the Humanities at Johns Hopkins University, where he teaches in the English department and in the Writing Seminars. His many books and essays in the field of American literature include *Doubling and Incest/Repetition and Revenge: A Speculative Reading of Faulkner* and *American Hieroglyphics: The Symbol of the Egyptian Hieroglyphics in the American Renaissance.* Irwin's influential essay, "Mysteries We Reread, Mysteries of Rereading," excerpted in this volume, was the basis for his subsequent book, *The Mystery to a Solution: Poe, Borges, and the Analytical Detective Story* (1994), which has won national and international prizes for literary criticism.

Patricia Merivale is professor of English and comparative literature at the University of British Columbia. Her very first publication—"The Flaunting of Artifice in Vladimir Nabokov and Jorge Luis Borges," in *Nabokov: The Man and His Work* (1967)—was an early and influential essay on the metaphysical detective story. Since then she has published *Pan the Goat-God: His Myth in Modern Times* (1969), as well as many essays on contemporary fiction, comparative literature, magic

realism, intertextuality, self-reflexive artist-parables, and postmodernist, especially apocalyptic narrative strategies.

Jeffrey T. Nealon is associate professor of English at Pennsylvania State
University. He is the author of *Double Reading: Postmodernism After Deconstruction* (1993), and has published essays on a wide range of contemporary theorists and artists, including Jacques Derrida, Michel
Foucault, Martin Heidegger, Jacques Lyotard, and Samuel Beckett.
His next book, *Alterity Politics: Ethics and Performative Subjectivity*, is
forthcoming.

Raylene Ramsay completed a doctoral thesis on the French *nouveau roman* in Poitiers, studied linguistics at Cambridge University, taught
French at Simmons College and Massey University, and is now professor of French and head of the school of European languages and
literatures at Auckland University, New Zealand. She is the author of
Robbe-Grillet and Modernity: Science, Sexuality, and Subversion (1992) and
The French New Autobiographies (1996), as well as many essays on the
works of Marguerite Duras, Nathalie Sarraute, and Robbe-Grillet.

Michel Sirvent teaches French literature at the University of North Texas.
His articles on Jean Lahougue, Vladimir Nabokov, Georges Perec,
Edgar Allan Poe, Jean Ricardou, Alain Robbe-Grillet, and Paul Valéry
have appeared in *Dalhousie French Studies* and *Protée* (Canada); *French
Review, Romanic Review, Sites, Nabokov Studies,* and *Studies in Twentieth
Century Literature* (USA); *Lettres Romanes* (Brussels); *Neophilologus* (Am-
sterdam); and *Littérature* (Paris). His most recent publication, "Dou-
blures transcriptuelles: récits récrits de Jean Lahougue" (*Neophilogus*),
extends the study of Lahougue's intertextuality that he begins here.
He has also contributed to Ricardou's seminars on *Textics* at Cerisy-la-
Salle for several years. Sirvent is currently working on a book-length
study of *Tel Quel* and the *nouveau nouveau roman.*

Susan Elizabeth Sweeney, associate professor of English at Holy Cross
College and past president of the International Nabokov Society, studies postmodernist revisions of popular genres. Her work on detective
fiction includes essays on locked-room mysteries and self-reflexivity
(*The Cunning Craft: Original Essays on Detective Fiction and Contempo-
rary Literary Theory*); on money in "The Red-Headed League" (*Sherlock
Holmes: Victorian Sleuth to Modern Hero*); on purloined letters in Poe,
Doyle, and Nabokov (*Russian Literature Triquarterly*); on Alfau's *Locos* as
metaphysical detective story (*Review of Contemporary Fiction*); on Carol
Shields's *Swann*, in *Anxious Power: Reading, Writing, and Ambivalence in
Narrative by Women*, a book she coedited; and on gender-blending and
genre-bending in Barbara Wilson's *Gaudí Afternoon* (*Multicultural Detective Fiction: Murder on the "Other" Side*). She is now working on feminist
revisions of the gothic.

Index

ABC Murders, The (Christie), 12, 82, 83, 160
Abe, Kobo, 5, 18 (fig.), 101, 105, 107, 109–
11, 113n5; The Face of Another, 13, 110, 112;
Inter Ice Age 4, 13, 110; Secret Rendezvous,
110
Acker, Kathy, 131n4
Ackroyd, Peter, 5; Chatterton, 18 (fig.),
19–20, 261–62; Hawksmoor, 18
"Adventure of the Speckled Band, The"
(Doyle), 195n6
Adventures of Pinocchio, The (Collodi), 151n4,
229n9, 254
"Agatha Christie" (Peeters), 157, 161, 162
Alcott, Bronson, 111
Alfau, Felipe, 4, 249, 251, 253, 254–56;
"Fingerprints," 255; "Identity," 17,
254–56, 257, 261, 262, 265; Locos, 254,
255
Alienist, The (Carr), 97n15
Amateur sleuth. See Armchair detective
American Renaissance, 11, 13–14, 111,
113n2, 134–35
Amis, Martin, 5, 18
Analysis. See Detection; Hermeneutics;
Logic
Analytic detective story, 3–4, 27–28,
51–52, 56
"Analytic Language of John Wilkins, The"
(Borges), 52–53n5, 64
Angel Heart (film), 5
Angélique (Robbe-Grillet), 200, 201, 203,
205, 207, 209, 213
Anthony, Patricia, The Happy Policeman,
195n2
Anti-detective story, 2–3, 104, 119–20,
126, 157–58, 189; defined, 2–3, 104;

mentioned, 8, 101. See also Metaphysical
detective story
Apocalypse, 88, 89–90, 94, 110
Aquin, Hubert, 5, 18 (fig.), 20, 101
Architecture. See Structure
Aristotle, 87–89
Armchair detective, 8–9, 11–12; defined,
8; inaugurated by Poe, 6, 14, 104, 251;
mentioned, 91, 111. See also Classical de-
tective story; Detective figures; Library
Art of Hunger, The (Auster), 135, 149
Asbee, Sue, 179
Aspern Papers, The (James), 18
At Swim-Two-Birds (O'Brien), 188
Atwood, Margaret, 18 (fig.), 20; "Murder
in the Dark," 2, 110
Auerbach, Jonathan, 105
Auster, Paul, 18 (fig.), 111–12, 117–33, 134–
53, 262–63; detective figures of, 91,
111, 118–22, 123–24, 137, 150n2, 262;
mentioned, 1, 5, 11, 91, 107, 249, 251,
253. Works: The Art of Hunger, 135, 149;
City of Glass, 10, 13, 111–12, 117–33, 134,
135, 136–41, 142, 144, 146–47, 148–
50, 262, 263; "The Death of Sir Walter
Raleigh," 151n5; Ghosts, 111, 134, 135,
136, 137, 139, 140–41, 142, 143, 144, 147,
148, 180, 247–48, 262, 263, 266n10; The
Invention of Solitude, 138–39, 142, 143,
151n4, 264; The Locked Room, 17, 111,
132n8, 134, 135–36, 137, 139, 140, 141,
142–43, 144, 145–46, 147–48, 262–63,
265; The New York Trilogy, 13–14, 111–12,
118, 120, 129, 134–53, 262, 263
"Autobiographical Essay, An" (Borges), 43
Autobiography, 158–59, 172, 194, 201, 204,
205, 213